D0572805

After Enron

After Enron

Lessons for Public Policy

Edited by
William A. Niskanen

ROWMAN & LITTLEFIELD PUBLISHERS, INC.
Lanham • Boulder • New York • Oxford

ROWMAN & LITTLEFIELD PUBLISHERS, INC.

Published in the United States of America
by Rowman & Littlefield Publishers, Inc.
A wholly owned subsidary of The Rowman & Littlefield Publishing Group, Inc.
4501 Forbes Boulevard, Suite 200, Lanham, Maryland 20706
www.rowmanlittlefield.com

PO Box 317
Oxford
OX2 9RU, UK

Copyright © 2005 by Rowman & Littlefield Publishers, Inc.

All rights reserved. No part of this publication may be reproduced,
stored in a retrieval system, or transmitted in any form or by any
means, electronic, mechanical, photocopying, recording, or otherwise,
without the prior permission of the publisher.

British Library Cataloguing in Publication Information Available

Library of Congress Cataloging-in-Publication Data

After Enron : lessons for public policy / edited by William A. Niskanen.
     p. cm.
  Includes index.
  ISBN 0-7425-4433-8 (cloth : alk. paper)
  1. Disclosure in accounting.   2. Corporations—Accounting—United States.
3. Corporations—Auditing—United States.   4. Corporations—Taxation.
5. Corporate governance—United States.   6. Enron Corp.—Corrupt practices.
I. Niskanen, William A., 1933-
  HF5658.A24 2005
  338.6'0973—dc22   2004024939

Printed in the United States of America

⊗™ The paper used in this publication meets the minimum requirements of American
National Standard for Information Sciences—Permanence of Paper for Printed Library
Materials, ANSI/NISO Z39.48-1992.

Contents

Preface

$\mathcal{T}$he collapse of the Enron Corporation in December 2001 triggered two broad concerns: There may be more "Enrons" out there, since many corporations share some of the characteristics that led to the Enron collapse. This concern was reflected by a continued weakness in the stock markets and the foreign exchange value of the dollar well into the recovery from the 2001 recession, even though most of the subsequent economic news was better than expected.

The accounting scandals and bankruptcy by Enron and other major corporations have also undermined the popular and political support for free market policies. This effect has already led to increased federal regulation of accounting, auditing, and corporate governance and increased criticism of any proposal for reducing the role of government. Any number of critics seem prepared to blame many of the problems of the modern world on the corporate culture, with a potentially adverse effect similar to that of the muckrakers in shaping and promoting the early twentieth-century progressive legislation.

These two concerns led the Cato Institute to initiate a project on the major policy lessons from the collapse of Enron and the other major corporate scandals.

This is the second of two books sponsored by Cato that address the policy lessons from the collapse of Enron. The first book, organized by Christopher Culp and edited by the two of us, is titled *Corporate Aftershock: The Public Policy Implications of Enron and Other Corporate Disasters* and was published in 2003. That book focuses primarily on the policy lessons specific to the energy and other markets in which Enron traded and on the specialized financial instruments that it used. The contributors to that book are among the leading practical specialists in these markets and with these financial instruments. The target audience for that book is the academics who specialize in these issues, others who trade in these markets, the many others who use these financial instruments, the regulators of these markets and financial instruments, and the policy officials who approve the rules by which these markets operate. Some of the policy lessons from these careful analyses of the collapse of Enron are also important to a broader audience—such lessons as the problems of conventional accounting and the limitations of the monitoring model of corporate governance.

This book, which I organized and edited, addresses the major policy lessons affecting the broader corporate sector illustrated by the collapse of Enron and the other major corporate scandals. This book focuses primarily on the government policies that contributed to these conditions, the reasons why their weak financial conditions were not revealed and possibly corrected earlier, and the major policy changes that would reduce the frequency and magnitude of future corporate failures. The major sections of this book, thus, focus on the policy lessons affecting accounting, auditing, taxes, and corporate governance that were highlighted by the collapse of these large firms. The contributors to this book are Cato analysts and academics who, in turn, have drawn on the extensive academic literature on these several subjects. The target audience for this book is the larger community of academics, the media, and policy officials who have been motivated to address the implications of the collapse of Enron and the other major corporate scandals for the broader policies affecting American corporations.

Both of these books have tried to focus on the rules by which people operate and how to improve these rules, rather than on the heroes and villains of these stories. There is ample evidence of outrageous and, in some cases, illegal behavior by some corporate managers and an unforgivable lack of attention by too many people in the audit chain, and these cases should be acknowledged and addressed. On the other hand, as is characteristic of prior periods following a large decline in the equity markets, there is a severe danger that the populace, the press, and politicians will overreact, making scapegoats of people for innocent behavior and responding with misguided rules that do not address the basic problems. Our objective is to identify changes in the rules such that the normal incentives of people in both the market and government would lead corporate management to better serve the interests of general shareholders.

ORGANIZATION

Accounting scandals and the bankruptcy of Enron and other large corporations raise two quite different policy issues: How to restore investor trust in the accounts of American corporations? And what changes in government policies would reduce the frequency and magnitude of corporate bankruptcy? Almost all of the attention of the public, the press, and politicians has focused on changes in accounting and auditing in an attempt to restore investor trust in corporate accounts. Enron's collapse, however, was a result of a series of bad business decisions, *not* because it manipulated its accounts, and almost all of the costs to Enron's investors, creditors, employees, and local communities were a consequence of the bankruptcy, *not* because of the accounting scandal. So, again, this book has an overriding objective—to identify the policy changes that would restore investor confidence in corporate accounts by changing the behavior of corporate managers in ways that better serve the interests of general shareholders.

Part I summarizes the major private and public responses to these issues through 2003 with our conclusion that many of these responses were unnecessary, harmful, or insufficient to address the larger issues raised by the collapse of Enron and other large corporations.

Part II summarizes the major accounting issues raised by the Enron collapse, the major alternatives that are being considered, and our conclusion that conventional accounting is inherently limited as a means to estimate the market value of modern corporations. This section concludes with a proposal for competing accounting standards, with each exchange choosing the accounting standard for all firms listed on that exchange.

Part III summarizes the complex story of why *every* link in the Enron audit chain failed to detect Enron's financial vulnerability until it was too late and why this is a likely outcome in many other cases. This section includes brief evaluations of the role of the audit committees and corporate boards, corporate attorneys and those for whom the corporation is a client, the independent auditors, the market specialists in the corporation's stock, the stock exchanges, shareholder suits, the business press, the major creditors, the credit-rating agencies, and the Securities and Exchange Commission. This section concludes with a proposal to shift the authority to select and monitor the disclosure rules and the public auditors to the stock exchanges.

Part IV addresses the several provisions of the current U.S. tax code that influence the character of executive compensation and promote the conditions leading to bankruptcy. First, the corporate income tax, in which the U.S. rate is now among the highest in the world, induces corporations to use too much debt financing. Second, the substantial difference between the personal tax rates on dividends and on long-term capital gains (prior to the 2003 tax legislation) led corporations to rely too much on capital gains as the means to distribute the returns to equity; this reduces the incentive of corporate managers to maintain the cash flow to distribute dividends, increases the incentive to use stock options as executive compensation, and increases their role in the allocation of capital. And third, an obscure provision of the 1993 tax code limits the salary of a corporate executive that may be deducted as a business expense to $1 million a year, a provision that substantially increased the use of stock options as executive compensation. This section concludes with a proposal for a broad-based cash flow tax to replace the corporate income tax.

Part V summarizes the major changes in the rules of corporate governance over the past several decades, most of which strengthened corporate managers relative to shareholders, and the effects of the changes in these rules. The section concludes with proposed changes in the federal and state rules of corporate governance to increase the role of shareholders and their agents.

Finally, Part VI summarizes the major policy lessons affecting the broader corporate economy from this examination of the collapse of Enron.

ACKNOWLEDGMENTS

I am grateful for the careful research and thoughtful policy recommendations by all of the contributors to this book. Readers are encouraged to make comments or raise questions directly with the contributors; the e-mail address for each is included in their brief biography. I am especially grateful to Jacobo Rodriguez, who edited the several chapters that were each published earlier as a Cato Policy Analysis, and to Anna Stroman, my assistant, who brought order to what seemed like a paper chaos for too long.

We have benefited by conversations with many knowledgeable people and, without implicating them as agreeing with everything in this book, we wish to thank them for their guidance: These include several members of the Cato board of directors plus Robert Eccles, Robert Glauber, Susan Koniak, Arthur Levitt, Robert Levy, Robert Litan, Marty Lipton, Henry Manne, Nell Minow, Leon Panetta, Hardwick Simmons, Sara Teslik, Peter Van Doren, Paul Volcker, Peter Wallison, and Frank Zarb.

ABOUT THE CATO INSTITUTE

The Cato Institute is a private, nonprofit, and nonpartisan policy institute committed to individual liberty, free markets, and limited constitutional government. We choose our own research agenda, do no work under contract, and receive no funding from any government. We are pleased to thank the Gillette Company, the D&D Foundation, UST Inc., and the B&E Collins Foundation for their specific support of this project. Most of our funding is from around fifteen thousand individual sponsors to whom we are always grateful.

A Crisis of Trust

William A. Niskanen

TWO TROUBLED INSTITUTIONS

*T*wo important American institutions are now experiencing a crisis of trust—in each case because of a pattern of outrageous behavior that has not yet been sufficiently detected, acknowledged, and corrected by the relevant hierarchy. In each case, the number of known perpetrators has been a very small share of the total number of people in similar positions and the problem is not unique to that institution, but the visible problem has been sufficiently broad and outrageous that it has caused widespread anxiety among those with any relation to the institution. Also, in each case, there is a risk that the response to the problem will be an overreaction, the consequence of those looking for a scapegoat for their own losses or of those using the crisis to further their own agenda. And finally, in each case, there is a continuing controversy about how much of the problem should be resolved within the institution or by the government.

One of these institutions is the Roman Catholic Church. The problem has been sexual abuse by some priests, and the church will hopefully sort out this problem without much outside interference. The *Boston Globe* won the 2003 Pulitzer Prize for Public Service for its coverage of this story.

The other institution experiencing a crisis of trust is American corporate management. The problem has been a massive loss of wealth by shareholders, only a small part of which is due to the accounting frauds by some corporate managers. The *Wall Street Journal* won the 2003 Pulitzer Prize for Explanatory Reporting for its coverage of this story.

The objective of this book is to sort out the policy problems raised by the collapse of Enron and the other major corporate scandals in a way that better serves the interests of the general shareholders.

The Enron Corporation filed for bankruptcy on December 2, 2001, with assets then estimated at $63 billion, the largest bankruptcy to that date, after six straight years of being considered the most innovative corporation in the United States. The collapse of Enron triggered a more general crisis of trust about American corporations with all of the characteristics described above. *Every* link in the Enron audit chain failed to detect and acknowledge Enron's financial problems until it was too late, in some cases until days before Enron filed for bankruptcy. Among the larger group of corporations charged with accounting fraud, no more than a hundred corporate managers, accountants, and attorneys are likely to be subject to criminal penalties, a tiny share of those with similar responsibilities in the seventeen thousand American public corporations. And managerial abuse and mismanagement are not unique to corporations or to the United States. As I write, investigations are under way about evidence of insider trading by managers of Ullico, a union-owned insurance company, and of personal theft by the officers of the District of Columbia teachers union. In Europe, the collapse of Ahold and Parmalat were similar in origin and magnitude to those by Enron and WorldCom. Nor is massive accounting fraud unique to corporations. The General Accounting Office (GAO) has not certified the financial statements of the federal government for seven years in a row because of weak accounting controls and mismeasurement of assets, liabilities, and costs.[1] And the fiscal imbalance of the federal government at the end of fiscal year 2002 is estimated to have been about $44 trillion![2]

Although the stock market has been one of the more reliable leading indicators of general economic conditions, investor concern following the Enron collapse led most U.S. stock indices to decline for over a year after the general economic recovery was under way. There also continues to be a serious danger of overreaction; as in prior cases following a major market decline, there is a continued search for scapegoats and continued pressure on politicians to be seen to be doing something to protect investors. The relative role of market institutions and the government to resolve what continues to be a major problem has yet to be sorted out, and a number of groups will surely use this crisis as an opportunity to make the case for their own agenda.

THE COLLAPSE OF ENRON

Enron's stock peaked at $90.75 a share in August 2000 but ended 2001 as a penny stock. In February 2001, Enron was again ranked as the most innovative firm in the United States, but it ended the year as a symbol of all that is wrong in corporate America. What happened?

Enron ultimately failed for the same general reasons that lead to all bankruptcies: investments that proved too risky to service the debt obligations of the firm. But that is almost a truism and tells us little specific to the collapse of Enron.

In fact, Enron was a very innovative firm and most of its innovative market activities were initially quite profitable; the *Fortune* magazine survey may have been correct to rank Enron as the most innovative corporation in the United States for six years in a row through February 2001. What the *Fortune* survey and most market analysts missed, however, is that Enron never resolved the potential conflict between two quite different business models. One traditional "asset rich" business model, building on Enron's history as a natural gas pipeline company and promoted in Enron by Rebecca Mark, an executive vice president of Enron and its chief dealmaker for major power plants and water companies, was to invest in the infrastructure of the energy, water, and telecommunications industries around the world, a model that required substantial debt. The more innovative "asset light" business model, developed for Enron by Jeffrey Skilling, was to make a limited investment in some commodity supply chain and to use the information from the operation of these physical assets to create a wholesale market and risk-spreading instruments for the commodity, a model that required Enron to maintain sufficient equity capital and ability to borrow to absorb the occasional loss of cash flow from its trading activities. Enron applied this business model most successfully to create wholesale markets for natural gas and electricity and also applied this model successfully in markets for coal, oil, and pulp and paper. The earnings from these innovations were initially quite high but were reduced over time by increasing competition in each of these markets.

Most of Enron's major losses, interestingly, were its traditional investments in utilities, the largest of which were the Dabhol power plant project in India and major water distribution utilities in Britain, Argentina, and elsewhere. The deregulation of water markets in Britain provided an opportunity to do what Enron had done very successfully in the U.S. market for natural gas after deregulation, that is, to make a market for risk-spreading instruments in the commodity, but this opportunity was never realized. Enron, like most other investors, lost a lot of money on its investments in broadband, in general because the demand for bandwidth did not develop as fast as expected and the late investors had to buy bandwidth from the inventors of the technology. One of the few "asset light" investments that proved to be a large loss for Enron was its purchase of Metallgessellschaft PLC, the metals trading component of a German firm, primarily because Enron had no industry-specific assets or experience in this market.

The conflict between Enron's two business models became increasingly apparent beginning in 1997 after Skilling replaced Richard Kinder as chief operating officer (COO).[3] Enron's financial condition had been quite strong during Kinder's tenure as COO, in part because of his obsession with the level of cash flow. Enron chief executive officer (CEO) Kenneth Lay and Skilling, in contrast, focused almost exclusively on increasing the level of reported revenues and earnings, inviting a pattern of aggressive accounting and financial manipulation, and the internal performance review committee reinforced a ruthless and reckless corporate culture by large rewards for innovative ways to increase these reported financial aggregates. The broad use of stock options as executive compensation further encouraged risky behavior. And the results were dramatic! Reported revenues increased rapidly to over $100 billion in 2000, and the widely watched estimate of earnings before interest, taxes, depreciation, and amortization (EBITDA) increased steadily to over $2.8 billion. Over the period from 1997 through 2000, however, Enron experienced *negative* free cash flows of over $10 billion![4]

This tangled web of deceit began to unravel in early 2001. Lay, who had been Enron's only CEO, resigned in February but maintained his position as chairman of the board; Lay's successor as CEO was Skilling. That month, a *Fortune* cover story by Bethany McLean was the first article in the national business press to question the value of Enron's stock, an article that Lay tried to convince *Fortune* to suppress.[5] In May, a revealing article by Peter Eavis in TheStreet.com was the first to report that Andrew Fastow, Enron's chief financial officer (CFO), controlled two special purpose entities (SPEs) that Enron had wrongly failed to consolidate on its own accounts. J. Clifford Baxter, the Enron vice chairman who had questioned the off-the-books transactions and accounting, resigned that month and committed suicide the next January. The price of Enron stock dropped to the $40 range in July *before* the major revelations in August, which proved to be a busy month. Skilling resigned his brief tenure as CEO with the typical letter about wanting to spend more time with his family, and Lay again assumed this position. A memorandum from Sherron Watkins, an accountant and mid-level Enron executive, warned Lay that Enron could collapse in an accounting scandal, a memorandum that led Fastow to attempt to have Watkins fired. And the Securities and Exchange Commission (SEC) started its first investigation of Enron since it reviewed Enron's 1997 annual report. On October 16, Enron reported a third-quarter loss of $618 million, the first reported quarterly loss in four years. Fastow, who had been honored as the nation's leading CFO in 1999, was placed on indefinite leave of absence on October 24, after which a number of senior managers requested and received accelerated distributions of deferred compensation payments of over $53 million. Enron also incorporated three partnerships that it had wrongly treated as independent, resulting in an additional reported loss of $586 million. A proposed merger with Dynegy, another Houston-based energy trading firm, was announced on November 9, only to be terminated on November 28. On November 19, Enron met with its bankers to reveal that its on-book debt was $13 billion at the end of the third quarter but that its off-balance-sheet debt was $25.1 billion, of which $13.8 billion was debt of its special purpose entities.

Lay had long cultivated the Bush family. Enron had hired several former officials of the first Bush administration, and Enron was the largest contributor to the Bush campaign in 2000. One should not be surprised that Enron tried to cash in on these political investments during this period of financial troubles. As a member of the National Energy Policy Task Force, Lay had a private meeting with vice president Dick Cheney in April 2001, following which the administration expressed strong opposition to price caps in the wholesale electricity markets and made a coordinated effort to rescue Enron's large investment in the Dabhol project in India. In late October, after Enron's financial vulnerability became more apparent, Lay called Federal Reserve chairman Alan Greenspan, Treasury secretary Paul O'Neill, and former Treasury secretary Robert Rubin, apparently with the hope that the Federal Reserve would organize a financial restructuring of Enron as it had with Long Term Capital Management in 1998. In November, Rubin, as a director of Citigroup, which was one of Enron's largest creditors, called Treasury undersecretary Peter Fisher to suggest that the Treasury urge the credit-rating agencies to defer a downgrading of Enron's debt to assure enough financing for the pending merger with Dynegy. In the end, the Bush administration rejected any more assistance to Enron, and the potential for a major political scandal evaporated.

On November 28, the three credit-rating agencies downgraded Enron debt to below investment grade, a decision that made Enron debt ineligible as an investment by commercial banks. Enron filed for bankruptcy on December 2, and the house of cards collapsed. When the proposed reorganization plan was filed nineteen months later, most creditors expected to be paid only 14.4 cents to 18.3 cents per dollar, and Stephen Cooper, Enron's acting CEO, remarked that "When you look at how much fluff was in Enron's balance sheet, this is actually very good."[6]

Enron was a very complicated corporation, and sorting out what happened is quite difficult. Enron owned or sponsored hundreds of legal entities, for example, although many were inactive. There is now no question, however, that Enron's senior management was engaged in a pattern of aggressive accounting and financial manipulation to mislead investors and creditors for several years prior to its collapse, especially in 2000 when total reported revenues increased from $40.1 billion to $100.8 billion! The post-bankruptcy report by the Powers Committee of the Enron board described this behavior as follows:

"Many of the most significant transactions apparently were designed to accomplish favorable financial statement results, not to achieve bona fide economic objectives or to transfer risks."[7] Revenues were artificially inflated by wash trades (in which Enron was effectively trading with itself) and by pulling forward deferred revenue to the time a trade was arranged. Enron also used some of its many SPEs to arrange wash trades, the improper use of mark-to-market accounting, to conceal debt and to generate tax losses. Some of these transactions, except those involving several SPEs, were not clear violations of accounting rules, but they were clearly misleading. These transactions, unfortunately, were not sufficient to trigger a special review of Enron's financial status by any element in the audit chain until it was too late. And most of the market specialists in Enron stock maintained a buy recommendation well into the fall of 2001. One wonders, however, whether Enron's senior management may have misled *themselves* by the combined effects of all the financial manipulation that they invited and approved.

Shortly before this book went to press, Lay was indicted on several criminal charges. I do not have the authority or the information to judge whether he is guilty of these charges; that is for the trial court to decide. My primary concern about this trial is that Lay may be incorrectly judged by what he *should have known* about the behavior of his subordinates. Lay should be judged on the basis of his personal actions, directions to subordinates, or the actions of subordinates that he implicitly condoned by knowing about without attempting to correct—not on the basis of what he should have known. There is no way to manage any large private or public organization if the senior manager is criminally liable for illegal behavior by others in the organization about which the senior manager has no knowledge. Congress has wisely chosen not to apply a should-have-known standard as the basis for a criminal charge against senior federal officials for misleading budget accounting.

The history of Enron summarized in this and other books suggests that Lay should have known about the widespread pattern of accounting manipulation and other misrepresentations of Enron's financial status. In that case, Lay was an incompetent CEO, whether or not he was guilty of criminal behavior. A should-have-known standard should be a sufficient basis for a corporate board to fire the CEO but not for a court to judge a criminal charge.

The most important lesson from the Enron collapse, however, is that Enron failed because of a combination of bad business decisions, not because its accounts were misleading. The major business decisions that most contributed to its collapse were a series of bad investments, most of which were in the traditional asset-rich industries; the failure to reconcile two quite different business models; and the decision to focus management objectives on reported revenues and earnings rather than on the present value of future cash flows. Enron first manipulated its accounts to impress investors with its reported financial aggregates but ultimately to hide its financial vulnerability. More accurate, transparent, and timely accounts—given the pattern of bad business decisions—would only have accelerated the Enron collapse.

ENRON AS A SYMBOL OF A BROADER PROBLEM

The collapse of Enron led to huge losses to Enron's investors, creditors, and employees but, by itself, with little direct effect on other parties except those in the energy-trading markets. The conditions specific to Enron will be adequately sorted out by the market and the courts. As expressed by one blunt-speaking investment manager, however, "Enron ain't the problem. . . . The unremarked gut issue today is that over the past decade there was a landslide transfer of wealth from the public shareholders to corporate managers. Enron was just the tip of the iceberg ready to happen."[8] Some context, however, is important at this point: The total value of American corporate equity declined nearly $7 *trillion* from March 2000 through the end of 2002, only several hundred billion dollars of which was in the large firms that were charged with a major accounting scandal and later went bankrupt. For the larger community, the important issues are not the specific reasons why Enron collapsed but whether the general rules affecting all corporations lead managers to manipulate their accounts, to use too much debt, and to incur too many risks. The other important issue raised by the Enron collapse is why these conditions often escape notice or are not acted on by any link in the audit chain.

The broader pattern of financial developments since the mid-1990s is clearly more consistent with a description of Enron as a symbol of a broader problem than with a view that the Enron collapse was merely a rare event in a stable distribution of potential corporate failures. This pattern includes the following major developments:

- The explosion of corporate executive compensation; average CEO compensation at the S&P 500 companies (including the estimated value of options when granted) increased from $2.7 million in 1992 to $14.7 million in 2000, only to drop with the stock market to $9.4 million in 2002.
- The substantial increase in the number of companies restating their earnings from 97 in 1997 to 330 in 2002.
- The huge decline in the broad stock-market indices since March 2000 and, contrary to the usual pattern, a continuation of this decline well into the current general recovery; major accounting scandals and other malfeasance by corporate officers at Adelphia, Cendant, Computer Associates, Dynegy, Enron, Fannie Mae, Freddy Mac, Global Crossing, HealthSouth, Hollinger International, ImClone Systems, Kmart, Lucent Technologies, Peregrine, Rite Aid, Sunbeam, Tyco, U.S Foodservice, Waste Management, WorldCom, and Xerox, and by the bankruptcy of Global Crossing, Enron, WorldCom, Conseco, and several other large corporations.
- A growing number of investigations of corporate misconduct by the SEC and the Justice Department.

These developments suggest that something is seriously wrong in corporate America. Richard Breeden—a lawyer, Republican, and former SEC chairman—may have best summarized this problem by commenting that

> I think that the worst abuses were limited to a few companies . . . but there were widespread problems of disclosure and widespread examples of companies hyping their numbers and turning their earnings announcements into something more like a tout-sheet than a financial statement. . . . We turned a culture of conservatism about financial statements into a culture of hype.[9]

Alice Rivlin—an economist, Democrat, and former senior official in several federal agencies—elaborated on this perspective to conclude that

> The problem of Enron and too many other corporations also demonstrates that we do not yet have the rules of the game right. . . . The accounting rules

have not caught up with the rapidly increasing complexity of business trans-actions, as the current discussion of special purpose entities demonstrates. Companies have been able to overstate earnings, hide debt off the balance sheet, and create a rosier picture than reality. Even more dismaying have been insider deals that enriched executives at the expense of shareholders, many of whom were employees, and the spectacle of executives touting the soundness of the company's stock while secretly dumping their own and tipping off their friends.[10]

General shareholders, now about half of American households, have a financial interest in correcting the conditions that led to these problems. Those who are concerned about maintaining the necessary popular and political support for a free-market economy have a special political stake in correcting these conditions.

THE SPECIAL PROBLEMS OF THE TELECOMMUNICATIONS INDUSTRY

Enron was not primarily a telecommunications company, although, like many other investors, it lost a lot of money on its broadband investments. But it is also important to sort out the policy lessons from the failure of other large firms in this same period. A substantial share of the total loss of equity value since March 2000 and of the various accounting scandals, for example, involved telecommunications firms. The record indicates that

> many telecom stocks have fallen more than 90 percent from their historical highs. In the past two years, some 500,000 jobs have been lost. . . . Of the 330 new entrants in the local telephone market at the end of 2000, only 80 exist today. Of the 39 million miles of optical fiber in place as of March 2002, only 10 percent is currently in use.[11]

As in most industries, many of the failing firms had not offered any better, distinctive, or cheaper service. The one common expectation of these firms is that business and residential access to broadband would increase rapidly, an expectation that was not realized. But many of the problems of this industry are attributable to major policy mistakes. The most important of these policy mistakes was the decision by the Federal Communications Commission to interpret the Telecommunications Act of 1996 as authority to order the incumbent local exchange carriers (ILECs) to provide access to the competitive local exchange carriers (CLECs) at low administered prices, a mistake that has not yet been corrected; this led to massive overcapacity among the CLECs and a low rate of return to the ILECs without providing any significant new services. Another element of the misguided industrial policy that has prevented a market restructuring of the telecommunications industry has been the use of antitrust regulations to block mergers among the wireless companies and the reintegration of the ILECs and the long-distance carriers. The accounting scandals by a number of telecommunications firms appear to have been attempts to hide their financial vulnerability, a problem that was at least substantially caused by policy mistakes.

A BROADER PERSPECTIVE

For all of the problems of corporate America and the special problems of the telecommunications sector, it is also important to bound the range of these problems. For all of these problems and the large decline in stock prices since early 2000, an important 2003 study by Bengt Holmstrom and Steven Kaplan documents that the U.S. stock market performed as well or better through the end of 2002 than the average of other major stock markets in Europe and the Pacific, both recently and since 1982. Also, the increase in U.S. real GDP per capita through the end of 2002 was as high as, or higher than, that in Great Britain, France, Germany, and Japan, again, both recently and since 1982.[12] Adding 2003 to this sample would only strengthen this conclusion. So, something is also profoundly right about corporate America.

Our special challenge has been to sort out the policy lessons from the collapse of Enron to resolve these problems effectively without jeopardizing the conditions that have led more general measures of U.S. economic performance to be superior to that of most other major economies. The U.S. economy, in summary, has been a marvelous engine of economic growth, but we can do even better.

NOTES

1. General Accounting Office, "FY2003 U.S. Government Financial Statements," GAO-04-477T, March 3, 2004.

2. Gokhale, Jagadeesh and Kent Smetters, *Fiscal and Generational Imbalances*, Washington, D.C.: AEI Press 2003.

3. Kinder had bought Enron's liquid gas division to form his own company, Kinder Morgan.

4. Bassett, Richard and Mark Storrie, "Corporate Accounting after Enron: Is the Cure Worse than the Disease?" in Christopher Culp and William Niskanen (eds.), *Corporate Aftershock*, Hoboken, N.J.: John Wiley and Sons, 2003.

5. Weaver, Paul, "The Business Press as a Corporate Monitor," chap. 11 of this book.

6. Cooper, Stephen, "Enron's Creditors to Get Peanuts," *Wall Street Journal*, July 11, 2003.

7. Powers, William C., Raymond S. Troubh, and Herbert Winokur, Jr., "Report of Investigation by the Special Investigative Committee of the Board of Directors of Enron Corporation," February 1, 2002.

8. Sosnoff, Martin T., "Enron Ain't the Problem," *Directors and Boards*, spring 2002, p. 38–39.

9. Breeden, Richard, quoted by Andrew Hill, "Comment and Analysis," *Financial Times*, December 30, 2002.

10. Rivlin, Alice M., "The Challenges to Capitalism and the Role of the Government," *Miller Center Report* 18, no. 4, fall 2002.

11. Wohlstetter, John C., "Telecom Meltdown," *American Outlook*, fall 2002.

12. Holmstrom, Bengt and Steven N. Kaplan, "The State of U.S. Corporate Governance: What's Right and What's Wrong?" National Bureau of Economic Research Working Paper no. 9163, April 2003.

I

EARLY PRIVATE AND PUBLIC RESPONSES TO THE CORPORATE SCANDALS

Major Private Responses

William A. Niskanen

The collapse of Enron proved to be a valuable wake-up call to a number of affected private groups. Major responses were proposed or initiated by a number of private organizations prior to the approval of the Sarbanes-Oxley Act (SOA) in late July 2002.

STANDARD AND POOR'S

Standard and Poor's (S&P), one of the three major credit-rating agencies, proposed new measures of corporate earnings[1] in May 2002, the output of a project that S&P had initiated in 2001. The new concept of core earnings attempts to measure the earnings from a company's primary lines of business. Compared with earnings as defined by the Generally Accepted Accounting Principles (GAAP), for example, the new S&P measure removes the effects of onetime changes, adds employee stock options and the interest cost on pension obligations as an expense, and excludes the gains and losses from a variety of financial transactions. S&P has now calculated a measure of core earnings for all firms in the S&P 500 beginning in 2001 and, later, for other listed firms.[2]

It is not yet clear whether this concept will become broadly accepted and utilized. The measure of core earnings still includes most of the problems of GAAP and adds the controversial provision that stock options should be expensed. As of late 2002, core earnings of the S&P 500 were about 70 percent of GAAP earnings, with the largest difference due to the estimated expense of stock options. And a longer history is probably required to make the data on core earnings valuable to market specialists.

THE BUSINESS ROUNDTABLE

The Business Roundtable (BRT), whose members are the chief executives of about 150 large corporations, endorsed new principles of corporate governance[3] in May 2002. The BRT urged corporations to adopt a number of voluntary changes in corporate governance rules, most important of which was that a substantial majority of the corporate boards be independent both in fact and appearance. More specific recommendations included that the audit committee, the nomination committee, and the compensation committee consist only of independent directors and that the audit committee have the responsibility to select the outside auditor and monitor the relations with the auditor. More interesting, perhaps, is the suggestion that the relation between the board and the management should be one of constructive skepticism. The BRT endorsement of these principles represented a near-complete victory for the monitoring model of the corporate board, the view that most of the problems of corporate America are due to some conflict of interest and would be reduced by more independent boards. And most of their specific recommendations were then or later endorsed by the stock exchanges, the SOA, and the SEC.

In June 2003, the BRT surveyed its member corporations to determine how many firms had implemented the major recommendations of the May 2002 *Principles*. The major findings of this survey are summarized below:[4]

- Eighty percent of the BRT companies reported that at least 75 percent of their board members are independent, and 90 percent report that at least two-thirds of their directors are independent.
- Fifty-five percent of the BRT companies have an independent chairman, independent lead director, or a presiding outside director—a large increase relative to 2002.
- Outside directors of 97 percent of the BRT companies now meet in executive sessions (without the management directors present) at least once a year, and 55 percent expect to do so at least five times in 2003.
- Two-thirds of the BRT companies reported a process by which the nominating committees respond to shareholder inquiries, proposals, and nominations of board candidates.

In summary, for better or for worse, the BRT appears to have endorsed and implemented almost all of the corporate reform agenda. It is too early to tell how important this will be, except to demonstrate a BRT interest to avoid continued controversy on these issues; the empirical studies summarized in section VI, however, suggest that these changes will have little effect on firm performance.

THE STOCK EXCHANGES

In June 2002, a report by a blue-ribbon committee of the New York Stock Exchange (NYSE) proposed major changes to the listing standards for NYSE-listed firms and a number of recommendations for approval by Congress or the SEC.[5] The National Association of Securities Dealers (NASD) had previously submitted proposed new director independence standards and later endorsed the major provisions of the NYSE proposal.

Central to the NYSE report is a provision that boards of NYSE-listed companies have a majority of independent directors. In addition, the committee report calls for:

- Tightening the definition of an independent director,
- Granting the audit committee sole authority to hire and fire auditors and to approve any significant non-audit work by the auditors,
- Mandating that director compensation represent the sole remuneration from the listed company for audit-committee members,
- Requiring audit, nominating, and compensation committees to consist solely of independent directors, with a requirement that the chair of the audit committee have accounting or financial management experience,
- Requiring the CEO of NYSE-listed companies to attest to the accuracy, completeness, and understandability of information provided to investors,
- Mandating that shareholders vote on all equity-based compensation plans, including stock option plans, and
- Allowing the NYSE to impose additional penalties, including public reprimand letters, in addition to suspension and delisting.

The committee also recommended a number of measures for approval by Congress or the SEC, including the following:[6]

- Establishing a new private-sector organization . . . to monitor and govern public accountants,
- Prohibiting relationships between auditors and their clients that would affect the fairness and objectivity of audits,
- Giving the SEC the authority to permanently bar officers and directors from holding office again after violating their duties to shareholders, and
- Asking Congress to allocate increased resources to the SEC to increase the agency's monitoring and enforcement activities.

Almost all of these proposals, with minor amendments at most, were later incorporated in the SOA or by SEC rulings. These measures substantially nationalized the rules of corporate governance in the United States, rules for which the states had previously had almost complete authority. And the BRT and the stock exchanges were the primary private organizations that led these rules to have the force of federal law.

EARLY RESPONSES BY OTHER PRIVATE ORGANIZATIONS

Other private organizations also proposed or implemented responses to the developing corporate scandals before congressional approval of the SOA.

The International Corporate Governance Network, institutional investors that manage about $10 trillion in assets, approved a set of international standards for corporate governance (much like that proposed by the NYSE committee) that its members would use their voting power to promote.

A task force of the American Bar Association (ABA) recommended tightening the standard for a lawyer's obligation to report a crime or fraud by a client to include a requirement for a "noisy exit" if the lawyer's superior takes no action in response to such a report. As of the fall of 2003, this proposal was still being debated because of a concern that it would weaken the incentive for corporate managers to seek legal advice.

More important, the long bear market beginning in March 2000 had changed the attitude of many corporate managers and directors. In good times, no one minds the store of management-friendly firms that make an adequate return, even though shareholder-friendly firms may have a significantly higher rate of return. In subsequent years, however, corporate managers have been quicker to reduce employment and close plants in response to weak demand; productivity growth has continued to be unusually high as a consequence, and boards appear to have been more cautious in approving major new investments and increased executive compensation. A study by Booz Allen Hamilton of the world's 2,500 largest listed corporations found that 3.9 percent of CEOs were dismissed in 2002, compared with 2.3 percent in 2001 and only 1 percent in 1995.[7] The important test is whether the costly lessons of this period will survive a recovery of demand and another long bull market.

NOTES

1. Standard and Poor's, *Measures of Corporate Earnings*, revised May 14, 2002.
2. All of these data are now available on the S&P Compustat database.
3. Business Roundtable, *Principles of Corporate Governance*, May 2002.
4. Business Roundtable, press release on the *Corporate Governance Survey Highlights*, July 2003.

5. New York Stock Exchange, press release on the *Report of the New York Stock Exchange Corporate Accountability and Listing Standards Committee,* June 6, 2002.

6. NYSE, press release on *Corporate Accountability*.

7. Skapinker, Michael, "CEO Dismissals Rise as Investors Strike Out," *Financial Times,* May 12, 2003.

• 3 •

Political Responses to the Enron Scandal

Alan Reynolds

𝒯he first major political responses to the massive bankruptcies of Enron and WorldCom were the Sarbanes–Oxley Act (SOA) of July 2002 and the securities regulators' settlement with ten Wall Street firms in April 2003. Both responses appear to have been based on essentially the same assumption about the nature of the problem to be solved and the goal of the prescribed actions. The implicit assumption was that the "corporate scandals" were primarily a matter of inadequate or misleading stockholder information. And the explicit goal of both the law and the settlement was to "restore investment confidence." That assumption and goal explain the overwhelming emphasis on certifying and overseeing accounting and auditing in the SOA.

The same assumption and goal also led several states' attorneys general, led by Elliot Spitzer of New York, to persuade the Securities and Exchange Commission (SEC) to join in a sweeping complaint outside any courtroom that investors had been duped by at least two stock analysts who proved too bullish after the bull market died. In both instances, the actions taken were mainly rationalized in terms of a single short-term intent—to "restore investor confidence"—rather than any specific long-term results. There was little pretense that either the law or the settlement was even intended to minimize the risk of Enron-like traumatic corporate collapses recurring in the future. Even the short-term intent was left conveniently undefined, making it impolitic to ascribe the significant decline of stock prices between the enactment of SOA and the announcement of the Wall Street deal as reflecting a vote of no confidence in the law or settlement.

The same narrow focus on improving the way a financial collapse is reported, either by accountants or stock analysts, was sometimes echoed among researchers. Writing about Enron and WorldCom, for example, Graham, Litan, and Sukhtankar said, "both bankruptcies resulted from accounting malpractice."[1] That widespread view was the main rationale behind "accounting reform." But

18

bankruptcies are real events, not simply a matter of the way records are kept. Companies go bankrupt because their cash inflow is insufficient to service their debts. Deceptive accounting by Enron, Global Crossing, WorldCom, and others was a consequence of financial crises, rather than the cause—a devious attempt to cover up the looming danger of bankruptcy by exaggerating income and/or hiding debts. With more honest accounting the financial distress of these firms might have been more widely known at an earlier date, with the result that their credit ratings and stock prices would have fallen sooner. Rapid and candid disclosure of the problems could conceivably have reduced the scale and damage of the ultimate bankruptcy, but it would have done so only by accelerating bankruptcy, rather than by preventing it.

Law professor Douglas Branson, author of *Corporate Governance*, helps put recent events in perspective. He notes that in many recent cases "as with Scott Sullivan at WorldCom or the Rigas family at Adelphia Communications, the cause of the eventual failure of the firm was the wrongdoing of one or two individuals, rather than some sort of corporate governance failure." And he adds that all the corporate scandals that made the headlines, whether bankrupt or not, "still adds up to only approximately 20 companies out of the 16,200 which file periodic reports with the SEC."[2]

Many recent bankruptcies did not involve scandals and therefore received little public or political attention. After Enron, the largest bankruptcies of 2001 were Pacific Gas and Electric, the FINOVA Group, Reliance Group Holdings, Federal-Mogul, and Comdisco. Smaller bankruptcies included PSI Net, Bethlehem Steel, Sunbeam, and W.R. Grace.[3] Measured by the number of employees at risk during bankruptcies, K-Mart had 252,000, WorldCom 75,000, and Enron only 20,600.[4] Yet employees of Enron captured the most media attention.

Just as most bankruptcies did not involve scandals, many allegations of accounting transgressions did not involve bankruptcy—such as Xerox, Tyco, Rite Aid, and AOL. Naturally, accounting failures that did not end in business failures failed to generate a strong political response, unlike Enron and WorldCom. And a wide variety of alleged misdeeds by prominent business people, some of them entirely legal, had nothing to do with accounting. Yet political officials and the media nonetheless tended to lump everything together as corporate "malfeasance" or "misconduct," thus combining indiscriminately all accusations (proven or not) of sales tax avoidance, sweetheart loans, insider trading, biased investment advice, and even lavish retirement perks.

REDUNDANT BUT NOT INNOCUOUS

The SOA was to some extent a political response to a wide variety of perceived misdeeds, some of which are always with us (greed), and some of which had nothing to do with accounting or crime. Yet the new law was nonetheless mainly focused on increasing criminal and financial penalties for deviations from the inherently confusing and malleable rules of the Generally Accepted Accounting Principles (GAAP), even though the law implicitly criticizes those same principles. Lawrence Cunningham of the Boston College Law School summarized the law as follows:

> The Sarbanes-Oxley Act of 2002 modifies governance, reporting and disclosure rules for public companies, bolsters criminal and civil liability for securities fraud, founds a new oversight board for independent audit firms to be paid for by stockholders of public companies, embraces restrictions on audit firms engaging in various non-audit services for their clients, requires internal control certifications by CEOs and CFOs and prohibits corporate loans to directors.[5]

"Facing crisis," Cunningham explains, "politicians (as well as others) need to feel in control. For legislators, regulators, and prosecutors, this means responding to crisis with legislation, regulation, and prosecutions." Putting aside post-crisis agitation among regulators (Harvey Pitt's hyperactive press releases while at the SEC) and prosecutors (Spitzer's competing media campaign), Cunningham finds much of the SOA legislation itself redundant. "Virtually all [changes] were already in effect as a matter of custom or practice and/or due to requirements imposed by stock exchanges, regulators, state law, or other provisions of federal law." That does not mean SOA was ineffectual, only that most of it was unnecessary at best ("the loan prohibition is a classic case of overreaction to a few miscreants"), the new Accounting Oversight Board could end up "meaningless or worse," and the ritual of CEO-CFO certification is risky. Cunningham elsewhere criticizes as both new and unwise the whole idea of making "fair" financial statements the basis of CEO-CFO certification.[6] Legal scholars have been busily trying to unravel the numerous contradictions and ambiguities in the law. Michael Perino of the Columbia University Law School writes that some aspects of the act,

> especially the changes to the statute of limitations for private securities claims, are inconsistent with current law. Other aspects of the Act, like the new certification requirements, are internally inconsistent. . . . Many provisions of the Act are simply delegations of authority to the Commission [SEC] to adopt rules. Often these involve areas in which the Commission or the SROs [self-regulatory organizations, such as stock exchanges] had already undertaken rulemaking initiatives, again raising the question of whether legislation was truly necessary.[7]

Ambiguities aside, perhaps the most prominent features of the new law are these: (1) a requirement that the chief executive officer (CEO) and chief financial officer (CFO) certify that their company's financial reports are accurate; (2) a requirement that the CEO and CFO disgorge any gains from bonuses and stocks sales during the year prior to any financial restatement attributed to any undefined "misconduct"; and (3) the creation of a new Accounting Oversight Board for publicly traded corporations with vast discretionary authority to spend money from fees (de facto taxes) levied on stockholders, to favor or abolish particular accounting firms, and to create and revise auditing standards if it chooses to do so.

This chapter is mainly devoted to an assessment of the promises and pitfalls of the SOA legislation. It also comments, however, on the April 2003 $1.4 billion settlement with ten Wall Street firms that evolved from a complaint one year earlier against Merrill Lynch by Spitzer.

Our general conclusion about SOA, as will be explained and documented later, is that this hastily written law was unnecessary, harmful, and inadequate.

Sarbanes-Oxley was *unnecessary* because the SEC already had ample authority to oversee, investigate, certify, and enforce honest accounting and auditing. The new Accounting Oversight Board is charged with the same job the SEC was supposed to have been doing, although with less expertise and no experience. Before SOA, the SEC's chief accountant testified, "The SEC . . . not only has authority under the securities laws of the United States to set accounting standards to be followed by public companies but also has the power to enforce those standards."[8] The SEC brought 163 enforcement actions in 2002, up from 79 in 1999, and did not need new legislation to do that.[9] The SEC required CEOs to certify financial statements two weeks before the enactment of SOA and did not need new legislation to do that either. Moreover, the Department of Justice and state prosecutors already had ample authority to prosecute executives for fraud.

Sarbanes-Oxley is likely to prove *harmful*, on balance, mainly because it greatly increases the costs and risks of doing business as a publicly traded corporation in the United States, and increases the risks of serving as an executive or director of such a corporation. One nearly immediate consequence of the SOA, for example, was greatly increased premiums for directors and officers liability insurance. Such costs and risks are already giving rise to many unintended consequences, such as reluctance to take private firms public and increased interest in taking public firms private, greater difficulty of recruiting and retaining qualified directors, and so on. Evidence of several adverse but unintended consequences will be presented later in this chapter.

Sarbanes-Oxley was *inadequate* because it failed to identify and remedy any fundamental causes of massive corporate failures. By concentrating on stricter *accounting* under nebulous GAAP, rather than working to provide more timely and meaningful investor information or to repair institutional weakness that may contribute to business failure, much of SOA became a symbolic exercise in codifying the wrong priorities. New guidelines from the stock exchanges to make directors more independent and the tax bill proposed by the Bush administration to reduce distortions that punish dividends and encourage debt-financed corporate acquisitions were more substantive efforts to fix underlying problems.

A secondary thesis of this chapter is that certain features in SOA and the Wall Street settlement are apt to significantly reduce, rather than improve, the quality of stock market analysis made available to individual investors in the future.

THE MYOPIC, ILLUSIVE GOAL OF INVESTOR CONFIDENCE

Sarbanes-Oxley and the lucrative (for state governments) effort to fine Wall Street firms were repeatedly sold to the public as ways to "restore investor confidence." That language even appears in section 501 of SOA, which asks the SEC to "foster greater public confidence in securities research." The single-minded objective of restoring confidence—which clearly implied a public promise of restoring higher stock prices—encouraged and exploited a widespread misperception that corporate scandals were the main reason stocks had declined. Yet that purely psychological explanation for the market's decline was inconsistent with three readily available facts.

First, most of the stock market's decline happened long *before* the Enron debacle was publicly revealed. And the market's second significant decline occurred *after* July 5, 2002, when President George W. Bush began supporting SOA's alleged power to restore confidence. As *Washington Post* financial columnist James Glassman explained, "Between November 8, 2001, the date that Enron told shareholders that its five previous years of financial statements should not be relied upon, and June 25, the date the WorldCom deceptions became public, the Dow-Jones Industrial Average dropped only 3 percent."[10] That is, most of the stock market's decline occurred during the eighteen months *before* the Enron scandal. Another serious decline occurred during the nine months *after* SOA first appeared politically viable. The period when the biggest scandals were most in the news was, as Glassman observed, a period when investor confidence was relatively strong and stable.

Enron's collapse was much more of a surprise to the markets than the well-known troubles of WorldCom and others. Even in the relatively surprising case of Enron, however, the market had discounted substantial risk long before the press or SEC took notice of Enron's bogus accounting. Enron stock had briefly traded as high as $90 a share in 2000 (a figure that some wrongly used to show how big the losses were to Enron employees who did not diversify). It closed the year at $83.12. "Before the first revelations on October 16 [2001]," noted Robert Bartley, "Enron's share price had fallen to $33.17."[11] The market took Enron stock down by about 63 percent before the rating services and stock market analysts figured out that something was wrong. In the case of WorldCom, lying about earnings did not prevent the stock from dropping below $1 a share before its accounting trickery was revealed.

Second, as economists Holmstrom and Kaplan show,

> the broad evidence is not consistent with a failed U.S. system. The U.S.
> economy and stock market have performed well both on an absolute basis
> and relative to other countries over the past two decades. And the U.S. stock
> market has continued to outperform other [countries'] broad indices since
> the scandals broke.[12]

Third, political claims that stock prices could be increased by the greater
confidence that would allegedly be inspired by increased regulation and litigation
amounted to saying stocks were too cheap in June 2002—that stock prices were
much lower than could explained by reported earnings, so those earnings reports
must be too rosy. All the ambitious political promises to "restore investor confidence" amounted to saying the average price-earnings (p/e) ratio was too low or,
equivalently, that the earnings-price ratio (e/p) was too high. In early 2003, however, the *Economist* noted that "a market with a p/e ratio of 28 on historic profits
. . . is not exactly discounting bad news."[13]

The president's Council of Economic Advisers converts the familiar p/e
ratio into an inverted e/p ratio. On June 30, 2002, that e/p ratio was 2.7, which
was quite low (and the p/e ratio was high). That suggests that investor confidence was *not* unusually depressed just before the passage of SOA, given the
known earnings of these five hundred firms over the previous year. And that, in
turn, means *low* reported earnings—not earnings that looked high because of
accounting tricks—were the real reason stock prices were low. The relationship
of stock prices to earnings and the relative stability of stock prices between the
Enron and WorldCom revelations provide no evidence that political promises
to restore confidence through regulations and fines bore any relation to any
genuine problem. What investors needed was not a restoration of confidence
but a restoration of profits. Increased fines, fees, lawsuits, and regulatory costs do
not improve profits. Judging by 2002 stock prices, they did not improve confidence either.

Table 3.1 shows that reported earnings per share shortly before SOA passed
were half of what they had been during the first three quarters of 2000 (based on
earnings over the previous four quarters). Stock prices were weak, not because investors feared that reported earnings were exaggerated by accounting tricks, but because reported earnings were depressingly depressed. It is only after SOA passed that
stock prices began to look lower than might be expected given an apparent improvement in earnings. If anything, that suggests the new law may have damaged investor confidence. Yet investors may have simply been anticipating the renewed drop
in earnings at the end of 2002. At the end of 2002, the ratio of earnings to S&P 500
stock prices (3.18) was actually the same as it was in 1999 (3.17), when the market
was supposedly experiencing a "bubble." What had changed from 1999 to 2002 was
not the relationship of earnings to prices ("confidence") but earnings alone.

Table 3.1   S&P 500 Stock Index: Prices Fell with Earnings

Date	Earnings per share (Cents)	Earnings/Price Ratio	S&P 500 Index
03/31/2000	13.74	3.40	1498.6
06/30/2000	13.48	3.57	1454.6
09/30/2000	13.71	3.74	1436.5
12/31/2000	9.07	3.79	1320.3
03/31/2001	9.18	3.92	1160.3
06/30/2001	4.83	3.00	1224.4
09/30/2001	5.23	2.72	1041.9
12/31/2001	5.45	2.15	1148.1
03/31/2002	9.19	2.15	1147.4
06/30/2002	6.87	2.70	989.8
09/30/2002	8.53	3.68	815.3
12/31/2002	3.00	3.14	879.8
03/31/2003	11.92	3.57	848.2
06/30/2003	11.10	3.56	974.5

Sources: Economic Indicators; Standard & Poor's Quantitative Services.[14]

The evidence is clear that prices of major U.S. stocks at the time SOA was enacted were not particularly low when compared with earnings (i.e., the e/p ratio was low, rather than high in the first half of 2002), so there was no measurable crisis in investor confidence. Yet restoring investor confidence (rather than preventing future financial crises) was nonetheless the primary issue ostensibly addressed by both SOA and by the Wall Street settlement. Judged by their own standard, SOA and the Wall Street settlement were instant failures. The Dow-Jones Industrials closed at 9,380 on July 5, 2002, the day before President George W. Bush began to speak out in favor of increased regulation of corporate accounting, but the Dow subsequently fell to 8,306 by April 25, 2003, when the details came out about the Wall Street settlement. Cheering up investors was a presumptuous political objective in the first place, and one unrelated to any facts. Yet by their own criterion, advocates of SOA and the Wall Street deal could not point to having provided any discernible reassurance to investors.

UNWARRANTED FAITH IN GAAP ACCOUNTING

Two weeks before SOA was enacted, an SEC order required chief executive officers and chief financial officers of larger U.S. companies to certify by August 14 that their companies' financial statements neither "contained an untrue statement of a material fact" nor "omitted to state a material fact necessary to make the statements . . . not misleading."[15] The SEC had announced six months earlier that it was considering such a certification scheme. This was just one example of SOA putting into law something that was already being put into practice. Proposals from the NYSE and NASDAQ to make directors more independent of managers are another example.

Despite its redundancy and ambiguity, certification is nonetheless the show-piece of SOA, partly because President Bush put great emphasis on certification before the act was signed. Section 302(a) threatens prison sentences of up to twenty years for executives who "willfully" certify reports that are later deemed to have not "fairly" presented "financial condition and results" (the fairness crite-rion is an unpredictable addition to the SEC version). Unfortunately, these sanc-tions rely on treating accounting by GAAP as something far more factual and objective than it is or can possibly be. As Donald Langevoort of the Georgetown University Law Center notes, "certification as written speaks to the language of the profession—GAAP."[16] As a result, an executive's property may be "disgorged" and/or he could be imprisoned for many years based only on what the *Economist* calls the "brittle illusion of accounting exactitude."[17]

Somewhat paradoxically, SOA also requires the SEC to report on how quickly the country could move away from GAAP's rule-based approach to the simpler principles-based approach used in most other countries. "Because Amer-ica's GAAP accounting system relies on thousands of pages of rules," notes the *Economist*, "it is more vulnerable to manipulation than Europe's more principles-based approach."[18] Nearly everyone understands that, including SEC officials and the authors of SOA. Yet the SOA sanctifies GAAP definitions of corporate earn-ings, and audits based on those same definitions, at the expense of arguably more meaningful information such as corporate cash flow. "The appropriate policy for Congress," writes Peter Wallison, "would have been to diminish the importance of audited financial statements by encouraging the disclosure of information that is more useful to investors."[19] Instead, Congress moved to strengthen GAAP while asking the SEC how quickly it might be scrapped.

The main criterion of good accounting is that it provides stockholders and creditors with information that is as clear, timely, useful, and accurate as possible. Few experts believe that periodic reports of the GAAP numbers, to which Con-gress has now attached severe sanctions, meet this basic need. Former SEC Chair-man Harvey Pitt described some gaps in GAAP:

> Because our current system focuses principally on so-called objective numbers and disclosure, it does not provide nearly enough useful informa-tion to investors, for example, the kinds of trend information that corpo-rate managers use continuously to make critical managerial decisions. By the time the information our system provides is actually available to in-vestors, it is often stale. And the information currently supplied is not always capable of being deciphered by sophisticated experts, much less or-dinary investors. Combined with a hyperactive litigation environment, our disclosure can appear focused less on disclosure and more on liability

avoidance. The recent phenomenon of 'pro forma' financials . . . is often—but unfortunately not always—a legitimate desire by companies to demystify mandated financial statement disclosures.[20]

Pitt's remarks highlighted two important points. First, "hyperactive litigation" (class action lawsuits ostensibly on behalf of stockholders) greatly reduces any incentive to volunteer genuinely useful information, because informed judgments about the inherently uncertain future might later be said to have been misleading. Second, GAAP reports are required to be so complex that they may be incapable of being deciphered by "sophisticated experts." How then can errors in such indecipherable reports be made the legitimate basis for imprisoning CEOs or confiscating their assets, since CEOs are usually not expert in accounting? (CFOs have less excuse to claim ignorance, but any plan to treat careless CFOs more harshly than CEOs seems unlikely to work well.)

Unfortunately, the clarity, usefulness, and even accuracy of GAAP reports have become increasingly subjective, largely because more estimates and forecasts are now required. As a result, there can be wide disagreement about how best to account for this or that. Since inflexible and mathematically precise rules are impossible in the rapidly changing world of business, accounting depends on a fluid consensus about the GAAP. The rules themselves exceed 4,500 pages, and textbooks that try to simplify GAAP rules still exceed a thousand pages. Accountants have to update these huge volumes frequently to keep up with increasingly frequent and dramatic changes since 1973, when the SEC delegated virtually all GAAP authority to the quasi-private Financial Accounting Standards Board (FASB). Changes in GAAP rules have required numerous financial restatements, although the press typically treats all restatements as evidence of previous deception. Even the name "generally accepted" accounting principles reveals the inherently tenuous nature of America's constantly changing and increasingly complicated accounting rules. According to the FASB, what is "generally accepted" at the moment refers to an ever-changing blend of "Accounting Principles Board (APB) Opinions, Financial Accounting Standards Board Statements, American Institute of Certified Public Accountants (AICPA) Audit and Accounting Guides, AICPA Statements of Positions (SOPs), FASB Interpretations, Emerging Issues Task Force (EITF) Issues, Securities and Exchange Commission (SEC) Staff Accounting Bulletins, and the like."[21] There is also a new International Accounting Standards Board, launched in 2001, as well as national standards boards in the United Kingdom and elsewhere. Of these standards-setting bodies, only the SEC is an agency of the U.S. government. The FASB puts considerable emphasis on due process, soliciting inputs from interested parties (including influential politicians), and sometimes delegates provisional authority to a task force (the EITF).

Additional evidence on the inherently subjective nature of rule-based accounting came from the fact that on April 24, 2003, the FASB changed its own voting rules to allow new accounting rules to be established by the vote of a simple majority, rather than the previous requirement that five of the seven board members must agree. The goal was to facilitate more frequent changes in more controversial accounting rules. But accounting rules that three out of seven supposed experts may find ill advised can scarcely be defined as black-and-white matters of objective fact. Majority rule can be a useful decision-making device, but consensus alone cannot define the difference between true and false.

With all of these professional organizations constantly working on complicated changes in accounting standards, the correct way to account for any particular item is difficult to determine, variable, and often quite subjective. Consider, for example, what the SEC defines as "critical accounting policies." As the annual report from one firm explains, "The SEC defines critical accounting policies as those that require application of management's most difficult, subjective, or complex judgments, often as a result of the need to make estimates about the effect of matters that are inherently uncertain and may change in subsequent periods."[22] As FASB has required more and more such "difficult, subjective, or complex" estimates to be included in corporate earnings reports (including the fashionable impulse to estimate the "fair value" of employee stock options when granted), the more reported earnings come to resemble a collection of difficult, subjective, and complex estimates and forecasts.

"The cruel reality," notes Jeffrey Bonchick, "is that the bottom line . . . in an accrual based accounting system like the generally accepted accounting principles, is the net result of a long series of guesstimates; the interpretation of which is not as black and white as, say, a prison uniform."[23]

A University of Utah study on accounting observes, "Recent research examining market reactions to earnings announcements provides evidence that investors often find *pro forma* [as if] earnings numbers to be more informative than audited GAAP earnings."[24] Section 401(b) of SOA directs the SEC to get more involved in the regulation of pro forma reports, reconciling them with GAAP numbers. Yet the larger point is surely that many investors do not believe FASB's GAAP procedures are resulting in timely and useful information.

By treating such GAAP earnings as something far more precise and meaningful than they can possibly be, SOA attributed excessive significance to reported earnings while also making it more difficult and dangerous for companies to provide more useful information to investors.

Most other countries, particularly in Europe, rely more on broad accounting principles. The International Accounting Standards Board, notes former Citigroup chairman Walter Wriston, "has just thirty-four standards, and instead of thousands of pages, most are expressed in memos of a few dozen pages."[25]

The SEC understands the problem but appears unable to budge the FASB, which is supposedly answerable only to the SEC. Robert Herdman, the SEC's chief accountant, explained the flaws in GAAP quite clearly:

> Rule-based accounting standards provide extremely detailed rules that attempt
> to contemplate virtually every application of the standard. This encourages a

check-the-box mentality to financial reporting that eliminates judgments from the application of the reporting. . . . Rule-based standards make it more difficult for preparers and auditors to step back and evaluate whether the overall impact is consistent with the objectives of the standard. An ideal accounting standard is one that is principle-based and requires financial reporting to reflect the economic substance, not the form, of the transaction. . . . The FASB has not issued comprehensive guidance such as revenue recognition and consolidation of special purpose entities [FASB finally did the latter in July 2002, long after Enron's abuse of special purpose entities to conceal debt came to light].[26]

Sarbanes-Oxley asks the SEC to report on how long it would take to move to a principles-based system in section 108(d). The law also endorses "international convergence on high-quality accounting standards" in section 108(a). Yet William Bratton of the George Washington University Law School notes, "'principles' and 'convergence' by themselves do little to constrain rent-seeking behavior on the part of managers and auditors."[27] Accounting, in short, is no substitute for corporate governance—institutions and incentives to keep the behavior of managers in line with the interests of shareholders and creditors.

The new law's introduction of twenty-year prison sentences on the basis of certification of GAAP accounting appears perverse, since the SEC's chief accountant and the SOA law itself clearly acknowledge that America's uniquely rigid rules-based approach to accounting has been part of the problem, not the solution.

WHEN IN DOUBT, EMPOWER ANOTHER BOARD

By establishing a full-time FASB whose reason for existence was to keep creating and changing the rules of accounting, the architects of FASB virtually guaranteed that too many rules would be created and that they would be changed too frequently. If the intent of establishing the FASB was to make corporate reports clearer and more informative to ordinary investors, then the board has clearly failed to justify its continued existence. Rather than question the record of the existing quasi-private board, however, nearly half of SOA law is devoted to creating yet another such board—the Public Company Accounting Oversight Board (PCAOB).

Like the other half of the SOA, this new board was an unnecessary and risky addition to regulatory uncertainty. As Donald Langevoort explains,

The question of who should set public accounting standards, and discipline accountants who fall short, is easy in the abstract—the SEC itself. The creation of a separate oversight board of the sort established in Sarbanes-Oxley is unnecessary in principle. But presumably the question was one of resources and public trust, and hence the quasi-independent creature was born.[28]

The question of "public trust" presumably explains the new board's "quasi-independent" facade. The SEC failed to discover serious accounting malpractice at Enron and WorldCom until internal whistle-blowers (Sherron Watkins at Enron and Cynthia Cooper at WorldCom) uncovered the problems. The same was true of lesser accounting problems at such companies as Lucent and Xerox. Congress apparently decided that to augment one inept government regulatory board with another government regulatory board would not merit the public trust. So they went through the pretense of calling the PCAOB a private, nongovernmental entity.

Langevoort's question of "resources," however, was answered by giving the new board vast discretionary powers to extract fees—essentially taxing the companies they regulate—and also to impose sanctions and essentially license accounting firms. These powers far exceed those of any truly private agency. This quasi-private board looks just like a public agency but with none of the rules that apply to other public agencies, such as the SEC. Board members do not have to go through the normal process of presidential appointment and Senate confirmation, for example, and their salaries and expenses are not subject to normal budgetary procedures.

At its first meeting, the five-person PCAOB surprised its congressional designers by setting its members salaries at $452,000 (above the salary of the president of the United States) and its chairman's salary at $560,000 (well above the $144,000 salary of the chairman of the SEC).[29]

The board was able to pay itself more generously than federal employees because the SOA asserts that, "no member or person employed by, or agent for, the Board shall be deemed an officer of or agent for the Federal Government." The board is nominally a very unique private monopoly—one with regulatory and taxing authority. And that raises serious questions about the constitutionality of allowing the board to circumvent appointment and salary rules that apply to officers and agents of the federal government. As attorney Erica C. Birg argues in some detail, "Congress's desire to create an 'independent' Board under the auspices of the SEC actually may run afoul of the Appointments Clause [of the Constitution], rendering the Board unconstitutionally created."[30]

Congress decided that some accountants were, by definition, responsible for bad accounting. Congress also decided that a majority of the PCAOB must consist of nonaccountants. This appears no more sensible than requiring that any professional licensing board be dominated by people who know nothing about the profession. The three nonaccountants on the Accounting Oversight Board (who had previously worked in law or finance) are likely to find themselves quite dependent on people with some expertise in the subject, such as the American Institute of Certified Public Accountants (AICPA).

It is impossible to predict how this new board of mainly nonaccountants overseeing accounting will work out. There is some overlap between the board's objectives and those of the SEC and FASB, so there may be some additional confusion about who is in charge of what.

One unintended consequence, documented in the *Washington Post*, is that many small accounting firms simply quit offering to audit public companies, partly because of the increased difficulty and expense of getting liability insurance. A week before the deadline in August 2003, only 88 of about 850 accounting firms had registered with the PCAOB as required to be allowed to audit public companies. Even some that continued to audit a few public companies nonetheless stopped auditing small companies that had been routinely shunned by the Big Four accounting firms.[31]

The political promises behind the PCAOB were typically grandiose but actually amounted to little more than hope in the expertise of nonexperts. Since stockholders have to pay for this "quasi-independent" board, perhaps they should decide whether it is worth the money. Otherwise, Congress has simply enacted a hidden tax on stockholders to create a powerful, free-spending agency with great power over accounting but very little accountability.

CRIMINAL VERSUS CIVIL SANCTIONS

Sarbanes–Oxley catered to the urge to "get tough" with errant executives. Destruction of corporate audit records was made punishable by up to ten years' imprisonment. Falsification of records with the intent to impede a federal investigation carries a sentence of up to twenty years in prison. Securities fraud carries a maximum penalty of twenty-five years. And the maximum sentence for the catchall offense of mail and wire fraud (i.e., anything deceptive sent by mail or e-mail) was increased from five to twenty years.

There is surely nothing wrong with prison sentences for actual fraud. But fraud is often hard to distinguish from incompetence or carelessness. Putting longer prison sentences on the books does not make it any easier to prove the business failure involved criminal intent on the part of some particular individual. On the contrary, threatening sentences for nonviolent crime that are as long as sentences often served for murder might make juries more inclined to give executives the benefit of reasonable doubt.

Even before the sentences were so threatening, the Department of Justice rarely attempted to pursue criminal charges against errant executives because such cases are so difficult to prove. That is why Jim Cramer, of the TV show *Kudlow and Cramer,* complained that the Clinton administration did not send any executives to jail in the earlier "frauds at Cendant, Waste Management, and Sunbeam."[32] But there were and are obvious reasons for that.

When it comes to offenses that are loosely defined (such as "biased" research reports in the recent Wall Street settlement), prosecutors generally prefer to threaten civil penalties and settle out of court. Even in cases in which it might be easier to prove fraudulent intent, prosecutors still tend to prefer civil sanctions to criminal sanctions. Criminal law, unlike civil law, requires (1) actual victims to be identified rather than some broad group of people, and (2) requires proof before a jury of guilt "beyond a reasonable doubt" rather than merely a preponderance of evidence. Besides, civil sanctions raise money for state or federal governments while prison sentences raise government expenses.

By early May 2003, seventeen Enron executives and one of their wives had been charged with crimes linked to that company, but no charges had been brought against former CEOs Skilling or Lay. A likely explanation is that the CEO's responsibility for crimes involving intricate accounting rules is much more difficult to prove than charges of tax evasion (a former CEO at Tyco) or looting a company for personal gain (executives at Adelphia). *Business Week* noted that "the more ambiguity there is, the easier it is for execs to plead ignorance." America's uniquely rule-based accounting system is nothing but ambiguous. Even accounting experts have been unsure, for example, whether or not Enron's infamous trick of hiding debts within special purpose entities was even against the notoriously complicated GAAP rules that FASB has saddled us with.

QUESTIONS THAT ARE NOT MERELY ACADEMIC

Professors of economics, accounting, and law have begun to take a serious look at what Congress wrought with such haste—the SOA. In the view of some leading scholars from all three disciplines, Sarbanes-Oxley creates potentially serious new risks.

Consider the evaluation of two economists—Bengt Holmstrom of MIT and Steven Kaplan of the University of Chicago's Graduate School of Business:

> First, the ambiguity in some of the provisions, particularly those that overlap with and even contradict aspects of state corporate law, will almost certainly invite aggressive litigation. The fear of such litigation will lead CEOs and CFOs to direct corporate resources [e.g., legal, accounting, and insurance expenses] to protect themselves against potential lawsuits. Fear of litigation is also making it harder to attract qualified board members—certainly an unintended consequence of all the efforts to improve board effectiveness. The second, broader concern is that SOA represents a shift to more rigid federal regulation and legislation of corporate governance. . . . Because some of the additional costs of complying with SOA are fixed rather than variable, the effects will be more negative for smaller companies than for larger ones. At the margin this may lead some public companies to go private and deter some private companies from going public.[33]

Accounting professors have their own concerns about the SOA. Jonathan Glover and three associates from Carnegie Mellon's Graduate School of Industrial Administration observe that

> financial statements are so full of forecasts that they are not something one can 'certify' with confidence and with any degree of accuracy, just as no one would be able to 'certify' with confidence local weather a month from now. The exposure of CEOs and CFOs to civil and criminal liabilities arising out of forecast errors can therefore be potentially huge. . . . Every restatement of forecast, however inevitable it may be, will be publicized as a sign of fraud because it is, ipso facto, an admission of guilt by the CEO/CFO who certified the number.[34]

Unless Congress and the media come to understand that estimates and forecasts in GAAP financial statements cannot possibly be considered hard facts, according to these accounting experts, "financial accounting in the United States may have to go back to cash basis accounting, without which litigation risks will become fatally high to the profession."

Several legal scholars have likewise been nearly as skeptical about the new law as economists and accountants. Larry Ribstein of the University of Illinois College of Law finds that "given the limited effectiveness of new regulation, its potential costs, and the power of markets to self-correct, new regulation of fraud in general, and Sarbanes-Oxley in particular, is unlikely to do a better job than markets."[35] Jill Fisch and Kenneth Rosen of the Fordham University School of Law are concerned that, "by obligating lawyers to report information rather than obligating directors to demand information, [section 307 of] Sarbanes-Oxley encourages directors to reduce their information seeking efforts and to blame information deficiencies on the failure of outside professionals. Indeed, the congressional hearings on Enron are rampant with directors' efforts to pass the buck to their professional advisers."[36]

The seriousness of many new business and professional risks arising from the heavy-handed regulatory approach of SOA are becoming increasingly apparent in both academic research and in actual complaints being reported by the popular press. Any offsetting benefits from this hastily enacted law, including the pretentious political promise to "restore investor confidence," remain illusive.

UNINTENDED CONSEQUENCES

In the rush to enact something called "accounting reform," there was no weighing of the costs and benefits of a major change in business regulation. The most commonly promised benefit was higher stock prices, thanks to the assumed restoration of investor confidence. Clearly, that promise soon proved illusive. To the extent that SOA increases costs (such as compliance costs) and risks (such as greater exposure to class-action suits), it should have been expected to reduce profits on a risk-adjusted basis and therefore to reduce typical stock prices. Since these costs apply only to publicly traded firms, SOA should also have been expected to put such firms at a competitive disadvantage in comparison with private companies in the same industries.

Unlike the promised benefits of this legislation, which remain unseen and hypothetical, some adverse effects of SOA began to be noticed soon after its enactment. These unintended consequences generally fall into two categories. Some result from increased costs of complying with new rules, such as being required to hire more lawyers and to buy more liability insurance for directors and officers at a much higher price. Other unintended consequences arise from the perceived increase in risk to corporate directors and executives, particularly greater exposure to lawsuits and possibly criminal penalties. Some of these perverse effects of Sarbanes-Oxley were mentioned in the previous section, quoting academic research. What follows is some anecdotal evidence of unexpected problems that are beginning to multiply.[37]

Sarbanes-Oxley provides a strong incentive to avoid taking private firms public, with initial public offerings, and begin taking public firms private, with buyouts. "Sarbanes-Oxley has been a major factor in the decision of whether or not to go public," reports corporate lawyer Andrew Humphrey. Barbara Stymiest, CEO of the Toronto Stock Exchange, likewise observed that "lawyers all over the country [the United States] are reporting that the question they are hearing most often is how to go private."[38] Thompson Financial reported that forty-nine public companies went private from July 2002 to April 2003, a 26 percent increase from the same period a year earlier.[39] If fewer companies go public and more go private, investors will have reduced opportunities to invest in promising new ventures (e.g., Google was private until 2004).

Foreign companies may decide not to list on the NYSE, or may delist from that exchange, in order to avoid risks of certification of compliance with U.S. accounting standards, or they may be prohibited from listing because foreign practices are inconsistent with the SOA rules. Porsche quickly changed its plans to list in the United States, saying "the crucial factor in Porsche's decision was ultimately the law passed [by] the U.S. government this summer (the Sarbanes-Oxley Act)."[40] Sarbanes-Oxley attempts to regulate some 1,300 foreign companies and bars them from listing on U.S. stock exchanges unless they comply with the new U.S. rules. But U.S. rules may be offensive or illegal in their home countries. Sarbanes-Oxley requires that audit committees be composed entirely of independent directors, for example, while German law requires employee representatives on that committee.[41] What is decried as "earnings management" in the United States (such as tapping reserves in hard times) is encouraged in Germany as a way to smooth over cyclical bumps. The section 402 prohibition on loans to officers or directors "applies to both U.S. and non-U.S. public companies (whether the lender is a U.S.

company or a non-U.S. company, whether the insider is located in the United States or outside the United States and whether the loan is made inside or outside the United States)."[42] Sarbanes-Oxley appears to foreigners to be trying to set rules far outside its jurisdiction. Yet the inevitable concessions to foreign firms may leave them at a competitive advantage in comparison with U.S. firms that would then bear higher regulatory costs and litigation risks.

Sarbanes-Oxley is making it more difficult, and therefore more costly, to attract and retain qualified directors. The problem is reportedly most serious when it comes to finding a financial expert, defined as someone who understands GAAP (which is nearly impossible). Sarbanes-Oxley requires at least one such GAAP expert on every corporate audit board, although the same law prohibits more than two such experts from serving on the Accounting Oversight Board. "Many companies are having trouble filling this slot because candidates fear they will be held responsible for auditing problems."[43] Directors will have to be offered more compensation to offset the new risks. The most talented CEOs and CFOs will also command risk premiums added to their pay packages, or they will migrate to private firms. Thanks to "the escalating clamor from regulators," say executive recruiters, "the job of wooing talent to privately held companies becomes easier."[44] Because of new risks of regulation and litigation arising from certification and other rules, companies also have to purchase more liability insurance at higher fees for executives, directors, and class action litigation. Companies are also paying much more for corporate governance consultants.[45] These higher costs mean smaller profits and lower stock prices, injuring the same stockholders the law was ostensibly intended to help.

Sarbanes-Oxley's emphasis on punishment for top executives is likely to make corporate bosses too timid, afraid to make the risky investments that a vibrant economy requires. Jeffrey Garten, dean of Yale's School of Management, predicts that "CEOs are going to become more risk-averse and big investments on risky projects are going to be held back."[46] Of the many problems attributed to SOA, this is potentially the most dangerous. The law certainly makes downside mistakes more personally risky for executives both in terms of financial loss (lawsuits) and possible prison time (criminalizing risk). Nothing is more likely to attract unwanted attention than dramatic failure, and the surest way to avoid such failure is to avoid making risky investments in promising new technologies, products, or services. Excessive risk avoidance, whether by corporate directors and officers or by stock market analysis, is a proven recipe for producing economic paralysis.

ELLIOT SPITZER V. WALL STREET

Many things done in the name of "protecting investors" have ended up having the opposite effect. Indeed, the whole idea that this is something the government can or should do is quite debatable. In his chapter "Regulation of the Securities Market" in *The Encyclopedia of Law and Economics*, Edmund Kitch of the University of Virginia Law School explains why protecting investors (or restoring their confidence) always seems to be a quixotic quest:

> Given that investment transactions involve the transfer of money between consenting adults for a product that is not socially harmful, it is difficult to identify what the regulation is protecting investors from. . . . The idea that securities regulation could or should improve the returns obtained by investors is particularly improbable. . . . If securities regulation permitted only conservative investments to be offered . . . then the investment risk would be reduced. But would that be a good thing? The reduction in risk would be achieved at the cost of suppressing the opportunity for risky investments that would be socially productive.[47]

Sarbanes-Oxley clearly illustrates this common governmental impulse to minimize the opportunity for investment risk by making risk illegal or at least immoral. The crusade to purge "conflict of interest" from Wall Street stock reports, through large fines and small-minded rules, provides an even more ludicrous example.

On April 8, 2002, New York State Attorney General Elliot Spitzer issued a press release announcing "dramatic evidence that [Merrill Lynch's] stock ratings were biased and distorted in an attempt to secure and maintain lucrative contracts for investment banking services." The charges were based on the state's 1921 Martin Act, which a supporting affidavit explained "proscribes a wide array of practices" such as "misrepresentation" and "unlike the federal securities laws, no purchase or sale of stock is required, nor are intent, reliance, or damages required elements of a violation."[48] Under such open-ended legislation, a company might be found guilty of something as vague as failure to disclose a conflict of interest without the prosecutor being required to demonstrate any intent to deceive or offering any evidence that anyone was damaged.

Merrill Lynch settled out of court on May 21, 2002, for a $100 million fine without "the Court making any findings of fact" and without any legal "evidence of the validity of any alleged wrongdoing or liability."[49] A year later, however, Spitzer was publicly accusing Merrill of "fraud"—a criminal offense that neither the company nor its employees were ever charged with, based on allegations never entered into any court findings of fact or law.[50]

The Merrill Lynch settlement proved it possible for state prosecutors to (1) raise large sums for state governments without the nuisance of a trial and (2) virtually rewrite national securities law without bothering to involve elected representatives. The same fundraising strategy was soon embraced by other state prosecutors and the SEC in the $1.4 billion deal with ten Wall Street firms on April 28, 2003.

The original Spitzer case against Merrill Lynch was unique because the allegations were actually written down in an affidavit. Later complaints against other financial firms were just tried in the press, using the threat of private litigation as a lever.

The Spitzer affidavit of April 2002 revealed no understanding of the business the attorney general aspired to redesign or regulate. The first and presumably toughest complaint said, "as previously covered stocks such as Pets.com . . . plummeted, sometimes all the way to zero, retail customers and the investing public were never advised to sell. The reason for this failure is at least in part the substantial unrevealed conflict of interest" [between analysis and investment banking]. How could there possibly be any "conflict of interest" in a "previously covered stock"? Firms do not attract big investment banking fees by refusing to issue reports on some stock plummeting toward zero. Companies do not pay analysts to keep track of stocks that are nearly worthless, and there is no way for an analyst to advise anyone to sell a stock that is no longer being reported on. Retail customers of Merrill Lynch could ask their brokers, which is what brokers are for. No Wall Street firm has any obligation to offer research to "the investing public" that is not paying for it.

The affidavit and also the "dramatic evidence" in the original press release from Spitzer's office established a pattern of ripping excerpts from e-mails out of context and sometimes even attributing such quotes to employees of Merrill Lynch when they were actually written by customers.[51] As a famous example of taking statements out of context, the press release said, "a senior analyst writes: 'the whole idea that we are independent of [the] banking [division] is a big lie."[52] What analyst Kristen Campbell actually wrote, after downgrading a stock, is that "Mazzucco said he is fine with a 3-2 (I said to him the whole idea that we are independent from banking is a big lie—without banking this would be a 3-2 and he said 'no—you guys are independent you can do what you want—I'm fine with that.'[53] Far from proving that banking prevented this analyst from downgrading a stock, the quote proves the opposite when taken in context.

Other comments leaked to the press were equally misleading. Tech stocks were falling so fast in the fall of 2000 that ratings in printed reports could hardly be taken down fast enough to avoid embarrassment. Analyst Henry Blodget's infamous "piece of junk" remark in document 373, for example, was followed by "downgrade it." Yet, the press accepted Spitzer's claim that Blodget was saying something in private that was entirely different from the way stocks were rated. Blodget's widely reported "piece of shit" comment in document 205 (about a stock that had quickly dropped to $4) was followed by "shame on me/us for giving them any benefit of doubt." No deliberate deception, just a big mistake. The equally famous "piece of crap" comment in document 8,655 was an indecipherable comment by another analyst complaining about a news item saying Excite At Home was threatening to derail a deal with AT&T. Her following comment was, "I bet Comcast is the C doing a deal with you know who," which may mean she thought the news report (not the company) was a piece of crap.

To suggest that Spitzer's evidence was more biased than any analyst's report is not to absolve analysts from the sin (not crime) of "conflict of interest." Merrill

Lynch, Salomon Smith Barney, and several others among the ten Wall Street companies are "full-service financial firms," not just investment bankers like Goldman Sachs. That means they charge a relatively high commission on stock trades in exchange for research reports and other services. But nearly two-thirds of stock trading is done by professionals—institutional money managers at pension funds, mutual funds, and hedge funds. If institutional pros lose money following one company's research reports they switch their trading to another firm, often a discounter. The brokers of a company issuing bad advice also quit or at least complain—complaints from Salomon's brokers account for much of the dubious evidence against that firm. Yet the conflict between investment banking and brokerage does not necessarily tilt in favor of investment banking, because brokerage commissions for some of these firms are much larger than investment banking fees—particularly commissions from institutional investors. Spitzer and his followers talk as though there are only investment banking and retail stockbrokers, ignoring the enormous incentive to provide research that attracts and retains institutional investors. Indeed, analysts spend much of their time pandering to such money managers, through road shows and phone calls, and could scarcely be said to have an interest in duping them. Complaints from institutional investors about poor stock picks were also handed to the press as evidence of analyst bias, but they actually demonstrate that analysts are under pressure from big investors to pick good stocks, not just bankers who want them to promote bad stocks.

Even if the interests and incentives always pointed in one direction toward investment banking, as though commissions and reputation did not matter, the prosecutors' presumption that markets move on bad ratings is clearly indefensible. At Salomon Smith Barney, telecom analyst Jack Grubman was one of the prosecutors' two prime targets because he "kept a 'buy' rating on WorldCom until April, despite the fact that the stock had already fallen 92 percent from its peak in June 1999."[54] Spitzer and others assume Grubman's ratings had some magical power to shove WorldCom stock prices higher, thus making some bank client happy. That 92 percent decline shows otherwise.

Although the $1.4 billion in fines was often reported as a minor slap on the wrist (often by comparing it to gross revenues rather than profits), the prosecutors' collection and dissemination of e-mails and handwritten memos was openly intended to help trial lawyers collect much more through class action suits. Meanwhile, the three-year bear market had taken its toll on the financial services industry before Spitzer carved his pound of flesh. Merrill Lynch set the model others may have to follow to pay their fines and legal bills: "Over the past two years, Merrill Lynch's new management has cut its work force far more than its peers have"—by 18,600 jobs, or 25.8 percent.[55] Fines and regulations are certainly not the only reason for job losses among beleaguered Wall Street firms, but they did not help. And those companies have many innocent stockholders too.

The global settlement of April 2003 devoted about a third of the loot to providing free independent research for individual investors for five years. That sounds like a welcome subsidy for companies that produce research that investors don't value highly enough to pay for. Besides, most online brokerage services already provide easy access to company reports from a few independent sources (one I use offers even tiny accounts free reports from Standard and Poor's and Zacks). In any case, "only a handful of firms, including Argus Research, Value Line Inc., and Mc-Graw-Hill Cos' Standard and Poor's unit cater to individual investors."[56] Morningstar is another, although it is best known for rating mutual funds (analysts' stock picks don't matter if you invest in funds).

Some "independent" research is actually extremely dependent on summarizing the work of Wall Street analysts, such as Zacks, First Call, and multexinvestor.com. Some useful investment research for individuals appears in magazines such as *Mutual Funds, Money, Forbes,* and *Fortune,* or newspapers like *Investors Business Daily, Barron's, The Wall Street Journal,* and even the Money section of *USA Today*. But that information has also been partly derived from interviewing Wall Street industry specialists. If Wall Street keeps cutting back on analysts and keeping their work for institutional eyes only, both of which are easily predictable consequences of the global settlement, derivative varieties of related information such as Zacks and First Call must deteriorate in quality.

Unfortunately, any research sufficiently sanitized to avoid regulators' wrath is likely to be valued by investors at the same zero price they will be charged. In the Wall Street deal, the prosecutors' heat fell entirely on two analysts, one in telecom and the other in Internet stocks. That suggests that what prosecutors really want is to ban upbeat research in risky industries. "Massachusetts regulators have been investigating whether Credit Suisse misled investors with *overly positive* research reports" (emphasis added).[57] Regulators don't care a bit if research reports are *overly negative*, thus causing investors to miss opportunities. George Gilder is certainly an independent telecom analyst (he runs his own firm), but he once proved overly positive on telecom stocks. Any such independent analyst guilty of "overly positive research reports" would surely be unacceptable to risk-averse prosecutors who believe equity research should be a government-regulated trade. So the heavily subsidized "independent" research will turn out to be cautious, stale, wishy-washy, and useless. It may well be biased as well, since those selling "independent" research to Wall Street will know who is paying them millions. Most potential stock investors are instead looking for less paper and more concrete advice from somebody smart enough to get enthusiastic (even overly positive) about something.

Shortly after the "global settlement," the *Economist* noted, "it is still not clear what the investment banks have done wrong, legally speaking. If the law was broken, then firms and their employees should have been prosecuted. If it was not, then the fines and bans seem hard to justify." If Spitzer really believes what he says, that somebody is guilty of fraud, then he has failed in his primary duty as a prosecutor—to prosecute criminals.

In the final analysis, one politically ambitious state prosecutor discovered an old state law that was so loosely crafted that he could easily use it to threaten exposing any securities firm to criminal prosecution and private litigation unless they paid hush money and jumped through a few hoops. However, as Judge Stanley Sporkin, a former head of SEC enforcement, points out, "it is illegal and improper to say that you're going to be prosecuted unless you do A-B-C on the civil side."[58] The SEC and several other states pushed such legal ethics aside and jumped on Spitzer's bandwagon; a compliant press helped push it along. New business rules and regulations were crafted with the force of law although no elected legislature had any part in their design. Accusations of criminal fraud have been tossed about without any evidence being properly examined through due process in court. Many have professed outrage at the discovery that sell-side analysts may have an interest in selling something, but only a few have expressed outrage at the prosecutors' end run around customary legal procedures and protections and the state-by-state regulatory balkanization this threatens to produce. As Michael Greves asked, "Who authorized Elliot Spitzer to 'restructure' the U.S. financial markets?"[59]

The most predictable consequence of the global settlement is that there will undoubtedly be much less high-quality research available to individual investors than there would have been in the absence of this backroom deal. That matters because as a group the Wall Street analysts have helped to keep the market informed and efficient.

James Glassman cites a major April 2001 study in the *Journal of Finance*, "Can Investors Profit from the Prophets?" by Brad Barber, Reuven Lehavy, and two associates.[60] That study, notes Glassman, examined "over 360,000 recommendations from 269 brokerage houses and 4,340 analysts" from 1985 to 1996. "They found the highest-rated stocks produced average annual returns of 18.8 percent while the lowest-rated returned just 5.8 percent. The market as a whole over this period returned an average of 14.5 percent."[61] Even mutual fund investors benefited because the best mutual fund managers do pay careful attention to the best analysts. Updated results show that the Wall Street analysts' buy recommendations continued to do far better than those rated hold or sell for fourteen years in a row—until 2000.[62] The crash after March 2000 was enough to make any bull look foolish, and bullish mistakes in a bear market came to be freely attributed to conflict of interest or some other sin. Unfortunately, "new regulations will inevitably load new costs onto firms," predicts Glassman, "and diminish their resources—not to mention their desire—to provide clients with strong analysis."

Pension fund and mutual fund companies that buy stocks still do their own research, and hire consultants to provide more. But the best and most timely material on the buy side is strictly internal, not shared with small investors (otherwise competitors would get it for free). Of the research that survives the Spitzer assault on the sell side (meaning firms selling brokerage services and/or investment banking), much less of it is apt to be made easily available to small investors who had previously been "free riding" by following tips on television or in financial papers and magazines. Prudential, for example, "decided in November 2002 to forbid analysts from being quoted in print or on television."[63]

The distinguished thirteen-member Shadow Financial Regulatory Committee issued its own verdict on the untried Wall Street settlement: "In all likelihood, these measures will entail a significant waste of resources in pursuit of an unobtainable goal [beating the market with little risk]."[64] "The most perverse outcome of the investigation," added the *Economist*, "is its impact on investment research. Analysts have been leaving Wall Street by the dozens. . . . Without subsidies from investment banking fees, research budgets are being crushed; there is little money for stars. Institutions have turned to research boutiques for advice. Unfortunately, these firms rarely cater for retail customers. Was this really the intended result?"[65] Perhaps not. But unintended and unpleasant consequences will surely be the main legacy of prosecutors' meddling with incentives to produce stock market research, much as other unintended but nasty consequences are beginning to plague SOA.

CONCLUSION

The SOA was unnecessary, harmful, and inadequate. It is already producing such unintended consequences as (1) more costly or less risky compensation packages for directors and executives to compensate them for new risks of prosecution and litigation; (2) fewer investment choices for stockholders due to fewer domestic and foreign companies being willing to subject themselves to the law by listing on U.S. stock exchanges; (3) reduced profitability and competitiveness of U.S. public corporations due to higher costs of regulatory compliance, greater exposure to the legal expenses of class action suits, and greater expenses for insurance and directors' compensation to compensate for added personal risks of civil and criminal penalties; and (4) a reduction in the quantity and quality of stock market analysis that will be made available to noninstitutional small investors—a deficiency promised by Sarbanes-Oxley but not virtually ensured by the Wall Street settlement.

Although harmful to the U.S. economy, on balance, SOA was also grossly inadequate. The law's false promise of "restoring investor confidence" through strictly enforced GAAP accounting eschewed any serious effort to discover any fundamental defects in the nation's laws, rules, and regulations that may contribute to the collapse of other major firms in the future. The key congressional assumption appeared to be that any problems in business or accounting must be the fault of businessmen and accountants, not the fault of any governmental institutions with which they operate, such as the IRS, SEC, or FASB. So the solution, as usual, was more rules and regulations piled on top of other rules and regulations that clearly failed.

The architects and supporters of SOA fundamentally misdiagnosed the problems behind the collapse of Enron and WorldCom and thus ended up prescribing a much stronger dose of the same old snake oil (GAAP accounting) as a panacea.

NOTES

1. Graham, Carol, Robert Litan, and Sandip Sukhtankar, "The Bigger They Are, the Harder They Fall: An Estimate of the Costs of the Crisis in Corporate Governance," The Brookings Institution, August 30, 2002, http://www.brookings.org/dybdocroot/Views/Papers/Graham/20020722Graham.pdf. Accessed April 25, 2003.

2. Branson, Douglas M., "Enron—When All Systems Fail: Creative Destruction of Roadmap to Corporate Governance Reform?" mimeo, University of Pittsburgh, 2003, p. 3 and 52.

3. BankruptcyData.com. The Largest Public Company Bankruptcies—2001. http://www.bankruptcydata.com/Research/Ch11__2001.htm. Accessed April 13, 2002.

4. "Spreading the Pain," table in the *Wall Street Journal*, September 30, 2002.

5. Cunningham, Lawrence A., "The Sarbanes-Oxley Yawn: Heavy Rhetoric, Light Reform (and It Might Just Work)," *University of Connecticut Law Review* 36, 2003, p. 19, http://papers.ssrn.com/sol3/paper.cfm?abstract_id=337280.

6. Cunningham, Lawrence A., "Semiotics, Hermeneutics, and Cash: An Essay on the True and Fair View," Boston College Law School Research Paper no. 0.6, March 5, 2002, p. 3. http://ssm.com/abstract=386041. Accessed May 1, 2003.

7. Perino, Michael A., "Enron's Legislative Aftermath: Some Reflections on the Deterrence Aspects of the Sarbanes-Oxley Act of 2002," Columbia University Law School Working Paper no. 212, October 2002, p. 3–4. http://ssrn.com/abstract_id=350540. Accessed May 2, 2003.

8. Herdman, Robert K., "Testimony Concerning the Roles of the SEC and the FASB in Establishing GAAP," House Subcommittee on Capital Markets, Insurance and Government Sponsored Enterprises, May 14, 2002. http://www.sec.gov/news/testimony/o51402tsrkh.htm. Accessed April 27, 2003.

9. Spinner, Jackie, "SEC Official Targets Big Firms," *Washington Post,* December 13, 2002.

10. Glassman, James K., "The Truth about America's Corporate Scandals," address to Confederation of Swedish Enterprise, Stockholm, September 5, 2002. http://www.aei.org/include/news_print.asp?newsID=14277. Accessed April 25, 2003.

11. Bartley, Robert L., "Enron: First, Apply the Law," *Wall Street Journal,* February 11, 2002.

12. Homstrom, Bengt, and Steven N. Kaplan, "The State of U.S. Corporate Governance: What's Right and What's Wrong?" National Bureau of Economic Research Working Paper no. 9613, April 2003.

13. "The Economic Risks," *Economist,* February 22, 2003, p. 67.

14. Standard & Poor's Quantitative Services, S&P 500 Earnings and Estimate Report, http://www2.standardandpoors.com/spf/xls/index/SP500EPSEST.XLS?GXHC_gx_session_id_=fd638ffbf6338fe2& Accessed April 29, 2003.

15. Beckett, Paul, "SEC Order Forces Executives to Swear by Their Numbers," *Wall Street Journal,* July 5, 2002.

16. Langevoort, Donald C., "Managing the Expectations Gap in Investor Protection: The SEC and the Post-Enron Reform Agenda," Georgetown University Law Center Working Paper no. 328080, September 4, 2002. http://papers.ssrn.com/paper.taf?abstract_id=328080. Accessed May 1, 2003.

17. "True and Fair Is Not Hard and Fast," *Economist*, April 26, 2003, p. 61.

18. "A Holdout," *Economist*, March 1, 2003, p. 12.

19. Wallison, Peter J., "Poor Diagnosis, Poor Prescription: The Error at the Heart of the Sarbanes-Oxley Act," American Enterprise Institute, *On the Issues,* March 2003, p. 1. See also Rodgers, T. J., "Corporate Accounting: Congress and FASB Ignore Business Realities," Cato Institute Briefing Papers no. 77, October 25, 2002.

20. Pitt, Harvey L., "Remarks before the AICPA Governing Council," Miami Beach, Fla., October 22, 2001, http://www.sec.gov/news/speech/spch516.htm.

21. Financial Accounting Standards Board, "Proposal for a New Agenda Project," http://www.fasb.org. Accessed July 23, 2002.

22. DRS Technologies, Inc., *Annual Report* (2002), p. 40.

23. Bronchick, Jeffrey, "We Need Better Stock Analysis, Not More Info," *Wall Street Journal,* August 6, 2002.

24. Bhattachahyarya, Nilabhra, et al., "Who Trades on Pro Forma Earnings Information?" mimeo, University of Utah, March 2003, p. 1.

25. Wriston, Walter, "The Solution to Scandals? Simpler Rules," *Wall Street Journal,* August 5, 2002.

26. Herdman, "Roles of the SEC and the FASB in Establishing GAAP," p. 5.

27. Bratton, William W. "Enron, Sarbanes-Oxley, and Accounting: Rules versus Standards versus Rents," *Villanova Law Review* 48, no. 4, 2003, http://ssrn.com/abstract=399120. Accessed May 1, 2003.

28. Langevoort, "Managing the Expectations Gap," p. 28.

29. Schlesinger, Larry, "High Salaries Threaten U.S. Oversight Board," *Accountancy Age.com*, February 18, 2003, http://www.accountancyage.com/News/1132567. Accessed October 19, 2003.

30. Johnson, Carrie, "Small Accounting Firms Exit Auditing," *Washington Post,* August 27, 2003.

31. Johnson, Carrie, "Small Accounting Firms Exit Auditing," *Washington Post,* August 27, 2003.

32. Cramer, James J., "Mr. Levitt's Legacy," *Wall Street Journal,* December 5, 2002.

33. Holmstrom, Bengt and Steven N. Kaplan, "The State of U.S. Corporate Governance: What's Right and What's Wrong?" National Bureau of Economic Research Working Paper no. 9613, April 2003, p. 22.

34. Glover, Jonathan, Yugi Ijiri, Carolyn Levine, and Pierre Liang, "CEO/CFO Certification and Emerging Needs to Separate Facts and Forecasts," Carnegie Mellon Tepper School of Business Working Paper, November 2002.

35. Ribstein, Larry E., "Market vs. Regulatory Responses to Corporate Fraud: A Critique of the Sarbanes-Oxley Act of 2002," *Journal of Corporate Law* 28, no. 1, 2003, http://ssrn.com/abstract_id=332681. Accessed May 1, 2003.

36. Fisch, Jill E. and Kenneth M. Rosen, "Is There a Role for Lawyers in Preventing Future Enrons?" forthcoming *Villanova Law Review,* 2003, p. 48. See also Zirin, James, "Risky SEC Rule for Noisy Withdrawal?" *Washington Post,* March 23, 2003.

37. Some additional examples and references were provided in my presentation at a Cato Institute event on December 18, 2003, "Sarbanes-Oxley in Retrospect," http://www.cato.org/events/sarbanes-oxley.pdf.

38. Cusack, Bob, "Business May Try to Undo New SEC Law," *The Hill*, April 23, 2003.

39. Gilpin, Kenneth N., "New Rules May Drive Push to Privatize," *New York Times,* April 27, 2003, p. BU5.

40. Schlesinger, Larry, "Sarbanes-Oxley Forces Porsche to Reverse," *Accountancy Age,* October 17, 2002, http://www.AccountancyAge.com /News/11321114. Accessed October 18, 2002.

41. Karmin, Craig and Kevin J. Delaney, "SEC's Exemption Gets Some Praise," *Wall Street Journal,* January 13, 2003, p. C16.

42. Gerkis, James and Rima Moawad, "Sarbanes-Oxley Act: Seven Months Later," American Bar Association, *Administrative and Regulatory Law News,* spring 2003, p. 13.

43. White, Ben, "Declining a Place at the Table: More Politicians, Executives Say 'No Thanks' to Director Seats," *Washington Post,* February 27, 2003.

44. Deutsch, Claudia H., "Private Companies Have a New Allure," *New York Times,* August 25, 2002, p. BU12.

45. Day, Kathleen, "After High-Profile Corporate Busts, Governance Consulting Booms," *Washington Post,* December 27, 2002, p. E1.

46. "Opinions Vary Widely on Oversight Bill's Impact," *Wall Street Journal,* July 29, 2002.

47. Kitch, Edmund W., "Regulation of the Securities Market," in Boudwijn Boukaert and Gerrit De Geest, eds., *Encyclopedia of Law and Economics,* New York: Edward Elgar, 1999, pp. 821–822, http://encyclo.findlaw.com/5660book.pdf. Accessed May 5, 2003.

48. "Affidavit in Support of Application for an Order Pursuant to General Business Law Section 354," Supreme Court of the State of New York, County of New York, April 2002, p. 7.

49. "Agreement between the Attorney General of the State of New York and Merrill, Lynch, Pierce, Fenner & Smith, Inc.," May 21, 2002, p. 2.

50. "Mr. Spitzer said, referring to Mr. [Stan] O'Neal and Merrill: 'What we have alleged about your company is that you committed fraud.'" Smith, Randal and Susanne Craig, "Spitzer Views Notes for Salomon Meeting as Crucial in Probe," *Wall Street Journal,* April 29, 2003, p. C9.

51. McConnell, John J., "Spitzer's Big Lie," *Wall Street Journal,* May 15, 2002.

52. "Merrill Lynch Stock Rating System Found Biased by Undisclosed Conflicts of Interest," press releases, Office of New York State Attorney General Elliot Spitzer, April 8, 2002.

53. Document 80, Affidavit in Support of Application. Other cited documents from the same source.

54. Backover, Andrew, "Salomon Telecom Analyst Grubman quits," *USA Today,* August 16, 2002.

55. Thomas, Landon, "Have Merrill's Bulls Been Led to Pasture?" *New York Times,* January 5, 2003.

56. Sidel, Robert, "Better Stock Picks? Six Research Firms Sense Opportunity," *Wall Street Journal,* December 18, 2002. Full disclosure: I worked as senior economist for Argus Research in 1976.

57. White, Ben, "Regulators Propose Fining CSFB $250 Billion," *Washington Post,* November 23, 2002, p. E2.

58. Freedman, Michael, "Witch Hunt," *Forbes,* December 9, 2002. See also Stephen W. Stanton, "Wall Street Thug," *Forbes,* December 20, 2002.

59. Greve, Michael S., "Free Elliot Spitzer!" *Federalist Outlook,* American Enterprise Institute, May 1, 2002.

60. Barber, Brad, Reuven Lehavy, Maureen McNichols, and Brett Trueman, "Can Investors Profit from the Prophets? Security Analyst Recommendations and Stock Returns," *Journal of Finance* 56, no. 2, April 2001, http://webuser.bus.umich.edu/rlehavy/Published_JF.pdf. Accessed May 5, 2003.

61. Glassman, James K., "Faulty Analysis," *Wall Street Journal,* April 12, 2002.

62. Hulbert, Mark, "Analysts vs. Newsletters: Whose Recommendations Are Best?" American Institute of Individual Investors, *AAII Journal,* June 2002, p. 14.

63. White, Ben, "Analyst Reform: An Issue of Dividends," *Washington Post,* January 4, 2003.

64. "Statement of the Shadow Financial Regulatory Committee on Enforcement Settlement with Wall Street Investment Firms," May 5, 2003.

65. "No Rest," *Economist,* March 1, 2003.

II

ACCOUNTING

· 4 ·

Don't Count Too Much
on Financial Accounting

William A. Niskanen

ACCOUNTING PROBLEMS SPECIFIC TO ENRON

$\mathcal{O}$n first reading about the collapse of Enron, I was outraged by its many misleading accounting practices. Such practices included the booking of wash trades (in
which Enron was essentially trading with itself) as revenues, the improper use of
mark-to-market accounting to increase the reported value of existing assets when
no substantive economic value had been added, booking future revenues when the
trade was made rather than when the revenues were received, and the use of some
of its many special purpose entities (SPEs) as passive partners in these practices. In
addition, the post-bankruptcy report by Enron's board observed that

> Other transactions were implemented . . . to offset losses. They allowed En-
> ron to conceal from the market very large losses resulting from Enron's mer-
> chant investments by creating the appearance that those investments were
> hedged, that is, that a third party was obliged to pay Enron the amount of
> the losses—when, in fact, that third party was simply an entity in which
> only Enron had a substantial stake. We believe these transactions led to En-
> ron reported earnings that were almost $1 billion higher than should have
> been reported.[1]

On reading further, I was doubly outraged to learn that many of these practices
were consistent with the letter, even if not the spirit, of accounting rules. But then,
I am not an accountant. As a *Wall Street Journal* column observed, "Many critics
have noted, for instance, that the real scandal at Enron Corp was how much of the
now collapsed energy company's accounting shenanigans were legal."[2]

The most apparent violations of accounting rules appears to have been the
failure to consolidate three of its many SPEs on the Enron books, a mistake that
when acknowledged in November 2001 led to a $586 million reduction in reported

earnings, and the failure to report the amount of debt of the SPEs that was effectively guaranteed by Enron. The most important early lesson from this examination, however, is that Enron failed because it made bad investments and management decisions, not because it violated the letter and spirit of accounting rules. Enron first seems to have adopted aggressive accounting practices to impress investors with inflated revenues and earnings and, at the end, to hide its financial weakness. Given Enron's bad business decisions, strictly accurate, transparent, and timely financial accounting would only have accelerated its bankruptcy.

SEVERAL ACCOUNTING ISSUES RAISED BY THE ENRON COLLAPSE

The collapse of Enron also highlighted several accounting issues that affect many corporations—most important of which are whether stock options should be expensed, the accounting treatment of SPEs, and the current monopoly of the Financial Accounting Standards Board (FASB) in setting accounting standards. None of these issues is specific to Enron or has yet been resolved.

Current accounting rules allow corporations either to include the estimated value of stock options as an expense when granted or to report the estimated value of the options granted in a footnote to its financial reports. The collapse of Enron provides no distinctive lesson about this issue; Enron was quite innovative in designing executive compensation but did not make unusually extensive use of stock options. Most corporations do not now include the estimated value of options as an expense when granted, and any requirement to do so would be strongly resisted by the high-tech firms and the NASDAQ exchange. In response to strong pressure from the FASB and the Securities and Exchange Commission (SEC), however, a few hundred major American firms have recently started to expense options. In 2003, the International Accounting Standards Board (IASB) was considering a general requirement to expense options for all firms using the International Financial Reporting Standards (IFRS), and the FASB announced that it would require U.S. firms to expense options but had yet to agree on how to value options.

Accountants and economists often differ on this issue, and this difference is perceived to reflect a reasonable disagreement. Accountants generally favor the explicit expensing of stock options, as valued by Black-Scholes or some other formula, in order to estimate the full cost of managerial compensation in the same period their services are rendered.[3] Many of the advocates of option expensing oppose the extensive use of options and believe that an increase in the accounting price of options would reduce the number of options granted. Economists are more likely to point out that there is no nonarbitrary way to value a stock option that is not tradable and to recommend a focus on fully diluted earnings as the best guide to investors.[4] More important, accountants are basically wrong on the timing issue. A stock option, unlike a bonus, is *not* compensation for recent performance but is an incentive for future performance. And options should be recorded as compensation in the year they are exercised and valued at the difference between the exercise price and the strike price, a rule that better addresses both the timing issue and the valuation issue. This is the rule that is used in tax accounting, and, in this case, the tax law is right. My sense is that this controversy is a tempest in a teapot. Current accounting rules seem to provide all the information that a careful investor could use to evaluate the effects of a grant of stock options. And there is no apparent reason why the FASB, the SEC, or Congress should insist that this issue be resolved one way or the other.

Current accounting rules permit the debt of an SPE to be off the books of the sponsor company if outside investors own a majority of the equity and their equity is at least 3 percent of the assets. (After the collapse of Enron, the FASB proposed that the minimum equity of SPEs owned by outside investors be increased to 10 percent of assets.) In addition, the SPE cannot be controlled by the sponsor company and must bear the full risks and returns of the assets conveyed to it; there has long been some ambiguity whether the latter rule also prohibits a guarantee of an SPE's debt by the sponsor company. Enron apparently violated these accounting rules in several cases, most importantly by not revealing that several of its SPEs were controlled by an Enron financial officer, by guaranteeing the debt of several SPEs, and by conveying its own stock as the only liquid equity of another SPE. These practices were clearly misleading about Enron's financial problems but were not the primary cause of these problems. Many other firms make extensive use of SPEs for good business reasons. The major accounting issues with respect to the SPEs seem to be whether the sponsor company has failed to consolidate the SPEs that do not meet the above three standards or has failed to disclose the amount of SPE debt that it had guaranteed.

A third set of accounting issues raised by the Enron collapse is whether investors would be better served if American firms adopted the international accounting standards, whether the standards should continue to be set, monitored, and enforced by the FASB and the SEC, or whether firms should be allowed to choose among competing standards. A July 2003 report by the SEC staff straddled this issue by recommending a transition to an "objectives-oriented" accounting standard and concluded, "We believe that neither U.S. [generally accepted accounting principles] nor international accounting standards, as currently comprised, are representative of the optimum type of principle-based standards."[5] Again, accountants and economists often differ on this issue—accountants usually favoring the harmonization of accounting standards, economists more likely to favor a competition among accounting standards—and there is a basis for reasonable disagreement on this issue. Harmonization would increase the comparability of financial accounts if there is one set of accounting standards that is clearly best for all firms. It is also important that any monopoly that sets the accounting standards is quickly responsive to a change of business practices, such as derivatives, that calls for an amendment or addition to the common standards. Decentralizing the authority to set the accounting standards, maybe to the stock exchanges or to industry associations, in contrast, would increase the comparability of financial accounts within a more homogeneous group of firms at the expense of a lower comparability across groups of firms. Some specialized accounting services and software, however, would almost surely be developed to report the financial accounts on alternative accounting standards.

THE GENERAL PROBLEMS OF FINANCIAL ACCOUNTING

More important, the broader community appears to expect too much of financial accounts, even if they are strictly by-the-books, fully transparent, and timely. The problems of financial accounting are legion. Let me count the ways:

Accounting is inherently backward-looking, at best a record of the financial effects of prior decisions. For firms in trouble, thus, financial accounts are a lagging indicator of bad decisions and are often insufficiently timely to trigger decisions that would offset the effects of these prior decisions. In contrast, investors are more concerned about the magnitude and timing of future cash flows, about which current financial accounting often provides little useful information.

Current financial accounting is inherently subjective and requires many estimates of revenues, costs, assets, and liabilities about which reasonable professionals may disagree. Dennis Beresford, a former chairman of the FASB, for example, observed, "For too long, most people have thought of accounting as very, very precise . . . if different estimates had been used, there's a range of answers that would be available for any public company."[6] And Richard M. Jenneret, a partner at Ernst and Young who was formerly with Arthur Andersen, concludes that "There are always lots of judgments and estimates in accounting. . . . The rulebook of generally accepted accounting principles, [he said], is not always black and white."[7] There is a reasonable basis, for example, that advertising or R&D expenditures that increase expected long-term revenues should be capitalized rather than expensed, but a CFO who made such a decision may now be subject to a criminal charge. The focus on these accounting aggregates, rather than cash flow, reflects this subjectivity, as reflected by the adage, "Earnings are an opinion; cash flow is a fact." The subjective nature of the accounting aggregates also makes these estimates subject to manipulation to meet earnings targets and to inflate the reported value of a firm. A 2003 article by Baruch Lev, a professor of accounting and finance at New York University, observes that earnings manipulation is widespread even now. Although egregious cases triggering SEC and legal actions are relatively scarce, a large number of managers regularly fine-tune their reported earnings to meet external targets. The subtle, hard-to-detect manipulations are quite prevalent.[8]

Lev, however, concludes:

Trying to regulate earnings manipulation out of existence with ever-more-detailed rules seems unlikely to produce more informative financial reporting or, ultimately, to reduce the extent of earnings manipulation, which actually thrives in a thicket of rules. Thus, we must think seriously about reforms that will change the incentives for earnings manipulations and will make corporate reports more truthful and revealing.[9]

Current accounting standards are extraordinarily complex. Publication of the Generally Accepted Accounting Principles (GAAP) in the United States now requires nearly five thousand pages, with about eight hundred pages specific to the accounting rules for derivatives. Many of these rules are to provide data to the government for our comparably complex systems of taxation and regulation, not to serve management or investor demand. The primary reason why the U.S. GAAP is especially complex appears to be an attempt to reduce the risks of litigation.

The FASB is a private monopoly subject to SEC authority. As such, it is often very late in responding to important new accounting issues—a four-year delay in publishing its statement on derivatives, for example, and a twenty-year delay in publishing the accounting standard for SPEs. It is also subject to both questionable accounting doctrines, such as fair-value accounting, and political influence. Managers and investors would be better served by competitive accounting advisory groups, maybe with each exchange choosing the accounting rules for the firms listed on that exchange.

There is no one set of accounting rules that best serves the managers or investors in all firms and industries or the data demands of all governments. For that reason, for example, about three-fourths of the Silicon Valley firms prepare their accounts on both a GAAP basis and a pro forma basis.[10]

Most important, a good balance sheet, at best, is a measure of the net value of the assets *owned* by the firm. The value of most modern firms, however, is increasingly dependent on "intangible" assets that the firm does not own and which there is no objective way to value other than by selling the firm. In the early 1980s, for example, the market value of the Standard & Poor's 500 index firms was 1.3 times the net book value. This ratio increased to 6.5 in 1997 before the asset bubble of 1998–2000 and fell to 4.3 at the end of March 2002. Even in the weak subsequent stock market, about three-fourths of the net value of major corporations is off the books. Some of this unrecorded value may be the difference between the market value of assets owned by the firm and the depreciated historical cost. Most of this difference, however, is the value of such intangible assets as the quality of the management and senior professionals; the distinctive rules by which the management operates; the reputation of its products, customer service, and investor relations; the skills, creativity, and loyalty of the employees; the breadth and stability of the supplier and customer bases; the market power of the firm in the product and supplier markets; and the relative invulnerability from litigation and changes in regulation and taxation. A change in these intangible assets can substantially change the value of a firm, even if there is no change in its financial accounts. The sharp drop in the market value of Martha Stewart's firm in response to her legal problems should be a reminder of how important one individual may be to the earnings potential and value of a firm. Many intangible assets cannot be independently valued, but some can be measured. In summary, a lot of conditions that affect the value of a firm, for better or for worse, are never reflected in its financial accounts. The primary contemporary challenge for accountants may be to develop a set of nonfinancial measures of these key performance indicators, as a complement to the best possible financial accounts.[11]

WHAT TO DO?

The first policy lesson that I draw from the above characteristics of accounting is that the interests of neither corporate managers nor investors are best served by assigning the authority to set accounting standards to the FASB, the SEC, and Congress. There is no reason to question the FASB's professionalism, but, as a private monopoly, it has proved incapable of developing accounting standards that are concise, nonarbitrary, and timely. The SEC has no special expertise or interest to understand whether the FASB has proposed a better accounting standard, other than as a response to political pressure. Congress has no expertise to recognize better accounting standards, and it is generally biased in favor of rules that create or protect private rents. This leads me to conclude that the authority to develop and set accounting standards should not be assigned to any private or public monopoly.

The one institution that has the greatest potential to capture the third-party benefits of good accounting rules, I suggest, is the stock exchange on which the corporation is listed.

Investors would pay more for the shares of corporations listed on an exchange that requires nonarbitrary, transparent, and timely financial accounts, and corporations would prefer to be listed on that exchange if the benefits of the accounting standards required by the exchange are higher than the costs. Competition among the exchanges may lead some exchanges to require less complex accounting rules, but only if the reduction in benefits is smaller than the reduction in cost. Some exchanges may choose to specialize in the accounting rules that best serve the investors in a specific industry; others may specialize by region, firm size, etc.

This leads me to recommend a radical increase in the authority of the stock exchanges that would include the following role: Each exchange would choose the accounting standards for the corporations listed on that exchange. In the United States, of course, each exchange would start with the GAAP but would have the authority to add, delete, or amend any of these rules. There would continue to be a role for the FASB and other accounting advisory groups, but their proposed changes would be subject to the approval by each exchange, not by the SEC.

Allowing each exchange to choose the accounting rules for corporations listed on that exchange is expected to lead to rules that are less complex and less ambiguous, increasing the transparency and comparability of the accounts of the corporations listed on that exchange.

Over time, however, the set of accounting rules chosen by each exchange would probably diverge somewhat, better reflecting the preferences of the subset of investors and the corporations listed. This would somewhat increase the cost of comparing the accounts of firms using different accounting standards, but I expect that specialized skills and software would be developed to reduce this cost.

This first proposal would be a role for the exchanges for which they have no history and which they have not previously considered in their internal deliberations. Our initial interviews with officials of the exchanges, however, suggest that there is some interest in this proposal. The NYSE, for example, may prefer to allow firms to use either GAAP or the IFRS, in order to reduce the cost to foreign firms listed on that exchange. And the NASDAQ has a strong preference to continue to allow firms the choice of whether to expense stock options.

CONCLUSION

In summary, investors are best served by the opportunity to see much of the same information by which managers make their decisions. Current financial accounting, unfortunately, provides little of this information, some of which may be misleading.

Following the collapse of Enron and WorldCom, however, most of the attention of the public, the media, and the politicians was focused on policies that might improve accounting and auditing on the mistaken impression that such policies would be sufficient to reduce the frequency and magnitude of financial fraud and corporate bankruptcies. In contrast, we need more competition among accounting rules, not more debate about what are the best general accounting rules. And more important, we need to complement good financial accounting with public information on the key nonfinancial performance indicators specific to each industry. Tweaking GAAP would divert attention from the measures that are necessary to address the major current problems of financial accounting.

NOTES

1. Report of Investigation by the Special Investigative Committee of the Board of Directors of Enron Corp., February 1, 2002.

2. *Wall Street Journal*, August 13, 2002.

3. See chap. 5.

4. Varian, Hal, "Knowing about Diluted Earnings Is a Powerful Tool," *New York Times*, May 9, 2002.

5. *Wall Street Journal*, July 28, 2003.

6. "Making It All Add Up, Again," *Washington Post*, March 28, 2003.

7. Ibid.

8. Lev, Baruch, "Corporate Earnings: Facts and Fiction," *Journal of Economic Perspectives* 17, no. 2, spring 2003.

9. Lev, "Corporate Earnings: Facts and Fiction."

10. Rodgers, T. J., "Corporate Accounting: Congress and FASB Ignore Business Realities," Cato Briefing Paper no. 77, October 29, 2002.

11. For a summary of the comments of the Financial Accounting Standards Committee of the American Accounting Association on the disclosure of nonfinancial performance measures, see Laureen A. Maines, Eli Bartov, Patricia M. Fairfield, D. Eric Hirst, et al., "Recommendations on Disclosure of Nonfinancial Performance Measures," *Accounting Horizons,* 16, December 2002, p. 353–62.

• 5 •

Corporate Accounting
before and after Enron

George J. Benston

$\mathcal{T}$he preamble to the Securities Exchange Act of 1934 states that it was designed "to provide full and fair disclosure of the character of the securities sold in interstate commerce and through the mails, and to prevent fraud in the sale thereof." To that end, corporations with at least $10 million in assets for which securities are held by more than 500 shareholders must file annual and quarterly financial statements with the Securities and Exchange Commission (SEC). Those statements are prepared by corporate accountants and must follow Generally Accepted Accounting Principles (GAAP). They must also be audited by a registered public accounting firm (RPA) that assures investors that the statements were, indeed, prepared in accordance with GAAP, based on their audit of the corporation's books and records.[1] Those are the rules.

However, after the discovery of misstatements in the audited reports of well-known and seemingly successful corporations—notably Enron, Adelphia, Global Crossing, WorldCom, Qwest, Rite Aid, IBM, Sunbeam, Waste Management, and Cendant—journalists, legislators, and investors have increasingly questioned the integrity and usefulness of this disclosure-based system. Are the GAAP rules inadequate? Or were they just not followed? If not followed, why did their independent public accountants (IPAs) attest that they were followed?[2] Did the SEC do its job and ascertain that the disclosure and attestation requirements of the Securities Exchange Act of 1934 were being followed? Are corporations playing a "numbers game," as claimed by former SEC Chairman Arthur Levitt, using "creative" and "aggressive" accounting to bend the rules and "reflect the desires of management rather than the underlying financial performance of the company"?[3] Or is this an overstated problem, considering the thousands of corporations that file financial statements with the SEC and are not charged with wrongdoing? If it is a systemic problem, what might be done to correct it? In any event, what or who is to blame for the scandals that led to overwhelming passage by the Congress of the Sarbanes-Oxley Act of 2002 (SOA)?

55

This chapter begins with a historical review of accounting regulation, which indicates that the current criticisms are not new, and then goes "back to basics" to outline why audited financial statements are valued by investors. Stewardship and investment decisions are the principal reasons for which trustworthy numbers, as attested to by RPA firms, are particularly useful. Although economic values would be more useful than historical costs, these amounts often cannot be measured and verified as trustworthy. Indeed, the movement by the Financial Accounting Standards Board (FASB) and the SEC toward a non-market-based measure of economic values, "fair value," will make financial statements less useful. Traditional accounting-based financial statements, though, are useful to investors for several reasons. The most important is that they describe the traditional accounting measure of net income, the procedures for revenue and expense recognition, and the role of conservatism in determining those numbers. The chapter also shows why it is not possible to eliminate managers' opportunities to manipulate reported net income or cash flows, a situation about which investors should be aware.

Next comes an analysis of what went wrong at Enron and what lessons might be drawn from this one very important case. Enron has had great importance in molding public perceptions about accounting statements and external auditors and is, to a large extent, responsible for SOA, the most sweeping regulation of accounting since the early 1930s. Overall, it appears that Enron's managers and auditors presented misleading financial statements because they did not follow the prescriptions of basic, traditional accounting and many of the rules codified in GAAP. Enron's failure, however, does reveal several shortcomings in GAAP, predominantly with respect to its rule-based approach and allowance of fair-value accounting.

Enron is not the only or the first corporation to have misstated its financial statements, however. A review of the data reveals substantial deficiencies that are the result of corporations not following established Generally Accepted Auditing Standards (GAAS) and GAAP rules and IPAs either not discovering these deficiencies or acquiescing to them. On the basis of those analyses, I consider who is to blame. Among the possible culprits are auditing and accounting standards and standards setters, boards of directors, external auditors (IPAs), and professional IPA associations and state and federal regulators, particularly the SEC. Finally, three changes to GAAP—allowing restatements of assets and liabilities only to the extent that those are based on trustworthy numbers, replacing the U.S. rule-based system with a principles-based traditional "matching concept" system, and allowing publicly traded corporations to use international accounting standards as an alternative to U.S. GAAP—are suggested.

PUTTING THE CRITICISM INTO PERSPECTIVE: THE HISTORICAL RECORD

As harshly criticized as accounting and accountants are now, such criticism is not at all new. Strident complaints about dishonest and deceptive accounting in the

1920s[4] and the distress of the Great Depression led to the creation in 1934 of the SEC, which was given the authority to prescribe, monitor, and enforce accounting rules that presumably would help investors to make informed decisions. In effect, the SEC's motto is "Ye shall know the truth, and the truth shall make ye rich." Actually, the preambles to the Securities Act of 1933 (which governs new securities issues) and the Securities Exchange Act of 1934 (which governs periodic financial reporting) call the acts "disclosure statutes." However, it is not disclosure, as such, that reigns, because publicly traded corporations cannot simply state, "we disclose that we will disclose nothing," or "we follow international accounting standards," or some other statement. Rather, the SEC adopted a rule that proclaims: "Where financial statements filed . . . are prepared in accordance with accounting principles for which there is no substantial authoritative support, such financial statements will be presumed to be misleading or inaccurate *despite disclosures* contained in the certificate of the accountant or in footnotes to the statements provided the matters involved are material."[5] Although the SEC promulgated Regulation S-X, which specifies what must be reported in filings submitted to it and how the material must be reported, in 1940, it has generally relegated the development and codification of GAAP and GAAS to the public accounting profession. Its influence on what the profession does, particularly with respect to GAAP, though, is profound and continuing.

In its early years, the SEC adopted a strongly conservative stance. It insisted that corporate registrants use only historical-cost-based numbers and not include intangibles as assets. Appraisals and other estimates of the current value of assets could not be reported in financial statements, and goodwill was eliminated from balance sheets. The SEC followed that conservative approach in response to criticism that it had allowed corporations to report asset values that later evaporated. The American Institute of Certified Public Accountants (AICPA), to which the SEC granted authority to codify GAAP, emphasized reducing the alternatives for reporting events that superficially appeared to be the same, such as recording long-term lease obligations either on or off the balance sheet, and providing guidance for reporting newly important events, such as the investment tax credit.

Over the years, various complaints about and scandals related to the inadequacies of GAAP led to the restructuring of the institutions dealing with and promulgating GAAP. The FASB was created in 1973 as a well-funded, professionally staffed rule-making body that is independent of the public accounting profession. It replaced the Accounting Principles Board, which was run by the AICPA and staffed with volunteer partners of CPA firms. The APB, in turn, had replaced the AICPA's Committee on Accounting Procedure (CAP), which was created in 1936. The CAP could only suggest, rather than demand, specific practices, while the APB and the FASB have been able to specify practices that must be followed by CPAs and companies that report to the SEC.

Since the mid-1970s, though, dissatisfaction with allegedly irrelevant historical costs has moved the SEC and the FASB toward requiring companies to report current values for financial assets. Marketable securities that are regularly traded or are held for sale must be shown at their market values (if these are available) on balance sheets, although revaluation gains and losses that are not realized are included in the income statement only for traded securities. Debt securities held until maturity are shown at cost, with their market values reported only in footnotes to the statements. Derivatives that do not qualify as hedges (based on a complex set of rules codified in Financial Accounting Statement 133 and 138 and Interpretations thereof) must be stated at fair values, with changes in these values reported as income or expense in the income statement. Because these financial assets often are not regularly traded, their values are determined with models rather than from quoted market prices. In addition, contracts involving energy and risk management activities must be stated at fair values, even though these amounts are based on calculations of the present value of the net cash flows the assets are expected to generate.

Thus, under current FASB rules corporate balance sheets are mixtures of past (historical) values, current values based on market values, and fair values estimated by corporate managers. An issue that is (or should be) debated is whether financial accounting should continue moving toward showing all or some assets and liabilities at current values and, if so, whether these should be based only on market values or on market values and estimates thereof (fair values). Also to be debated is whether accounting should return to values based on actual transactions (historical costs), or on some combination of values. The answers depend on the purposes for which financial statements are useful to investors.

THE VALUE OF AUDITED FINANCIAL STATEMENTS

Investors, whether present or prospective shareholders, benefit from learning about how their investments have been and might be used by the managers of their companies. Managers render financial reports to their boards of directors and shareholders. Those reports are the principal formal means by which managers convey how they have managed a company's resources over a period of time, usually no longer than a year, and the financial condition of the company at the end of that period, as determined by their accounting records. Prospective investors realize that once they have committed their funds to a corporation, either by purchasing shares directly or from a shareholder, they usually have little control over how the corporation is managed. Consequently, they have reason to be interested in how those in control of corporate resources use those assets and the extent to which controlling persons (senior managers, directors, and other shareholders) have conflicts of interest that might result in costs being imposed on them as noncontrolling shareholders. Reporting in these areas is called the "stewardship" function of accounting. Financial reports also help to motivate managers to operate their corporations in the interest of shareholders. This is called the "agency" or "contracting" function of accounting.

In addition to a report of stewardship, investors want data that help them determine the present and possible future economic value of their investments. If a corporation's shares are actively traded in a market, shareholders can obtain seemingly unbiased estimates of the economic value of their investments from share prices. However, those prices are based, in part, on the information provided in financial reports. If that information is not useful and accurate, its receipt will not provide investors with insights that they want, nor would it change the values ascribed to those shares. Hence, prospective investors might have to incur costs to obtain information elsewhere or discount the amount they are willing to pay for the shares given the information currently available to them. That would make the shares worth less to them. Thus, present shareholders, including those who can exercise some control over the corporation, also benefit from their managers providing all investors with financial reports that investors find trustworthy.

Because the corporate managers who prepare their firms' financial reports have incentives to misreport the performance and financial condition of their enterprises, financial statement users have reason to question the trustworthiness of those statements. Assuring that figures are reliable and presented according to GAAP is the principal purpose of audits by IPAs—for example, Certified Public Accountants (U.S.), Chartered Accountants (U.K.), or Wirtschaftsprüfer (Germany). IPAs' attestations of the validity of the numbers presented provide surety that they have examined the corporate records in a manner that is expected to be sufficient to uncover material misstatements and omissions and that they have conducted an audit that conforms to GAAS.

TRUSTWORTHINESS OF FINANCIAL STATEMENTS AND IPAS' ATTESTATIONS

For a substantial portion of stewardship, it is sufficient for the numbers presented to be trustworthy and the audits to be designed to uncover and reveal misuse of corporate resources, misstatement of income and expenses, overstatement of assets, and understatement of liabilities. Only an audit can provide this information.

For evaluating managers' performance and for investment decisions, it would be desirable if financial statements could also report the value to investors of their corporation's resources at the beginning and end of an accounting period. Net income or loss for the period, then, would be the difference between the beginning and end-of-period values, adjusted for distributions to and additional investments by shareholders. For those purposes, economic values for assets and liabilities, rather than historical costs, would be most relevant. Indeed, that is an important motivation for the increasing inclusion of market values and, where these are not available, "fair values" (which proxy for market values) in place of historical costs in the accounting standards adopted by the FASB and the International Accounting Standards Board.

A fair value is the amount for which an asset presumably could be (but hasn't been) exchanged, or a liability settled, between informed, willing parties on an arm's-length basis. That amount may be computed from management's estimates of the present values of expected cash flows (as described in the FASB's Statement of Financial Accounting Concept 7). The problem is that fair values (as distinct from market values) must often be derived from estimates rather than actual market values. Unfortunately, a financial report based on fair values can rarely be achieved within the requirement that the numbers also be trustworthy. It often is said that there is a trade-off between trustworthiness and relevance, but information is relevant and useful for decision making to the degree that it is accurate and unbiased (where the bias is not known). Therefore, trustworthy numbers are more relevant than fair values that are not based on market prices, because fair values are much more subject to managerial manipulation than are historical costs. Investors and others who want to know the economic market value of the enterprise must and can look to other sources of information apart from a company's financial statements. For example, fair values could be presented to investors in supplementary schedules and even attested to by IPAs as having been derived from models or sources that the IPAs find acceptable.

CAN ECONOMICALLY MEANINGFUL AND TRUSTWORTHY NUMBERS BE OBTAINED?

One problem in determining economic values stems from the cost and difficulty—often impossibility—of measuring the value of assets to an enterprise (value-in-use) and, hence, to an investor. That is, the present value of the net cash flows expected from its use (including disposal) by the enterprise in combination with other assets and liabilities. This is very difficult to estimate, even subjectively. Furthermore, the estimates are likely to change over time, as other enterprise operations, market conditions, and general and specific prices change. Although managers make formal or informal estimates of the present values of assets before their purchase, these estimates need only indicate that the present value of net cash flows exceeds the cost of the asset. Furthermore, this analysis (called "capital budgeting") often requires data that are not routinely available, such as current and expected prices and amounts related to asset purchases and use. Repeating these analyses for each periodic balance sheet would be very costly. Fixed assets, such as buildings, equipment, and land used for operations, provide prime examples of these valuation difficulties. Even more difficult to estimate are the values of intangible assets that are produced by the enterprise.

In addition, the value of an enterprise to an investor almost always is greater than the sum of the values of its assets less the sum of its liabilities. That is one of the principal reasons that companies exist. Their owners obtain rents (positive externalities) from the combination of assets and liabilities that comprise the company, which increase expected net cash flows above the amounts these assets and liabilities separately or in other combinations would have generated. (If the whole were not worth more than the sum of the parts, the company should be liquidated, in which event the value-in-use would be the net disposal value.) Thus, for almost all corporations, even if investors and IPAs were willing to accept as trustworthy the managers' estimates of the economic values of individual assets and liabilities, the amount shown as "fair-value shareholders' equity" would not equal the economic value of the enterprise. Nor would the change in shareholders' equity (adjusted for distributions to and additions by shareholders) provide a valid measure of shareholders' net economic income.

A second and more important problem is that the only economic values that can be measured are rarely trustworthy unless they are based on relevant and reliable market values, rather than managerially determined fair values. In this light, there should be great concern about the FASB's move to require restatement of all financial assets to fair values, even when these amounts are not based on trustworthy market prices, with the changes in those values shown as current income (or loss). Managers who want to make it appear as if they had done well in a particular accounting period can readily increase the fair value of assets and, thereby, increase reported net income. All they have to do is increase their estimates of cash inflows, decrease their estimates of cash outflows, or decrease the rate that discounts the net cash flows to obtain present (fair) values. They can easily work backward toward the numbers they want, constructing a rationale for the estimates they make that IPAs would find difficult or impossible to refute. If the cash flows they estimated turn out to be incorrect (as they inevitably will, even if the managers sought only to make unbiased estimates), the managers can argue that conditions have changed (as they inevitably do). They can argue further that they could not reasonably have predicted the changes or that they did correctly predict a range of outcomes with associated probabilities, and that the outcome was within this range, although not equal to the expected amount. This lack of trustworthiness led the SEC in its early years to disallow estimates and appraisals.

THE USEFULNESS OF
FINANCIAL STATEMENTS TO INVESTORS

Although financial statements that report the economic position of an enterprise at the end of an accounting period and changes in that position over the previous period cannot be reliably produced by managers and audited by IPAs, the statements nevertheless have great value to investors. In addition to providing evidence of an audit and revealing the presence or absence of significant conflicts of interest and misappropriation of resources (stewardship), financial statements provide investors with five additional valuable benefits.

One benefit is disclosure of important numbers, whose values investors can trust to be accurate. These presently include cash and marketable securities, accounts and notes receivable, prepaid expenses, current liabilities, floating-rate interest-bearing assets and liabilities and fixed-rate obligations when interest rates have not changed, and the physical presence, if not the economic values, of inventories, plants, equipment, and land. GAAP could be changed to have many inventories and fixed-interest-bearing assets and liabilities reliably stated at economic (market) values. Even then, however, in volatile markets the numbers reported as of the balance sheet date may not reflect current prices.

A second value is assurance that all the numbers presented in financial statements are consistent with GAAP. Even though many of these numbers (e.g., some long-term tangible and most, if not all, intangible assets) do not reflect economic values well, at least investors can readily understand the rules under which they are recorded. For example, when trustworthy valuations cannot be made, GAAP should not permit managers to increase the value of buildings or decrease the amount of depreciation to give investors the impression that the reported numbers actually measure the value of their investments or that accounting net income was greater. Revenue should not be recorded unless the corporation has substantially completed all it must do to be entitled to future cash inflows. Indeed, even though the income statement is not (and cannot be) a report of the change in shareholders' wealth embodied in the corporation over a period, net of dividends and new investments, it provides investors with a generally useful indicator of periodic changes in wealth. Because this is the statement that has been (and will continue to be) of greatest interest to investors, the next section outlines how it could be improved.

The third benefit is confirmation of earlier announcements by managers of a company's financial condition and earnings. By the time audited financial statements are published, market participants have usually learned and acted on information about the corporations' financial condition and changes over the period. This information often comes from corporate announcements, such as current and expected earnings, write-offs of discontinued facilities, and changes in earnings prospects as the result of new or revised contracts, employee lay-offs, and management changes. Much of this information is also reported in the financial statements. Because the statements are attested to by IPAs, both senior managers and investors can be assured that the announcements that reflect or affect the numbers in the statements are unlikely to be fabrications. That assurance improves the efficiency of share transactions, such that the cost of information is lower and share prices very quickly reflect changes in the economic value of corporate shares.

The fourth benefit, the usefulness of the numbers presented for analyses of trends, follows from the other benefits. As long as analysts and investors have assurance that the numbers presented are consistently produced, they can use these data to identify trends—such as growing or shrinking sales and profit margins, inventories, capital investments, and income and expense ratios to sales and assets—and changes therein, that help them evaluate and predict company performance.

The fifth benefit is provision of a useful measure of economic performance—the traditional accounting definition of net income from operations. Deliberate violation by managers of this measurement has been the greatest problem for public financial accounting.

THE ACCOUNTING MEASUREMENT OF NET INCOME

Determining net income involves two key steps. The first is recognition of revenue, which has two essential requirements: timing and reliable measurement. Revenue may be recorded when a corporation has essentially fulfilled its obligations to the purchaser in whole or in part. When the transaction is complete, title to the product should have passed to the purchaser. When the product is delivered contractually over more than one accounting period, the proportion of revenue called for in the contract that is completed in a period should be reported as revenue in that period. That point of recognition is often called the "critical event." For example, although the conversion of materials, labor, and overhead into finished goods available for sale usually increases their value above the sum of the resources expended, revenue is not recognized until the critical event, which is the sale to a customer. When there is a firm contract that essentially transfers title to the goods when they are manufactured, however, their completed manufacture is the critical event. In contrast, a consignment would not be treated as producing revenue to a company, because the critical event is sale of the consigned goods by the recipient and its acceptance of an obligation to pay the company. A similar situation is a sale that is financed by the seller, either directly with a loan or indirectly with a guarantee of a loan made to the buyer by a third-party lender (e.g., a bank), where the prospect that the buyer will pay for the goods as promised is unclear. The critical event is the payments received from the buyer or the buyer's repayment of the loan and release of the seller's obligation. In effect, this is an "installment sale," and revenue should be recognized as the payments are made, not when the product was transferred. (Alternatively, the account or note receivable could be reduced to the amount of expected repayment.) These "rules" for revenue recognition are well established, although they often are violated when management seek to manipulate and misstate net income. Reliable measurement is necessary to determine the value of assets received or liabilities extinguished in exchange for the goods and services, and hence the amount of revenue earned. The amount of revenue earned should be determined by the value of the asset received. Where the market values of assets received in exchange cannot be reliably measured, revenue should not be recorded until reliably measured values can be determined. For example, if a company receives in exchange for its product the product of the purchasing company, the revenue amount should be no greater than the amount for which the product received could be sold in an arm's-length transaction. Thus, an Internet company that "sold" time on its Web site in exchange for time on another Internet company's Web site should record as revenue no more than the amount for which it could sell the time received. If either or both of the companies have surplus time that they cannot sell in arm's-length transactions for cash or other assets that can be reliably valued, the "sale" has no value and no revenue should be recorded.

Another often encountered example is a tied sale, where a company sells its product for a reliably measured asset, such as cash or a receivable, but agrees to purchase the buyer's product, perhaps at an inflated price. In that and other situations, the issue is whether the asset purchased is valued at an arm's-length price. If the price paid is greater than the arm's-length price, the difference actually is a discount of the sales price, which should be recorded as a reduction of revenue.

Such would not be the case, however, in another fairly common situation that often involves commodities, where companies inflate their sales with largely offsetting sales and purchases to each other. For example, company S sells electricity contracts to company B for a reliably specified amount, but in exchange informally agrees to buy the same or very similar amount of company B's electricity contracts for almost the same price. These may be "sham" sales, but they are very difficult to distinguish from legitimate sales that may have been undertaken to diversify risk. Unless IPAs can determine that such sales really are shams, they have no alternative except to attest that the companies' financial statements accord with GAAP. Financial statement users should recognize this and other basic limitations of auditing and financial accounting. They also often can discover and adjust for such situations by examining whether increases in revenue are associated with decreases in gross margins.

It also is important for managers to distinguish between revenue earned from the operations of the enterprise and income derived from the sale and revaluation of assets and liabilities. Many financial statement users (particularly investors) base their calculations of a company's prospects on its past performance, as reflected by its revenue and net income from its continuing operations. In the past, accountants sought to limit the income statement to those numbers, with nonoperating and extraordinary revenue and expenses taken directly to shareholders' equity in the balance sheet (then called "earned surplus"). However, experience revealed that managers tended to exclude the effect of many unfavorable events from the income statement. Consequently, the accounting profession adopted the "clean surplus" approach, whereby almost all income and expense is reported in the income statement. Hence, it is important that revenue (or sales) and the associated expenses include only the results of the ordinary operations of an enterprise.

A very important task for the IPA, then, is to determine that the requirements for recognizing and classifying revenue have, in fact, been met. (Indeed, as explained later, this has been, perhaps, the most prevalent and important aspect of misreporting that has not been caught and corrected by external auditors.) An important part of this determination is the GAAP requirement that the financial records must be presented in a manner consistent with earlier reports, unless otherwise noted and explained. Thus, a consistently applied recognition rule would tend to prevent managers from recording, say, a substantial increase in revenue from one previously specified source in a particular period to cover up losses or a substantial revenue decline from a different previously specified source. For example, a company should not report as "revenue or cash flows from operations" the gains or amounts received from its sale of a segment of its business.

The second key step is matching the expenses incurred (whether beneficially or not) to obtain the revenue recognized. These are the costs of acquiring the revenue less their economic value at the end of the accounting period. This is the "matching concept" that has served accounting very well over a long time. Some expenses, such as the cost of resold merchandise and salespersons' commissions, can readily be matched with revenue. Many expenses, though, are incurred before or after the associated revenue is recognized. In general, accruals are designed to deal with this situation. Expenditures for tangible assets that will generate revenue in future periods, such as buildings and equipment, are "capitalized" and charged against revenue (i.e., as depreciation expense) over the period of their estimated useful economic lives. Expenses incurred to generate currently reported revenue that will not be paid for until future periods, such as the cost of warranties and pension benefits, are charged against that revenue and a liability for the future expected expenditure is created. (The charge should be for the present value of the liability, preferably discounted at no higher rate than the yield on the company's debt, since the pension liability is a preferred obligation.) Expenses that are predominantly time related, such as administrative and property expenses, are generally charged against revenue in the period in which they are incurred. The rationale is that the resources created, such as going concern value and other intangibles, rarely can be reliably measured and, if they were recorded as assets, would be untrustworthy and subject to manipulation by managers.

Similar reasoning, however, has not been applied to manufactured inventory, perhaps because it is a tangible, rather than an intangible, asset. Overhead expenses that are fixed (i.e., do not vary with inventory produced) are allocated to inventory with arbitrary but not readily manipulated procedures (e.g., per dollar or hour of direct labor). Those fixed amounts, though, ought to be charged to the period in which they were incurred, based on the assumption that the opportunity value of the inventory in process of manufacture or finished goods is the cost to replace it—the variable costs that were incurred. (Where the inventory cannot be replaced at variable cost because the plant is operating at capacity, the asset value of the inventory would be the lower of the estimated replacement cost or net realizable value.)

As suggested by E. Edwards and P. W. Bell in 1961, assets and liabilities that can be valued reliably as of the end of the accounting period should be recorded, and the difference between those values and the recorded values should be reported as income (or expense) from holding gains (or losses).[6] The important element is trustworthiness. In general, this means that the amounts are those that are, or, if based on accepted independent valuations, would be, based on prices determined from arm's-length market transactions.

CONSERVATISM

"Conservatism" refers to the bias in traditional accounting to delay the recognition of income and speed up the recognition of expense when there is substantial uncertainty about both the timing and the amounts involved. For example, if a construction firm has undertaken a contract spanning several years, where the amount it will eventually gain cannot be determined until the contract is completed, revenue is not reported until it is clear that it has been earned and will be (or has been) received. Expenses incurred to earn that revenue will be similarly delayed (the matching concept), although if they exceed the expected revenue, they will be reported as expenses (reductions in equity) in the current period.

Accountants necessarily must estimate some items of revenue and expense. For example, the amount of revenue that will be earned on a project and employees' pensions that will not be paid until some future time can only be estimated. The estimated revenue, though, will rarely be reported until there is reliable evidence of its amount and that it has, indeed, been earned and will be received. The estimated expense, though, will be reported currently.

The essential reason for the conservative bias is accountants' long-term experience that people get very upset when they learn that events are worse than they believe they were led to expect but usually are happy when events are better than expected. Hence, it is better to delay the good news until it is likely to occur and recognize the bad news earlier rather than later.

ELIMINATING ALL MANAGERIAL
DISCRETION IS NOT POSSIBLE

The traditional accounting measure of net income (with or without the change suggested that would incorporate trustworthy current values of inventories and other assets and liabilities) must necessarily be derived, to some extent, from assumptions and judgments, which give managers some ability to affect reported net income. For example, the amount of depreciation of a plant, equipment, and other fixed assets is determined by assumptions about the useful economic life of those assets and the rate at which their costs are written off as expenses. The relevant measure would be the reduction (or possibly increase) in the value-in-use of depreciating assets. However, those measurements are generally unreliable and often subject to deliberate misrepresentation. Accountants, therefore, have used predetermined procedures, such as straight-line or accelerated allocations of the historical cost of fixed assets, to determine periodic depreciation expenses. As long as financial statement users understand that, at best, those numbers only approximate the cost to equity holders of holding and using depreciable assets, they can make adjustments to the reported net income numbers, including ignoring depreciation as a meaningful measure of economic user cost.

Liabilities that must be estimated also give managers an opportunity to affect reported net income. For example, a company's liability for warranties and employee retirement benefits is based on assumptions about expected future cash flows and discount rates. The amounts that are charged as current-period expenses can vary considerably, depending on those assumptions.

Managers can also time transactions and take advantage of alternative accrual procedures to alter revenue recognition and expense incurrence. For example, they can delay or speed up revenue recognition between accounting periods by specifying when title passes to a purchaser. Periodic expenses that are not inventoried as part of manufactured goods—such as advertising, research and development, and maintenance—can be reduced, delayed, or incurred earlier than need be in order to affect the amount charged against revenue in an accounting period. IPAs cannot object to those actions, because they represent the effect of actual events. Newly appointed CEOs can decide that the value of substantial assets are impaired and write them off (a procedure known as the "big bath"), thereby reducing future expenses. IPAs can and should examine the rationale for such write-offs for conformity with the matching concept.

However, the ability of opportunistic managers to manipulate reported net income with timing and accrual assumptions is limited by three factors. One is the self-correcting nature of accruals. Earlier revenue recognition that overstates net income in a period results in understated net income, usually in the next period. Direct charges of "extraordinary" events to retained earnings that bypass the income statement are not self-correcting and, thus, rarely are (or should be) accepted by IPAs. The second is managers' decisions to advance or delay the acquisition, purchase, and use of resources. Unfortunately for shareholders, this form of manipulation is more than cosmetic; it can be detrimental to economic performance. This detriment, though, limits the extent to which these manipulations of expenses can be made, because their negative effect will be reflected by such actual events as lower sales and higher expenses. Third, GAAP does not allow IPAs to accept numbers that are inconsistently determined from period to period. Hence, although managers can, say, initially reduce depreciation expense by assuming a longer economic life for a fixed asset, in the future the depreciation expense must be greater.

Furthermore, users of financial statements should be aware of possible management manipulations of financial accounting data that are accepted by IPAs. The data may be accepted because they conform to GAAP rules and could accurately reflect the operations of a company or because the IPAs are not competent or have been (perhaps unknowingly) suborned. Users can then evaluate and interpret the reported data.[7]

To summarize, net income should be the amount that can be reliably reported as having increased the claim of equity holders over the assets of their corporation, although some of the numbers are derived from estimates and judgments. The balance sheet should only partially reflect the economic market values of individual assets and liabilities, as of the balance sheet date. To some extent, managers can manipulate the numbers presented in the income statement. That is the best that accounting can do, and, when the numbers reported are trustworthy, that is very valuable to investors and other users of financial statements.

THE ROLE OF ACCOUNTING STANDARDS

Standards governing the content and presentation of financial accounting data (GAAP) in formal statements (balance sheets, income statements, and statements of cash flow) substantially improve the usefulness of financial reports. Users of those reports can efficiently determine the extent to which the attesting IPAs have examined the books and records of their clients. Users also should be able to readily determine the meaning and validity of the numbers presented in the statements, particularly if IPAs have done their jobs well. Consequently, it is very important that IPAs determine that the financial statements really were prepared in accordance with GAAP.

Standards provide substantial benefits to IPAs as well, who are likely to be under pressure from some managers to overlook or even accept misrepresentations of poor performance. Codified accounting concepts and standards and auditing procedures can provide IPAs with guidance and protect them from demands by clients to attest to numbers that might mislead financial statement users. They can rightly claim that there is no point for the client to go to another IPA who might be more compliant, because all IPAs would have to adhere to the same general standards.

WHAT WENT WRONG AT ENRON?

Enron's bankruptcy has generated substantial concern about the inadequacies of GAAS and GAAP, probably because Enron became bankrupt so quickly after having been so highly regarded. Its stock price, which had increased from a low of about $7 in the 1990s to a high of $90 a share in mid-2000, plunged to less than $1 by the end of 2001, wiping out shareholders' equity by almost $11 billion. That decline was preceded by an announcement, on October 16, 2001, that the company was reducing its after-tax net income by $544 million and its shareholders' equity by $1.2 billion. On November 8, it announced that, because of accounting errors, it was restating its previously reported net income for the years 1997 through 2000. These restatements reduced previously reported net income as follows: 1997, $28 million (27 percent of previously reported income of $105 million); 1998, $133 million (19 percent of previously reported income of $703 million); 1999, $248 million (28 percent of previously reported income of $893 million); and 2000, $99 million (10 percent of previously reported income of $979 million). These changes reduced stockholders' equity by $508 million. Thus, within a month, Enron's stockholders' equity was lower by $1.7 billion (18 percent of previously reported equity of $9.6 billion at September 30, 2001). On December 2, 2001, Enron filed for bankruptcy under Chapter 11 of the United States Bankruptcy Code. With assets of $63.4 billion it was the largest corporate bankruptcy in U.S. history until WorldCom declared bankruptcy in 2002.[8] Not only did investors and employees, whose retirement plans included large amounts of Enron stock, lose wealth, but Enron's long-time auditor, Arthur Andersen, was destroyed, and the U.S. system of financial accounting was severely questioned, with strong and insistent calls for reform that culminated in the enactment of the SOA.

ENRON'S ACCOUNTING ERRORS
AND SHORTCOMINGS

The role of accounting misstatements and corrections in causing, rather than reflecting, Enron's demise still is unclear.[9] Over time, as congressional, SEC, bankruptcy court, and other investigations proceed and lawsuits against Enron's officers and directors, accountants, and lawyers unfold, we should learn more. Nevertheless, five groups of issues may be delineated:

- The failure to account properly for, and investments in, special purpose entities (SPEs) (organizations sponsored by and benefiting Enron but owned by presumably independent outside investors) and Enron's dealings with them;
- Enron's income-recognition practice of recording as current income fees for services rendered in future periods and recording revenue from sales of forward contracts, which were, in effect, disguised loans;
- Fair value accounting resulting in restatements of "merchant" investments that were not based on trustworthy numbers;
- Enron's accounting for its stock that was issued to and held by SPEs; and
- Inadequate disclosure of related party transactions and conflicts of interest and their costs to stockholders.

All but one of these issues (the third, fair-value accounting) involved violations of the provisions of GAAP and GAAS. One other (inadequate accounting for SPEs) appears to have violated the spirit, if not the letter, of GAAP and has resulted in a change in GAAP adopted by the FASB.[10]

Accounting for and Associated with Investments in SPEs

Enron sponsored hundreds (perhaps thousands) of SPEs with which it did business.[11] Many were used to shelter foreign-derived income from U.S. taxes. The SPEs for which its accounting has been criticized, though, were domestic and were created to provide a means whereby Enron could avoid reporting losses on some substantial investments.[12] The structure and activities of the specific SPEs in question are quite complicated, in part because the SPEs themselves created other SPEs that dealt with Enron.[13]

Outside investors held all of the equity in Enron's SPEs, usually amounting to no more than the minimum of 3 percent of assets established by the accounting authorities (the SEC and FASB) for a sponsoring corporation to avoid consolidating the SPEs into its financial statements. The balance of the assets was provided from bank loans guaranteed, directly or indirectly, by Enron or with restricted Enron stock and options to buy Enron stock at less than market value, for which Enron got a receivable from that SPE. Had Enron accounted for transactions with these SPEs in accordance with the spirit as well as the letter of GAAP requirements on dealings with related enterprises and disclosure of contingent liabilities for financial guarantees, nonconsolidation, as such, should not have been an issue.

Six accounting problems are associated with Enron's SPEs, all of which appear to have involved violations of GAAP as it existed at the time. First, in some important instances, the minimum "3 percent rule" was violated, but the affected SPEs were not consolidated. When Arthur Andersen realized that this was not done, it required Enron to restate its financial statements. Second, Enron failed to follow the dictates of FAS 5, the accounting standard that deals with contingencies, and report in a footnote the amounts and conditions of financial contingencies for which it was liable as a result of its guaranteeing the SPEs' debt. Had that been done, analysts and other users of Enron's statements would have been warned that the corporation could be (and eventually was) liable for a very large amount of debt. Indeed, the bankruptcy court examiner found that Enron's debt of $10.23 billion reported as of December 31, 2000, would have increased by $1.35 billion.[14] In this regard, Enron's not consolidating the SPEs was not the problem. Indeed, where Enron did not own or control the SPEs, it should not have consolidated them. Third, Enron did not but should have consolidated the SPEs that, in fact, it controlled, because they were managed by its chief financial officer (CFO), Andrew Fastow, or his employees. Fourth, although Enron controlled some SPEs through its CFO, transactions with them were treated as if the SPEs were independent enterprises; Enron should not have recorded net profits from those transactions. Fifth, Enron funded some SPEs with its own stock or in-the-money options on that stock, taking notes receivable in return. That violated a basic accounting procedure, under which companies should not record an increase in stockholders' equity unless the stock issued was paid for in cash or its equivalent. Reversal of this error resulted in a $1.2 billion reduction in shareholders' equity in October 2001. Sixth, Enron used a put option written by an SPE to avoid having to record a loss in value of previously appreciated stock when its market price declined, without recognizing that the option was secured by the SPE's holding of unpaid-for Enron stock and loans guaranteed by Enron.

Incorrect Income Recognition

Several of the SPEs paid Enron fees for guarantees on loans made by the SPEs. Although GAAP and the matching concept require recognition of revenue only over the period of the guarantees, Enron recorded millions of dollars of up-front payments as current revenue. It also appears to have engineered several sizeable sham "sales," where the buyers simultaneously or after a prearranged delay sold back to Enron the same or similar assets at close to the prices they "paid." This allowed Enron to report profits on the sales and, almost simultaneously, increase the book value of some assets.

In addition, Enron recorded as "sales" transfers of assets to SPEs even though it still controlled and substantially kept the risks and rewards derived from the assets. Enron first transferred the assets to subsidiaries, then exchanged nonvoting stock in the subsidiaries to SPEs in exchange for funds that the SPEs borrowed. Simultaneously, Enron swapped rights to the cash flow from the assets for an obligation to pay the bank loans. Thus, in essence, Enron still owned the assets and had borrowed funds from banks but recorded the transaction as sales and did not record the debt.[15]

Fair-Value Restatements of "Merchant" Investments
Not Based on Trustworthy Numbers

The AICPA's Investment Company Guide requires investment, business development, and venture-capital companies to revalue financial assets held (presumably) for trading to fair values, even when these values are not determined from arm's-length market transactions. In such instances, the values can be based on "independent" appraisals and on models using discounted expected cash flows. The models allow managers who want to manipulate net income the opportunity to make "reasonable" assumptions that would give them the gains they want to record. Enron designated various projects and investments in subsidiaries as "merchant investments," which allowed it to restate these investments at fair values in accordance with AICPA's Investment Company Guide.

A particularly egregious example is Enron's broadband investment and joint venture with Blockbuster, Inc., which was called Braveheart. Enron invested more than $1 billion on broadband and reported revenue of $408 million in 2000, much of it from sales to Fastow-controlled SPEs. In addition, on July 19, 2000, Enron entered into a twenty-year agreement with Blockbuster, Inc., to provide movies on demand to television viewers. The problem was that Enron did not have the technology to deliver the movies, and Blockbuster did not have the rights to the movies to be delivered. Nevertheless, Enron, as of December 31, 2000, assigned a fair value of $125 million to its Braveheart investment and a profit of $53 million from increasing the investment to its fair value, even though no sales had been made. Enron recorded additional revenue of $53 million from the venture in the first quarter of 2001, although Blockbuster did not record any income from the venture and dissolved the partnership in March 2001. In October, Enron had to reverse the $110.9 million in profit it had earlier claimed, an action that contributed to its loss of public trust and subsequent bankruptcy.

How could Enron have so massively misestimated the fair value of its Braveheart investment, and how could Arthur Andersen have allowed Enron to report those values and their increases as profits? Indeed, the examiner finds that Arthur Andersen prepared the appraisal of the project's value.[16] Andersen assumed the following: (1) the business would be established in ten major metro areas within twelve months, (2) eight new areas would be added per year until 2010, and those would each grow at 1 percent per year, (3) digital subscriber lines (DSLs) would be used by 5 percent of the households, increasing to 32 percent by 2010, and those would increase in speed sufficient to accept the broadcasts, and (4) Braveheart would garner 50 percent of this market. After determining (somehow) a net cash flow from each of these households and discounting by 31 percent to 34 percent, the project was assigned a fair value.

Another example is the Eli Lilly transaction.[17] On February 26, 2001, Enron announced a $1.3 billion fifteen-year agreement with Lilly for energy management services. The fair value of the project was determined by estimating the energy savings that Lilly was projected to achieve over fifteen years and discounting those amounts by 8.25–8.50 percent. That yielded a present value of $39.7 million. Within two years, this contract was considered worthless.

Accounting for Stock Issued to and Held by SPEs

GAAP and long-established accounting practice do not permit a corporation to record income from increases in the value of its own stock or to record stock as issued unless it has been paid for in cash or its equivalent. Nevertheless, that is what Enron did, to the tune of $1 billion. For reasons that are not clear, Arthur Andersen did not discover those accounting errors or, if it did, it allowed Enron to proceed. Correction of the errors in October 2001 contributed to concerns about Enron's accounting.

Inadequate Disclosure of Related Party Transactions and Conflicts of Interest

Enron disclosed that it had engaged in transactions with a related party, identified in its proxy statements (but not its SEC 10K report) as Andrew S. Fastow, its chief financial officer. Enron asserted in footnote item 16 of its 2000 10K that, "the terms of the transactions with the Related Party were reasonable compared to those which could have been negotiated with unrelated third parties."[18] However, those transactions do not appear to have been at arm's length. Indeed, the Powers Report, commissioned by the Enron Board of Directors to investigate Fastow's activities, concludes that he obtained more than $30 million personally from his management of the SPEs that did business with Enron, and other employees who reported to Fastow got over $11 million more. Furthermore, a detailed analysis of the Fastow-related SPEs indicates that the outside investors in the SPEs that Fastow controlled solicited and obtained multiple millions from investments on which they took little risk and that provided Enron with few benefits, other than providing a vehicle to overstate income and delay reporting losses and debt. The requirements of FASB Statement 57 and SEC's Regulation S-X item 404 for disclosure of transactions exceeding $60,000 in which an executive officer of a corporation had a material interest were not followed, except in the most general of ways.

THE IMPLICATIONS OF THE ENRON EXPERIENCE FOR CHANGES IN GAAP

Thus, except for fair-value accounting and Enron's use of financial engineering to obviate the intent of traditional accounting GAAP while conforming to or aggressively interpreting the rules, most of Enron's misstated and misleading accounting resulted from violations of GAAP. Based on the public information available at this time, one must conclude that Arthur Andersen violated the basic prescriptions of GAAS in conducting an audit that would allow it to state, as it did, "In our opinion, the financial statements referred to above present fairly, in all material respects, the financial position of Enron Corp. and subsidiaries . . . in conformity with accounting principles generally accepted in the United States."[19]

The Enron experience indicates that only two changes in GAAP are necessary. One is a rule that fair values should not be included in financial statements unless they are based on trustworthy information—prices determined by arm's-length market transactions. The second is that the traditional accounting definition of revenue and expenses described earlier should govern and, if necessary, override rules specified in authoritative (FASB and SEC) pronouncements and interpretations.

The destruction of Arthur Andersen as a firm should serve as a sufficient lesson to other IPA firms. Moreover, as is discussed below, more effective punishment of individual IPAs who materially violate GAAS and GAAP might serve to motivate them to act more effectively as gatekeepers.

MAJOR FINANCIAL STATEMENT PROBLEMS ASSOCIATED WITH OTHER CORPORATIONS

The accounting problems revealed by Enron's bankruptcy should be put into perspective. Enron, after all, was only one of thousands of publicly traded corporations. A broader view can be obtained from recently published research that describes financial misstatements and frauds over several years. These studies and the more recent highly publicized restatements by such companies as World-Com, Global Crossing, and Qwest show that many of Enron's accounting issues were not unique to Enron. Similar to Enron, most misstatements are violations of basic GAAP requirements (particularly involving revenue recognition) that IPAs should have found and dealt with effectively. From the studies, it does not appear that these problems have been widespread or indicative of a systemic breakdown.

In their book *The Financial Numbers Game*, Charles Mulford and Eugene Comiskey describe many creative and fraudulent accounting practices employed in recent years. The authors base their discussion on an examination of reports by the SEC, the press, and corporate financial filings.[20] Many of the violations they found are identified as frauds, most of which involved misstatements of revenue. These include fictitious sales and shipments; booking revenue immediately for goods and services sold over extended periods; keeping the books open after the end of an accounting period to record revenue on shipments actually made after the close of the period; recording sales on goods shipped but not ordered and ordered but not shipped; recognizing revenue on aggressively sold merchandise that was returned ("channel stuffing"); recording revenue in the year received even though the services were provided over several years; booking revenue immediately even though the goods were sold subject to extended periods when collectibility was unlikely; making shipments to a reseller who was not financially viable; and making sales subject to side agreements that effectively rendered sales agreements unenforceable. Another distortion is misclassification of a gain from the sale of a substantial investment as other revenue rather than nonoperating income.

Expenses also were misrecorded. Some involved booking promotion and marketing expenses to a related, but not consolidated, enterprise and recognizing revenue on shipments, but not the cost and liability, of an associated obligation to repay purchasers for promotion expenses. Several corporations took "big bath" write-offs when a new CEO took over. Warranty and bad debt expenses were understated. Aggressive capitalization and extended amortization policies were used to reduce current-period expenses.

Assets were overstated by such means as recording receivables for which the corporation had established no legal right, such as claims on common carriers for damaged goods that were not actually submitted and those that it probably could not collect. Inventories were overstated by overcounts and by delaying write-downs of damaged, defective, overstocked, and obsolete goods. Declines in the fair market values of debt and equity securities were delayed, even though the chances of recovery were remote. Liabilities were understated, not only for estimated expenses (such as warranties), but also for accounts payable, taxes payable, environmental cleanup costs, and pension and other employee benefits.

Additional insights can be obtained from three other studies. Thomas Weirich examined the SEC's Accounting and Auditing Enforcement Releases (AAERs), which criticize audits of registrant corporations, issued between July 1, 1997, and December 31, 1999.[21] Of the ninety-six AAERs issued against Big Five audit firms and their clients, thirty-eight cases, or 68 percent, involved misstated revenue and accounts receivable.

Mark Beasley et al. studied all AAERs issued between 1987 and 1997 that charged registrants with financial fraud.[22] Their analysis of 204 randomly selected companies (of nearly 300) revealed, among other things, that the companies were relatively small (78 percent had assets less than $100 million) and had weak boards of directors and that the fraud involved senior officers (72 percent named the CEO, 43 percent the CFO). Half the instances involved improper revenue recognition, resulting largely from recording fictitious revenue and premature revenue recognition. An overlapping 50 percent overstated assets, 18 percent understated expenses and liabilities, and 12 percent misappropriated assets. The SEC explicitly named external auditors in 56 cases, of which only 10 involved auditors from the major IPA firms. Auditors were charged with performing a substandard audit in 26 of the 56 cases (46 percent), of which 9 (35 percent) were from major IPA firms. A minority of the corporations and their senior officers paid fines and made monetary settlements to plaintiffs (30 and 35 corporations, respectively) and the officers of some 76 corporations lost their jobs and were barred from working for another SEC registrant for a period of time (54 corporations); only 31 were criminally prosecuted and 27 were jailed. But Beasley et al. do not report any actions against the individual IPAs or their firms.

Finally, the General Accounting Office (GAO) searched Lexis-Nexis for mentions of restatements between January 1, 1997, and June 30, 2002. The GAO found that 845 public companies announced material restatements involving accounting irregularities. The number increased each year, from 83 in 1997 to 195 in 2001 and 110 in the first six months of 2002. Over this period, the percentage of publicly traded corporations that restated their financial statements increased substantially, from 0.89 percent in 1997 to 2.95 percent in 2002, in part because the number of corporations listed on the exchanges decreased from 9,275 to 7,446. The GAO also found that the proportion of large corporations (those with assets of more than $1 billion) among those that restated increased from about 25 percent in 1997 to over 30 percent in 2001. Consistent with other studies, the most important reason for restatements was improper revenue recognition (38 percent). This reason is followed by improper recognition or capitalization of costs or expenses (16 percent). The GAO studied the effect of 689 of the restatements on the stock prices of the affected corporations.[23] It found a three-day loss (adjusted for changes in the market) of 10 percent of those corporations' capitalization, or a total of $95.6 and $14 billion for the 689 and 202 restatements. This loss, though, is only 0.11 percent of the total market capitalization of listed corporations.

Thus, the several studies of financial statement restatements yield similar findings.[24] The number of restatements has increased, largely because of changes in SEC practices, but is still quite small in relation to the approximately 8,500 corporations that report to the SEC. Until recently, smaller companies tended to restate their financial statements more often than larger companies. The most pervasive reason for restatement is misstatement of revenue. A substantial minority of companies that restate financial statements and a smaller number of their auditors are sued. Losses to investors who hold diversified portfolios, which may result from misstatements that are corrected, are small overall, although the losses can be substantial (particularly recently) for investments in those companies.

WHO IS TO BLAME?

Accounting standards in the United States, more than in Europe, tend to be rule based rather than principle based, in part because the former offers greater protection against potential plaintiffs, who are more likely to bring lawsuits in this country than in Europe. Consequently, at least some managers have viewed GAAP as a set of rules that they must meet only minimally, even if (and, in many cases such as Enron, particularly because) it results in misleading financial reports of net income.[25]

Given the rule-based system, some blame should be placed on the FASB. The FASB has been considering a restatement of consolidation policy regarding SPEs for more than twenty years.[26] The SPE situation as exemplified by Enron could have been avoided had the FASB done its job expeditiously. The SOA (401[j]) now requires disclosure of

> all material off-balance sheet transactions, arrangements, obligations (including contingent obligations), and other relationships of the issuer with unconsolidated entities or other persons, that may have a material current or future effect on financial condition, changes in financial condition, results of operations, liquidity, capital expenditures, capital resources, or significant components of revenues or expenses.

In addition, as discussed earlier, the FASB's move toward fair-value accounting has given opportunistic managers the means to grossly overstate reported net income.

The FASB also should be criticized for giving in to pressure from which it was supposed to be immune. For example, pressure from commercial banks led to its curious decision to have debt securities not restated at market values, even though their market values can be reliably measured when the securities are designated as "held to maturity." More recently, pressure from the Business Roundtable and the CEOs of high-tech companies (among others) apparently has kept the FASB from requiring corporations to show as expenses the economic values of compensation in the form of options granted to executives, even though options have economic value and, thus, constitute compensation in the same way that compensation that includes physical goods given to employees rather than cash for their services. The problem is that stock options often cannot be readily valued. But, then, neither can employee pensions and future health benefits. Indeed, options often can be more easily valued with a model (e.g., the Black-Scholes options-pricing model),[27] valuations by independent experts (such as investment bankers), or market prices. Market prices (which usually provide the best estimate) could be obtained from similar options that corporations could sell directly or distribute to shareholders as dividends or rights offerings. These prices should be reduced to reflect the effect of restrictions placed on options granted to employees.[28]

With these exceptions, the inadequate, misleading, and even fraudulent financial reporting that has been revealed in recent years is due primarily to failures in enforcing the rules.

CHANGES TO GAAP

Fair Value Accounting

The accounting authorities (SEC, FASB, and IASB) have attempted to make accounting statements more relevant by adopting fair value accounting for financial assets and liabilities. Their argument is that investors would want to know the current values of assets and liabilities, rather than the amounts originally expended or obligated. What they do not appear to recognize sufficiently is that numbers that are likely to be manipulated by opportunistic or overoptimistic managers are considerably worse for investors than numbers that are not current. Consequently, the authorities have required fair values, at least for financial assets, even when they are not based on reliable market values. As the Enron situation revealed, substantially misleading reporting of net income is likely to be the result.

It might appear that the FASB has limited "fair value" reporting to financial assets and liabilities. This presumed limitation yields several important disadvantages. First, most corporations hold other assets that can be reliably measured and that are more important to investors than financial assets. In particular, as noted earlier, inventories can often be valued at their opportunity cost, particularly when they will be replaced. In this event, their value can be measured at their replacement cost, numbers that are usually known before the financial statements are published. Second, fair value accounting has been applied inconsistently, with debt instruments identified as "held to maturity" not being marked to market, even though readily and reliably measured gains and losses in their value accrue to the benefit of shareholders and creditors, whether or not the assets are sold. Third, trust-worthy values cannot be obtained for many financial assets, which allows for substantial misstatements of both asset and net income. This is a very serious situation that compromises the reliability and usefulness of published financial accounting numbers, and thus merits discussion in greater detail.

Enron was able to increase the unrealized (and, as it turned out, unrealizable) values of large-scale nonfinancial assets to what its managers' decided were "fair values" by recording as income the increase in those values. The company did this by declaring that its investments in large-scale projects were "merchant" investments for which the provisions of the AICPA's Investment Company Guide permit (indeed, mandate) fair-value accounting. Section 1.32 of the guide states: "In the absence of a quoted market price, amounts representing estimates of fair values using methods applied consistently and determined in good faith by the board of directors should be used."

According to the FASB, this is how fair values are to be measured: If a quoted market price is not available, the estimate of fair value should be based on the best information available in the circumstances. The estimate of fair value should consider prices for similar assets or similar liabilities and the results of valuation techniques to the extent available in the circumstances. Examples of valuation techniques include the present value of estimated expected future cash flows using discount rates commensurate with the risks involved, option-pricing models, matrix pricing, option-adjusted spread models, and fundamental analysis.[29]

Corporations generally could also use the following procedure (as did Enron) to extend "fair value" accounting to many nonfinancial assets. First, either develop a new product, facility, or business in a wholly owned subsidiary or transfer the assets the managers want to restate at "fair values" into a subsidiary. Call it FV Inc. The corporation now owns FV Inc.'s stock, which is a financial asset. Large corporations can do this many times and have a series of subs—FV1 Inc., FV2 Inc., and so forth. Then exchange the stock in the FVs for stock in another subsidiary that is designated a securities broker-dealer or an investment company (e.g., venture capital or business development company). Because the FV Inc. shares are not traded, these values necessarily must come from the corporate managers' estimates of the fair values of the underlying assets, including intangibles. Finally, because the subsidiaries are 100 percent owned, they must be consolidated with the parent, which now puts the revalued assets on the corporation's consolidated financial statements. Voilá—almost any group of assets can be revalued to what the managers say they are worth, and changes in those valuations (usually increases) are reported as part of income.

The evidence on corporate and industry practices, the Enron experience, and the logical possibilities for manipulation or overoptimistic estimation of "fair values" leads me to conclude that allowing corporate managers to value assets and liabilities in situations where trustworthy market values are not present and cannot be verified should not be permitted by GAAP. The AICPA has taken one step in the right direction with its proposal to limit fair valuation of nontraded securities to registered investment companies and legally and actually separate investment companies, no owner of which owns 20 percent or more of its financial inerests.[30] However, it is likely that clever corporate managers will figure out a way around this limitation. Furthermore, managers can still manipulate income through "fair valuation" of derivatives and energy contracts.

Principle-Based, Rather than Rule-Based, GAAP

Under the current rule-based approach, managers and their consultants design accounting procedures that are in technical accordance with GAAP, even though those procedures tend to mislead investors and violate the substance or spirit of GAAP. Enron provides an excellent example of that approach. Accountants not only find it difficult to challenge the use of such procedures; they often propose or assist in their design. In this sense, the practice of public accounting has become similar to tax practice, with clients demanding and accountants providing expertise on ways to avoid the substantive requirements of GAAP while remaining in technical compliance.

There are several reasons for this rule-based approach. First, auditors believe that they can avoid losing lawsuits if they can show that they did in fact follow the rules. Second, there is the fear of losing a client by refusing to attest to an accounting procedure that does, after all, technically conform to GAAP. Third, government agencies such as the SEC tend to establish or support rules and then demand strict adherence to them. This protects the agencies from claims of favoritism and arbitrariness, forestalling political interference. Last, but by no means least, GAAP has been criticized because it permits managers some degree of choice under some circumstances. As noted earlier, the FASB was created in 1973 largely in response to concern about excessive accounting flexibility. Its well-funded professional staff and directors have fulfilled their mandate and have developed a very large set of detailed rules designed to limit alternative means of compliance with GAAP.

However, the rule-based approach is clearly not working. Accounting firms are sued when a company they audited goes bankrupt, or even when the company's share price drops for some reason. Courts have not accepted as a sufficient defense that specific GAAP rules were followed or not explicitly violated. The SEC and FASB have been severely criticized for allowing companies and accounting firms to violate the spirit of GAAP. Of greatest importance, users of financial statements, who have reason to believe that the numbers presented therein are at least not *deliberately* deceptive, have at times been misled.

The principles of accounting are clear enough. Revenue should not be recognized until there is objective and reliable evidence that it has been earned. Expenses should be matched to the associated earnings or to the time periods in which assets are determined to have lost future value. Most important, the numbers reported in financial statements should be trustworthy, as verified by independent public accountants who have conducted audits and ascertained that the numbers reported accord with the basic principles embodied in GAAP. Having satisfied these conditions, the traditional income statement would be a fair and consistent record of a company's operations and would therefore fulfill the stewardship function of public accounting.

Competition among Accounting Standards[31]

A central problem with any monopoly standard-setter—whether the FASB, the IASB, or any other similar body—is that it has no incentive to respond quickly to market forces, let alone act in a manner free from political influence. As in private markets, the solution to monopoly is competition. As is the situation for private enterprises, quasi-governmental agencies seek acceptance of their products and modify those products to meet substitutes produced by other agencies. Consequently, at a minimum, Congress or the SEC should permit corporations with publicly traded stock to base their financial accounting statements on U.S. or international accounting standards.[32]

CONCLUSION

Investors should recognize the inherent limitations of financial information reported in audited financial statements. Accounting cannot yield both trustworthy and completely adequate measures of the economic performance and the condition of an enterprise. Managers, to some extent, do manipulate the reported numbers by timing expenditures and choosing among reasonable assumptions. Notwithstanding those limitations, financial statements can be very useful. GAAS should ensure that audits conducted by IPAs result in corporations presenting numbers that investors can trust.

The misstatements in the financial reports of Enron and other corporations were, by and large, the result of violations of GAAP and inadequate audits. Many, perhaps most, of those misstatements could and should have been caught and stopped by auditors if these had been more diligent in examining and evaluating their clients' records and financial statements, as required by GAAS. The one major exception is the GAAP requirement that companies revalue assets classified as traded financial assets (to which many assets can be converted) at their fair values, a measure that gives managers too much scope for manipulation.

The SEC has had the authority under rule 201.102(e) to discipline IPAs who attest to financial statements submitted to it, once it becomes known that those statements include gross violations of GAAP or GAAS. Nevertheless, it appears that the SEC has rarely disciplined the IPAs who attached their names to the financial statements that included the substantial violations outlined above.

The SOA now offers the possibility that individual IPAs who are grossly derelict in fulfilling their professional responsibilities will be sanctioned. In addition to punishing the few IPAs who fail in their duties, the authorities could help restore trust in and respect for the accounting industry by empowering IPAs to withhold unqualified opinions when they find reporting that violates the *spirit* of GAAP, even if the letter is followed.

However, the bureaucracy and regulation established by the SOA is likely to be quite costly to shareholders. The board's costs will be met by fees imposed on registered corporations in proportion to their equity market capitalization. The fees now imposed by the SEC on registrants will not be reduced. In addition, public corporations will have to pay higher auditing fees to offset the costs and risks imposed on their external auditors and their own internal costs to meet the requirements of the act. Shareholders necessarily will bear these costs. Whether those costs will exceed the benefits that shareholders might gain from better audits is unclear at this time.

GAAP should be improved by an overall rule that the numbers reported be trustworthy and that the matching concept be followed. The overall rule proposed here would change GAAP to include reporting as operating or as nonoperating income (depending on the asset or liability) changes in values that can be reliably measured. Expenses that were incurred in a period, such as managerial compensation in the form of stock options, would have to be recorded.

"Fair value" accounting, which allows managers to restate many financial assets and liabilities to their managerially estimated values even when these values are not based on reliable market transactions, is subject to misstatement by opportunistic or overly optimistic managers, as shown by the Enron disaster. Only numbers that are trustworthy should be used for financial accounting statements that are attested to by IPAs.

Although these proposals, if adopted by the FASB and SEC, would improve accounting, there are differences in opinion about what should be included in GAAP as well as significant political costs that would make changes difficult to effect. Therefore, a competitive system that would allow corporations to prepare their financial statements in accordance with alternative standards, such as the International Accounting Standards that have been adopted by the European Community, should be adopted in the United States.

NOTES

1. The designation "registered public accounting firm" was established by the SOA, which limits audits of public companies to independent auditors who are registered with the PCAOB, also established by the act.

2. IPAs is the general designation for independent auditors. I use this title, rather than RPA, because the latter did not exist prior to the SOA, or CPA, because CPAs need not be

employed by external auditors. Indeed, CPAs often work directly for companies or, like myself, are teachers who no longer practice public accounting.

3. Levitt, Arthur, "The Numbers Game," remarks to the New York University Center for Law and Business, September 28, 1998.

4. Ripley, William Z., *Main Street and Wall Street*, Boston: Little, Brown, 1927.

5. Securities and Exchange Commission, Accounting Series Release 4, 1938.

6. Edwards, Edgar O. and Philip W. Bell, *The Theory and Measurement of Business Income*, Berkeley and Los Angeles: University of California Press, 1961.

7. Howard Schilit, president of the Center for Financial Research and Analysis, describes the various ways in which managers have used accounting to misinform investors. With many examples from actual situations, he delineates seven practices that he calls "shenanigans." Three involve misreporting revenue: recording revenue too soon or of questionable quality, recording bogus revenue, and boosting income with onetime gains. Three involve violations of the matching concept: shifting current revenue to a later period, shifting current expenses to a later or earlier period, and shifting future expenses to the current period as a special charge. The seventh is failing to record or improperly reducing liabilities. He shows how analysts can detect these "shenanigans" and offers his proprietary computer-based service for detecting these practices. See Howard Schilit, *Financial Shenanigans: How to Detect Accounting Gimmicks and Fraud in Financial Reports*, 2nd ed., New York: McGraw Hill, 2002.

8. Texaco, the third-largest bankruptcy to that time, went bankrupt in April 1997 with assets of $35.9 billion.

9. This section is largely drawn from George Benston and Al L. Hartgraves, "Enron: What Happened and What We Can Learn from It," *Journal of Accounting and Public Policy* 21, 2002, p. 105–27, which is based on reading of press reports, and William C. Powers, Jr., Raymond Troubh, and Herbert S. Winokur, Jr., "Report of Investigation by the Special Investigation Committee of the Board of Directors of Enron Corp." (hereafter the Powers Report), and supplemented by information made public by Neal Batson, "First Interim Report of Neal Batson, Court-Appointed Examiner," United States Bankruptcy Court, Southern District of New York, In re *Enron Corp., et al., Debtors*, Chapter 11, Case No. 01-16034 (AJG), Jointly Administered, September 20, 2002, and Neal Batson, "Second Interim Report of Neal Batson, Court-Appointed Examiner," United States Bankruptcy Court, Southern District of New York, In re *Enron Corp., et al., Debtors*, Chapter 11, Case 01-16034 (AJG), Jointly Administered, January 21, 2003.

10. Enron's accounting practices were much more complicated than can be described here. See Benston and Hartgraves and the Powers Report for much more detailed descriptions. See also Batson's first and second interim reports for extensive descriptions and the legal implications of Enron's use of SPEs.

11. For a detailed account of SPEs, their origins, and their accounting conventions, see Barbara T. Cavanagh, "The Uses and Abuses of Structured Finance," Cato Institute Policy Analysis no. 479, July 31, 2003.

12. For a complete description of the accounting rules governing consolidation of SPEs and other investments, see Al L. Hartgraves and George J. Benston, "The Evolving Accounting Standards for Special Purpose Entities (SPEs) and Consolidations," *Accounting Horizon* 16, 2002, p. 245–58.

13. Because summaries can be found in Benston and Hartgraves and more detailed descriptions in the Powers Report and Batson's first and second interim reports, I will present here only the essential features.

14. Enron also avoided recording $4.02 billion of debt with a complicated series of transactions called "prepays," wherein it traded energy contracts with organizations established by banks, such that it recorded as prepaid income (a liability) what were actually loans from banks for which they were liable. These were summarized by Batson's second interim report, p. 58–66, and described in detail in app. E. See also chap. 13 of this book for R. T. McNamar's analysis of these transactions.

15. See Batson and McNamar for descriptions of these FAS 140 transactions.

16. See Batson's second interim report, p. 30–31.

17. Batson's second interim report, p. 33–35.

18. Enron Corp. *2000 Annual Report*, p. 48.

19. Enron Corp. *2000 Annual Report*, p. 30.

20. Mulford, Charles W. and Eugene E. Comiskey, *The Financial Numbers Game: Detecting Creative Accounting Practices*, New York: John Wiley, 2002.

21. Weirich, Thomas, "Analysis of SEC Accounting and Auditing Enforcement Releases," in *The Panel on Audit Effectiveness Report and Recommendations*, Public Oversight Board, Shaun F. O'Malley, chair, August 31, 2000, app. F., p. 223–38.

22. Beasley, Mark S., Joseph V. Carcello, and Dana R. Hermanson, "Fraudulent Financial Reporting, 1987–1997: An Analysis of U.S. Public Companies," Research commissioned by the American Institute of Certified Public Accountants, Committee of Sponsoring Organizations of the Treadway Commission, Jersey City, N.J., 1999.

23. A follow-on study of an additional 202 of the restatements found a three-day market price loss of 5 percent, or $14 billion.

24. Two other comprehensive studies of restatements are by the Financial Executive International, "Quantitative Measures of the Quality of Financial Reporting," FEI Research Foundation, 2001; A. Palmrose and Susan Scholz, "The Circumstances and Legal Consequences of Non-GAAP Reporting: Evidence from Restatements," Contemporary Accounting Research Conference, 2002; and Report Pursuant to Section 704 of the Sarbanes-Oxley Act of 2002 (analysis of 227 investigations of financial reporting and disclosure violations over the five years ended July 31, 2002, Securities and Exchange Commission, January 2003. All three studies yield similar results to those summarized in this chapter.)

25. The SOA, 108(d)(1)(A), directs the SEC to "conduct a study of the adoption by the United States financial reporting system of a principles-based accounting system."

26. This is detailed in Hartgraves and Benston, "Evolving Accounting Standards."

27. The Black-Scholes model tends to overvalue the options when stock price volatility is not stationary.

28. Options are still an imperfect form of performance-based compensation, because managers are rewarded for increases in corporate stock prices due to general upward movements in the market and stock repurchases, rather than dividends, and are not punished when their corporation's stock price declines, except for the loss of the value of the options. Even then, compliant boards of directors often reduce the option strike price. More incentive-compatible shareholders' and managers' rewards could come from compensating managers with actual or restricted stock.

29. FAS 140, sec. 5.

30. "Clarification of the Scope of the Audit and Accounting Guide Audits of Investment Companies and Equity Method Investors for Investment in Investment Companies," Proposed Statement of Position, December 17, 2002. It has been cleared by the FASB. If adopted, it would become part of GAAP for fiscal years beginning after December 15, 2003.

31. See chap. 3 of George J. Benston, Michael Bromwich, Robert Litan, and Alfred Wagenhofer, *Following the Money: The Enron Failure and the State of Corporate Disclosure,* Washington, D.C.: AEI-Brookings Joint Center for Regulatory Studies, 2003, for a much more complete discussion.

32. This suggestion follows that made by Ronald Dye and Shyam Sunder in "Why Not Allow FASB and IASB Standards to Compete in the U.S.?" *Accounting Horizons* 15, September 2001, p. 257–71.

III

AUDITING

· 6 ·

Don't Count Too Much on Auditing

William A. Niskanen

GENERAL PROBLEMS OF THE AUDIT PROCESS

$\mathscr{T}$he most important lesson about the audit process from the collapse of Enron is that every private and public link in the audit chain failed to detect Enron's weak financial condition until it was too late to avoid bankruptcy—including the audit committee and the board, the presumably independent public auditor, the market specialists in Enron stock, Enron's major creditors, the credit rating agencies, and the Securities and Exchange Commission (SEC).

A report by the staff of the Senate Committee on Governmental Affairs on the financial oversight of Enron observed that

> what emerged was a story of systemic and arguably catastrophic failure, a failure of all of the watchdogs to properly discharge their appointed roles. Despite the magnitude of Enron's implosion and the apparent pervasiveness of its fraudulent conduct, virtually no one in the multilayered system of controls devised to protect the public detected Enron's problems, or, if they did, they did nothing to correct them or alert investors.[1]

Moreover, a *Fortune* survey ranked Enron as the most innovative company in the United States for the sixth year in a row as late as February 2001. And the many lawyers advising Enron appear to have had insufficient information or incentive to discover and report those actions that they believed were illegal. No one in the formal audit chain or the corporate legal community appears to have had a sufficient incentive to discover and report the truth, even for personal gain. Every party that might have made a difference seems to have acted as a free rider, hoping that someone else would perform the necessary audit role. If each link in the audit chain had a probability of detecting Enron's financial problems of only 50 percent and acted independently of the other links, the probability that all would

87

fail was less than 1 percent. The only plausible conclusion is that the probability that any one link would detect Enron's financial problems is much less than 50 percent or, more likely, that each link assumed that there was no problem if some other link gave Enron a pass. In fact, as chapter 11, by Paul Weaver, documents, the first serious questioning of Enron accounting and the value of Enron stock was by a Dallas-based reporter for the *Wall Street Journal*, a New York–based short seller, and a reporter for *Fortune*, in each case long before any of the misleading accounting was acknowledged and revealed. After the subsequent collapse of WorldCom, a leading consultant to the accounting industry warned that audit reports are "probably not even worth their weight in paper,"[2]—a conclusion that is disturbing even if overdrawn.

Moreover, a failure of every link in the audit chain is almost inherent in all corporate bankruptcies. So our attention should be focused on the general characteristics of the audit process, not only on the conditions specific to the Enron collapse. For many years, the Generally Accepted Auditing Standards (GAAS) were set by the auditing profession's self-regulatory body, the American Institute of Certified Public Accountants (AICPA), a role that has now been assigned to the new Public Company Accounting Oversight Board (PCAOB). The most important challenge of this new board is to determine the reasons why each link in the audit chain fails to discover the relevant information or fails to act on the available information in time to avoid a bankruptcy. This section addresses the lessons from the Enron collapse about each link in the audit chain and concludes with a proposal for a radical restructuring of securities regulation and the audit process.

NOTES

1. Staff of the Senate Committee on Governmental Affairs, "Financial Oversight of Enron: The SEC and Private-Sector Watchdogs," October 8, 2002.

2. Quote from Allan D. Koltin, "Value of Audit Reports Disputed," *Washington Post*, June 27, 2002.

· 7 ·

The Formal Audit Process

George J. Benston and William A. Niskanen

AN OVERVIEW OF WHO IS TO BLAME

Auditing and Accounting Standards

*A*s far as we know, there are no studies that explain why the external auditors have not discovered and prevented managers of companies from substantially misstating their financial reports. In particular, we do not yet know, for example, how the chief financial officer of Global Crossing could have avoided discovery of his capitalizing billions of dollars of current expenses, thereby massively overstating net income and total assets for several years. Nor has it been revealed how the auditors of Tyco apparently were unaware that its senior officers took hundreds of millions of dollars, allegedly to the detriment of shareholders. Nor did the authors of the several studies of massive accounting misstatements provide a general explanation of whether these misstatements were due to failures of the external auditors to discover the errors because the auditing procedures were inadequate, the auditors failed to conduct audits that complied with the Generally Accepted Auditing Standards (GAAS), or the auditors colluded with the managers. Consequently, we cannot draw conclusions about the necessity of changing the auditing standards. From Benston's personal experience with two large corporate failures in which auditors were charged with gross negligence, he determined that the auditor's failure to use statistical sampling to determine whether the records substantially reflected the correct valuation of important assets (loans and inventory) was the principal reason that the auditors did not discover the misstatements.[1]

Accounting standards in the United States, more so than in Europe, tend to be rule based rather than principle based, perhaps because this offers greater protection against potential plaintiffs who are more likely to bring lawsuits in this country than in Europe. Consequently, at least some managers have viewed Generally Accepted Accounting Principles (GAAP) as a set of rules that they must meet only minimally, even if in many cases, such as Enron, it results in misleading reports of net income.[2] Thus, Enron's managers could argue, with the concurrence of Arthur Andersen, that Enron should not consolidate their special purpose entities (SPEs) because they met the 3 percent outside investment rule, even though this might mislead users of the financial statements as to their earnings and liabilities.

Given the rule-based system, some blame should be placed on the Financial Accounting Standards Board (FASB), which has been considering a restatement of consolidation policy for over twenty years.[3] The SPE problem as exemplified by Enron could have been avoided had FASB done its job expeditiously. The Sarbanes-Oxley Act (SOA) (401[j]) now requires disclosure of all material off-balance-sheet transactions, arrangements, obligations (including contingent obligations), and other relationships of the issuer with unconsolidated entities or other persons that may have a material current or future effect on financial condition, changes in financial condition, results of operations, liquidity, capital expenditures, capital resources, or significant components of revenues or expenses. In addition, as Benston discussed in his prior chapter on accounting, the FASB's move toward fair value accounting has given opportunistic managers the means to grossly overstate reported net income.

The FASB should also be criticized for giving in to pressure from which it was supposed to be immune. For example, we believe that pressure from commercial banks led to its curious decision to have debt securities not restated at market values, even though their market values can be reliably measured, when the securities are designated as "held to maturity." More recently, pressure from the Business Roundtable and the CEOs of high-tech companies (among others) apparently have kept the FASB from requiring corporations to show as expenses the economic values of compensation in the form of options granted to executives, even though options have economic value and, thus, constitute compensation in the same way that compensation includes physical goods given to employees, rather than cash, for their services.[4] One problem is that stock options cannot be readily valued. But then, neither can employee pensions and future health benefits. Indeed, options often can be more easily valued with a model (such as the Black-Scholes options-pricing model, although it tends to overprice the options when stock price volatility is not stationary), evaluations by independent experts such as investment bankers, or by market prices. Market prices, which usually provide the best estimate, could be obtained from similar options that corporations could sell directly or distribute to shareholders as dividends or rights offerings. These prices should be reduced to reflect the effect of restrictions placed on employee-granted options.

With these exceptions, the inadequate, misleading, and even fraudulent reporting that has been revealed is due primarily to failures to enforce the rules, rather than the inadequacy of the rules. Individual investors should be able to rely on the several "gatekeepers" to see that financial statements were, in fact, produced in accordance with GAAP and GAAS. These gatekeepers include the corporate boards of directors, the independent public auditors and their professional associations, and state and federal regulators.

Boards of Directors

The initial gatekeeper is the board of directors. Managers prepare financial statements for the benefit of shareholders, investors, and others who are expected to use the statements.[5]

The board of directors is supposed to represent the shareholders. All executive compensation must be approved by a board and, in many cases, boards have approved substantial compensation in the form of stock options. These options, which offer managers enormous gains if the price of their corporation's shares increase, may have given them strong incentives to manage reported earnings to meet or exceed stock analysts' expectations, in the belief that this would increase share prices.[6] The board of directors also is responsible for determining whether the cost to other shareholders of the options should be accounted as an expense (an option allowed by the FASB).

The audit committee of the board has particular responsibility for the reliability of the financial statements and the audits (both internal and external) that should be designed to assure the reliability of the statements. The New York Stock Exchange (NYSE) adopted a requirement in 2002 (subject to the approval of the SEC) that a majority of the board of directors, and all members of the audit committee, the nominating committee, and the compensation committee must be independent of their corporation and its CEO, including not having been an employee of the company or its affiliates or auditors within the previous five years. The SOA (301) also requires that all members of the audit committee must be independent directors and makes them responsible for the appointment, compensation, oversight, and dismissal of the external auditors. The audit committee may also engage independent counsel or other advisers as it determines necessary to carry out its duties, supported by appropriate corporate funding.

These changes may make boards of directors more effective gatekeepers, but the Enron experience leads one to be skeptical. In 2000, the Enron board was judged one of the five best boards in the country by *Chief Executive* magazine. The Enron board met all the requirements of the SOA, and the audit committee was unusually well qualified. The Senate subcommittee report on the role of the Enron board found the directors to have a wealth of sophisticated business and investment experience and considerable expertise in accounting, derivatives, and structured finance.[7] This report, however, observed that "overall the Board received substantial information about Enron's plans and activities and explicitly authorized or allowed many of the questionable Enron strategies, policies, and transactions now subject to criticism. Enron's high-risk accounting practices, for example, were not hidden from the Board. The Board knew of them and took no action to prevent Enron from using them. . . . Enron's extensive off-the-books activity was not only well known to the Board, but was made possible by Board resolutions authorizing new unconsolidated entities, Enron preferred shares, and Enron stock collateral that was featured in many of the off-the-book deals."[8] Almost all of the decisions by the Enron board, moreover, were unanimous.

The post-bankruptcy report by the Powers Committee to the Enron board concluded that the Enron "Board of Directors failed . . . in its oversight duties [with] serious consequences for Enron, its employees, and its shareholders. . . . While the primary responsibility for the financial reporting abuses . . . lies with Management . . . those abuses could and should have been prevented or detected at an earlier time had the Board been more aggressive and vigilant."[9]

The former members of the Enron board, of course, disagreed with this conclusion, contending that "they had reasonably relied on assurances provided by Enron management, Andersen, and Vinson & Elkins (the primary outside counsel), and had met their obligations to provide reasonable oversight of company operations."[10] One longtime member of the board and a former chairman of the finance committee, however, acknowledged that the collapse of Enron was "a cautionary reminder of the limits of a director's role [which is by nature] a part-time job."[11]

Our judgment is that the Enron board was simply overwhelmed by the number of complex financial transactions, given the time that was committed to review these transactions. As a rule, the board had five regular meetings a year, with the first day committed to committee meetings and the second day to the meeting of the full board. Committee meetings as well as the full board meeting, generally lasted one to two hours. And for this, the total compensation of a member of the Enron board was about $350,000 a year—nice work if you can get it. There is no reason to question the capability or integrity of the Enron board: they just took the easy way out because they did not have enough at stake to do otherwise.

The Independent Public Auditors

The independent public auditors (IPAs) who attest to the financial statements should be the most important gatekeepers. External audit firms have strong incentives to be effective gatekeepers, at least to the extent of not allowing their partners and employees to grossly violate the prescriptions of GAAS and GAAP. If, to satisfy one or a few clients, they do not, they risk losing their reputations and their other clients, a cost that should greatly exceed any benefits they might have achieved. Nevertheless, it appears that Arthur Andersen did a poor job as gatekeeper for several publicly important corporations, for which they paid a very heavy price. What might explain why Andersen and other audit firms were ineffective gatekeepers?

One explanation given for the failures described above is the alleged weakening of the federal securities laws governing auditor liability. Specifically, did the

Private Securities Litigation Reform Act of 1995 (PSLRA), which generally made it more difficult for class-action plaintiffs to sue public firms for accounting abuses, and the Securities Litigation Uniform Standards Act of 1998 (SLUSA), which abolished state court class actions alleging securities fraud, increase the difficulty of plaintiffs of suing accounting firms so much that these firms decided to risk the cost of being successfully sued for larger audit and other fees?[12] Columbia University law professor John C. Coffee points to this legislation and two court cases as possible explanations for the presumed weakening of auditing performance. Although he supports the changes on grounds of fairness, he concludes that "their collective impact was to appreciably reduce the risk of liability."[13]

It is most unlikely, however, that the legislation can be blamed for the recent rise in earnings restatements and accounting abuses. For one thing, a substantial portion of the increase in the numbers of earnings restatements is attributable to changes in SEC practices. More significantly, the PSLRA did not exempt IPAs from liability; it only eliminated their joint-and-several liability for accounting misdeeds when there are several defendants before the court.[14] The PSLRA also raised pleading standards and restricted the extension of the statute designed to punish organized crime (Racketeer Influenced and Corrupt Organizations Act, or RICO) by trebling damages. These reforms were enacted to prevent plaintiffs from digging into the deepest pockets among a group of defendants and from bringing extortionist lawsuits against IPAs in the hope of settlement. Furthermore, the SLUSA only abolished state court class actions alleging securities fraud; federal class actions can still be brought against accounts. Significantly, the overall volume of investors' lawsuits has not changed much since the PLSRA. In the five years preceding this act, shareholders filed 948 suits; in the five subsequent years, the number is virtually unchanged at 935, although the ones that survive lead to larger settlements. As argued in chapter 10 by Adam Pritchard, "The combination of higher settlements and a smaller percentage of such cases getting to trial suggests that the class-action lawsuits under the PSLRA are doing a more cost-effective job of deterring corporate fraud."[15] In any event, we are not aware that any accounting firm named as a defendant in any of the large recent accounting controversies has been excused from liability or not been added as a defendant in any of these actions because of this legislation. To underline this point, plaintiffs have not been dissuaded from suing Arthur Andersen for liability in Enron and other cases.

Another alleged cause of IPAs having been inadequate gatekeepers is the fear of losing substantial fees from consulting services provided to their audit clients. Critics have pointed to Arthur Andersen having received $29 million in consulting fees in addition to $27 million in audit fees from Enron in 2000. No evidence has been presented, however, that these collateral activities have been more prevalent at corporations that experienced reporting problems, failures, or frauds. It also seems likely that IPAs that could be suborned by consulting fees could as easily be influenced with higher audit fees. Indeed, the audit partner gets direct credit for the audit fee and only indirect credit for the net revenue earned from collateral business with the client.[16] Furthermore, if audit firm–provided consulting were banned, economies of scope from IPA firms providing both audit and consulting could no longer be achieved. These economies include lower business development costs by the consultants and search costs by the corporations, because the audit firm is already known and trusted. Operations costs for both the audit firm and its client are likely to be lower, because the audit firm already understands the client's financial system and problems. And consultants and auditors are likely to help each other by uncovering operations and audit problems. Nevertheless, the SOA (201) made it unlawful for a public accounting firm to provide virtually any non-audit service to a corporation that it audits, with the exception of tax-related services. The result will be higher audit costs that necessarily will be paid by the shareholders. These higher costs, however, will probably exceed the savings from better audits, particularly for investors who hold diversified portfolios.

A final possible explanation of why the IPAs have not proved to be effective gatekeepers has yet to be adequately studied. Until the 1990s, most accountants and lawyers worked for general partnerships in which all partners were liable for the malpractice of any partner; this provided a strong incentive for the firm to monitor the practice of all partners with the hope of correcting any practice that may be later judged as a malpractice. During the 1990s, however, all state governments, beginning with Texas, authorized professional general partnerships to become limited liability partnerships (LLPs), and many large accounting and law firms opted to become LLPs. The state laws affecting LLPs differ somewhat, but, in general, they provide liability protection against the malpractice of other partners. Many states, however, require LLPs to obtain a certain level of liability insurance. And, in general, an LLP partner may still be jointly and severally liable for the contractual debts of the business. The protection of each LLP partner against the malpractice by another partner substantially reduces the incentive of the firm to monitor the practices of each partner. All partners still bear the potential loss of the reputational capital of the firm and an increase in the premium for liability insurance due to a revealed malpractice by any partner. But this is a much lower potential loss than that faced by a professional working for a general partnership. This change in the liability structure of large accounting and law firms may explain much of their recent failure to be effective monitors of corporate malfeasance, but more study is necessary to confirm this effect and to suggest the appropriate responses.[17]

In any event, it appears that many, perhaps most, of the recent earnings misstatements could have been caught and stopped if IPAs had been more diligent in examining and evaluating their clients' records and financial statements, as required by the GAAS. The cost of avoiding all audit and reporting shortcomings, however, is probably excessive. The studies of accounting-related fraud and restatements find relatively few instances of financial statement problems among the over eight thousand registrants. Hence, investors would be worse off if much more extensive auditing requirements were imposed on all corporations. Indeed, there is no apparent evidence that a deficiency in auditing standards has been a cause of any of the recent accounting problems. The problem, instead, has been a failure by individual external auditors, their firms, and the audit committees of boards of directors to do their jobs; that is, to follow the rules that are already in place.

Professional IPA Associations and State and Federal Regulators

Several bodies oversee both individual auditors and the firms for which they work, and all seem to have failed in their duties. The auditing profession's self-regulatory body is the American Institute of Certified Public Accountants (AICPA), which has a committee that is supposed to discipline wayward auditors. The reality, however, has been quite different. In a study conducted by the *Washington Post* of more than a decade of SEC professional misconduct cases against accountants, the AICPA took disciplinary action against fewer than 20 percent of those accountants already sanctioned by the SEC.[18] Moreover, even when the AICPA found that the accountants so sanctioned had committed violations, it closed the vast majority of ethics cases without taking disciplinary action or publicly disclosing the results, but, instead, issuing confidential letters directing the offenders to undergo training. Clearly, self-regulation by the AICPA has not been very effective, nor can it be expected to be; the most stringent penalty the AICPA can apply is simply to expel the offending member from the organization.

The record of the state accountancy agencies that issue and can withdraw CPA certificates is not much better. By and large, these agencies are not well-funded or staffed with sufficient numbers of highly trained individuals to both ferret out and investigate accounting misconduct. This is especially so for complex accounting matters of the kinds revealed in some of the large corporate scandals of recent years. In general, the agencies tend to act after a client or other government agency has successfully brought a legal action against a CPA or an offending CPA cannot respond adequately to a serious complaint. Indeed, the *Washington Post* study of a decade of SEC enforcement finds that "[t]he state of New York, which had the most accountants sanctioned by the SEC, as of June had disciplined [only] 17 of 49 accountants."[19]

The SEC, though, has both the staff and the authority, as well as the responsibility, to investigate and discipline IPAs that attest to statements filed with it. To its credit, the SEC has been more aggressive in recent years in investigating corporate financial statements to determine whether earnings have been misrepresented, as indicated by the 2001 report of the Financial Executives International.[20] This effort started under former chairman Arthur Levitt and was continued by his successor Harvey Pitt. The 2002 study by the General Accounting Office (GAO) of 689 earnings restatements found that in the period January 2001 through February 2002, thirty-nine CPAs were suspended or denied the privilege of appearing or practicing before the SEC, twenty-three for three years or less. In addition, one non–Big Five accounting firm was permanently barred, one Big Five firm and one other were given cease and desist orders, and one Big Five firm was censured. (After the collapse of Arthur Andersen, of course, there are now only the Big Four accounting firms.) From a reading of the GAO's case study descriptions of the restatements by sixteen major corporations, each of which includes information on civil and criminal actions taken against the auditors, Benston concludes that the penalties were inadequate for the crime.

The GAO also presents sixteen case studies that detail the reasons for, effects of, and actions taken by the SEC as a consequence of these corporations restating their financial reports.[21] In three cases, the violations of GAAP were discovered by the auditor, and in three, the restatements resulted from changed interpretations of GAAP requirements. Ten cases involved important and substantial violations of GAAP (e.g., liabilities not reported, improper recognition of income, expensing costs that should have been capitalized, falsification of expenses, and rampant self-dealing by management). In three of these cases, the SEC took action against the auditors. In the Sunbeam case, the auditor was charged with having his firm (Arthur Andersen) sign unqualified statements; even though he did not know about the misstatements, he faces trial. In the Waste Management case, Andersen issued unqualified statements; even though its auditors had identified and quantified the improper accounting practices, Andersen was fined $7 million. Two of the three auditors were fined $50,000 and $40,000 and barred from practice before the SEC for five years; the other was barred for one year. In the Enron case, Arthur Andersen was charged with destroying documents in advance of an SEC investigation and, in a jury trial, was found guilty. No mention is made of Andersen's partner in charge of the audit, who destroyed the documents. The GAO does not indicate any actions taken by the SEC against the audit firms or the CPAs who conducted the audits for the seven other corporations where there were serious errors, misclassifications, and omissions that substantially overstated reported net income and assets and understated liabilities.

SEC action is important because it can trigger several consequences: private lawsuits against company officers and directors for negligence or even willful commission of fraud or misrepresentation, similar lawsuits against accounting firms, and, if the facts warrant, criminal fraud investigations by the Department of Justice. Because these consequences have been apparent for some time, the puzzle is why they have not done more to deter the kind of accounting abuses that seem to have become more frequent in recent years. One reason may be that lawyers, who may find financial statements boring, dominate the SEC. Indeed, the SEC has reviewed only about 2,300 annual 10K reports in recent years.

This situation, though, has changed with the passage of the SOA in 2002, which established the Public Company Accounting Oversight Board (PCAOB).[22] The PCAOB will have five financially literate full-time members, only two of whom shall be or have been CPAs. The PCAOB will register accounting firms, establish standards related to the preparation of audit reports, conduct inspections of accounting firms, and conduct investigations and disciplinary proceedings. It may then impose appropriate sanctions, presumably against both firms and individual IPAs.

Sanctions imposed by the PCAOB, together with a fear that what happened to Arthur Andersen might happen to them, probably will be effective in motivating the external audit firms to be more effective gatekeepers. But this mechanism is likely to be seriously incomplete unless it is applied to individual external auditors, particularly those whose salaries and bonuses depend on how much business they bring in (or work on) and whose liability costs may be covered by insurance or the firm. Individual partners of large IPA firms who are in charge of a single very large client have considerable incentives to accede to the demands of these clients. If they do not and lose the account for the firm, they stand to lose a substantial amount of their personal income, if not their positions in the firm. If they do accede to client demands, there are three possibilities: The misstatements might not be discovered. If discovered, the partner-in-charge may not be blamed. Or, if blamed, the other partners are likely to defend the errant partner to avoid having to assume substantial damages.

Considering the externalities that accompany major audit failures, it is critical that there be an institutional mechanism for applying discipline to individual external auditors who fail to live up to their professional responsibilities. This was and still is the responsibility of the SEC. Although it has had the authority under rule 201.102(e) to discipline IPAs who attest to financial statements that violate GAAP or GAAS, it has used this power sparingly. We can understand why the commission has rarely used its ultimate weapon—prohibiting an offending firm from attesting to financial statements of public companies—the most notable exception being Arthur Andersen. But we do not understand why the commission has so rarely sanctioned individual auditors who have attached their names to the financial statements that included the substantial violations described above. If individual CPAs had reason to believe that their professional careers and personal wealth were seriously in jeopardy, they would be much more likely to risk losing a client rather than agree to that client's demand for inadequate audits and overly aggressive or misleading accounting. The new PCAOB is now expected to fulfill the role largely abdicated by the SEC.[23]

PROPOSED CHANGES TO THE AUDITING STANDARDS

In 2003, the PCAOB took over the development of auditing standards that had been left to the AICPA. This change in responsibility may be either negative or positive for investors. The negative prospect is that the development of auditing standards and procedures will pass from the professional IPAs, who must balance the costs of auditing against the value of audits as determined by the investors' representatives, to the audit committees of corporate boards. If the staff of the PCAOB acts similarly to the staff of the FASB, investors are likely to have to purchase more extensive audits than they are worth. As noted earlier, the prohibition against most concurrent consulting work by IPA firms is likely to increase the costs of an audit even more.

Positive change, however, might result to the extent that inadequate audits have resulted in externalities from reduced investor confidence in equity securities generally and IPAs particularly, and that changes mandated or suggested by the PCAOB improve audits and, thereby, reduce the externalities. One such improvement that we urge is mandated use of statistical sampling, which at present is only suggested and, we believe, inadequately used or even understood by many IPAs.[24] Without sampling, it is difficult for us to believe that in many important situations IPAs have a meaningful basis for determining the extent to which a corporation's statements are materially correct and that corporate resources have not been stolen or grossly misused. The PCAOB might be able to establish an understanding and acceptance of the reality that, at best, audits provide a high, but not 100 percent, probability that all material irregularities have been identified.

CONCLUSIONS

Many, perhaps most, of the major recent accounting misstatements could have been caught and stopped if auditors were more diligent in examining and evaluating their clients' records and financial statements, as required by GAAS. Had the traditional accounting revenue recognition and expense matching procedures been followed, audits (including statistical sampling) conducted to discover violations by managers (particularly related to revenue recognition), and had the attesting IPAs insisted that their clients' statements adhere to the substance of GAAP, we believe that most of the misstatements would not have occurred.

There seems to be little excuse for the failure of some auditors to follow basic accounting and auditing requirements, particularly those related to revenue recognition, expense matching, and liability disclosure. The major problem, we believe, is inadequate disincentives for individual IPAs who fail to fulfill their responsibilities as gatekeepers. It appears that the individual auditors who benefited personally and substantially from revenue derived from Enron and some other clients were willing to take the risk that the violations of GAAP would not be discovered or, if discovered, would cost them less than they would incur if they lost these companies as clients.

NOTES

1. Benston was an expert witness for the plaintiffs against the external auditors in Continental Illinois Securities Litigation (1987) and Phar-Mor Securities Litigation (1995).
2. The SOA, section 108(d)(1)(A), directs the SEC to "conduct a study on the adoption by the United States financial reporting system of a principles-based accounting system."

3. Hartgraves, Al L. and George Benston, "The Evolving Accounting Standards for Special Purpose Entities (SPEs) and Consolidations," *Accounting Horizons* 16, 2002.

4. On this issue, there is a reasonable disagreement among the contributors of this book (e.g., see chap. 6, by Niskanen, and chap. 17, by Reynolds). There is broader agreement, however, that options are an imperfect form of performance-based compensation, because managers are rewarded for increases in corporate stock prices due to general upward movements in the market and stock repurchases, rather than dividends, and are not punished when their corporation's stock price decreases, except for loss of the value of the options. Even then, compliant boards of directors often reduce the option strike price. More incentive-compatible shareholders' and managers' rewards would come from compensating managers with actual or restricted stock.

5. The SOA (302) requires principal executive and financial officers to sign and certify that, to their knowledge, their corporation's reports "fairly present in all material respects the financial condition and results of operations of the issuer" and similar collateral statements. This is a tighter standard than certifying that the firm's financial reports are consistent with GAAP.

6. The increased use of options to compensate senior managers appears to have been driven, at least in part, by the 1994 Internal Revenue Code 162(m) disallowance as a deductible expense of executive compensation over $1 million unless it is "performance based."

7. Report of the Permanent Subcommittee on Investigations of the Committee on Governmental Affairs, U.S. Senate, "The Role of the Board of Directors in Enron's Collapse," July 8, 2002.

8. Report of the Permanent Subcommittee on Investigations, p. 13.

9. Powers, William C., Jr., Raymond S. Troubh, and Herbert S. Winokur, Jr., "Report of Investigation by the Special Investigative Committee of the Board of Directors of Enron," February 1, 2002.

10. Eggleston, W. Neil and Dimitri J. Nionakis, "The Outside Directors' Response to the Permanent Subcommittee on Investigations of the Senate Governmental Affairs Committee Report on the Role of the Board of Directors in Enron's Collapse," August 1, 2002.

11. Report of the Permanent Subcommittee on Investigations, p. 14.

12. For an analysis of the effects of the PSLRA on securities class actions, see chap. 10, by Adam Pritchard.

13. In John C. Coffee, Jr., "Understanding Enron: It's About the Gatekeepers, Stupid," (*Business Lawyer* 57, 2002), Coffee cites and discusses two cases: (1) *Lampf, Pleva, Lipkind, and Petigrow v. Gilbertson* 501 U.S. 350, 359–361, 1991 (which created a federal rule requiring plaintiffs to file in one year when they should have known of the violation underlying their action, but in not more than three years after the violation; previously the state law–based rule was from five to six years); and (2) *Central Bank of Denver, N.A. v. First Interstate of Denver, N.A.* 511 U.S. 164, 1994 (which eliminated private "aiding and abetting" liability in securities fraud cases).

14. In particular, the act assigns joint-and-several liability only when the jury specifically finds that the defendant knowingly violated the securities laws.

15. Page 144.

16. Rick Antle and Mark Gitenstein analyzed the financial records of the Big Five accounting firms and found that, while the per hour rate for consulting is higher than the rate for auditing, the present value to IPAs of audit fees is considerably greater, because the net

cash flow from audits is steadier and continues for a longer time. Antle and Gitenstein, "Analysis of Data Requested by the Independence Standards Board from the Five Largest Accounting Firms," report presented to the Independence Standard Board, February 17, 2000.

17. For a case that this condition is not a problem, see Larry E. Ribstein, "Limited Liability of Professional Firms after Enron," prepared for the Conference on Evaluation and Response to Risk in Law and Accounting in the U.S. and EU, University of Illinois College of Law, April 5, 2003.

18. Hilzenrath, David S., "Auditors Face Scant Discipline; Review Process Lacks Resources, Coordination, Will," *Washington Post*, December 6, 2001.

19. Hilzenrath, "Auditors Face Scant Discipline."

20. General Accounting Office, "Financial Statement Restatements: Trends, Market Impacts, Regulatory Responses, and Remaining Challenges," GAO-030-138, app. 5, October 2002.

21. Some critics of SOA have questioned whether the creation of the PCAOB, a body that is structured as a private monopoly that has the power to regulate and to levy taxes (or fees) on all publicly traded companies, is constitutional. See Peter Wallison, "Action in Haste on Corporate Governance," *On the Issues*, November 1, 2002.

22. Wallison, "Action in Haste."

23. Two provisions of the SOA might additionally reduce the willingness of individual auditors to accede to clients' demands: the lead audit or coordinating partner and the reviewing partner must rotate off the audit every five years (203), and a company's senior financial/accounting officer (e.g., the CFO) cannot have been employed by its audit firm during the one-year period proceeding the audit. We are not aware of any analysis of whether the benefits from these rules are likely to exceed their costs to shareholders from higher audit fees and executive search costs and compensation.

24. Statistical sampling procedures that could be applied to accounting data are outlined in Statement of Auditing Standards (SAS) 39 and in many textbooks. From a properly taken sample (random or stratified random), an auditor can assess the probability that the population values are within the specified bound. From tables based on such samples, auditors can determine the number of items to examine, given their acceptance of a specified risk. The results of the examination, then, can provide auditors with a reliable measure of the validity of the aggregate number being audited (e.g., accounts receivable) and the necessity of conducting a more extensive examination.

· 8 ·

The Market Analysts

William A. Niskanen

*M*arket analysts of a corporation's stock, although not a formal link in the audit chain, should provide useful information to general investors about the prospect for that stock. The Enron collapse, however, led to more general questioning about the value of "sell-side" analysis. As documented by the staff of the Senate Committee on Governmental Affairs,

> Nearly all of the Wall Street analysts who covered Enron recommended Enron as a stock to buy ... well into the fall of 2001, even as Enron's hidden partnerships were revealed, the SEC initiated its investigation, and Enron restated its financials going back more than four years.[1]

Moreover, this problem does not seem specific to Enron. According to Thomson Financial, about two-thirds of the recommendations by sell-side analysts in 2001, a bear market year, were to buy, about one-third were to hold, and less than 2 percent were to sell. Over the two years from January 2000 to January 2002, during which the S&P index fell from 1,500 to about 1,100, a high proportion of the recommendations by sell-side analysts on those five hundred companies remained a buy. This record led Arthur Levitt, a former Securities and Exchange Commission (SEC) chairman, to declare that, "I think that Wall Street sell-side analysis has lost all its credibility."[2] John Bogle, the founder and former chief executive officer (CEO) of Vanguard, concludes that

> it's time to face reality: There is no evidence that research—even the research of the Institutional Investor all-stars—adds value. Academic studies only confirm what we all believe: The stock market is highly efficient, and that stock prices incorporate virtually all information. . . . As a result, for the market as a whole, research is a dead-weight cost that turns a zero-sum game into a loser's game.[3]

That conclusion about the billions of dollars that are spent for market analysis may seem overdrawn—but probably not by much. In the Enron case, the record of the independent analysts was somewhat better than that of the sell-side analysts. In the nine months prior to October 2001, for example, analysts with investment banking firms expected the Enron stock to appreciate 54 percent over the next twelve months, whereas analysts not employed by investment banking houses expected a 24 percent appreciation; but even the independent analysts, of course, proved to be wildly optimistic. The first analyst report to question the value of Enron stock was a February 21, 2001, report from an independent investment research firm. Six of the eight independent investment newsletters downgraded their Enron rating to a sell recommendation prior to November 2001, three as early as March or April 2001. The first financial managers to short Enron stock on the basis of their own analysis may have been James Chanos of Knikos Associates, who began to short Enron in November 2000, and Richard Grubman of Highfields Capital Management, who began to short Enron in the winter of 2001, but general investors did not have access to these analyses.

A study by Paul Asquith, Michael Mikhail, and Andrea Au, published in October 2002, is the most comprehensive recent analysis of the information content of equity analyst reports.[4] This study found that only 54 percent of analysts' price targets were achieved within twelve months. Features of the analyst reports that proved to be significant predictors of future stock prices were a downgrade recommendation and a measure of the strength of the analyst's argument but not, interestingly, the analyst's earnings forecast, an upgrade recommendation, or a measure of the relation between the analyst's brokerage and the firm. This study, in summary, found some positive information content in analyst reports, a very high variance of future stock prices relative to the forecast, and that investors are rather discriminating in reading these reports. This study is impressive, but there are at least three possible biases in these results:

- All of the reports in the sample were written by members of the Institutional Investor's All-America Research Team, analysts with an unusually good prior record.
- All of the reports were written in 1997, 1998, or 1999, a period of a general stock market boom and prior to the SEC rule that required a general disclosure of all material information.
- Only those reports from brokerage firms willing to make their reports available were included in the sample.

Given these biases, the amount of useful information in reports beginning in 2000 is probably less than in the sample of reports analyzed by the above study. For the moment, I am prepared to acknowledge that there is probably some useful information in the reports of market specialists, but it is less clear that it is worth the cost and time of a lot of bright people.

As is common with the other links in the audit chain, the press and politicians jumped too quickly to an assumption that the primary reason that sell-side analysts do not provide very accurate stock price forecasts is because of a conflict of interest, in their case with the investment banking activities of their Wall Street firms. After a two-year probe, New York State Attorney General Eliot Spitzer, several other state attorneys general, and the SEC claimed that they found hundreds of documents that show how analysts routinely misled investors by promoting stocks of firms that they knew were weak in order to generate investment banking business. And their final agreement with ten Wall Street firms included a $1.4 billion settlement, over $400 million of which was a commitment to fund stock research by wholly independent analysts, fines on two leading analysts who were also subject to a lifetime bar from further work in the securities industry, and an attempt to separate most of the banking and research activities of these firms.

Maybe the Wall Street firms should not have settled with Spitzer. On July 1, 2003, two federal district judges issued separate rulings to dismiss class action lawsuits against several of these firms for stock market analyses that proved to be misleading. One judge described the plaintiffs as "high-risk speculators [who hoped to] twist the federal securities laws into a scheme of cost-free speculators' insurance."[5] The other judge ruled that "the plaintiffs' allegations about a general industry-wide conflict of interest fails to [prove a deliberate attempt to deceive]."[6]

One interesting first effect of these rulings is that the stock markets increased strongly after they were announced. Many investors, apparently, do not like class action suits.

The Spitzer probe made a sufficient case that many of the analysts employed by these investment banks were biased, but an interesting part of this story has not been reported: The probe provided no evidence that investors were broadly misled by the reports of these analysts—in other words, that they were *more* misled by analysts connected with these investment banks than by those without this potential conflict of interest. The Asquith, Mikhail, and Au study summarized above found that the degree of association of the analyst's firm with the firm whose stock was analyzed had *no* significant effect on the price of that stock. Most investors have apparently learned to discount buy recommendations and weak arguments in the reports of all analysts. A statement on this issue by the Shadow Financial Regulatory Committee concludes that "[i]n all likelihood, these measures will entail a significant waste of resources in pursuit of an unattainable goal."[7]

A better explanation of the lack of much useful information in the average stock analysis is that it is very difficult for the best-informed and least-biased analyst to beat the market. A lot of information is in the market before the publication of any stock analysis or new financial information. Analysts are typically dependent on inside information, but this information is valuable only to those analysts who are first to receive, correctly evaluate, and act on or publish the information. For this reason, analysts generally act to maintain good relations with the firm, often asking the firm to review their draft report before publication, and maintain a generally favorable review of its stock. Most stock analysts will drop reviewing a specific stock, rather than write a negative review. A stock analyst, like a business journalist, will seldom write a negative review of a specific firm more than once, expecting that they would be cut off from further inside information. The SEC fair disclosure rule of 2000, by requiring general disclosure of all material information, may substantially eliminate any discrimination in the access to inside information, possibly at the cost of a general reduction of the information of value to investors. Over time, I expect the number of analysts to decline to those who are superior analysts of information available to the general public, most of whom will be either independent or buy-side analysts for the major funds. Most small investors, in turn, are probably best advised, as suggested by John Bogle, to skip the research and buy an all-market index fund.

NOTES

1. Staff of the Senate Committee on Governmental Affairs, "Financial Oversight of Enron: The SEC and Private-Sector Watchdogs," October 8, 2002.

2. Levitt, Arthur, testimony before the Senate Committee on Governmental Affairs, January 24, 2002.

3. Bogle, John, "Reality Bites," *Wall Street Journal*, November 21, 2002.

4. Asquith, Paul, Michael B. Mikhail, and Andrea S. Au, "Information Content of Equity Analyst Reports," National Bureau of Economic Research Working Paper no. 9246, October 2002.

5. *Washington Post*, July 2, 2003.

6. *Washington Post*, July 2, 2003.

7. "Statement of the Shadow Financial Regulatory Committee on Enforcement Settlement with Wall Street Investment Firms," May 5, 2003.

· 9 ·

Public and Private Rule Making in Securities Markets

Paul G. Mahoney

$\mathcal{D}$ebates over appropriate standards for corporate governance and accounting, once the province of specialist journals and conferences, have become front-page affairs in the wake of recent corporate scandals. Politicians, regulators, journalists, corporate executives, institutional investors, and academics have all weighed in on a variety of once esoteric issues. Should incentive stock options be treated as an ordinary business expense? Should publicly traded companies be required to separate the posts of chairman and chief executive officer? Should companies be required to change accounting firms periodically?

Each of those questions is important and deserves attention. But relatively little attention has been paid to an issue that is arguably much more important, because it will affect each of the others: who should set standards for corporate governance and disclosure for publicly traded companies?

This chapter attempts to analyze that question. The potential standard-setters include government bodies such as Congress, state legislatures, the Securities and Exchange Commission (SEC) or other regulatory bodies, and private entities such as stock exchanges or industry groups. Stock exchanges have substantial advantages, in comparison with government bodies, as the primary regulators of corporate governance, disclosure, and accounting standards. This is an argument, not for the status quo, in which stock exchanges are statutorily appointed as "self-regulatory organizations" under the firm control of the SEC, but rather for a more substantial privatization of the regulatory function.

Perhaps many observers will find this prescription entirely backward, even dangerous. Conventional wisdom about the various accounting and governance crises of recent months holds that they demonstrate the need for "tougher" regulation and a firmer governmental hand on the wheel. But that badly misconceives the dynamics of the regulatory process.

INCENTIVES MATTER

The U.S. securities laws incorporate a limited degree of self-regulation. Securities exchanges and the National Association of Securities Dealers (NASD), which operates the National Association of Securities Dealers Automated Quotation System, are "self-regulatory organizations" with authority to adopt and enforce rules for their members and listed companies, to the extent those rules do not conflict with the federal securities laws. The exchanges and the NASD also have disciplinary authority over their members. Both functions, however, are subject to the supervision and ultimate control of the SEC.

The standard argument for self-regulation is that the securities industry has more expertise in the problems and potential solutions associated with securities trading than does a government agency. The argument is not terribly persuasive. All of the information and expertise in the world will be wasted unless the regulator has an incentive to make rules that benefit investors. A regulator with appropriate incentives, on the other hand, could easily hire people with the relevant experience.

The case for allowing exchanges to determine standards of corporate governance and disclosure, then, rests on incentives, not expertise. Exchanges and their members profit from investors' trades. The traditional nonprofit exchange is owned by its members, who typically are brokers. Higher trading volumes on the exchange generate greater profits for brokers. A for-profit exchange can be owned by dispersed investors, many of whom may not be brokers. Such exchanges earn profits from fees paid by listed companies and brokers and by selling market data. More transactions mean more fees and more data that the exchange can sell. Anything, then, that increases the public's eagerness to trade in listed securities is good for exchanges, whether nonprofit or for-profit, mutual or publicly owned.

Political actors, by contrast, are motivated to seek approval in the form of votes and campaign contributions. Their interests span a much wider set of public policy issues than those related to securities markets. Most important for present purposes, it is clear from centuries of observation that securities markets become salient political topics only in the immediate aftermath of broad and sharp declines in securities prices. As legal historian Stuart Banner has noted, every important regulatory statute in England and the United States, from the very start of organized securities markets in the late seventeenth century, was enacted after a market crash.[1]

The differences between the incentives facing stock exchanges and those facing politicians, then, are quite stark. Exchanges have an ongoing financial incentive to increase trading volumes. Elected officials, by contrast, have an incentive to avoid blame for market crashes and to respond to crashes in ways that will mollify their constituents. Political actors may respond directly through legislation or indirectly by putting pressure on regulatory agencies.

Political incentives are unlikely to promote optimal market regulation. First and foremost, the incentives facing political actors are considerably more one-sided than those facing market actors. Exchanges and brokers gain when trading volumes are high and lose when volumes are low. By contrast, the political harm that elected officials suffer when a market decline occurs on their watch is typically much greater than the credit they receive when markets are healthy. When markets are rising, the public typically judges its political leaders on some other set of issues—education, prescription drug benefits, and so on. The stock market is politically important only when it is in sharp decline.

That tendency reinforces a ubiquitous, and exceptionally unhealthy, political reaction to market crises. When markets decline, faith in and enthusiasm for the chaotic nature of capitalism—Joseph Schumpeter's "creative destruction"—declines as well and is replaced by a desire for stability. Thus, at the same time that the likelihood of significant regulatory changes is at its highest, the public's tolerance for risk is at its lowest. That is a toxic combination.

Those two phenomena combine to create bad regulation because they are so easily exploited by rent-seeking businesses. The lure of stability is the only positive inducement that the would-be monopolist or cartel can offer to consumers. In ordinary times, consumers and political actors are more likely to recognize that they are being offered a terrible deal. The absence of competition does, indeed, promote stability, in the sense that consumers are spared the difficult task of comparison shopping and are not faced with the tough choice between lower prices and established reputation. The cost, however, is exorbitant. Consumers pay a high price for the monopolist's goods or services. A really creative monopolist may even discover a way to price discriminate and appropriate most of the consumer surplus.

The history of regulatory efforts in the U.S. securities markets bears this out. The earliest widespread attempt to regulate securities offerings was the so-called blue-sky laws of the early twentieth century. Those statutes, enacted by individual states, often required advance permission by a state official to market securities in that state. One obvious and notable feature of those statutes is that they placed greater hurdles in the way of high-risk, high-return securities. Often, companies without a long operating history, or those whose balance sheets contained a large amount of intangible assets, were singled out for harsher treatment. As legal scholars Jonathan Macey and Geoff Miller hypothesized, and I have confirmed empirically, those statutes were shaped by the lobbying efforts of banks that feared competition for depositors' funds from securities salesmen.[2] From the outset, then, securities regulation was plagued by the problem of sellers of low-risk investments trying to use the regulatory system to put barriers in the way of sellers of high-risk investments.

The same phenomenon shaped the federal securities laws of the 1930s.[3] Some segments of the securities industry warmly welcomed federal regulation and benefited substantially from it. The "bulge bracket" (i.e., the most elite) investment banks of the late 1920s—led by J. P. Morgan & Co. and including a few other select firms such as Kuhn, Loeb & Co. and Dillon, Read & Co.—specialized in relatively low-risk securities such as blue-chip bonds and railroad stocks. They also sold through a slow, painstaking process involving multiple syndicates. During the 1920s, however, the securities market changed substantially. Investors in pursuit of higher returns began to include riskier securities in their portfolios. Newer, more aggressive investment banks such as the National City Company began to sell securities rapidly through nationwide sales networks linked by telegraph, rather than through the traditional syndication methods, and to offer volume discounts.

As a result, when Congress decided to regulate public offerings through the Securities Act of 1933, the established investment banks lobbied eagerly for a statute that would slow down the offering process. The Securities Act did just that. Moreover, the investment bankers' trade group helped to shape a separate innovation, the Maloney Act of 1938, which created the NASD. The Maloney Act was accurately described as a mini-National Recovery Act (NRA) for the securities industry. Like the NRA, it granted the regulated industry the right to ban some forms of price competition. A longstanding goal of the NASD's predecessor, the Investment Bankers Association of America (IBAA), was to make underwriting a "one-price business" by ending all volume discounts. This, the IBAA said, was its primary objective in drafting a code of fair practice under the NRA.[4] After the Supreme Court held the NRA unconstitutional, Congress revived the fair practice code by enacting the Maloney Act, which explicitly permitted the NASD to outlaw volume discounts.

Investors, therefore, should not feel reassured by reports that Sen. Paul Sarbanes (D-Md.) modeled the recently enacted Sarbanes-Oxley Act (SOA) on the Maloney Act.[5] Instead, that analogy should remind us that Congress is constantly tempted by the siren song of industry groups who promise that, if given a free hand to stifle competition, they will make sure that today's problems won't recur. Accepting such a deal is foolish. By their very nature, extreme events are usually followed by more normal times—that is, there's regression to the mean. Whatever problems have occurred, therefore, may be temporary. But the barriers to competition and innovation that they prompt live on well after the memory of the problems which they were intended to address has faded.

WHY NOT THE EXCHANGES?

Counterarguments against the exchanges as regulators typically fall into four categories.

- *Monopoly.* Because trading in a particular security is a natural monopoly (or, as it is sometimes now expressed, a "network good"), the necessary competitive pressures are absent.

- *Competition.* When push comes to shove, the New York Stock Exchange (NYSE) would never enforce its rules against a listed company, because that company would threaten to move to NASDAQ, or vice versa. Competition between exchanges for listings will lead to toothless enforcement.
- *Externalities.* Good disclosure and corporate governance rules do not merely benefit the marginal investor who happens to trade in a particular stock at a particular point in time. They have spillover benefits to third parties, including other investors, competitors, and suppliers. An exchange and its members cannot capture all those benefits because they do not contract with those third parties. Accordingly, the exchange will put less than the socially optimal amount of effort into designing and enforcing the rules.
- *Ineffective tools.* Because exchanges control access to the trading mechanism, they have an array of graduated sanctions available against member firms. A brokerage firm might be fined a small amount for a minor violation, suspended for a few days for a slightly greater one, and expelled for an egregious fraud. The same is not true, however, when it comes to disciplining listed companies. Were an exchange to suspend trading in a listed company's stock, it would harm investors and exchange members as much or more than the listed firm. The primary threat the exchange has against a listed firm is delisting. That, unfortunately, is too great a sanction for lesser violations and perhaps too small a sanction for extreme violations. The absence of graduated punishments means that the exchange's rules will be violated with impunity.

Let us examine these arguments one at a time.

MONOPOLY

The monopoly argument comes in two varieties. The less sophisticated version simply holds that a monopolist will provide a shoddy product, and therefore, an exchange that has a monopoly over trading in a particular asset will provide shoddy rules of corporate governance and disclosure. This is an old argument with an old answer—even monopolists are subject to the demand curve. They can sell their product for more money than a competitive firm can, but not for more than the product's value to the marginal consumer. A rational monopolist will, therefore, adopt any improvements to the product that cost less than their value to the marginal consumer. Applied to exchanges, we would expect a monopolist exchange to offer the same "product" (that is, the same corporate governance and disclosure rules) as a competitive exchange but to charge a higher price.

The persistence of the notion that monopolists offer a lower-quality product is likely a consequence of the fact that our experiences with monopolists usually involve heavily regulated firms that may not be permitted to raise prices sufficiently to justify improvements in service (utilities are a good example, as was AT&T before deregulation). Such monopolists provide low-quality products because they can charge only a low-quality price. Absent price regulation, however, the monopolist has ample incentive to improve the product.

The more sophisticated version of the argument notes that an exchange is not a unitary actor but an amalgamation of members offering different services and subject to different demand and marginal cost functions.[6] Exchange members are heterogeneous; they are brokers, arbitrageurs, market makers, specialists, and others. An exchange's rules, therefore, do not simply determine the amount of the members' profits; they also determine the distribution of those profits. Each group has a strong interest in shaping the rules for its own benefit. The resulting competition among groups for rents will distort the rule-making process, potentially generating rules that are less beneficial to investors than those that would be adopted by a unitary actor.

That is a variant of the monopoly argument because it turns on the exchange having market power—that is, being able to charge a price in excess of marginal cost for its services. Absent market power, there are no rents to distribute and, therefore, no fights over their distribution.

The question of exchange market power is, unfortunately, unresolved. It is clear that traders desire liquidity, which means that a market is not viable unless it captures "enough" of the trading in a particular stock to ensure liquidity. The more debatable question is whether "enough" is 100 percent of the demand for that stock (in which case trading in a particular security is a pure natural monopoly) or something less (in which case there could be two, or perhaps more, markets for a given stock). A second issue is whether, supposing the market for a stock is a natural monopoly, that monopoly is contestable. If the entire market for a specific stock can migrate at a reasonable cost from one exchange to another, then the incumbent exchange cannot extract a monopoly rent even if it controls 100 percent of trading in the stock. Distributional fights are, therefore, eliminated. These are empirical questions on which the evidence is not conclusive.[7]

Whatever the merits of the competing theoretical and empirical arguments, they are being overtaken by events. The NYSE and NASDAQ unquestionably act as if the market for any given stock is contestable. Each devotes considerable effort to arguing that its trading platform is superior. There is persistent migration from the NASDAQ to the NYSE, but in the past few years there have also been moves in the other direction.[8] Equally important, it is not inevitable that large firms will end up at the NYSE. As of the beginning of September 2002, seventy-five of the companies in the Standard & Poor (S&P) 500 are traded on NASDAQ.[9]

Equally important is the growth of electronic trading networks. Initially, these networks focused on NASDAQ securities because of the NYSE's rule 390, which restricted off-exchange trading of listed stocks by member firms. Rule 390 was repealed in 2000, however, clearing the way for electronic networks to trade NYSE-listed stocks.[10] Since the repeal, Instinet, the largest electronic network, has accounted for approximately 3 percent of quarterly trading volume in NYSE-listed stocks.[11]

One measure of the competitive pressure that exchanges feel from electronic networks is the growing movement toward demutualization and for-profit status. Exchanges have traditionally been organized as mutuals—that is, they are owned by their member brokers. They have also been nonprofit entities. The principal constraint on a nonprofit entity is that it may not make distributions in the nature of dividends. Thus, a nonprofit exchange cannot charge profit-maximizing transaction fees and distribute the resulting surplus to its members on the basis of their percentage ownership. Instead, it charges reduced fees, with the effect that the benefits of exchange membership are captured only to the extent the member actually consumes the exchange's services.

When an exchange has market power and its members are heterogeneous, members might prefer to distribute economic rents based on usage rather than ownership.[12] As noted above, the exchange's members care not merely about the size of the rents but also about their distribution. They may choose a set of rules that is not optimal from the investors' perspective and, therefore, reduce the size of the rents, in order to achieve a preferred distribution. For-profit exchanges, however, are concerned not about the distribution of rents, but about the maximization of profits (and thereby the maximization of investor welfare). Nonprofit status allows the exchange's leadership to focus less on the size of the pie and more on how the pie is sliced. This opens up the possibility that inefficient rules will survive because they achieve the desired distribution.

Once an exchange faces substantial competition, however, it can no longer afford the luxury of designing rules to create the desired distribution of rents among its members, because there are no longer any rents to distribute. At that point, the exchange is better off dropping its nonprofit status and creating—and charging for—optimal rules.

This analysis sheds light on a fallacy that has become widespread. Recently, commentators and regulators have expressed great concern that when exchanges convert to for-profit status, they will abandon investor protection in favor of profits.[13] This conventional wisdom is exactly backward. The move to for-profit status will *increase* an exchange's incentives to adopt optimal investor protections precisely because such protections lead to greater profits. A for-profit exchange may charge the full marginal cost for its services. It will, therefore, benefit directly from any improvements in those services that cost less than what investors are willing to pay. The argument against for-profit status is, therefore, simply a variant of the argument against competition, to which we now turn.

COMPETITION

Imagine that exchanges have become the principal source and enforcers of disclosure rules. Now, imagine that a large, prominent company is accused of violating those rules. Will the exchange vigorously investigate the allegation and apply the agreed-upon penalty? Or will it sweep the matter under the rug so as not to of-fend a powerful constituent? A common assumption is that the company need only threaten to move to a competing exchange. The incumbent exchange, un-willing to risk the loss of a high-profile listed company, will then back down.

University of Chicago Law School professor Daniel R. Fischel and Wharton School economist Sanford J. Grossman have studied that issue at length, but it is worth discussing it here briefly.[14] The analysis in the last paragraph concludes that competi-tion is bad because companies can play exchanges off against one another. It ignores, however, the fact that investors are not innocent bystanders but active participants who can also vote with their feet. If investors care about good disclosure, then they will penalize exchanges that do not enforce their disclosure rules. Competition for companies is profitless unless it is accompanied by successful competition for investors.

That is simply an application of the First Fundamental Theorem of Welfare Economics, which holds that a competitive equilibrium is Pareto optimal. In other words, the allocation (in our case, of rules and enforcement) produced by a com-petitive process maximizes consumer welfare within the constraints of the con-sumers' willingness to pay. The corollary for our purposes is that the exchange's gains from keeping the miscreant company will be more than offset by losses caused by investors' reduced desire to trade.

The First Fundamental Theorem of Welfare Economics, like any analytical result, requires some restrictive assumptions. When those assumptions do not hold, we can show that the outcome of the competitive process will not be optimal. One common departure is imperfect information. If investors do not know that the ex-change is failing to enforce its rules, they will not react appropriately.

Investors in securities markets, however, have an especially valuable tool for overcoming informational deficits. Securities prices reflect information. For prices to adjust to an exchange's poor enforcement record, it requires only that a sophis-ticated few uncover the truth. Those investors respond by trading, which means that prices will reflect the information they have uncovered. The bulk of investors need not have particularly good information—they can free ride on the informa-tion produced by others.

The other common departure from optimality comes about through exter-nalities, or circumstances in which third parties who are not participants in the market gain or lose because of transactions in that market. (Externalities are dis-cussed in the next section.)

Finally, one might declare that we should look up from economic theory and view the world around us. Participants in markets are not automatons but people with human emotions and frailties. Will investors really know or care enough to desert an exchange that doesn't punish violations of disclosure rules? Perhaps not, but that is not an argument against exchange regulation *relative* to government reg-ulation. Government bureaus are made up of people, too. Government agencies have ample authority, resources, and motivation to prevent frauds such as Enron and WorldCom, yet they failed as much as investors, broker-dealers, and exchanges.

The point deserves elaboration. Many of the market shortcomings that culminated in the Enron and other scandals are painfully clear in retrospect—but only in retrospect. Before the scandals, it would not have been unreasonable to argue, for example, that firms would be unlikely to go to great lengths to create temporary mispricings of their stock because the move would backfire in the long run. However, this argument is not quite correct in a world in which corporate officers can make tens of millions of dollars instantaneously through the exercise of incentive stock options. In that situation, the benefits of a brief, one-time increase in price may really outweigh the discounted value of future compensation and reputation. That, in turn, suggests that options align managerial and investor incentives only imperfectly. For options to work properly, managers must face strong constraints from accountants and securities analysts who attempt to spot misleading disclosures. Put differently, when managers have great incentives to mislead, accountants and analysts must also have strong incentives to prevent deception.

Unfortunately, the incentives facing accountants and analysts have been moving in precisely the opposite direction. One of the striking trends in financial services over the past few decades has been the service providers' dreams of becoming "one-stop shops." This led accounting firms to offer auditing, financial advisory, tax, and legal services. It led Citigroup to bring commercial banking, investment banking, securities analysis, mutual funds, and insurance under one roof. Such combinations offer operating efficiencies and customer convenience. But both the service providers and their customers seem to have underestimated the associated costs that stem from ubiquitous conflicts of interest. Those conflicts dulled the accountants' and analysts' incentives to keep managers honest.

That, in broad outline, is the case for more regulation. But there is one enormous hole in the analysis. Regulators did no better than investors at appreciating and taking steps to prevent problems before the consequences became obvious. Let us begin with incentive options. The sources to which a sensible regulator might turn for guidance—academic opinion, the financial press, and so on—did not identify the problem with sufficient clarity and forcefulness to make a difference. Prior to the recent scandals, it was widely accepted among academic lawyers and economists that incentive options closely aligned the interests of managers and investors. Only in hindsight does it appear that options may have an undesired side effect because they increase in value as the volatility of the stock increases. Thus, options enable managers to profit from volatility and not only from increases in value. That, in turn, can provide a huge payoff from a temporary mispricing. Perhaps the market failed to notice the problem, or perhaps boards of directors concluded that the risk was outweighed by the substantial tax benefits to the firm of using options rather than cash compensation. A 1993 tax law amendment disallowed as a deductible business expense any executive compensation exceeding $1 million unless it is "performance based." Certainly, Congress failed to recognize that it was creating potentially bad incentives.

The story differs only in the details when we turn to conflicts of interest facing the accounting industry. Some commentators—in both the private sector and the SEC—warned that those conflicts were a substantial problem.[15] Investors, however, did not appear to view the problem as serious until it was too late. After the recent scandals, investors changed their views about the problem, which prompted some accounting firms to divest their advisory businesses and investment banks to make changes in their analysts' practices.

Meanwhile, Congress and the SEC did not act to address the problem in advance, in part because of the strong resistance to the proposed reforms by accounting firms and investment banks. Only after the scandals did the political salience of accounting and analyst conflicts of interest reach a level that permitted legislative change. To sum up, then, prior to the recent scandals, investors did not act aggressively because they did not appreciate the magnitude of the problem, and regulators did not act aggressively because it was not politically expedient. At the end of the episode, the score stands at Market 0, Regulators 0. That is not an argument in favor of government regulation.

The government's after-the-fact response may seem more vigorous because it is more highly visible. With considerable fanfare, Congress has prohibited accounting firms from providing certain nonaudit services to audit clients and instructed the SEC to make rules to improve the independence of securities analysts. The market's solutions, however, are considerably harder to spot. Markets send their commands through prices. Having learned the hard way that excessive option-based compensation, or the combination of audit and consulting services, can create bad incentives, investors will react. But investors do not call press conferences or hold hearings—they simply revalue assets. We won't know the results until time has passed and researchers have had an opportunity to look carefully at the clues that prices provide.

We should also keep in mind that political actors and regulators seeking more regulatory authority have every incentive to overstate the contribution of failures of accounting and corporate governance to the stock market's decline. Although the conflict of interest problems outlined above undoubtedly contributed to Enron's collapse, it seems plausible that the proximate cause of that collapse was a failed business model.[16] Managers who tried to hide debt through off-balance-sheet entities, and analysts who credulously or deceitfully predicted continued rapid growth, may have made the collapse more violent. The absence of conflict of interest problems, however, probably would not have prevented it. Moreover, we cannot easily determine how much of the price declines that followed the revelations of accounting frauds were a consequence of investors' revaluation of the earning power of the assets and how much reflected investors' fears of lawsuits and regulatory overreaction. Thus, if it turns out that investors viewed the conflict of interest problems as relatively minor, that is not proof that the investors were foolish.

It is obvious that investors, like all humans, fall short of the perfect cognition and calculation required for optimal outcomes. This is a large part of the standard argument for regulation. But it is a deeply flawed argument. We cannot expect either markets or regulators to achieve perfection. The critical question is whether private or public actors will do better at setting rules. That question just takes us back to the beginning—to incentives, which favor the exchange.

EXTERNALITIES

The argument that exchanges have strong incentives to provide optimal disclosure and governance rules turns on the idea that the exchange can profit from providing such rules by capturing larger trading volumes and, perhaps, charging higher fees. High-quality disclosure and governance rules increase investor wealth by increasing the accuracy of prices and reducing the ability of corporate promoters and managers to misappropriate corporate assets.[17]

Not all of these benefits, however, accrue to the marginal investor—the party whose willingness to pay for improved disclosure and governance is critical to the analysis. Accurate prices and faithful corporate management also help competing firms, suppliers, and employees. The exchange does not sell its services to all of those other benefited parties, so it cannot charge them for the benefits the exchange confers. Similarly, some of the benefited parties are inframarginal traders who would have traded under either low- or high-quality rules. The exchange also does not capture a share of the benefits received by those inframarginal traders. Because it bears all of the costs and captures only part of the benefits of writing and enforcing high-quality rules, the exchange will underprovide them. Externalities create a wedge between private and social optimality.

Of course, all economic activities generate some externalities. When the manufacturer of my favorite breakfast cereal invests in improving the taste, I am in a better mood after eating breakfast, to the benefit of my family and colleagues. The manufacturer can't force those third parties to pay for the benefit thus conveyed, and it will, therefore, invest too little, from a social perspective, in improving the taste of the cereal. But we readily recognize such external effects as trivial—as occupying one end of a spectrum. A factory dumping toxic wastes into a river upstream from a town that uses the river for drinking water and recreation is at the other end of the spectrum.

A substantial majority of academics and policy makers would agree that the external effects in the breakfast cereal case are too small to justify government intervention, whereas those in the second case are too large to justify confidence that the invisible hand of the market will solve the problem. Empirical hunches about the size of externalities tend to drive attitudes toward regulation in many settings. Advocates of regulation believe that externalities are often very large and the perverse incentives created by the government's intervention are typically small, while advocates of private solutions believe the opposite. For the purposes of this chapter, it is not necessary to settle that debate here; it suffices to ask whether the externalities present in securities markets are closer to the breakfast cereal or toxic waste end of the spectrum.

The claim most frequently advanced in the academic literature is that disclosure rules affect competitors of the disclosing company.[18] In particular, disclosures enable competitors and potential competitors to learn about the disclosing firm's costs and revenues. Companies would, therefore, prefer to disclose less than the socially optimal amount in order to hide information from competitors.

At bottom, the concern must be that, absent disclosure, there will be too little entry. Public policy doesn't (or shouldn't) care about the purely distributive question of whether company A or company B gets a profitable business opportunity. Instead, we care that neither A nor B has the opportunity to make more than the competitive level of profit. If it is easy to identify industries or products in which above-average profits are available, entry into those businesses will whittle the profit down to the competitive level. If the externality problem is large, then, it is because companies can hide their profitability and thereby earn excessive profits quietly without fear of new entry.

The net effect of disclosure and governance rules on entry, however, is likely negative. Compliance with these rules is costly. Some of the costs vary with the size of the company. An outside accounting firm charges more for a more complex audit, and a larger company usually requires more in-house compliance staff. But some costs are fixed—even a very small publicly traded firm usually needs some in-house legal and accounting staff to prepare disclosure documents and monitor compliance with governance rules. Those costs are a barrier to new entry. It is, accordingly, unlikely that maximizing the amount of required disclosure is a good way to maximize competition among publicly traded firms. The dominant externality argument in the academic literature, then, is not very convincing.

POOR ENFORCEMENT TOOLS

The strongest reason to be concerned about an exchange's ability to write and enforce disclosure and governance rules is that it lacks good enforcement tools. The exchange's principal threat is to delist a company that violates its rules. That is an excessive sanction for minor violations and accordingly not credible. It is an insufficient sanction for egregious violations, particularly those prompted by "last period" concerns.

Assume, for example, that a company finds itself in severe financial distress, but that fact is not yet publicly known. The company's officers face the decision of whether to make complete and accurate disclosures or to conceal the company's true position. They may believe that concealment could enable them to raise new capital and weather the crisis. By contrast, full and prompt disclosure will quickly lead to bankruptcy. To make the hypothetical as compelling as possible, let us assume that mere concealment would not constitute actionable fraud, so the exchange's sanctions are the only relevant ones.

In that situation, the company has nothing to lose from concealment if the only sanction is delisting. If the company discloses, it will become bankrupt. If it conceals and the exchange discovers the deception, the company will be delisted. Assuming that the stigma of delisting in those circumstances destroys the market for the company's securities, the worst that can happen is bankruptcy. There is no marginal deterrence of concealment.

An exchange faces a similarly troubling problem if it tries to withhold its primary benefit—listing and its attendant liquidity—in response to less serious violations. The exchange could merely suspend listing for a brief period rather than terminate it, but most of the cost of the lost liquidity would be imposed on investors rather than the corporate wrongdoers.

There is no technical barrier, however, to an exchange developing a more targeted and varied set of sanctions. The listing contract between a company and the exchange is just that—a contract. Like any other contract, it may include detailed remedy provisions in the event of breach. For example, the listing agreement could provide a schedule of fines for delays and shortcomings in disclosure documents. The listed company could be required to post a deposit from which the exchange could deduct those fines. As lawyers often say, a contract is a "private law" between the parties and can detail their rights and obligations as the parties think appropriate.

It is only natural to ask why exchanges do not write such detailed contracts. If contracting could solve the enforcement problem, we would expect to see exchanges write enforcement procedures into their listing agreements. That is unrealistic, however, under the current regulatory regime. The exchanges have relatively little authority over listed companies compared to the SEC. An exchange's principal enforcement responsibility is with respect to its member broker-dealers. We, therefore, learn very little about what is feasible and desirable from observing exchange behavior in a world where the SEC writes and enforces disclosure rules for publicly traded companies.

Of course, exchanges didn't write detailed enforcement procedures into their listing contracts during the pre-SEC era either. Perhaps this shows that exchanges were unwilling to spend the resources necessary to ensure that their disclosure and governance standards were followed. But drawing that conclusion may simply be succumbing to the "nirvana fallacy"—that is, letting the best get in the way of the good. In the pre-SEC era, the level of disclosure by listed companies was better than that of over-the-counter firms. Similarly, companies listed on more prestigious exchanges disclosed more than those listed on less prestigious exchanges. Clearly, the exchanges did not achieve perfection, but by the standards of their day they did quite well.

A more important issue for a contemporary exchange might be investigation rather than sanctioning. In order to impose punishments that actually deter, an exchange must be able to determine when a company has broken the rules. Government investigators have powerful tools, such as subpoena and search-and-seizure powers, that an exchange lacks. Faced with a recalcitrant company, it is much more effective to break down the door than to threaten a lawsuit or delisting.

Once again, the problem can be solved to a significant extent by contract. The listing agreement can ensure the exchange's employees unrestricted access to a listed company's personnel and records, with a provision for significant fines if the listed company chooses not to cooperate. Exchanges already typically require that member organizations (such as brokerage firms) permit examination of their books and records by exchange personnel.[19] Were exchanges, rather than the SEC, the primary regulators of listed company disclosure, they might decide to put a similar provision into their listing agreements. Despite those contractual solutions, it would be naïve to argue that exchanges would have as effective a set of investigation and enforcement tools as the SEC possesses today. It is undeniable that a government agency backed by the state's monopoly of force has an edge in investigating and punishing wrongdoing. Perhaps the most effective arrangement, then, would be a mixture of private rule making and government enforcement.

ANCIENT HISTORY: THE 1920s

We need not limit ourselves to a purely theoretical discussion, because there are actual examples of securities exchanges acting as the principal regulators of disclosure, accounting, and governance standards for publicly traded firms. Prior to the enactment of the federal securities laws, stock exchanges played that role in the United States. State "blue sky" laws regulated public offerings, but they were based on a regulatory theory entirely different from that underlying disclosure laws. Disclosure rules seek to make information available to the market so that investors can judge the merits of securities offered for sale. Blue-sky laws, by contrast, were based on the paternalistic notion that state officials should decide which securities were "safe" enough to be offered for sale. Accordingly, those laws did not aim to make information available to the investing public, which was assumed to be incapable of evaluating information.

Public offerings were also subject to disclosure rules that had been developed by courts under the rubric of the fiduciary duties of corporate directors, officers, and promoters.[20] Generally speaking, those who sold securities to the public had a duty to disclose conflicting interests, such as the fact that the sellers stood to gain from the sale of property to the corporation or the fact that the sellers would earn a commission were the offering successful. Those disclosure requirements were focused, however, on conflicts of interest, not on making information about corporate performance available to the investing public. Stock exchange listing standards were the most important means of achieving the latter objective.

The NYSE first adopted listing standards in 1856.[21] Listed companies were required to make specified financial information available to the exchange and its members. By the late 1920s, the mandated information for newly listed companies included audited annual balance sheets and income statements, and listed companies were strongly encouraged to provide quarterly financial reports.[22] The existence and effectiveness of stock exchange listing standards in the pre-SEC era are obviously relevant to the current debate. The theoretical arguments for and against exchange regulation of corporate governance and disclosure must be evaluated in light of the historical evidence.

There is little debate over whether the NYSE's pre-SEC listing standards were substantively defective—they were not. They mandated, in rough outline, the principal types of financial information that form the backbone of mandated disclosures today. The SEC based its early disclosure forms on the NYSE's listing standards, reinforcing the notion that those standards were reasonably comprehensive. Obviously, views about the appropriate level of disclosure have evolved since the 1930s, but it is not a controversial proposition that the NYSE's stated listing standards were adequate for their time.

The debate is over whether those standards were actually enforced and respected. The accepted wisdom is that the federal securities laws were adopted precisely because exchange regulation was ineffective. Listed companies, critics argue, flouted the NYSE's standards without consequences. Unfortunately, lawyers and policy makers have uncritically accepted the claims of the New Deal proponents of federal regulation. When scholars have ventured beyond the polemics and looked at the evidence directly, a different picture has emerged.

Contemporary observers were impressed with the extent of disclosures made by exchange-listed companies. Columbia University corporate law professor Adolf Berle, who helped shape much of the banking and securities legislation of the New Deal, noted in his 1932 classic study, *The Modern Corporation and Private Property*, that a substantial amount of financial information was available to investors.[23] We can easily verify the accuracy of Berle's assessment by picking up a bound volume of Moody's or S&P's investment manuals from the 1920s. Those volumes contain income statements and balance sheets for thousands of companies. A quick perusal is sufficient to verify that companies traded on an exchange provided more comprehensive and detailed financial statements than companies traded over the counter.

More recently, economist George J. Benston has extensively studied pre-SEC disclosure practices. He discovered a very high rate of compliance with the NYSE's listing requirements.[24] I have separately examined the claim that poor disclosure enabled large traders to manipulate stock prices and found that the evidence did not support the claim.[25] Banner, although principally concerned with enforcement actions against brokers, describes the NYSE's enforcement efforts in the late

1800s.[26] His description is sharply at odds with the notion that the NYSE was unable or unwilling to police its members (and, by extension, its listed companies). The evidence available to us suggests that in the pre-SEC era, listed companies substantially complied with the NYSE's listing standards and the resulting disclosures were sufficient to permit investors to make informed investment decisions.

MODERN HISTORY: THE AFTERMATH OF ENRON

Both the NYSE and the NASDAQ have proposed changes to their listing standards, subject to the SEC's approval, in light of the governance and accounting scandals. It is, of course, difficult to determine precisely how the exchanges would have altered their listing standards if left to their own devices. The SOA, which was making its way through Congress as the exchanges' proposals were being formulated, mandates some of the rule changes ultimately proposed. The SEC also took considerable interest in the exchanges' deliberations. Nevertheless, within the narrow scope of the discretion left to the exchanges, the proposed changes provide insight into the exchanges' views of good corporate governance.

The revised listing standards include the following provisions:[27]

- Listed companies must have a majority of independent directors.
- Independent directors must meet periodically in executive session without management.
- Listed companies must increase the role of independent directors in nomination and compensation decisions. The NYSE proposals require nominating and compensation committees composed entirely of independent directors, while the NASDAQ proposals permit decisions by an independent committee or a majority of independent directors. Both the NYSE and NASDAQ rules tighten the definition of "independence" for audit committee members as required by the SOA.
- Shareholders must approve adoption of stock option plans (NASDAQ) or equity-based compensation plans generally (NYSE), subject to exceptions.
- Listed companies must adopt codes of conduct covering legal and ethical responsibilities.

The NYSE proposals also contain a new enforcement tool. The exchange may send a public reprimand letter to a listed company that violates a listing standard. The commentary to the proposed new rule observes the problems noted above—delisting or suspension hurts investors as much as it does the company's management. Adverse publicity is an alternative sanction that, although less severe, also has fewer third-party effects.

Those changes, together with the SOA, create an interesting experiment regarding the difference between exchange regulation and SEC regulation. Two groups of listed companies have protested quickly and vociferously against portions of the new listing standards. One consists of foreign companies. In general, the NYSE has exempted foreign listed companies from its requirement of an independent audit committee. European companies with two-tier board structures (particularly those, like German companies, with mandatory union participation) find it difficult to set up committees of genuinely independent directors. The SOA, however, directs the SEC to make independent audit committees mandatory. A group of German companies has accordingly requested that the SEC exempt them from the audit committee requirement.

A second concerned group consists of small businesses. They are worried, among other things, about the cost of recruiting a sufficient number of independent directors to have a majority-independent board. This listing requirement, however, is not mandated by SOA, so the NYSE and the NASDAQ will have to decide whether to build in exceptions to the rule for smaller firms. Thus, the SEC on one hand, and the NYSE and the NASDAQ on the other, must directly confront a cost/benefit question regarding new listing standards. Are the costs to investors of deterring some foreign companies, or small businesses, from listing greater or less than the costs of failing to hold a steady line on the new listing standards? The theoretical discussion above suggests that the exchanges will be more likely to arrive at the correct answer because they have a direct financial incentive to do so. Watching the SEC, the NYSE, and the NASDAQ as they try to determine how strictly to apply the new listing standards may shed new light on the comparative efficacy of exchange and agency regulation.

THE BEST OF BOTH WORLDS?

Imagine that the Securities Act of 1933 and the Securities Exchange Act of 1934 were amended to remove all substantive provisions regarding disclosure, accounting standards, proxy regulation, and takeover regulation and to divest SEC of its rule-making authority over such matters. However, the statutes retained their anti-fraud provisions and authorized the SEC to investigate and impose civil sanctions against listed companies (and their officers, directors, and affiliates) that violate any disclosure or corporate governance rules promulgated by the exchange or other market on which they are traded.

The resulting system would combine the advantages of the exchanges' superior incentives to adopt optimal rules and the government's unique enforcement tools. We could expect competing exchanges to adopt disclosure, accounting, and governance standards that are closer to optimal than those adopted by Congress and the SEC. Of course, anyone who believes that more regulation is always better will find such a proposal manifestly unwise, because exchanges might choose not to replicate some parts of the current regulatory structure. But competition will provide the necessary incentive for exchanges to select rules that they believe will appeal to investors, given their costs.

For what it is worth, I suspect that the immediate result of such a change would not be dramatic, just as the immediate results of federal regulation in the 1930s were not dramatic. The infant SEC borrowed liberally from the NYSE's listing standards to write its initial disclosure forms. Similarly, exchanges would surely borrow liberally from existing precedents—including not only SEC forms but market-tested alternatives such as the typical Eurodollar disclosure documents. Unlike existing law, however, those standards would have to survive the market's fitness test on an ongoing basis.

CONCLUSION

Conventional wisdom has it that recent corporate governance and accounting scandals demonstrate the need for more government and less private regulation of securities markets. The case rests on the fact that the securities industry developed practices (such as the close integration of investment banking and securities analysis, or auditing and consulting) that were in retrospect not optimal, and investors arguably failed to react with sufficient alarm. Conveniently ignored is the fact that regulators failed as well.

Regulation by hindsight may be emotionally soothing, but it is not the best way to prevent yet unknown problems. In a dynamic setting like the securities markets, self-interest is the most powerful tool available for adjusting rapidly to changing conditions. That suggests that rule making by actors whose wealth is at stake and who face competitive pressure to get the rules right will be better than rule making by government actors.

NOTES

1. Banner, Stuart, *Anglo-American Securities Regulation: Cultural and Political Roots, 1690—1860,* New York: Cambridge University Press, 1998.

2. Miller, Geoffrey P. and Jonathan Macey, "Origins of the Blue Sky Laws," *Texas Law Review* 70, 1991, p. 347; and Paul G. Mahoney, "The Origins of the Blue Sky Laws: A Test of Competing Hypotheses," *Journal of Law and Economics* 46, no. 1, April 2003, p. 229–51.

3. This section follows Paul G. Mahoney, "The Political Economy of the Securities Act of 1933," *Journal of Legal Studies* 30, no. 1, 2001, p. 1–31.

4. See "Meeting of Board of Governors of Investment Bankers Association of America to be Held Feb. 10–11 to Consider Fair Practice Rules for Investment Banking Code," *Commercial and Financial Chronicle* 138, February 3, 1934, p. 782.

5. See "New Rules on Accountants, but Also Questions," *New York Times*, July 26, 2002, p. C1. Title I of SOA creates a PCAOB that regulates auditing firms and their activities. The compliance and financial costs imposed by this new body will create barriers to entry for smaller firms, thus consolidating the position of the Big Four accounting firms, which now have significant market power to raise the rates for their audit services.

6. Craig Pirrong has provided the most rigorous form of the argument. See Craig Pirrong, "A Theory of Financial Exchange Organization," *Journal of Law and Economics* 43, no. 2, 2000, p. 437–72; and Craig Pirrong, "The Self-Regulation of Commodity Exchanges: The Case of Market Manipulation," *Journal of Law and Economics* 38, no. 1, 1995, p. 141–206.

7. For evidence of exchange market power, see Craig Pirrong, "The Organization of Financial Exchange Markets: Theory and Evidence," *Journal of Financial Markets* 2, no. 4, 1999, p. 329–57. By contrast, other commentators look at the structure of financial exchanges and see considerable competition, both among trading platforms and between exchanges and their members, for the provision of order execution services. See, e.g., Marshall E. Blume, "The Structure of U.S. Equity Markets," in Robert E. Litan and Richard Herring, eds., *Brookings-Wharton Papers on Financial Services*, Washington, D.C.: Brookings Institution Press, 2002, p. 35–60; and Benn Steil, "Changes in the Ownership and Governance of Securities Exchanges: Causes and Consequences," in *Brookings-Wharton Papers on Financial Services*, p. 61–91.

8. The first voluntary move to NASDAQ of a company that met the NYSE's continued listing standards was in 2000. See "NASDAQ Concludes Record Share and Dollar Volume; Year Composite Index Finishes Lower," *M2 Presswire*, January 23, 2001.

9. S&P's Web site, www.spglobal.com/indexmain500_data.html. Accessed September 17, 2002.

10. See Exchange Act Release no. 42758, 65 *Fed. Reg.* 30175, May 10, 2000.

11. Instinet Web site, www.instinet.com/trade_data/trade_data_quarter.shtml. Accessed September 17, 2002.

12. See Pirrong, "The Theory of Financial Exchange Organizations."

13. See, e.g., International Organization of Securities Commissions, "Discussion Paper on Stock Exchange Demutualization," December 2000; Norman S. Poser, "The Stock Exchanges of the United States and Europe: Automation, Globalization, and Consolidation," *University of Pennsylvania Journal of International Economic Law* 22, no. 3, 2001, p. 497–540 ("Regulators see a conflict between the duty of the managers of a publicly owned stock exchange to maximize profits for the benefit of its shareholders and their regulatory obligation to protect investors"). A good overview of the arguments regarding the compatibility of for-profit status and self-regulation appears in Roberta S. Karmel, "Turning Seats into Shares: Causes and Implications of Demutualization of Stock and Futures Exchanges," *Hastings Law Journal* 53, no. 2, 2002, p. 367–430.

14. See Daniel R. Fischel and Sanford J. Grossman, "Consumer Protection in Futures and Securities Markets," *Journal of Futures Markets* 4, 1984, p. 273.

15. See, e.g., Tamar Frankel, "Accountants' Independence: The Recent Dilemma," *Columbia Business Law Review,* 2000, no. 2, 2000, p. 261–74; and "Auditory Discomfort: Auditors under Fire," *Economist*, January 13, 2000 (discussing SEC concerns about

accountants' nonaudit services), www.economist.com/research/articlesBySubject/PrinterFriendly.cfm?Story_ID=274092&subjectID=1290116.

16. See Christopher L. Culp and William A. Niskanen, eds., *Corporate Aftershock: The Public Policy Lessons from the Collapse of Enron and Other Major Corporations,* New York: John Wiley and Sons, 2003.

17. Although debates over securities regulation typically focus on the first of these harms, I have argued that the second—the fact that poor disclosure helps corporate promoters and managers to misappropriate assets without being detected—is the greater harm, and the one to which securities disclosure norms were originally addressed. See Paul G. Mahoney, "Mandatory Disclosure as a Solution to Agency Problems," *University of Chicago Law Review* 62, 1995, p. 1047.

18. See Merritt B. Fox, "Securities Disclosure in a Globalizing Market: Who Should Regulate Whom?" *Michigan Law Review* 95, no. 8, 1997, p. 2498–629; and Frank H. Easterbrook and Daniel R. Fischel, "Mandatory Disclosure and the Protection of Investors," *Virginia Law Review* 70, no. 3, 1984, p. 669–715.

19. See, e.g., NYSE rule 304(h)(4).

20. See Esterbrook and Fischel, "Mandatory Disclosure."

21. See Stuart J. Banner, "The Origin of the New York Stock Exchange, 1791–1860," *Journal of Legal Studies* 27, no. 1, 1998, p. 113–40.

22. The discussion herein draws from Paul G. Mahoney, "The Exchange as Regulator," *Virginia Law Review* 83, 1997, p. 1453.

23. Berle, Adolf A. and Gardiner C. Means, *The Modern Corporation and Private Property,* 1932; reprint, New Brunswick, N.J.: Transaction Publishers, 1991.

24. See George J. Benston, *Corporate Financial Disclosure in the UK and the USA,* New York: Lexington Books, 1976; George J. Benston, "An Appraisal of the Costs and Benefits of Government-Required Disclosure: SEC and FTC Requirements," *Law and Contemporary Problems* 41, summer 1977, p. 30; and George J. Benston, "Required Disclosure and the Stock Market: An Evaluation of the Securities Exchange Act of 1934," *American Economic Review* 63, 1973, p. 132.

25. See Paul G. Mahoney, "The Stock Pools and the Securities Exchange Act," *Journal of Financial Economics* 51, 1999, p. 343–69.

26. See Banner, "The Origins of the New York Stock Exchange."

27. See "Report of the New York Stock Exchange Corporate Accountability and Listing Standards Committee," June 6, 2002, www.nyse.com/pdfs/corp_govreport.pdf. A summary of Nasdaq's most recent (as of September 10, 2003) corporate governance proposals can be found at www.nasdaq.com/about/Corp_Gov_Summary.pdf.

· 10 ·

Should Congress Repeal
Securities Class Action Reform?

Adam C. Pritchard

$\mathscr{T}$he enactment of the Private Securities Litigation Reform Act of 1995 (PSLRA) was a victory for accountants, securities firms, and the high-technology industry, all of which sought to curtail what they perceived as a torrent of securities fraud class actions. Those groups believed that they had been unjustly victimized by lawsuits alleging "fraud by hindsight," based on little more than a sudden drop in a company's stock price. Despite the vigorous resistance put up by the plaintiffs' class action bar, which saw the law as a threat to their very lucrative livelihoods, proponents succeeded in persuading Congress to override President Bill Clinton's veto of the bill and enact the PSLRA.

Subsequent events have substantially diminished the lobbying clout of the industries that promoted the PSLRA. Arthur Andersen's involvement in the accounting legerdemain at Enron and subsequent criminal convictions have brought disrepute on the accounting industry as a whole. Incriminating e-mails from Merrill Lynch, Credit Suisse First Boston, and Salomon Smith Barney suggest that the stock picks that brokers offer their clients may be little more credible than the pitch of the average used-car salesman. The collapse of the high-tech bubble erased $4.3 *trillion* in market capitalization from the National Association of Securities Dealers Automated Quotation System (NASDAQ). Each of those developments has left multitudes of angry investors in its wake. As a result, Congress—always attuned to the anguish of angry investors—is a much less hospitable place for accountants, investment bankers, and high-tech entrepreneurs than it was a few years ago.

Not surprisingly, opponents of securities fraud class action reform see an opportunity to roll back the PSLRA. The recent spate of corporate scandals has brought the class action bar to the surface, lured by the prospect of tens of millions of dollars in attorneys' fees. Andersen's criminal conviction drove it into bankruptcy, but the remaining Big Four accounting firms, the big investment banks, and numerous high-tech companies face a raft of lawsuits seeking billions of dollars in damages and healthy contingent fees for the plaintiffs' attorneys. That class action windfall is not enough for the class action bar. They see Enron, WorldCom, and the host of lesser scandals that have followed as their great chance to undo the securities litigation reforms that Congress adopted in 1995.

The Enron fiasco, the plaintiffs' lawyers say, shows that the curbs on abusive lawsuits created by the PSLRA give corporations carte blanche to engage in fraud. Plaintiffs' lawyer William Lerach, dean of the class action bar, labels the PSLRA the "Corporate License to Lie Act." He says that there is "no question that the [PSLRA] emboldened executives to think they could do whatever they wanted."[1] The class action bar's friends in the media have joined the call for a rollback of securities litigation reform. The *New York Times* frets that the PSLRA

> may prove to be an obstacle to investors as they try to recover tens of billions of dollars from Enron, which has filed for bankruptcy protection, as well as its auditors, lawyers, bankers, partners, and others who may have been involved.[2]

That chorus is being heard in the halls of Congress. Sen. Patrick Leahy (D–Vt.) held hearings last year on the implications of Enron for securities class action reforms. Leahy voted against the PSLRA, he says, because "its special legal protections might lead to future financial scandals. Beginning with Enron, the chickens have come home to roost."[3] Bills have been introduced in the House and Senate that would repeal critical provisions of securities class action reform. The Sarbanes-Oxley Act of 2002 (SOA) did not incorporate those provisions, although it did extend the time period for filing fraud claims. But the drumbeat for further corporate governance reform is certain to include a call for loosening restrictions on securities class actions.

This chapter evaluates the wisdom of repealing the PSLRA. First, it briefly describes how securities fraud class actions operate. Then it discusses the impetus behind the PSLRA and provides an outline of its principal provisions. The study then surveys the impact of the PSLRA on securities fraud class actions. It also evaluates the proposals to roll back certain provisions of the PSLRA and offers an alternative reform for securities class actions to enhance their deterrence of fraud.

SECURITIES FRAUD AND SECURITIES FRAUD CLASS ACTIONS

To understand securities fraud class actions, we first need to understand the market abuse that they are intended to remedy. Securities fraud class actions target misrepresentations that are very different from what we customarily think of as fraud; the corporations that are held responsible for the damages generally do not benefit from the misrepresentations. As a result, the law of fraud does not quite fit those misrepresentations, thereby creating policy dilemmas with no easy solution.

SOME ECONOMICS OF FRAUD

Why do we worry about corporate fraud? In addition to the obvious moral objection to lying, economic analysis supports strong sanctions for fraud. Most conspicuously, fraud may influence how investors direct their capital. Firms that issue securities tend to disclose more information about themselves in an effort to attract investors. If those disclosures are fraudulent, investors will pay an inflated price for those securities and companies will invest in projects that are not cost justified. Fraud may also allow companies to retain money or other resources that would be better deployed elsewhere. Managers who fraudulently inflate their company's stock price may be able to invest in ill-advised empire building instead of paying cash flows as dividends to shareholders. Alternatively, managers may use fraud to keep the firm in business when its assets should be redirected through bankruptcy. The bottom line: if capital markets are infected by fraud, publicly traded firms will face a higher cost of capital because investors will discount the amount that they are willing to pay for securities to reflect the risk of fraud.

Misrepresentations by corporate managers also hurt the shareholders' ability to monitor the firm's performance and, more specifically, to evaluate the job the firm's managers are doing. Insofar as fraud insulates managers from scrutiny, it also may distort the market for corporate control. Poor managers may be able to discourage hostile acquirers by creating the illusion of strong performance. Deterring corporate misrepresentations, therefore, can help make managers more accountable to shareholders.

The U.S. scheme of securities regulation deploys a variety of countermeasures to discourage fraud. Financial statements are audited by reputable accounting firms. Audit committees of outside directors provide independent oversight of company disclosures. Rating agencies provide assessments of companies' creditworthiness. Analysts rate the credibility and completeness of company disclosures. In addition to those market mechanisms, fraud is further deterred by Securities and Exchange Commission (SEC) enforcement and criminal prosecution of defrauders by the Justice Department and state prosecutors.

Class actions promise additional deterrence. In fact, the SEC considers private class actions a "necessary supplement" to its own efforts to police fraud. Class actions, however, promise more than added deterrence; they also promise compensation to the victims of fraud. That promise of compensation—and the enormous damages that might be necessary to fulfill that promise—strikes genuine fear into the hearts of corporate executives. Surprisingly, the potential for large damages may undermine the deterrent value of securities fraud class actions, as discussed below.

SECURITIES FRAUD CLASS ACTIONS

The reason that securities class actions carry such large potential damages awards is the supposed need for compensation, but class actions promise compensation in cases in which it is not justified. Compensation is important in cases in which the corporation has been selling securities through fraud. Compensation corrects the distortion caused by fraud in two ways. First, requiring compensation to the victim discourages the corporation from committing the fraud. Second, compensation discourages investors from expending resources trying to avoid fraud. Expenditures by both the perpetrator and the victim of fraud are a social waste, so compensation makes sense in that context.[4] The federal securities laws encourage such fraud suits by providing a very generous standard for recovery, but despite that encouragement, claims asserting a misrepresentation made by a company in connection with an offering of securities make up only a small percentage of securities class actions.[5]

The overwhelming majority of securities fraud class actions have little effect on capital allocation because the corporations sued are not selling securities. In the typical securities fraud class action, plaintiffs' attorneys sue the corporation and its officers under rule 10b–5 of the Securities Exchange Act[6] for alleged misrepresentations regarding the company's operations, financial performance, or future prospects that inflate the price of the company's stock in secondary trading markets such as the New York Stock Exchange (NYSE) or NASDAQ. Because the corporation has not sold securities (and thereby transferred wealth to itself), it has no institutional incentive to spend real resources in executing the fraud.

That type of fraud, commonly referred to as fraud on the market, also differs from what we typically consider fraud in that there is no net wealth transfer away from investors, at least in the aggregate. Instead, the wealth transfers caused by fraud on the market overwhelmingly occur between equally innocent investors. For every shareholder who *bought* at a fraudulently inflated price, another shareholder *sold*: The buyer's individual loss is offset by the seller's gain. Assuming all traders are ignorant of the fraud, over time they will come out winners as often as losers from fraudulently distorted prices. Therefore, shareholders should have no expected loss from fraud on the market, so they would have no incentive to take precautions against fraud.[7] They simply need to diversify to protect themselves against the risk of fraud.

Despite the fact that the corporation being sued has not gained from fraud on the market, class action lawsuits allow a full measure of compensation to investors who come out on the losing end of a trade at a price distorted by misrepresentation. Those investors are entitled to recover from the corporation their losses due to the corporation managers' misstatements. Given the trading volume in secondary markets, the potential recoverable damages in such suits can be a substantial percentage of the corporation's total capitalization, easily reaching hundreds of millions of dollars. Occasionally the damages measure goes much higher. Cendant Corporation recently set records by settling a securities fraud class action for close to $3 billion.[8] With potential damages in this range, class actions are a big stick to wield against fraud.

Punitive sanctions of that sort are only appropriate, however, when they closely correspond to the actual incidence of fraud. Securities fraud class actions fall far short of that ideal. Distinguishing fraud from mere business reversals is difficult. The external observer may not know whether a drop in a company's stock price is due to a prior intentional misstatement about its prospects—that is, fraud— or a result of risky business decisions that did not pan out—that is, misjudgment or bad luck. Unable to distinguish the two, plaintiffs' lawyers must rely on limited publicly available indicia (e.g., SEC filings and press releases from the company, evidence of insider trading by the managers alleged to be responsible for the fraud) when deciding whom to sue. Thus, a substantial drop in stock price following news that contradicts a previous optimistic statement may well lead to a lawsuit.

That leaves courts with the difficult task of sorting out the cases with potential merit from the strike suits. The principal tool that courts use in that task is the scienter standard required to establish fraud. The scienter standard—the defendants' knowledge that their statements were false when made, or the defendants' reckless disregard for the truth—is notoriously amorphous. It is somewhat more stringent than negligence (would a reasonable person have made the statement?), but even in theory it is difficult to say how much more stringent, and it is nearly impossible to specify in practice. Courts and jurors, with hindsight, may have difficulty distinguishing knowingly false statements from unfortunate business decisions. Both create a risk of liability and, thus, provide a basis for filing suit. An uncertain standard for liability makes filing a diverse portfolio of cases a reasonable strategy for plaintiffs' lawyers. Sue all of the plausible candidates and let the courts sort them out.

Filing numerous cases is not only reasonable but also profitable for plaintiffs' attorneys because of the incentives that defendants face. If plaintiffs can withstand a motion to dismiss, defendants generally will find settlement cheaper than litigating to a jury verdict, even if the defendants believe that a jury would share their view of the facts. Any case plausible enough to get past a judge may be worth settling if only to avoid the costs of discovery and attorneys' fees, which can be enormous in these cases. Securities fraud class actions are expensive to defend because the focus of litigation will often be scienter— that is, the extent and timing of the defendants' knowledge. The most helpful source for uncovering that information will be the documents in the company's possession. Producing all documents relevant to the knowledge of senior executives over many months or even years can be a massive undertaking for a corporate defendant. Having produced the documents, the company can then anticipate a seemingly endless series of depositions, as plaintiffs' counsel seeks to determine whether the executives' recollections square with the documents. The cost in lost productivity may dwarf the expense of attorneys' fees and other direct litigation costs. Beyond the cost in executives' time, the mere existence of the class action may disrupt relationships with suppliers and customers, who will be understandably leery of dealing with a business accused of fraud. For those reasons, the Supreme Court has recognized that securities fraud suits pose "the threat of extensive discovery and disruption of normal business activities."[9]

Putting to one side the costs of litigation, the enormous potential damages also make settlement an attractive option for the company, even when it thinks it has a good prospect of prevailing at trial. The math is straightforward: A 10 percent chance of a $250 million judgment means that a settlement for $24.9 million makes sense. The combination of the cost of litigating securities class actions and the potential for enormous judgments means that even weak cases may produce a settlement if they are not dismissed before trial. If both weak and strong cases lead to settlements, the deterrent effect of class actions is diluted because innocent and wrongful conduct both lead to sanctions.

Deterrence is further diluted by the settlement dynamic in securities fraud class actions.[10] As discussed above, corporations typically do not benefit from fraud on the market because they are not selling securities at the time of the fraud. Who, then, benefits? The answer is the corporate managers who disguised poor corporate performance in an attempt to keep their jobs, or who inflated profits so that they could reach targets for incentive compensation or bring their stock options into the money.[11] Of course those objectives benefit the managers rather than the shareholders of the corporation. They are examples of managers' taking advantage of their positions.

Notwithstanding the self-dealing implicit in such fraud, the corporate officers who actually make the misrepresentations almost never contribute to the settlement of class actions. The dirty secret of securities fraud class actions is that the company and its insurers pay to settle the claims even though the officers are the ones responsible for the fraud. As a result, shareholders who have already been harmed by the loss of the corporation's credibility due to the managers' malfeasance also get stuck with the bill for the class action in the form of the cost of settlement, payment of attorneys' fees, and higher directors and officers insurance premiums. Securities fraud class actions are largely a device for shifting money between groups of shareholders, with the lawyers taking a healthy slice as compensation for arranging the transfer.

THE PRIVATE SECURITIES LITIGATION REFORM ACT

The legislative history of the PSLRA reflects the legislation's two central goals. The first is to rein in the class action bar so that defrauded investors receive more compensation. Given the relative unimportance of compensation, that goal might be seen as largely a pretext for Congress to launch a partisan attack on the plaintiffs' bar. The second, more important goal is to discourage frivolous litigation. That promises to enhance deterrence by more precisely targeting the sanctions imposed by securities class actions. The PSLRA includes numerous provisions intended to achieve those goals.

Reining in the Plaintiffs' Bar

Congress concluded after extensive hearings that plaintiffs' lawyers were acting for their own benefit instead of faithfully representing investors. Plaintiffs' lawyers were taking an exorbitant share of settlements for themselves, leaving defrauded investors with only a fraction of the damages that they had suffered. Plaintiffs' lawyers could charge handsome fees because the nominal plaintiffs in securities fraud class actions were typically "hundred-share plaintiffs." According to the Report of the Committee on Banking, Housing and Urban Affairs of the U.S. Senate on PSLRA:

> Under the current system, the initiative for filing 10b-5 suits comes almost entirely from the lawyers, not from genuine investors. Lawyers typically rely on repeat, or "professional," plaintiffs who, because they own a token number of shares in many companies, regularly lend their names to lawsuits. Even worse, investors in the class usually have great difficulty exercising any meaningful direction over the case brought on their behalf. The lawyers can decide when to sue and when to settle, based largely on their own financial interests, not the interests of their purported clients.[12]

The Senate report further charged that plaintiffs' lawyers recruited malleable "professional plaintiffs" through "the payment of a 'bonus' far in excess of their share of any recovery."

Congress also found abuses in the settlement process. Plaintiffs' lawyers typically received a third of the settlement, with the plaintiffs often receiving pennies on the dollar for their claims. Members of the plaintiff class often received inadequate notice of the terms of the settlement. Congress also criticized the courts, charging that judges rubber-stamped abusive settlements on "the premise that a bad settlement is almost always better than a good trial."[13]

To correct those abuses, Congress enacted a series of provisions intended to "empower investors so that they—not their lawyers—exercise primary control over private securities litigation."[14] The PSLRA places substantial restrictions on plaintiffs' attorneys in connection with settlements of securities class actions. Most notably, the law limits attorneys' fees to a reasonable percentage of the class recovery. One of the more novel reforms is the PSLRA's lead plaintiff provision. The law requires national publication of a notice advising class members that the action has been filed.[15] The PSLRA then directs the court to appoint a "lead plaintiff" from among class members who seek to act in that capacity. There is a rebuttable presumption that the most suitable plaintiff is the class member or group of members that has the largest financial interest in the relief sought. That presumption is intended to "encourage institutional investors to take a more active role in securities class action lawsuits."[16] The act further discourages reliance on the "100-share plaintiff" by prohibiting bonus payments to class representatives and limiting plaintiffs to serving as a class representative no more than five times during any three-year period. Notably, the lead plaintiff selects counsel for the class, subject to court approval. The lawyer who initially filed the action hopes to fill that role, but need not.

Discouraging Frivolous Suits

Congress's second motivation in passing the PSLRA was that class actions were being filed in a shotgun fashion. Plaintiffs' lawyers were filing suits with "a laundry list of cookie-cutter complaints" against companies "within hours or days" of a substantial drop in the company's stock price, according to the Report of the Committee on Commerce of the House of Representatives on the Common Sense Legal Reforms Act of 1995.[17] Moreover, the Senate report indicated that plaintiffs' lawyers had incentives to "file frivolous lawsuits in order to conduct discovery in the hopes of finding a sustainable claim not alleged in the complaint."[18]

Congress believed that, in the pre-PSLRA environment, a substantial number of weak cases settled because the underlying legal merits could not be determined from the complaint alone. Faced with the cost of discovery, defendants found that "the pressure to settle became enormous."[19] Even if a company were willing to bear the expense of litigation, Congress concluded that the company would inevitably settle rather than face a potentially ruinous jury verdict. The overall effect was that liability exposure was chilling issuers from making statements about their businesses:

> Private securities class actions under 10b-5 inhibit free and open communication among management, analysts, and investors. This has caused corporate management to refrain from providing shareholders forward-looking information about companies. . . . As a result, investors often receive less, not more, information, which makes investing more risky and increases the cost of raising capital.[20]

Congress also worried that innocent bystanders were being caught in the securities fraud class action crossfire. According to the Senate report, "underwriters, lawyers, accountants, and other professionals are prime targets of abusive securities lawsuits. The deeper the pocket, the greater the likelihood that a marginal party will be named as a defendant in a securities class action."[21] Congress found in its conference report that the "system of joint and several liability creates coercive pressure for entirely innocent parties to settle meritless claims rather than risk exposing themselves to liability for a grossly disproportionate share of the damages in the case."[22] Joint and several liability means that a secondary defendant could be left holding the bag if the defendant that engaged in the fraud later became insolvent, a not infrequent occurrence.

Congress attempted to make securities class actions a more precise deterrent for fraud through a series of procedural obstacles. The first barrier to frivolous class actions is a "safe harbor" provision for projections that are not knowingly false, or that have been qualified by "meaningful cautionary language."[23] That makes it very difficult for plaintiffs to bring lawsuits based on predictions about the company's future that have not come true, the archetypal "fraud by hindsight" claim.

The second barrier has a broader scope. The PSLRA imposes a rigorous pleading standard, which requires plaintiffs to specify in their complaint each statement alleged to have been misleading and the reasons why the statement is misleading. The pleading standard also requires plaintiffs to state with particularity facts giving rise to a "strong inference" that the defendant acted with "the required state of mind."[24] Those rules are applied by the judge reviewing the complaint before any discovery has been conducted. Thus, the pleading standard established by the PSLRA makes the complaint the critical document in the case—if the plaintiff cannot make out a credible case of fraud when he files his suit, he cannot proceed with his claims. Consequently, judges must play a much more significant role in deciding the merits of the lawsuit than they typically do.

Plaintiffs are left without the usual access to discovery to bolster their complaint. All discovery is stayed during the pendency of any motion to dismiss, unless the court finds that discovery is necessary to preserve evidence or prevent undue prejudice.[25] That combination of the pleading standard and the discovery stay is designed to weed out nonmeritorious actions at an early stage and low cost. Early dismissal with no discovery greatly reduces the expense to corporations forced to defend such suits, thereby limiting the settlement value of weak cases.

The PSLRA further reduces the coercive threat of securities suits by eliminating securities fraud as the basis for a civil racketeering under the Racketeer Influenced and Corrupt Organization Act of 1970 (RICO), with its potential for treble damages. The PSLRA also limits the liability of certain "peripheral" defendants. The act adopts proportionate, rather than joint and several, liability for defendants who are not found to have knowingly violated the securities laws.[26] That protection is most important for secondary defendants, such as accountants, lawyers, and investment bankers, who may be implicated in fraud by corporate defendants. If those secondary defendants can show that they did not know of the fraud, their liability exposure will be limited substantially.

EFFECT OF THE PSLRA

The PSLRA has been on the books for eight years now, enough time to shed some light on how it has changed corporate disclosure. There is some evidence that the safe harbor for forward-looking statements has encouraged issuers to be more forthcoming.[27] That begins to correct one of the more perverse results of securities fraud class actions, the chilling of corporate speech caused by fear of lawsuits.

The central goal of the PSLRA, however, was to alter practice in securities fraud class actions, and in that regard the law clearly has had a substantial impact. The process by which lead plaintiffs are selected has become reasonably settled, and after a slow start, institutional investors are now starting to step forward in greater numbers to take charge of securities fraud class actions. Although the lead plaintiff provision still awaits systematic study, there is anecdotal evidence that it is now beginning to have an effect on attorneys' fees.[28] If that trend continues, the introduction of a vigorous representative for plaintiffs-shareholders promises to benefit investors by reducing the cost of class actions.

The more fundamental question, however, is whether the PSLRA has discouraged frivolous suits. In that regard, the news is somewhat mixed. Courts have been vigilant in enforcing the PSLRA's discovery stay. On the other hand, courts appear to be ignoring the provision of the PSLRA targeted most directly at frivolous actions, the mandatory sanctions inquiry for complaints that have been dismissed. As a result, plaintiffs' lawyers continue to face no real sanction for sloppy investigation before filing suit or fabricating "facts" to allege in their complaint.

Fortunately, the PSLRA's sanctions inquiry requirement is not the law's only constraint on frivolous actions. The PSLRA's most important screen for meritless suits is the strong inference pleading standard that requires particularized allegations of fraud in the complaint. There are now hundreds of judicial opinions interpreting the pleading standard, so there is reason to think that provision is influencing the filing decisions of plaintiffs' lawyers and the settlements that they are able to obtain. Here are summaries of the few empirical studies to date focusing on the impact of the PSLRA on filing and settlement, as well as the stock market's reaction to the law.

FILINGS AND SETTLEMENTS

The PSLRA has not reduced the number of securities class actions being filed. In fact, the average number of suits is up nearly 25 percent from pre-PSLRA levels,[29] so it does not appear that the PSLRA has discouraged plaintiffs' lawyers from filing suit. That increase in filings does not necessarily translate to greater liability exposure for corporations. There is also evidence that the PSLRA has resulted in a higher percentage of cases being dismissed. A study by National Economics Research Associates reports that the dismissal rate for securities fraud class actions has roughly doubled since the passage of the PSLRA, so nearly a quarter of all suits are now dismissed.[30] If weaker lawsuits are dismissed at an early stage before companies must bear the cost of discovery, then companies will bear minimal expense from those suits, although they may still suffer some reputational harm.

The twin findings of more filings and more dismissals are seemingly contradictory. Why would plaintiffs' lawyers waste time and effort filing suits that are likely to be dismissed? Plaintiffs' lawyers argue that the upsurge in filings simply reflects a massive expansion in the amount of fraud being committed. The plaintiffs' bar can find support for their position in concerns expressed by the SEC and other policy makers about the quality of financial reporting. The only difference post-PSLRA, say the lawyers, is that meritorious suits are now being dismissed.

An alternative explanation for the surge in filings is that the plaintiffs' lawyers are incapable of sorting fraud from misjudgment or bad luck on the basis of the information available to them. Consequently, they sue on the basis of bad news that may reflect either. If they can withstand the defendant's inevitable motion to dismiss, they can gain access to discovery of the corporation's internal documents in an attempt to determine whether there has been fraud. A higher dismissal rate means that plaintiffs' lawyers need to file more suits in hopes that a reasonable number will make it through to discovery. If plaintiffs' lawyers are simply filing more suits in the hope that a few will "stick," the PSLRA may not have achieved its goal of discouraging frivolous class actions. But if those frivolous actions are quickly dismissed, the costs of defending them are greatly diminished. Moreover, the higher dismissal rate suggests that the sanctions that flow from securities fraud class actions are more precisely targeted—that is, weaker suits are more often dismissed. If only strong claims lead to settlements, class actions are producing more cost-effective deterrence.

Deterrence is determined not only by the precision but also by the magnitude of sanctions. Studies have found that monetary settlements are higher for post-PSLRA cases, but they are lower when expressed as a percentage of potential damages.[31] If securities fraud class action settlements now include a higher percentage of meritorious claims (as a result of the higher dismissal rate), then higher absolute sanctions are appropriate. The fact that monetary settlements may be a lower percentage of potential damages is not a cause for concern. Higher stock prices and more trading lead to higher potential damages, so it is no surprise that damages are greater after 1995 because of rising stock prices and increased trading during that time. Given that potential damages are unrelated to the social harm stemming from fraud on the market, it is not essential from a deterrence perspective that recoveries correspond to those damages.

The available evidence also shows that suits naming accountants and underwriters have led to greater settlements than suits that do not name them, both before and after the PSLRA was adopted, suggesting that the PSLRA has not exempted secondary defendants from paying damages. It is more difficult to name secondary actors as defendants, but when the plaintiffs provide evidence that ties those defendants to the fraud, they are being forced to pay.

THE STOCK MARKET'S RESPONSE

One method of assessing the PSLRA's impact is by measuring the stock market's reaction to the law. That reaction provides important evidence on the effect of the PSLRA because shareholders are the intended beneficiaries of the deterrence produced by securities fraud class actions. Shareholders suffer, however, if firms are subjected to frivolous suits that impose costs but do little to deter fraud. That trade-off between the costs and benefits of class actions should be reflected in shareholders' valuations of firms subject to the PSLRA.

Two stock market reactions are relevant to an assessment of the PSLRA's effect. The first is investors' reaction to Congress's override of President Clinton's veto of the PSLRA. Two studies found that the enactment of the PSLRA was wealth increasing, on average, for shareholders in high-technology firms (a favorite target of the class action bar).[32] Specifically, there was a significant negative market reaction to the rumors of President Clinton's veto, followed by a significant positive reaction to the override. Firms at the highest risk of being sued enjoyed the strongest positive reaction. Those findings suggest that shareholders generally believed that they would benefit from the PSLRA's restrictions on private securities litigation.

The second relevant finding from the stock market came in response to a decision by the U.S. Court of Appeals for the Ninth Circuit. The Ninth Circuit, which encompasses Silicon Valley, surprised many observers with its *Silicon Graphics* decision interpreting the PSLRA's requirements for pleading a securities fraud complaint. Prior to the PSLRA, the Ninth Circuit had the least stringent requirements for pleading fraud of all circuit courts. The Ninth Circuit's interpretation in *Silicon Graphics*, by contrast, is the most stringent of any circuit, requiring plaintiffs to allege facts that would show the defendants were "deliberately reckless" in making the misrepresentation that gave rise to the fraud claim.[33] Not surprisingly, courts that have adopted that more stringent standard are more likely to dismiss lawsuits.[34]

The tougher pleading standard allows a court to dismiss fraud suits at an early stage if the court deems they lack merit, but it also increases the risk that a court will dismiss meritorious suits. If cases of genuine fraud were dismissed or never filed, deterrence would be undermined. Marilyn Johnson, Karen Nelson, and I did a study of the stock market's reaction to the *Silicon Graphics* decision for a sample of high-technology companies. We found a positive market reaction to the decision, particularly for firms headquartered in the Ninth Circuit and those at greatest risk of being sued in a securities class action.[35]

Those results relating to the enactment and interpretation of the PSLRA bolster the conclusion that market participants believed that its restrictions on private securities litigation generally benefited shareholders of high-technology firms. That reaction presumably reflects an assessment by those participants that the

PSLRA discourages the filing of nonmeritorious claims, without unduly chilling meritorious claims and the deterrent benefits that they may produce. That conclusion comes, however, with a caveat: The assessment of investors may have been fueled by popular perceptions and anecdotal evidence. Market participants may not have had the information or expertise to assess whether the PSLRA had its desired effect of reducing nonmeritorious claims.

DO THE MERITS MATTER MORE?

Although market reactions are instructive, the more fundamental question is whether the PSLRA has achieved its central goal, the deterrence of frivolous lawsuits. As noted above, the overall number of suits has not declined, despite the barriers to class actions erected by the PSLRA. After a brief initial dip, the number of securities fraud class actions has returned to, and even exceeded, its pre-PSLRA level. On its face, the increase in filings suggests that the PSLRA may have done little to discourage the filing of frivolous suits. It is worth noting in this regard, however, that it appears that a smaller percentage of cases is being filed in the Ninth Circuit subsequent to the *Silicon Graphics* decision, suggesting that the stringent standard adopted there has discouraged some suits.[36]

A second study that I did with Johnson and Nelson provides more direct evidence on whether the PSLRA has discouraged frivolous suits. Once again studying a sample of high-tech companies, we found that factors relating to the likelihood of fraud—principally restatements of accounting results and insider trading—play a more important role in explaining the incidence, the type of allegations, and the resolution of class actions post-PSLRA. Factors relating to fraud were generally insignificant before the passage of the PSLRA. Factors relating to damages (such as share turnover and market capitalization), not surprisingly, have been important in explaining class actions both before and after the passage of the PSLRA. Damages factors, although unlikely to correlate with fraud, will always play a role in determining the incidence of suit because greater potential damages claims correlate with greater attorneys' fees. Nonetheless, the results show a closer relation between factors related to fraud and securities class actions after the passage of the PSLRA, suggesting that Congress achieved at least part of its objective in enacting the law.

In sum, the empirical evidence produced to date suggests that the PSLRA has made the plaintiffs' bar work harder for a living. The PSLRA discourages plaintiffs' lawyers from using lawsuits to fish for evidence. Today, complaints are better drafted, with stronger support for allegations of fraud. Marginal cases are more likely to be dismissed and less likely to lead to a settlement. In sum, the PSLRA has made the merits matter more to attorneys considering a suit.

SHOULD THE PSLRA BE REPEALED?

The evidence above suggests that the PSLRA has reduced the costs to corporate issuers of defending meritless class actions and encouraged plaintiffs' lawyers to target their lawsuits more precisely. Despite that evidence, calls for the repeal of securities fraud class action reform have been growing in the wake of revelations of fraud at a number of high-profile companies.

DID THE PSLRA CAUSE A FRAUD EPIDEMIC?

The impetus for calls to repeal the PSLRA is easy to understand. A spate of accounting and corporate governance scandals followed shortly after the passage of a law that made it more difficult to sue for fraud. And it's not just the fraud headlines that support this impulse—the number of restatements of accounting results has generally been on the rise.[37] Some use that chronology to imply a causal relation between the PSLRA and corporate fraud.

That logic is based on publicity rather than sound statistical inference. After a flurry of headlines trumpeting corporate wrongdoing, it is easy to be misled by a small number of high-profile cases, but the Enrons and WorldComs are not representative of America's corporations. The United States has more than fifteen thousand public companies, and only a handful of them have been implicated in wrongdoing. Fraud will always be with us, and it would be a mistake to conclude from what may be little more than a statistically insignificant blip that we are headed toward a financial apocalypse. The increased number of restatements is also misleading. Many of those restatements are the result of shifts by the SEC in interpreting accounting rules. A company's failure to anticipate a change in the SEC's position does not equate to fraud.

We should also remember the other factors in the financial environment that helped lead to the corporate scandals. Most conspicuous was the public's voracious appetite for any business concept, no matter how shaky, that had some connection to the Internet. Companies with actual earnings became passé, rendering quaint guideposts such as price-to-earnings ratios irrelevant. We are more sober now but still reluctant to admit that we were taken in by the hysteria for all things high tech—just like the now-failed whiz kids who dreamed of a business revolution.

Another ingredient was the popularization of stock options at the expense of more traditional forms of compensation, such as cash. The stock option frenzy of the late 1990s was driven in part by companies with good ideas, but little cash, that needed to attract talented employees. But that frenzy was also driven by an excise tax that Congress imposed on "excessive" executive compensation in 1993—yet another example of the law of unintended consequences.[38] The excise tax excluded "incentive" compensation, so not surprisingly, compensation consultants found a way to drive a Mack truck through that loophole. The result was an enormous spike in the use of stock options, with a corresponding motivation to keep those options "in the money." For the options to be lucrative, the current price of the stock had to exceed the exercise price of the option. And if accounting results had to be massaged a little to inflate the stock price, what was the harm? We have now found out what the harm was—a dramatic loss in investor confidence. Stock options are a useful component of many compensation packages, helping to align managers' and investors' interests, but they are no panacea. Whatever the relative merits of options and cash compensation, there is certainly no reason for Congress to put its fat thumb on the scale in favor of one over the other.

PROPOSED REFORMS

A number of bills were introduced in Congress during 2002 aimed at undoing securities class-action reform. Not surprisingly, given Arthur Andersen's role in the demise of Enron, accountants were the central target. Those bills include proposals to bring back joint and several liability for secondary defendants and restore aiding-and-abetting liability and racketeering liability under RICO for securities violations.[39] Another proposal would eliminate the discovery stay if auditors were named as defendants, allowing the plaintiffs' attorney immediate access to the accountants' work papers.[40]

Is diminished liability for secondary defendants a real concern? Hardly. The reputational sanction for complicity in fraud is severe, as Andersen's bankruptcy filing after its conviction for obstruction of justice shows. Professionals such as accountants are in the business of renting their reputation to corporations. Once the accountants lose their reputation for integrity, they have nothing left to sell. The market sanction for misbehavior is swifter and surer than any punishment that Congress is likely to devise.

Moreover, the PSLRA does not let secondary defendants off scot-free. Proportionate liability does not mean that accountants, lawyers, and underwriters are immune from liability. It only means that they are responsible only for the incremental harm caused by their participation in the fraud. Prior to the PSLRA, plaintiffs' lawyers routinely went after accountants, lawyers, and underwriters, who under joint and several liability could be forced to pay the entire judgment, even if their culpability for the fraud was slight. Under the PSLRA, defendants who are only tangentially involved in the fraud will not face potentially bankrupting liability. But secondary defendants who actively participate in the fraud get no such relief. Under the PSLRA, defendants are only entitled to the protection of proportionate liability when they lack knowledge of the fraud. Even then they can be required to pay an additional 50 percent above the damages based on their fault if the issuer is insolvent. Proportionate liability offers no protection at all for secondary defendants if a jury concludes that they were knee-deep in the fraud. Ernst & Young no doubt took that possibility into account when it paid $335 million to settle the lawsuit against it resulting from the accounting scandal at Cendant. Accountants must still consider the risk of a securities fraud class action when a client tries to pressure them into acquiescing in a dubious interpretation of accounting principles.

Another proposal relating to accountants would reverse the Supreme Court's 1994 *Central Bank* decision, which eliminated "aiding-and-abetting" liability for securities fraud.[41] Congress considered reversing *Central Bank* when it was debating the PSLRA, but it instead concluded that only the SEC should be authorized to pursue individuals who have facilitated but not perpetrated securities fraud.[42] A bill was introduced to extend that authority to private litigants. The argument was that expanded liability would encourage accountants and lawyers to be more vigorous "gatekeepers," denying defrauders access to the financial markets. Without audited financial statements and offering documents produced by accountants and lawyers, defrauders would not be able to sell securities at all.

As noted above, secondary defendants do not enjoy immunity from liability under current law. If they make misrepresentations upon which investors rely (such as certifying false financial statements), secondary defendants can and will be held liable. *Central Bank* only excludes liability when secondary defendants have made no false statement themselves. That is hardly a startling principle. The basic purpose of securities law is to protect investors who reasonably rely on information. If the accountant or lawyer has made no statement, then investors have not relied on that person in making their investment decision. On the other hand, if the secondary defendants have induced reliance by investors, they will be on the hook, as the recent decision by the trial judge in the Enron class action confirmed.[43]

Aiding-and-abetting liability transforms the law of fraud from a sanction for misleading people into a sanction for failing to uncover fraud committed by others. That might make sense if we thought it would be proper to transform professionals into quasi-fraud police. But there are good reasons why audits of public companies are not full-scale investigations for fraud. A forensic audit to uncover fraud requires an enormous investment of time and resources and, therefore, costs a multiple of the typical charge for an annual audit. A forensic audit is a huge waste for the overwhelming majority of public companies that are not engaged in fraud. And the cost of training lawyers to uncover fraud would be staggering—the average corporate lawyer is doing well to understand the transactions that she is asked to document, not to mention looking behind them for nefarious purposes. Uncovering fraud requires specialized expertise that can be developed only through extensive and expensive training.

The balance struck by the PSLRA is a sensible compromise. The SEC has the authority to pursue secondary defendants with knowledge of the fraud. Because the commission has more fraud to pursue than it has time or manpower, we can be confident that the agency will not abuse its aiding-and-abetting authority. Facing the knowledge standard, the SEC will pursue secondary defendants only when there is clear evidence of wrongdoing. For the plaintiffs' bar, by contrast, aiding-and-abetting authority is one more weapon with which to shake down a settlement from a deep pocket.

The exclusion of securities fraud from RICO's civil provisions was endorsed at the time of enactment even by then SEC chairman Arthur Levitt, no friend of defrauders. That exclusion prevents plaintiffs' attorneys from using the *in terrorem* threat of treble damages as a means of coercing settlements from defendants. Given that potential damages are already excessive under the damages measure of the securities laws, the added threat of civil RICO served no useful purpose. More important, it is specious to suggest that anyone who is not deterred by the prospect of billions of dollars in damages is going to be deterred by trebling those damages under RICO. Bankrupt is bankrupt.

The proposal to eliminate the discovery stay for auditors' work papers would essentially repeal the discovery stay altogether. Access to the work papers, with all of the details that they provide about a company's business, not only compromises corporate confidentiality, it also ensures that auditors will be routinely named as defendants so that plaintiffs' lawyers can go back to their old practice of using discovery as a "fishing expedition" for fraud. Whether or not the work papers reveal fraud, they will allow the plaintiffs' lawyers to amend their complaint and plead sufficient detail to get past a motion to dismiss. That will bring the coercive threat of discovery against the company and its officers to bear in settlement negotiations. The PSLRA's barriers against nuisance suits, which have greatly reduced the expense of defending such actions, would be completely eroded.

Another bill would repeal the Securities Litigation Uniform Standards Act,[44] a 1998 supplement to the PSLRA. Plaintiffs' lawyers initially responded to the restrictions that the PSLRA imposes on federal securities class actions by filing their suits in state court, where the PSLRA does not apply. Congress closed that loophole in 1998 by preempting class actions based on state securities fraud law for certain classes of securities. Undoing that preemption would reverse the improvements in securities fraud class action procedures that have been produced by the PSLRA.

A final proposal calls for lowering the standard required for fraud under the securities laws from scienter, which means actual knowledge or at least a reckless disregard for the truth, to negligence, which translates to "would a reasonable person have believed that he was telling the truth?" The negligence standard has obvious appeal—we're all reasonable people, aren't we?—but there are good reasons for using scienter instead. The scienter requirement is the chief bulwark against "fraud by hindsight," the temptation to conclude that a defendant accused of fraud must have known that the bad thing was going to happen at the time of his statements because the bad thing eventually did happen.

Although it may be difficult for the average juror to believe, it is often true that the chief executive officer and the board did not know that a fraud was being committed. Public corporations cannot always manage information flows among multiple divisions and elaborate management hierarchies. The stricter standard counteracts those biases by requiring strong evidence of an intentional misstatement before a defendant can be held liable for fraud. If there is evidence in corporate documents or from other employees that the defendant did know the truth at the time of the misstatements, the jury is free to ignore the defendant's denials of knowledge. Claims by corporate officers that "they didn't know" of the fraud are a risky litigation strategy.

A BETTER ALTERNATIVE

Instead of rolling back securities fraud class action reform, Congress should consider new reforms that would target the deterrent effect of securities fraud class actions where that would do the most good. One of the salutary developments in securities fraud litigation to come out of the recent spate of accounting scandals has been the targeting of corporate officers in fraud suits. Traditionally, class action settlements have not included a contribution from corporate officers individually. Plaintiffs' lawyers forgo that source of recovery because they can reach a settlement much more quickly if they do not insist on a contribution from the individual defendants. The only reason that officers and directors are named is to improve the plaintiffs' lawyer's bargaining position.

Faced with a substantial number of bankrupt companies with no assets to pursue, however, the class action bar has turned its sights on the individuals who are actually culpable for the fraud. Some of the officers were able to abandon ship with substantial gains by cashing out stock options before the collapse. When Al Dunlap, the former CEO of Sunbeam Corporation, recently was forced to contribute to the settlement in the class action arising out of that firm's bankruptcy, it was a "man bites dog" story for people familiar with securities fraud class actions. But the Dunlap story could become a trend. Those stock option millions are a tempting target for plaintiffs' lawyers stymied by bankrupt corporate issuers.

Deterrence is maximized by sanctioning the person who is most at fault for the fraud. Accordingly, the pursuit of culpable corporate officers should not be limited to cases involving bankrupt firms. Congress can encourage plaintiffs' lawyers to go after the real wrongdoers in every fraud case by altering the damages remedy for Rule 10b-5 fraud on the market cases. The current rule holds corporations responsible for the entire loss of all of the shareholders who paid too much for their shares as a result of fraudulent misrepresentations. But that measure exaggerates the social harm caused by fraud on the market, because it fails to account for the gains of equally innocent shareholders who sold at the inflated price. In most cases, the losses and gains will be a wash for shareholders in the aggregate, even though some individual shareholders will have suffered substantial losses.

A better damages rule would focus on deterrence rather than compensation. Instead of making corporations liable for all losses resulting from misstatements, we should instead force defendants to disgorge their gains (or expected gains, for those who fail in their scheme) from the fraud. So, if a corporation were issuing securities at the time it was distorting the market price of its stock, it would be required to disgorge the amount by which it inflated the price of the securities that it sold to the investors who bought them. In most fraud on the market cases, however, the corporation has not benefited from the misrepresentation that is the basis of the class action. Indeed, the corporation is usually the *victim* of the fraud. The corporation is victimized when an executive is awarded a bonus that is undeserved because he creates the appearance of having met the target stock price. The corporation is also victimized when a chief executive officer keeps his job for a bit longer because he creates the appearance of adequate performance. The proper remedy in such cases is for the executive to return the bonus or salary earned from the fraud to the corporation. If the executive benefits from the fraud by cashing out stock options at an inflated price, those profits can be paid over to the corporation. And for egregious cases, civil sanctions imposed by the SEC and criminal prosecution by the Justice Department will always be available.

The objective here should be to ensure that fraud does not pay. The recently enacted SOA makes a beginning toward making executives pay by requiring them to reimburse the corporation for any incentive compensation (as well as profits from any stock sales) if the corporation is required to restate its financial results.[45] The big money for plaintiffs' attorneys, however, remains in pursuing the corporation and its insurers. If we took away the corporation's exposure when it did not benefit from the fraud, we would substantially increase the attorneys' incentive to pursue the executives responsible for the fraud.

CONCLUSION

The call to roll back securities litigation reform comes as no surprise in the wake of a series of high-profile scandals at major public corporations and investment banks. The intuitive link between the PSLRA's barriers to lawsuits and the misbehavior that has unfolded in corporate boardrooms and financial markets is all too easy to make. Unfortunately, public policy is too frequently driven by such intuitions based on the latest headlines rather than hard evidence.

In this case, the hard evidence does not support the call to repeal the PSLRA. Securities fraud class actions are being filed at a record pace. The PLSRA has not discouraged the filing of lawsuits. Although a higher percentage of those suits is being dismissed, the ones that survive lead to larger settlements. That result should come as no surprise because the PSLRA demands stronger evidence from plaintiffs' attorneys before they can drag defendants through the expense of defending a securities fraud class action. Cases that meet that tougher standard are worth more in settlement negotiations.

The combination of higher settlements and fewer cases suggests that securities fraud class actions are now doing a better job of deterring fraud. Current proposals to repeal securities fraud class actions would give plaintiffs' lawyers another weapon with which to coerce settlements. But the wide net those proposals would cast offers little in the way of enhanced deterrence. Strong sanctions are appropriate for defrauders, but we must ensure that those sanctions are imposed only on culpable parties. Honest businesspeople and professionals need to be protected against threats intended solely to generate larger settlements and attorneys' fees. Investors are the intended beneficiaries of the deterrence produced by securities fraud class actions, but they also bear the costs when class actions get out of control. Investors bear those costs through higher insurance premiums for directors and officers insurance, as well as higher fees that accountants, lawyers, and investment bankers will charge if they face unjustified litigation risk.

The PSLRA struck a balance between the goal of deterrence and the costs that securities fraud class actions impose on investors. The evidence to date suggests that the balance struck was a reasonable one. Congress will not be doing investors a favor if it opens the door to frivolous class action lawsuits and coercive settlements in its frenzy to get tough on corporate wrongdoers.

NOTES

1. Cabro, Lori, "I Told You So," *CFO* 63, September 2002, p. 67 (interviewing Lerach).

2. Labaton, Stephen, "Enron Scandal Shocks Even Those Who Helped It Along," *New York Times*, February 3, 2002.

3. Patrick Leahy, chairman, Senate Judiciary Committee, Statement at Senate Hearing on Accountability Issues: Lessons Learned from Enron's Fall, February 6, 2002.

4. Mahoney, Paul G., "Precaution Costs and the Law of Fraud in Impersonal Markets," *Virginia Law Review* 78, 1992, p. 623.

5. Section 11 of the Securities Act, 15 U.S.C.A. § 77k, makes issuers strictly liable for misstatements in a registration statement for a public offering. From 1999 to 2000, approximately 14 percent of securities litigation cases involved allegations of violations of the 1933 Securities Act that regulates the offering of securities. See PricewaterhouseCoopers, LLP, "2001 Securities Litigation Study." www.10b5.com/2001SecuritiesLitigationStudy.pdf.

6. 17 C.F.R. § 240.10b-5.

7. There could, of course, be a decline in share price attributable to greater uncertainty in valuing the company because of the loss of credibility. That decline, however,

is likely to be insignificant relative to the price drop from artificially inflated levels when the fraud is revealed.

8. "Cendant Corp. Agrees to Record Payment to Settle All Financial Fraud Allegations," *Securities Regulation & Law Reporter* 31, December 13, 1999, p. 1618.

9. *Blue Chip Stamps v. Manor Drug Stores*, 421 U.S. 723, 742–743 (1975).

10. Pritchard, A. C., "Markets as Monitors: A Proposal to Replace Class Actions with Exchanges as Securities Fraud Monitors," *Virginia Law Review* 85, 1999, p. 925.

11. A stock option is said to be "in the money" when the exercise or strike price is equal to or greater than the stock price.

12. S. Rep. no. 104-98, at 6 (1995).

13. H.R. Rep. no. 104-50, at 17 (1995).

14. S. Rep. no. 104-98.

15. The provision is unusual in that Congress based it on a proposal by two law professors. See Elliot J. Weiss and John S. Beckerman, "Let the Money Do the Monitoring: How Institutional Investors Can Reduce Agency Costs in Securities Class Actions," *Yale Law Journal* 104, 1995, p. 2053.

16. H.R. Rep. no. 104-50, at 34 (1995).

17. H.R. Rep. no. 104-50, at 16, 17.

18. S. Rep. no. 104-98, at 14.

19. H.R. Rep. no. 104-50, at 17.

20. S. Rep. no. 104-98, at 5.

21. S. Rep. no. 104-98, at 5.

22. H.R. Conf. Rep. no. 104-369, at 37–38 (1995).

23. 15 U.S.C.A. § 78u-5(c)(1).

24. 15 U.S.C.A. § 78u-4(b)(1), (2).

25. 15 U.S.C. § 78u-4(b)(3).

26. 15 U.S.C. § 78u-4(g)(2)(B).

27. Johnson, Marilyn F. et al., "The Impact of Securities Litigation Reform on the Disclosure of Forward-Looking Information by High Technology Firms," *Journal of Accounting Research* 39, 2001, p. 297.

28. For example, the University of California was able to negotiate a fee of less than 10 percent in the litigation against Enron. Maureen Milford, "UC Takes Charge of Enron Suit," *National Law Journal*, March 4, 2002, p. A15.

29. Perino, Michael A., "Did the Private Securities Litigation Reform Act Work?" *University of Illinois Law Review*, 2003.

30. Foster, Todd S. et al., "Trends in Securities Litigation and the Impact of the PSLRA," National Economic Research Associates, 1999, unpublished manuscript in author's files.

31. Simmons, Laura E., "Securities Lawsuits: Settlement Statistics for Post-Reform Act Cases," Cornerstone Research, 1999, unpublished manuscript in author's files; and Mukesh Baja et al., "Securities Class Action Settlements: An Empirical Analysis," Law and Economics Consulting Group, 2000, unpublished manuscript in author's files.

32. Johnson, Marilyn F. et al., "Shareholder Wealth Effects of the Private Securities Litigation Reform Act of 1995," *Review of Accounting Studies* 5, 2000, p. 217; and D. Katherine Spiess and Paula A. Tkac, "The Private Securities Litigation Reform Act

of 1995: The Stock Market Casts Its Vote," *Managerial and Decision Economics* 18, 1997, p. 545.

33. *In re Silicon Graphics Inc. Sec. Litig.*, 183 F.3d 970 (9th Cir. 1999).

34. Grundfest, Joseph A. and A. C. Pritchard, "Statutes with Multiple Personality Disorders: The Value of Ambiguity in Statutory Design and Interpretation," *Stanford Law Review* 54, 2002, p. 629.

35. Johnson, Marilyn F. et al, "*In re Silicon Graphics Inc.*: Shareholder Wealth Effects Resulting from the Interpretation of the Private Securities Litigation Reform Act's Pleading Standard," *Southern California Law Review* 73, 2000, p. 773.

36. Perino, "Did the Private Securities Litigation Reform Act Work?".

37. Financial Executives Institute, "Quantitative Measures of the Quality of Financial Reporting," 2001, unpublished manuscript in author's files.

38. 26 U.S.C. § 162.

39. Aiding-and-abetting liability targets professionals who facilitate fraud committed by others. Racketeering liability under the RICO statute provides for treble damages for defendants found to have engaged in a pattern of criminal activity. That criminal activity need not have led to a criminal prosecution, nor must it be proved beyond a reasonable doubt. As a consequence, ordinary business torts can be the basis for a racketeering claim. The proposal to restore joint-and-several liability and aiding-and-abetting liability can be found in Sections 12(a) and 14 of the Comprehensive Investor Protection Act of 2002 (H.R. 3818) introduced by former representative John LaFalce (D-N.Y.). In the Senate, Sen. Richard Shelby (R-Ala.) introduced the Investor Protection Act of 2002 (S. 1933) that contained those same provisions and that would have repealed the Securities Litigation Uniform Standards Act of 1998. RICO liability would have been restored by the Securities Fraud Prevention Act of 2002 (H.R. 3644), introduced by Rep. John Conyers Jr. (D-Mich.).

40. This proposal can be found in section 12(e) of the Comprehensive Investor Protection Act of 2002.

41. *Central Bank of Denver v. First Central Bank of Denver*, 511 U.S. 164 (1994).

42. 15 U.S.C. § 78t (e).

43. *In re Enron Corporation Securities, Derivative & ERISA Litigation*, 2002 WL 31854963 (S.D. Tex.).

44. Pub. L. no. 105-353, 112 Stat. 3227 (1998).

45. Pub. L. no. 107-204, § 304 (July 30, 2002).

• *11* •

The Business Press as a Corporate Monitor: How the *Wall Street Journal* and *Fortune* Covered Enron

Paul H. Weaver

*N*ews coverage of the rise and fall of the Enron Corporation exhibits three distinct patterns, each corresponding to a phase of the company's history and a distinctive mode of normal journalism.

PHASE ONE

In the first phase, which ran into 2000, Enron was a new company on the rise— making an increasingly stellar record of innovation, acquisition, growth, rising stock price, and appreciating market capitalization. In the *Wall Street Journal* and *Fortune*, news coverage of this period of Enron's history faithfully reflected the positive achievements as they were announced by the company, usually in the standard reporting formats required by the Securities and Exchange Commission (SEC). The actual amount of coverage was quite modest, reflecting Enron's short history and, at the beginning, relatively low profile. The tone of the coverage was favorable but restrained, reflecting the company's initial obscurity and the unbroken string of rising quarterly revenue, profit, and growth reports. This was the dominant pattern of news coverage until the fall of 2000.

This broadly favorable pattern was both reflective of the reality of the company's affairs and typical of the news media in America. If, as one definition has it, journalism is criticism of the moment at the moment, the version of the genre that we call news is defined by its focus on current information about current events, especially as announced and characterized by official institutions. News, as a result, often coincides with the official account of an event, and news workers typically have a conscious or unconscious orientation to the organizations that are the sources and subjects of their reporting.

147

Toward the end of this long initial phase of news coverage, the Enron story intensified as the underlying trends were revealed. Ongoing growth, quarter after quarter, eventually elevated the company to the top rank of American business; by 2001 Enron had risen to seventh place on the *Fortune* 500 list of the largest U.S. industrial corporations. The pace of innovation accelerated as Enron redefined itself as an advocate of deregulation and a maker of markets in almost any sort of product, and it mounted major creative forays into industries ranging from old ones like municipal water provision to new ones such as telecommunications bandwidth. As the securities markets helped send Enron's stock to new peaks of speculative energy and dollar value, the good-news focus of Enron coverage became ever more laudatory. The *Journal* began to run profiles of the dazzlingly successful company and its senior executives. In *Fortune*, the annual lists of "most innovative" and "most admired" companies gave more and more prominent attention to Enron, which ranked at the top of *Fortune*'s "most innovative" hierarchy six years in a row through the winter of 2001.

Also intensifying the original Enron story was an increasingly enthusiastic suspension of disbelief on the part of the journalists covering the company. A typical case in point was the quarterly earnings news story of April 13, 2000, by *Wall Street Journal* staff reporter Rebecca Smith entitled, "Enron Net Nearly Tripled in 1st Period, Beating Estimate, as Revenue Rose 72%." After several paragraphs summarizing the statistics of Enron's latest quarter, Smith quoted an ecstatic observer on the meaning of it all: "'The real story isn't the earnings,' said utilities analyst David Fleisher at Goldman Sachs & Co. 'It's what lies ahead. This isn't your father's natural-gas company.'" Smith went on to describe the growth of Enron's online energy trading business and the new market it was making in broadband capacity. "It's absolutely astounding," she quoted Enron president Jeff Skilling as gloating. "It feels like we're being swamped with new opportunities."

In fact, however, Smith's story and the corporate quarter it purported to describe were a Potemkin village of contrived illusions and ignored realities. Enron was using an accounting method by which the company could attribute to some yet unrealized future revenues and profits more or less whatever present value it chose to. At the same time, Enron was concealing significant amounts of debt in legally dubious unconsolidated entities. Analysts covering Enron at the big, vertically integrated financial services firms like Goldman Sachs had been at least manipulated, if not flat-out corrupted, by Enron's systematic efforts to award and deny its investment banking business on the basis of how favorably or unfavorably the firm's analysts rated Enron stock. As a result, prevailing opinion among the leading analysts was far more favorable than hard business realities warranted. In fact, Enron's profits in its online energy trading business were collapsing as competitors moved in, cut prices, and eroded margins. Its entry into the already overexpanded and unprofitable bandwidth industry was not the "astounding" new growth and profit opportunity Smith let Skilling tout in her copy, but an elementary strategic error for which the company was already paying dearly in increased debt load and decreased real profits and cash flow.

If Smith's story misrepresented the hidden reality of Enron's current economic condition, at least it preserved the appearance and still honored the ideal of objective news writing. In *Fortune* that same month, there appeared a story about Enron by senior writer Brian O'Reilly that opened with a passage that abandoned even the pretense of responsible economic analysis in favor of a bizarre rhapsodic fiction:

> Imagine a country-club dinner dance, with a bunch of old fogies and their wives shuffling around halfheartedly to the not-so-stirring sounds of Guy Lombardo and his All-Tuxedo Orchestra. Suddenly young Elvis comes crashing through the skylight, complete with gold-lamé suit, shiny guitar, and gyrating hips. Half the waltzers faint; most of the others get angry or pouty. And a very few decide they like what they hear, tap their feet ... start grabbing new partners, and suddenly are rocking to a very different tune.

In the staid world of regulated utilities and energy companies, Enron Corp. is that gate-crashing Elvis.

PHASE TWO

Amid Enron's self-serving accounting and image making, and the growing unreality that infected news stories about the company's affairs, a limited and initially almost fugitive process of correction set in as some insiders began to balk at the confidence game they were effectively contributing to and as significant new players were drawn into the Enron scene. The news stayed in its generically derivative cooperative relationship to official institutions, and the lion's share of coverage continued to retail the world according to Enron. But alongside this ongoing, dominant pattern there slowly emerged, bit by bit, a second strain of Enron coverage that reflected a very different point of view.

Intriguingly, this second, downbeat story line was launched by Enron itself, in a partial bow to financial disclosure rules that, like any company, it was supposed to observe. On March 30, 2000, Enron filed with the SEC its Form 10-K annual report for 1999. Footnote 16, entitled "Related Party Transactions," described a number of special purpose entities whose operating results were not consolidated into Enron's. The note disclosed, apparently for the first time in public, that two of these entities were named LJM and LJM2, and that these were managed by a senior officer of Enron, whom the note did not name. The text went on to identify a number of transactions with the LJMs, and said that the terms were "representative of terms that would be negotiated with unrelated third parties."

The LJMs, the world learned later, were the tip of the iceberg on which the good ship Enron was soon to founder, and indeed the footnote did limn one troublesome element of the LJM story—the fact that there was a potential for self-dealing on the part of the unnamed senior officer who was managing the LJM partnerships (CFO Andrew Fastow, it later emerged). However, the footnote withheld other, even more negative aspects of these ventures, notably the billions of dollars of Enron liabilities that had been sequestered in the partnerships, away from the corporate balance sheet, and the facts that, notwithstanding accountant Arthur Andersen & Co.'s assurances to the contrary, the LJMs didn't meet the criteria for nonconsolidation, and thus that their debt was wrongfully withheld from the company's balance sheet.

Footnote 16 received no coverage in the press when Enron's annual report was released. Even so, it represents a first step in the plodding journey of discovery and disclosure that was to bring the company's misdeeds to public attention.

Four months later, the secret scandal at Enron slouched a further step toward the limelight thanks to the efforts of Jonathan Weil, a financial reporter in the Dallas bureau of the *Wall Street Journal* who covered Texas company equities and wrote a Texas-oriented stock market column. A source Weil hasn't identified informed him that the accounting practices of Enron and Dynegy, whose stocks were at all-time highs due to soaring electricity and natural gas prices, were less than models of transparency, and that this situation had the makings of an interesting, timely, contrarian stock market story. Weil and his editor agreed, and many weeks later, on September 20, 2000, Weil published the fruits of his research in an important 2,400-word article entitled, "Energy Traders Cite Gains, but Some Math Is Missing," in the weekly *Texas Journal* insert that at the time was distributed to the *Wall Street Journal's* readers in Texas. On the day of publication, Enron's stock closed at $82, down from an all-time high of just over $90, which it had attained a few weeks earlier in the summer while Weil was reporting his story.

The burden of Weil's article was that, unbeknownst to many of the investors who lately had been bidding up energy stock prices, "much of these companies' recent profits constitute unrealized, noncash gains" and that the quality of their earnings was questionable, to say the least. The problem, Weil explained, was the "mark-to-market" method that Enron and others were using in their effort to impute current values to future energy contracts. For future years for which no public market quotes are available, the method amounted to "essentially saying 'trust me,'" according to a Dallas accounting expert whom Weil cited in the story. Added a Michigan State University accounting professor and expert in risk disclosure whom Weil quoted at the end of the fifth paragraph to give a frontal statement of the theme of his article: "There certainly might be great volatility that could cause what now looks like a winning, locked-in gain to not arise sometime in the future." When the scandal eventually broke, of course, these dangers turned out to have been a central source of exaggeration in the picture Enron had been giving of its profitability. Weil's article, and the experts he quoted, had been devastatingly on target, and prescient to boot.

Weil's journalistic coup went largely unnoticed when it appeared. The story was picked up by the Dow Jones Newswires the day it appeared in Texas, but it did not run in the *Journal's* national edition, where the most recent mention of Enron had been another Smith celebration of "blowout earnings" by the "Wall Street darling" earlier in the summer. Editors in New York did express interest in a shortened version of Weil's story, but Weil wasn't interested in "squishing a sixty-five-inch story into twenty inches," as he put it to me, and nothing came of the idea, other than to induce the reporter, who in the meantime had been reassigned to the *Journal's* home office in New York, to keep an eagle eye out for a fresh angle on the dangers of mark-to-market accounting that he could turn into a new assignment. Meanwhile, no other publication picked up on the original story about Enron and Dynegy.

Even so, the article began quietly making waves. On the day it appeared, two major brokerage houses—Merrill Lynch and DLJ—reacted defensively by issuing talking points its sales people and investors could use to dispute Weil's critique. And early the following month, the *Texas Journal* piece came to the attention of James Chanos, a partner of Kynikos Associates, a short seller in New York City. "Kynikos" is the ancient Greek word for cynic, and in the spirit of his firm's name, Chanos, intrigued by what he read, began going through Enron's public filings with a fine-tooth comb.

Chanos, as he later recalled before a House subcommittee, was immediately struck by a number of facts. First, his experience with companies using mark-to-market accounting was that when the future arrives and the prospective profits it has booked fail to materialize, the company is tempted to offset the loss it must then record by doing fresh deals that deliver bigger paper profits now, even though these may well also turn to losses when once again the future finally catches up with the prediction. If the process continues for long enough, the result is a hidden implosion to which the company succumbs when it finally runs out of cash. Second, Chanos calculated Enron's pretax profits to be an underwhelming 7 percent of invested capital, versus a cost of capital in excess of 7 percent and perhaps as high as 9 percent. In other words, Enron wasn't really profitable at all in spite of constantly rising reported profits—which suggested it may have fallen prey to the lethal paper-profit addiction already. Last but not least, Chanos, an experienced reader of corporate filings, made a careful study of footnote 16 and concluded it was undecipherable with respect to the effect on Enron's business results, which in his mind raised another red flag about the company's real condition.

In November, Chanos started shorting Enron shares. Soon he took the further step of encouraging Bethany McLean, a reporter at *Fortune* magazine with whom he was acquainted, to write a story reflecting his negative analysis of the company, which he laid out for her.

McLean was interested, and in February 2001 her cover-listed article, "Is Enron Overpriced?" brought together for the first time in a national news outlet the nascent negativity on Enron. The core of the piece was a skein of statements by a dozen analysts, most identified by name and company, who confessed again and again that although they might be rating Enron a buy in the analytic reports they wrote for investor-customers, they couldn't explain how it made money or what was really going on inside the "black box" of the company's finances. This litany of ignorance (and, since it came from supposed experts publicly rating Enron a buy, hypocrisy) was bolstered by a number of specific critiques that McLean spelled out in her own voice—that Enron had a lackluster return on investment (Chanos's point), that its debt was mushrooming and its cash flow drying up, that it appeared to be liquidating assets, and that it was betting its future on grandiose expansion plans (notably in the no-longer-new broadband industry) that had a dubious, dot-com-ish feel to them.

In midarticle McLean took a lengthy fairness break to quote the denials of Skilling and Fastow, soon to become infamous as architect-beneficiaries of the still-hidden accounting scams. But these passages took little away from her thesis, which by piece's end had amassed genuine intellectual and emotional weight. It would have been a thickheaded reader indeed who came away from the story without at least the shadow of a doubt about the merit of investment in Enron shares at prevailing prices.

On the first trading day after the article officially appeared on newsstands, Enron's stock closed at $75. By the end of *Fortune*'s two-week publication period, it was down to $70.

The McLean article was marred by a curious undertow of emotional resistance to the point it made, however. The lead paragraph, for instance, was not a succinct statement of the thesis, but a rambling, off-message, 250-word rehash of Enron's strengths. Not until the second sentence of the third paragraph did the author finally get around to stating her business, and even then she did so by means of a sidling transition rather than a frontal declaration: "Even owners of the stock aren't uniformly sanguine." Not even when McLean finally had her argument up and running did she manage to give a simple, straight, declarative answer to the question posed by her title, though there could be no doubt about the thrust of her piece.

Compounding this puzzling bashfulness was the even odder way in which the text dealt with a series of events that took place just offstage during the article's gestation. At one point in her reporting, McLean conducted a telephone interview with Skilling. When she began asking pointedly about how Enron makes money, he denounced the queries as "unethical" and abruptly hung up to terminate the interview rather than answer her questions. This extraordinary behavior, which was evidence for McLean's point, was compounded by what happened next. Soon a company damage control team under the leadership of Fastow flew to New York to make an elaborate show of friendly openness. Yet Fastow responded to many of McLean's substantive questions with a polite refusal to comment "for competitive reasons." Most revealing and questionable of all Enron's efforts to subvert McLean's story was the one that unfolded as the article went to press, when Enron's chairman, Kenneth Lay, telephoned *Fortune*'s managing editor, Rik Kirkland, to denounce McLean's piece and urge him to kill it. Kirkland rightly refused to do so, and the story appeared on schedule.

These unusual, suspicious, unintentionally revealing instances of corporate resistance to a legitimate journalistic enterprise lent weight to McLean's thesis, yet she withheld them from the story. The odd silence is compounded by another, equally puzzling silence.

In the passage giving the company's response to the emerging-doubts thesis, McLean reports that Enron officials dismiss all talk about undefined financial weaknesses as propaganda by short sellers trying to drive the stock price down. The knock is a cheap shot that practically begs for a rejoinder that would have underscored the argument for viewing Enron stock as overpriced.

In the first place, McLean might have said, the present article was indeed prompted by a short seller. His name is James Chanos, and he is betting millions of his and his investors' money that Enron's share price is higher than warranted and will soon be lower. ("I would never have thought of looking at Enron if [Chanos] hadn't tipped me off," McLean later told journalism critic Scott Sherman, whose enterprising coverage of the Enron story for the *Columbia Journalism Review* I want to acknowledge.) The fact that the new doubts about Enron have begun to attract serious players on the sell side shows how substantial the questions have become.

And in the second place, McLean might have gone on, the fact that Enron's answer to these doubts is to airily attribute them to short sellers, as if there were something intrinsically wrong or disreputable about shorting as an investment strategy, is evidence that the company's position has become desperate. In fact— contrary to the supposedly pro-market company's hypocritical knock—short selling is a legitimate, benign element of our financial market system. If short sellers are active in the market for Enron's shares, this says something unflattering, not about the new doubts about Enron's share price, but about the heights to which that price has recently risen and the strength of the reasons for thinking it will fall.

McLean's failure to make these points bespeaks a deeper ambivalence, visible in the way the substance of the story diverges from its rhetoric. In substance, this is very much Chanos's story—an account of the overvaluation of Enron's stock, sourced in the evidence and views of a short seller, and aimed at an audience of investors, executives, and others interested in the practical reality of business and stock market affairs. In rhetoric, by contrast, the story belongs to Enron and the larger institutional-corporate world McLean is taking aim at. Thus, the text never once mentions Chanos by name or market specialty even though he is its central source. Instead, McLean imputes to the story a bogus sourcing among Wall Street analysts, who are quoted at length and with an appearance of respect even though McLean's real point is that, with respect to Enron, they have become totally unreliable narrators who say one thing about the company in public and something totally different in private. In a similar vein, the story goes on to quote, without answer, Enron executives' denunciations of the short seller fraternity on whose insights and authority McLean actually depends.

This is a story with divided loyalties and confused identity. It can't decide if it wants to criticize Enron or comfort and defend it. It is torn between a commitment to the reader as a rational and independent actor interested in learning about the widely unperceived dim reality of a prominent stock's condition and prospects, and an opposite commitment, more or less equally intense, to Enron's management and to its apparent concept of corporate communications as an exercise in the manipulation of readers as passive objects, rather than as an effort to connect with them as active, rational, self-reliant subjects. And it bounces back and forth between wildly different notions of what was wrong at Enron. One view—originally identified by Weil, developed by Chanos, and nicely stated at various points by McLean—is that mark-to-market accounting, with its carte blanche to fabricate future revenues, had opened the door to a more or less corrupt (because more or less witting) overstatement of Enron's reported profits. At other points, however, McLean put forth the very different idea that everything at Enron was on the up and up, but that management, for some undefined reason, simply wasn't explaining itself clearly enough, or that the analysts simply hadn't dug deeply enough to give the investing public a clear and reliable picture of the company's inner workings. In the wake of McLean's story, the negative view of Enron gained strength.

In April, Enron senior management made a notable, if inadvertent, disclosure. In the quarterly conference call for financial analysts, Skilling outlined the latest round of record results. Not everyone was impressed. Richard Grubman of Highfields Capital Management, which was shorting Enron at the time, asked why Enron hadn't provided data prior to the phone call. "You're the only financial institution that can't produce a balance sheet or a cash flow statement with their earnings," he complained. "Well, thank you very much," replied the CEO of the seventh-largest industrial corporation in the United States sarcastically. "We appreciate that. Asshole."

It was a stunning breach of decorum indicating an unusual, problematic, possibly guilty sensitivity in Enron top management to tough but fair questions about the company's financial reporting practices. Though there was no coverage by the news media at the time, word of the gaffe quickly made the rounds of the analytic community and in one form or another presumably began filtering out to its clients. That day Enron shares closed at $61—down nine points since the *Fortune* issue carrying McLean's article spent its last day on the newsstands, and one-third below the previous summer's peak price.

The next month an enterprising reporter for TheStreet.com named Peter Eavis, drawing on facts and interpretations provided by his own sources in the short-selling world, began connecting the dots. Previously, the emerging alternative paradigm for Enron coverage had been a desultory blossoming of negative points defined largely in isolation from one another. Now, Eavis took the obvious but revolutionary step of linking nascent bad news elements together.

Like McLean's piece three months earlier, Eavis's "Why One Firm Thinks Enron's Running Out of Gas" was sourced mainly in the views of a short seller. Unlike McLean, however, Eavis not only admitted the fact, but touted it, naming the short seller he was relying on (Off Wall Street of Cambridge, Massachusetts) in the lead paragraph and quoting the firm's new report on Enron extensively in the body of the piece. The simple act of linking the general doubts first described by McLean (and repeated and developed in Eavis's piece) with specific sources who had names and addresses and who were publishing bearish reports on and pursuing short-selling investment strategies with respect to Enron gave the "overpriced" theory a fresh specificity and coherence. It showed the overpriced thesis to be not just an idea, but the underpinning of an active investment strategy that was attracting adherents and putting Enron under new pressure in the marketplace. In his concluding sentence, Eavis further intensified the overpriced idea by redefining it as a scenario that would shape the future and by lending it an air of inevitability: "How soon before Wall Street follows Off Wall Street on Enron?"

Eavis's article was also novel in relating the overpriced thesis to the material in footnote 16. Identifying CFO Fastow as the previously unidentified senior executive in charge of the related entities, Eavis quoted an analyst as saying of Fastow's role in the LJMs, "Why are they doing this? It's just inappropriate." Eavis went on to relate the LJMs to the inflation of Enron earnings, noting with asperity that the "Off Wall Street analysis shows how a sale of optical fiber to a related party may have been used to goose earnings in the second quarter of 2000. Estimated profits from the . . . transaction allowed Enron to beat analysts' second-quarter earnings estimate by 2 cents a share, rather than missing by 2 cents."

This statement brought the Enron story to the brink of an intellectual revolution. In the nine months following the all-time peak of the previous summer, a few maverick news stories had set out a growing critique of Enron's stock price and prospects. Weil had observed the way mark-to-market accounting enabled financial deception. McLean had listed several further reasons for doubting the stock's future. Now, Eavis had added the points that Enron's accounting had been corrupted and that short sellers were in active pursuit. The dominant paradigm for Enron reporting was still the laudatory, good-news jubilation that had prevailed for a decade, but under pressure of discrepant events and the maverick stories that described them, it was crumbling. By the second quarter of 2001, the stage had been set for a new paradigm to recast the entire pattern of news coverage of the company.

PHASE THREE

Suddenly events at Enron took a sharply negative turn. A highly touted partnership with Blockbuster to market movies over the Internet was disbanded. Negotiations with the government of India over the refinancing of Enron's huge Dabhol generating plant south of Bombay foundered, and management suspended operations at the multi-billion-dollar facility. In August, after only six months in the top job, Skilling resigned "for personal reasons." And then, on October 17, the record results expected for the third quarter failed to materialize as Enron reported its first loss ever—a horrendous billion-dollar bath. The next day the share price hit $30, or half of what it had been when Skilling committed his gaffe with the analysts.

The business press's coverage shifted immediately. The previous pattern of a substantial body of overwhelmingly favorable coverage paralleled by a tiny, slowly coalescing new strain of negative coverage abruptly and massively reversed itself. The negative view became the dominant story, and the news media began to seek out and expose financial collapse and scandal throughout Enron's affairs.

In the *Wall Street Journal*, Enron beat reporters Smith and John R. Emshwiller began a drumfire of almost daily investigative pieces, many of them lengthy and most using normally confidential information made available by unnamed sources, that ripped the hide off the Enron carcass to expose a squalid hidden inner structure of failure and apparent abuse:

- "Enron Jolt: Investments, Assets Generate Big Loss—Part of Charge Tied to 2 Partnerships Interests Wall Street"
- "Enron CFO's Partnership Had Millions in Profit"
- "Enron May Issue More Stock to Cover Obligations"
- "Enron Replaces Fastow as Finance Chief"
- "Most Analysts Remain Plugged In to Enron," an article describing concerns that analysts have compromised themselves to help their firms land lucrative investment-banking fees.

After a barrage of two weeks, the share price had fallen by half again, to under $14, and Smith, Emshwiller, Weil, and others zoomed in on what quickly turned into a dramatic, bloody, and exceptionally compact ending:

- "With Enron Stock Trading at Book Value, Some See Company as a Takeover Target"
- "What Enron's Financial Reports Did—and Didn't—Reveal—Auditor Could Face Scrutiny on Clarity of Financial Reports"
- "Enron Slashes Profits since 1997 by 20%—Partnership Dealings Cited As Dynegy Talks Go On; Debt Ratings an Issue"
- "Why Credit Agencies Didn't Switch Off Enron—S&P Cries 'Junk' but the Warning Comes Too Late"

On November 30, six weeks after the crisis/scandal coverage began, the *Journal* brought word that Enron was about to file for Chapter 11. The share price closed at 26 cents.

That was pretty much the end for Enron. It was only the beginning for the *Wall Street Journal*, however. Already the distinguished business daily had ranged beyond the immediate financial crisis to run some substantial articles that laid out its causes and placed the event in its contexts. Smith nicely framed the central irony: the "fancy finances" that had sent Enron soaring years before had now brought it rapidly back to earth, she wrote. Weil weighed in with a revisitation of the critique of accounting practices that had first foreshadowed the coming Enron crash a year before. On the op-ed page a Manager's Journal essay tried manfully to appreciate what Enron's much-maligned business leadership had done right, but against the onrush of negative news the effort had the intellectual heft of a feather in a hurricane.

With events at Enron frozen in the bankruptcy court and the stock price near zero, financially and economically framed coverage gave way to a torrent of news stories out of Washington and the Houston courts about the investigations, recriminations, and punishments that came crashing down on the perpetrators of what was fast attaining the unenviable status of the business and financial scandal of the decade, if not the century. Smith, who a year earlier had reported the company's misleading account of its quarterly results without providing the corrective of some well-chosen context, had been reborn as a tigress of truth. Emshwiller and Weil and half a dozen other reporters followed suit. The result was a torrential cascade of disclosures as the *Journal* ran story after story after story—more than half a dozen substantial stories per issue on some days—reflecting the work of some twenty reporters working on a more or less full-time basis, day after day, for the three months starting in December 2001 and continuing without letup well into the spring of 2002.

It was an extraordinary spectacle. This was coverage of a sort that a national newspaper would give only to a presidential impeachment crisis, except that in this case, for the first time in living memory, the object of attention was the complex, often secret internal affairs and public record of a huge, far-flung business corporation. It was unprecedented—it was fascinating—it was also, in retrospect, a failure of editorial judgment.

There was, for one thing, a failure on the *Journal's* part to keep the story of Enron's collapse in proportion to the story of Enron's rise and to the stories of other big companies' failures. Compared to the limited coverage the *Journal* gave to Enron on the way up and to the moderate coverage given to Enron at the pinnacle, the amount of space and ink and manpower the *Journal* devoted to Enron on the way back down was simply disproportionate. It is often said that daily journalism in America is skewed in favor of bad news, and this truism was borne out with a vengeance in this case. The fact that this bias is widespread and of long standing doesn't make it any less a source of distortion.

In the second place, the *Journal* seemingly forgot that, sorely troubled and beleaguered though it was, Enron was still a big company even after the much ballyhooed bankruptcy layoffs. As the investigations in Washington went forward, the company still had over twenty thousand employees, and most of them presumably were doing something. To judge from the figure the company cut in the *Journal's* news pages, however, one would never have guessed that most of Enron's business operations continued more or less as usual.

Besides overplaying Enron's collapse, the *Journal* did even the most obsessed readers no favor by forcing them to wade through scores, even hundreds of disparate stories. The usual methodology newspapers use in reporting a complex, backward-looking, far-flung investigative story is to assign a team of reporters to gather the material over many weeks or months, have them sift and integrate their findings, and then write up a unified narrative that is published as a series. There is an inherent good sense in this time-tested way of reconciling the need for coherence with the complexity of many subjects and the chaotic way in which information often comes to light. The approach the *Journal* took to the story of the end-game worked about as well, from a reader's point of view, as publishing a book one page at a time in random order. It is surely no accident that when the *Journal* won a Pulitzer Prize for explanatory reporting of the business scandals of 2002, among the ten stories submitted by the *Journal* and cited by the Pulitzer committee—all truly splendid reportorial essays—not one was about Enron.

Partly explaining this failure of perspective is the fact that, to begin with, at least, it seemed possible that the Enron story just might *be* a presidential impeachment crisis. It was known from the outset that a longstanding nexus of personal, political, and financial ties linked Lay and George W. Bush, both while the latter was governor of Texas and in his first year as president. Democrats, still smarting from the narrow loss of the 2000 presidential election and still empowered by their narrow control of the Senate, hammered away at Enron in the awareness that the scandal had an inherent anti-Bush spin and the potential for damaging the president politically, conceivably fatally. In the event, this potential was never realized; the facts as they came out, though certainly an embarrassment to a president so close to Lay, did no real damage; the partisan and presidential side of the Enron scandal was pretty much stillborn, as it remains. That, however, is a judgment one makes retrospectively. At the time, at least to begin with, anything seemed possible.

The prime mover in the presidential version of the Enron scandal was the *New York Times*. The *Journal's* team was, by and large, skeptical of this take on Enron events, Weil told me. The *Journal's* massive coverage reflected a competitive determination not to be outdone by the *Times*, plus the conviction of many *Journal* reporters and editors that the importance of the Enron scandal lay not in its potential for unseating President Bush, but in the way it opened a window on the wide-ranging corruption that many believed had become epidemic in the financial and corporate world of the late 1990s. Even in this respect, though, the Enron story was a less compelling journalistic achievement than were the many other corruption stories that broke in its wake. It didn't have a celebrity malefactor of Martha Stewart's star power (indeed, Lay has so far kept a surprisingly low profile), didn't involve the brute criminality of an Adelphia or Tyco, and in dollar terms fell short of the sorry standard set by the accounting frauds of WorldCom. Once again, the absence of any Enron story from the roster of articles that the *Journal* nominated and the Pulitzer committee selected for journalism's most prestigious prize pretty well says it all as far as the editorial judgment displayed in Enron coverage is concerned.

But if the *Wall Street Journal* overplayed and undercondensed the Enron investigations, that was the only thing it did wrong. Hypertrophied and sometimes out of control though it was, the seemingly endless series nonetheless had a palpable magnificence. Almost every story framed its revelation carefully and succinctly fit the event at hand into the appropriate context. At their best, journalists on the trail of a breaking story are explorers pushing exuberantly ahead without knowing exactly where they will end up. They enact a drama of people exercising skills of discovery and story-telling, performing a high democratic function, seeking truth against the resistance of power as the whole world watches. These stories exude a wonderful moral and intellectual energy. To read them is to be roused from routine and summoned to one's duties as an employee, shareholder, and citizen.

In post-bankruptcy coverage uptown at *Fortune* a very different approach to Enron's collapse materialized. As bankruptcy approached, McLean returned to Enron for the first time in six months to update readers with a medium-length piece on the fate of the suddenly imploding firm. A month later she followed up with a long, comprehensive roundup on what had happened at Enron and why. Both essays were intelligent, timely articles that nicely laid out the main elements of the Alternative Paradigm, now bolstered by the wealth of new detail that had emerged of late. McLean's analysis gave due weight to both the stupidity and the cupidity at work in Enron's demise. She also accomplished something the *Journal* never managed—to pull a sprawling and unruly story together into a unified narrative.

The codependent protectiveness toward abusive management that had marred McLean's first article faded somewhat in these pieces. Now that the top people were no longer corporate heroes in the pink of power but villains receiving their just deserts, McLean relaxed her solicitous silence and spilled the beans about Skilling's peevish response earlier in the year to her probing questions and the locker-room epithet he had hurled at the short seller on the conference call. She stopped short, however, of disclosing Lay's effort to get her managing editor to kill "Is Enron Overpriced?"—it took the *New York Times* to dig up that revealing fact and make it a matter of public record. In other words, even in Enron's hour of crisis, *Fortune* continued to show not a little tenderness toward Enron's senior management. Through thick and thin, *Fortune's* silence was telling its clients in the executive suite, you can count on us to keep a channel open for secret communication, even when you abuse it to ask us to kill a story that correctly describes realities at your company that you are hiding from investors and the general public as part of a larger pattern of corrupt business conduct.

McLean's second article, which appeared in mid-December just as the *Wall Street Journal's* muckrakers hit the investigative stride that would carry them into the spring, brought *Fortune's* coverage of what had actually happened at Enron to a close. Thereafter the magazine dealt with Enron less as an event to be described or a scandal to be unmasked and more as an issue of politically correct speech and action—of public relations, in short. As the *Wall Street Journal* pursued its great white investigative whale to the corners of the earth in the name of truth and justice, *Fortune* threw a kind of journalistic hissy fit, issuing an occasional series of articles that offered aid and comfort to defensive corporate executives who found themselves in a suddenly chilly public environment. Not only did the magazine print very little about Enron in this period, but what it did print seemed trapped in a cycle of unproductive emotions that ranged from denial, to black humor, to self-pity, and back to the cynicism that had touched off and driven the entire performance.

The tone was set in February by an article that purported to lay out a strategy by which private investors, in the new age of Enron now a-dawning, could deal with accounting uncertainties on their own: "Ignore the accountants, the analysts, and the brokers who snigger at your stupidity. . . . They're smooth-talking villains who have a vested interest in confusing you. The Enron collapse . . . make[s] it imperative that you, the investor, get to the truth on earnings. When figures confound and experts confuse, you need to take a deep breath and do the math yourself. Can you? Sure. Think of what follows as Accounting for Dummies."

In a tough-talking, wise-guy voice, the author deconstructed some of the games financial executives play and spelled out ways for investors to compensate, most of which came down to the advice not to invest, or at least to invest less, in the company in question. However, for the central problem raised by Enron—the abuse of generally recognized accounting principles, fraud, and the secrecy that typically attends these—the article offered no solution or advice of any kind. The article's promise of enabling the beleaguered private investor to declare independence of the world's smooth-talking villains and begin to handle his informational needs by himself was so much moonshine. The implication that there might not be much real need for government action to deal with the mess at Enron was equally nonsensical. In effect, this story was propaganda to deflate the public uproar, prosecutorial zeal, and public-policy reformism that the Enron affair rightly stimulated. What billed itself as a service to discouraged investors was actually balm for the bruised egos of an executive class having the reputational equivalent of a bad hair day.

In the following issue, *Fortune* ran a sardonic item about an emerging category of business consultants who were busily deriving economic advantage from "Enronitis," as the piece derisively named the growing public concern over the misdeeds at the giant corporation. These were the so-called forensic accountants such as Mark Roberts of Off Wall Street and David Tice of Behind the Numbers, experts who probe corporate financial reports for signs of hidden trouble. The article suggested gloatingly that these services do not come cheap, identifying entry-level fees from $15,000 (Tice) to $50,000 (Roberts). However, whether these fees were really so stiff depends on what it costs to hire top accountants and others on the other side of the financial disclosure wars—which the article did not identify.

The language of these articles had a slangy, aggressive, condescending tone, as if to say that while *Fortune* might occasionally stoop to discussing the issues raised by the Enronitis-afflicted, it would be damned if it was going to speak to such people as equals or actually deliberate the choices posed. An article arguing for expensing stock options began: "Should we throw lawbreaking CEOs in jail? Of course we should. Could the SEC use more money to beef up enforcement? Well, duh. Do we need to figure out better ways to regulate and motivate the accountants who audit companies' books? That's a no-brainer."

The following month Geoffrey Colvin, a top *Fortune* editor, deconstructed the Enron affair as a tempest in a political teapot: "It's actually no mystery why Enron is getting unprecedented blanket coverage," he wrote with dismissive insight. "The story has a political angle, which has triggered the scandal apparatus in Washington, the center of the world for most mainstream media. Congressional investigators possess unique power to extract and publicize information. And, heaven knows, it's juicy stuff."

The cynical voice in which *Fortune* addressed Enron-related matters had little faith in either public or private efforts to address the issues raised by Enron. In the spring, a list of quick fixes for Enron problems recommended, as one step, "reengineer the board." Suddenly the narrative broke off to interject with a sneer, "Remember reengineering?" In other words, remember the trendy management buzzword and panacea of ten years ago? Having implicitly belittled what it was about to advocate, *Fortune* plunged on to spin its own panacea—and to exemplify the contradictions of cynicism, which out of disappointment and defensiveness often denies both its disillusionment and the values that underlie that disillusionment.

In June, Washington editor Jeffrey Birnbaum chortled in his column, "D.C. Declares Enron's 15 Minutes of Fame Over." The title is a takeoff on the amusing old complaint by Andy Warhol that in the future everyone will be famous for fifteen minutes, by which he meant that celebrity had become so empty that *anyone* could be famous, briefly. Birnbaum's borrowing of the line is a way of saying that Enron was a corporate nobody and the Enron scandal the public-discussion equivalent—an unworthy tale told by an idiot, full of sound and fury, signifying nothing, to borrow a line from the original literary celeb.

After months of peevishness and posturing, *Fortune* briefly seemed to back away from defensiveness and belatedly tried to come to grips with the issue of what was to be done about Enron. In the summer, a longish piece by a team of editors and writers laid out an agenda for restoring confidence in business that, while limited and fairly obvious, was a sincere effort—the only one *Fortune* made—to describe a plan for making the world after Enron a better place. The platform recommended: improve profit accounting (it named a few specific changes), separate securities research from investment banking, increase oversight and enforcement by the SEC, lower CEO compensation packages and expense all stock options, make boards more independent and active, and so on. But the article was such a perfunctory compilation of conventional wisdom, came so late, and reflected so little apparent engagement with the real issues that the whole effort ended up reinforcing the cynicism it was meant to dispel.

Suddenly, in midsummer, *Fortune* broke with the pattern of the previous half year and published two long and splendid articles that, for one brief shining moment, showed that the *Wall Street Journal* wasn't the only place where a reader could find serious journalism in the age of Skilling and Lay. These were two long, thoughtful, sympathetic, above-all interesting profiles of two leaders of the movements for ac-counting and corporate governance reform—Sir David Tweedie in the United Kingdom and Robert A. G. Monks in the United States. The pieces are easily the high points of the entire corpus of Phase Three Enron journalism in *Fortune*, and un-questionably the equal, or more than the equal, of the best in the *Wall Street Journal*. They are reminders not only of *Fortune's* storied past and tantalizing potential, but also of the enduring fact that as long as journalists are allowed to go forth and report and then to sit in a quiet place and faithfully record what they have found, enlight-enment is always a prospect and excellence always an option.

In November, *Fortune's* Year-of-Enron series came to a jarring conclusion with an odd essay, at once snarky and utopian, entitled, "From Heroes to Goats . . . and Back Again?" by veteran management writer Jeremy Useem. The piece observed, insightfully, that whereas earlier generations of business leaders had preached a doc-trine of corporate social responsibility, the current crop has touted the very different ideal of increasing shareholder value. In practice, Useem argued, both philosophies had degenerated into cover stories for the self-enrichment and self-aggrandizement of, by, and for CEOs. This, Useem urged, was no accident. "The more things change, the more creative CEOs get at turning circumstances to their advantage," he wrote, in a well-taken realist's critique of corporate ideology and leadership. "In other words, they've got the power."

The piece ended by hoping for a new breed of CEO espousing a new doctrine that would combine the best points of both the social responsibility ethos and the shareholder value school along with a new candor about the possibilities and limits of business leadership. Useem spun a scenario in which a handful of new CEOs, eman-cipated from the dead hand of the past by today's corporate crisis, would look within themselves and find the resources of imagination, will, and leadership to forge this new model that would redefine norms of business behavior to the benefit of all. However, Useem said not a word about what this model might be like, nor did he offer a way out of the dilemma, presumably enduring, created by the inherent power of the CEO to turn any institutional or doctrinal arrangement to his advantage at others' expense.

In short, no sooner did *Fortune* drop the pouty act and try to get serious about Enron, however unprepossessing the programmatic result, than it abandoned the whole idea of reclaiming the corporation for any value beyond the wealth, power, status, and convenience of its senior managers. It thereby succumbed to the cynicism it had been in the grip of from the beginning, albeit a cynicism that in the meantime it had hoisted onto a higher intellectual plane with Useem's facile neo-Machiavellian credo.

LESSONS FROM THE COVERAGE OF THE ENRON COLLAPSE

So what evaluative judgments do these news stories invite, and what lessons do they teach about the role of the business press in monitoring corporate performance?

The high point, clearly, was the success of both publications in picking up on the hazy first indications that Enron was overpriced. Weil's prescient analysis of the problem of mark-to-market accounting was both outstanding in its own right and truly exceptional in breaking free of the official view so early in the game. McLean's identification of a wider range of Enron negatives six months later was a major achievement regardless of any rhetorical ambivalence. And the fact that by May 2001, drawing on short-seller sources, Eavis had pieced together an analysis touching on the corruption concealed within the LJMs is little short of astounding, considering that the story had as yet attracted no prosecutors or federal investigators and that the active exercise of the subpoena power and the liberal application of press agentry almost always precede the appearance of news stories identifying corruption as such. When Enron's unexpected billion-dollar loss for the third quarter hit in October 2001, the pack of eligible receivers who instantly flooded the zone intending to get their hands around the big story floating down the field had an exceptionally detailed and accurate road map to navigate by thanks to the pioneering work of these three journalists. Without it, the *Journal* and *Fortune* wouldn't have had been able to get to the bottom of the core Enron story as fast as they did—by Thanksgiving, more or less; that is, in five or six weeks, or roughly the same period of time as it takes to report, write, and edit a typical *Fortune* article.

At the other end of the spectrum, the low point of the press-and-Enron saga was reached in 1999, 2000, and early 2001, when nearly everyone involved cooperated in an intensification of Enron's good news and in a progressive suspension of good sense and judgment. By the peak of the Clinton boom, even distinguished purveyors of journalism such as *Fortune* and the *Journal* had, to a significant extent, become active enablers of Enron fabulists, as exemplified by Smith's fawning quote of Skilling's lie about the firm's "astounding opportunities," and by the absurd annual myth fests staged by *Fortune* in the guise of rank-ordering the "best," "biggest," and "most innovative." These exercises in unreality provided cover for corruptors. They lulled the company's audiences into an unwarranted complacency about the silences and manipulatively partial disclosures that typically accompany official misdeeds and, wherever and whenever they appear, must be viewed as leading indicators of corruption's hidden presence and progress.

Both these admirable and regrettable phases of Enron coverage, together with the long period of relatively normal coverage that preceded them, strikingly illustrate the core competency of journalism in our time.

News is a factual story about events at or near organizations, and news workers gather the crucial raw materials needed for their work through a partly cooperative, partly adversarial relationship with officials in which access and information are traded in exchange for publicity. In this relationship, the journalist is an officially independent but generally subordinate partner, and the core skill he exercises is the ability to bargain for information in excess of what institutions would make public on their own. In normal journalism, particularly in the business news field, what transpires between both parties is mainly cooperative. They play complementary roles in generating a pattern of coverage that, in the typical case, is relatively scant and highly routinized, dominated by fairly short stories that often consist mainly of bare summaries of the company's basic quarterly filings with the SEC. That, certainly, was the pattern of Enron coverage from the company's founding until the late 1990s. It was favorable in the unobjectionable sense that the numbers showed Enron to be consistently growing and prospering.

The journalist's dependent and subordinate position vis-à-vis official sources works pretty well in practice, from a citizen-reader's viewpoint, as long as both journalist and source are behaving more or less honorably. But when either party goes off the reservation and starts flouting the usual civilities and the law, the relationship can easily degenerate into a vehicle of gross misinformation. That, essentially, is what happened with Enron coverage in the late 1990s. The story got bigger and much more favorable thanks, in no small measure, to the company's quiet new practice of concealing negative developments by means of completely inappropriate strategies, from the corruption of the mainstream equity analysts to the sequestering of debts and losses in related entities whose balance sheets and operating results should have been consolidated but, unlawfully, weren't. At the time, the journalists covering the company knew nothing of these practices and felt justified in assuming that the rules were being followed. Any inchoate suspicions that may have arisen in the backs of their minds on this score were laid to rest by the company's string of dazzling quarterly results, the skyrocketing stock price, and the personal fun and advantage of covering a visible and stellar corporation. For years it looked as if Enron was, not a corruptor of everything it touched, but that rare company that recast reality with its soaring brilliance and enviable success.

Even when news coverage is trapped in a mini dark age of the sort that public awareness of Enron was in this period, the journalist is still in possession of his core competency, and the corruption of news is always potentially reversible. The news worker, at least in theory, is always open to new facts and views that may attract interest or stir controversy. He or she continues to have an incentive to take the calls of informed new entrants to the Enron field such as the short sellers who were attracted to Enron by the very unreality that Enron's manipulations created in the marketplace. If it's a slow news week, or if it looks as if shorting might replace going long as the way the really big money is being made on the company in question, the journalist may even be the one to initiate the contact.

Moreover, the journalist gathers not only officials' stated facts and views, but also gleans an impression of their personalities and observes their offstage behavior. He takes note of the fact, for instance, that Skilling starts overreacting to questions about his company's financial reporting practices or denounces short sellers who ask questions or make comments. Sooner or later, the hidden lies and crimes that corrupt a news story leave a trace of their fugitive presence in the words, actions, or body language sources display to journalists in the course of their transactions. Journalists are always learning from these experiences. Even in the midst of the most wanton and repressive regime of corporate mendacity, journalism has an ongoing capacity for truth and self-correction.

As we have seen, that capacity began to reassert itself, and to reclaim the truth of the Enron story, in late 2000 and early 2001. Not, to be sure, through the efforts of beat reporters such as Smith, who had the regular energy beat, and Brian O'Reilly, who continued to retail the world according to Skilling. The journalists who picked up on the new information and sources were newcomers without previous Enron experience. Weil was a stock market reporter in Texas with a long suit in accountancy. McLean was a very junior financial reporter at *Fortune* with no background in Enron or energy stocks. The journalists who exercised their competency to launch a new and improved version of the Enron story were low-visibility worker bees with no stake in the old story that, with their new information and new sources, they were about to overturn.

I emphasize the work of these mavericks because what they did is noteworthy and heartwarming, and because it illustrates the inherent capacity of journalism to escape from errors deliberately imposed by official sources. At the same time, no one should imagine that these two stories were anything more than what they were—two lone stories over six months, which is to say, drops in the bucket of the misleading Enron story that had been up and running for years and that would continue to predominate until the company suddenly reported its shattering billion-dollar loss. At Enron, in other words, journalistic competence eventually saw through myth, reclaimed the truth, and got the results into cold print, but the pattern of Enron coverage didn't change on any appreciable scale until events forced the change. If financial conditions in 2001 had been a little more favorable—if the share price hadn't fallen quite as far as it had, if the air had gone out of the stock market bubble a bit more slowly, if Enron's executives had had a little more luck in their effort to keep the enterprise afloat—the huge loss might have been averted. In that case, Weil and McLean's stories would be languishing in the limbo of news stories that are true but irrelevant, and mainstream journalism would still be singing the praises of "Kenny Boy" Lay, who by now would have become President Bush's second treasury secretary and be rising to the top of the list of candidates to replace Alan Greenspan as chairman of the Federal Reserve.

In these pages I have been discussing journalism as a form of knowledge, as if truth were its main goal and standard. This is a legitimate perspective, but it isn't the only view to take. Journalism is also a business in which attracting an audience and selling access (to the publication for readers, to the audience for advertisers) is the name of the game, and in which success and profitability depend less on the truth as such than on the content's interest for, and credibility with, the chosen audience. It is natural to ask how the patterns of Enron coverage discussed in this paper relate to the business identity and needs of *Fortune* and the *Wall Street Journal*. The answer I will propose, briefly, is that the Enron story was shaped—and misshaped—by two powerful business-strategy influences.

The most important of these, already touched on but not identified as such, is the historic commitment of news companies in America to a business strategy keyed primarily to advertising sales, relegating subscription revenues to secondary rank. Historically, this approach to generating revenues and turning a profit gave rise to, and today is still embodied in, what we understand and accept as the news genre—the mix of expository rules and intellectual traditions that define news as a dramatic narrative of facts and events. In my view, this institutionalized, economically grounded habit of seeing reality from a short perspective in time, as a congeries of events, rather than a gallery of conditions or broad trends, is the central reason why the mavericks' alternative paradigm was so slow to reshape Enron coverage at the *Journal* and *Fortune*. News has a unidimensional, Manichean, either-or cast, thanks to the intense selectivity of the leading story formats, the way the text is geared to the theme sounded by the headline, and the ruthless weeding out of ideas and information that diverge from the organizing theme. This powerful simplifying reductionist impulse is what made the mainstream press's hyped-up take on Enron in the late 1990s so resistant to discrepant information.

This aspect of media business strategy is a good deal less than optimal, it seems to me. Readers' and citizens' interests would be far better served if the media industry were to base itself on the transaction with the reader, with his inherent need for truth, and to de-emphasize the transaction with advertisers, with their long-standing preference for simplified story forms that can assemble a maximum of people with maximum availability to the verbal ploys that advertising is based on. The point here is that the drawbacks of Enron coverage are no incidental curiosity, but consequences of the fundamental nature of the news business. They bring us face to face with the big issues of press and society in our time.

The other broad business influence visible in Enron coverage emerges from the starkly contrasting behavior of the *Wall Street Journal* and *Fortune* after October 17, 2001, with the *Journal* mounting an instant investigative crusade of maximum scale and intensity, and *Fortune* contenting itself with a couple of essays, followed by a retreat into silence punctuated by cynical outbursts of defensive annoyance and formulaic agenda-spinning. These patterns reflect the different market-segmenting strategies pursued by the two publications.

The *Wall Street Journal*, of course, is America's largest daily business news publication, with a circulation on the order of two million and an audience that embraces all major business reader categories (investors, managers, and executives) and is most clearly unified by a common interest in financial markets. Once the Enron investigations began to generate a daily flow of disclosures of wide interest to Wall Street, the *Journal* had little choice but to begin substantial daily coverage of the company's decline and fall, even if it risked inundating readers with more material than they had time or interest for. With the story affecting the markets on a daily or hourly basis, the traditional newspaper methodology for handling complex scandals by means of a retrospective series of carefully integrated investigative articles wasn't an option. In other words, both the special virtues and (limited) vices of this phase of the *Journal's* coverage are best seen as outgrowths of the nature of its business.

Fortune, by contrast, is a fortnightly with a circulation about a third the *Journal's*. Its audience is skewed heavily to top corporate executives, and a disproportionate share of its advertising revenues come from ads promoting positive perceptions of their corporate sponsors and, at least implicitly, of corporations or The Corporation in general. Both these elements of its business strategy had an apparent influence on Enron coverage. Fortnightly frequency affected *Fortune's* coverage, particularly of the second and third phases of the Enron story. In the second phase, from September 2001 to July 2002, when the Alternative Paradigm emerged, fortnightly publication helped *Fortune* step aside from the flow of daily happenings and official pronouncements to take the larger, longer, often unauthorized, and unofficial view of events that resulted in McLean's important article of February 2002. True, the prescient piece by Weil that antedated it appeared in a daily publication, but though journalism that goes against the conventional wisdom is possible in daily publications, it is less at home there. The daily has a built-in bias for the official events that appear in a daily time frame. The fortnightly, like the weekly and monthly, has a natural preference for articles that, while still tied to events and the daily flow of news, reflect less specific, more independent, potentially more critical perspectives.

In the third phase, when Enron collapsed and the Alternative Paradigm replaced the initial good-news paradigm, fortnightly publication stopped being a journalistic advantage and started being a disadvantage. To begin with, to be sure, *Fortune* handled the company's collapse with aplomb and expertise. It had on staff a writer, McLean, who knew Enron and was way up the learning curve with respect to its recent affairs, and as soon as Enron's shocking third-quarter loss was announced, the magazine's editorial management assigned her to write a fast-closing mid-length piece on the event. Within days of the appearance of this first cut at the suddenly redefined Enron story, the company plunged into bankruptcy, and *Fortune* immediately assigned its Enron expert to do a comprehensive, full-length analysis of what had gone wrong and why. Her piece appeared before Christmas.

With the coming of the new year, the fortnightly's Enron coverage pretty much collapsed. McLean asked for and was given a leave of absence to write a book about Enron, depriving *Fortune* of the services of its one writer with up-to-date Enron experience. Meanwhile, the *New York Times* and *Wall Street Journal* got their massive, day-by-day exposés up and running. Suddenly, the fact that *Fortune* came out only every fourteen days, plus the seven-day minimum delay between the closing of the magazine and its appearance, added up to a near-fatal handicap for any effort to follow and advance the Enron story: Any material *Fortune* might run on the company and investigation would be, on the day it appeared, at least one week, and more likely two or more weeks, behind the curve defined in the pages of the *Times* and the *Journal*. "They simply had the whip hand," managing editor Kirkland told me. "Rather than trying to add anything to the torrent coming out of the *Journal* and the *Times*, we waited to weigh in and synthesize when there was a denouement." By then, of course, there wasn't much left to say. Essentially, fortnightly periodicity drove *Fortune* out of the serious Enron-coverage field during the meltdown phase, leaving the magazine to content itself with the occasional think piece and rhetorical pot shot from the sidelines.

Fortune's focus on the big corporation and managerial class—as subject matter, audience, and advertising market—also left its imprint on the magazine's meltdown-period coverage. On the positive side, the magazine's identification with the interests of the big business audience can be seen in the three generally good to excellent Enron-related articles *Fortune* ran during that period: Useem's insightful neo-Machiavellian account of changing corporate ideologies, and the splendid profiles of the two serious-minded accounting-practice reformers. The first was defined by its reassuring (to executives) message that, come what may, CEOs would continue to "have the power." The profiles identified new business statesmen who, post-Enron, would have to be invited onto boards and into management retreats and feted in the spas of Davos, Aspen, and Sun Valley. These were Enron-related subjects that the senior executive audience was actually, positively interested in. It is no accident that *Fortune* covered them with its customary depth, intelligence, civility, and sincere energy.

The negative side of *Fortune's* identification with the big business audience was expressed in the sparseness and cynicism of the bulk of its meltdown-period coverage. The sparseness of *Fortune's* Enron coverage, as noted, may be attributable in significant part to the fortnightly frequency. But some of the sparseness and all of the cynicism are pretty clearly reflections of an institutional culture that takes to heart the values and interests of the big business audience, according to which the Enron story was a distasteful affair that decent people were going to have as little to do with as they could get away with. In effect, *Fortune* was taking the same posture as beleaguered executives did, whiling away the winter and spring of Enron's discontent with a program of quiet complaining and formulaic gestures of rectitude while waiting anxiously for the whole nightmare to pass and hoping that no lasting damage would be done.

This was a negative pattern of coverage, not only in the sense that *Fortune* was resisting and minimizing the Enron story, but also in the larger sense that the magazine was arguably failing to make good on its responsibility to serve the informational needs of the audience. In a crisis that throws up for grabs the big corporation's reputation, governance, and overall future, cynicism is never really an option for people at the top. When the going gets tough, policy makers and responsibility holders are called on to rise to the occasion and come up with answers that work for their organizations and for the larger society as well as for themselves. If they are personally cynical people who have risen to power on the basis of their success at serving private and individual interests at the expense of the broader collective goods at stake in business enterprise, they must either transcend their limitations and sincerely and seriously involve themselves in policy discussion or expect to be pushed aside as failures and losers. In this sense *Fortune* fell short of meeting the needs that by its business strategy it has chosen to serve.

In a series of e-mails to me, managing editor Kirkland took exception to this aspect of the present analysis. He argued that the meltdown-period coverage was shaped largely by the imperatives of fortnightly frequency, and by his decision, at the story's height, to let McLean take a leave of absence to write her Enron book, *The Smartest Guys in the Room*, as a result of which the magazine was without the services of an up-to-date Enron expert from January 2002 onward. Kirkland went on to deny that the magazine has a pro-big-business mind-set or that pro-business bias played any role in its Enron coverage, asserting that *Fortune* is happy to "crusade on behalf of free markets and old-fashioned morals" even when this entails criticizing big companies. As evidence he pointed to a number of substantial and hard-hitting articles that have taken aim at some very big names in corporate America, including the AOL half of AOL–Time Warner (which recently reverted to its previous corporate name, Time Warner), the owner of *Fortune*.

It is true that *Fortune* has sometimes taken big business to task, but it doesn't do so often, and when it does, the target is almost always a company or executive that has taken huge losses, gone bankrupt, run into trouble with the law, or independently become an object of public censure or ridicule. In other words, the magazine's crusades are directed against people and institutions that have failed, and thus are no longer entitled to the privileges and immunities attached to membership in the managerial class, which first, last, and always is about success. *Fortune* stories taking aim at successful companies that are behaving badly in some obscure, important, but as yet undiscovered way—Enrons in the making, as it were—are as rare as hen's teeth, and of those few, many are the work of the extraordinary Carol Loomis, the veteran financial writer whose stellar skills, crusty intellectual independence, and general distinction have long made her practically a force unto herself at the magazine she honors with her presence. That, incidentally, is why "Is Enron Overpriced?" was such an unusual event in *Fortune*'s history: it was a story critical of a big company not in obvious trouble by a writer other than Carol Loomis.

Further evidence of the pro-business institutional-cultural origins of *Fortune*'s meltdown-period coverage was provided by what Kirkland had to say about his decision to withhold from the original McLean story the facts about Enron's extraordinary efforts to discourage the author from pursuing the overpriced thesis and, when she persisted, to urge Kirkland to kill or reshape the story.

> I think it was not odd for *Fortune* [not to go into the] fierce efforts those guys made over Bethany's first story. We had no reason at that point to believe that Enron was anything other than a company worried about spin and protecting an overly high valuation. To have shown the play behind the scenes would have felt like piling on or an example of bias. Later, it was immaterial in light of what came out.

The statement shows how journalistic point of view or bias can reside in a concept of good manners as well as in an explicit ideology. And when the emergence of the Enron scandal made the Skilling-Fastow-Lay stop-the-story shenanigans "immaterial" even in Kirkland's view, his bias-laden concept of correct conduct didn't completely disappear. While McLean's next story did belatedly report the Skilling and Fastow machinations, it did not disclose the most damning act—Lay's call to McLean's managing editor, which apparently was still too hot for the courtly business magazine to handle in its own pages. Kirkland left it to the *New York Times* to break the story of his part in the telling, behind-the-scenes drama of *Fortune's* enterprising coverage of the inflated stock price of the corrupted corporation.

To sum up, both the *Wall Street Journal* and *Fortune* cooperated with Enron for several years in publishing misleadingly positive accounts of the company's business results made up and put out by Enron executives using unlawful or unethical means in part. At the same time, both publications more or less promptly picked up on and printed a limited body of contrary evidence indicating that Enron's profits were overstated and its stock was overpriced. This alternative, negative paradigm of the Enron story became the dominant one in both publications as soon as the results for the third quarter of 2001 showed a huge and unexpected loss even though the unlawful accounting and other prices continued.

The news coverage we have analyzed here shows that the business press plays a role in the monitoring of corporate performance that is at once partly dependent and partly independent. While the news of Enron was subject to capture by corrupt news management in one phase of the story, it was also capable of resisting false images and abusive image making, especially when natural adversaries of the false images, such as short sellers and investigators armed with subpoena powers, enter the fray and begin feeding their perspectives to the press. The culture, ethics, and business strategy of a news organization affect the accuracy of journalistic coverage and the speed and effectiveness with which it responds to new information. The *Journal* overcovered the scandal phase of the Enron story, seemingly out of the biases built into daily publication, a talented and ambitious professional staff that could smell the Pulitzer it won for covering companies other than Enron, and an audience drawn broadly from all sectors of business. *Fortune* undercovered the scandal phase, seemingly as a result of its fortnightly periodicity and focus on the big-corporation, top-management sector of the business world.

Lawyers as Corporate Monitors

R. T. McNamar

*F*rom a public policy perspective, one of the most vexing challenges is to understand the role of the lawyers in the Enron collapse and to identify what, if any, changes need to be made in federal or state policies affecting the type of behavior demonstrated by the lawyers in Enron. This chapter reviews the current cases, laws, and the regulation of lawyers. It has an extensive analysis of the civil law concerning attorneys aiding and abetting a corporate officer's breach of his (or her) fiduciary obligations. It then addresses the specific role of the attorneys in the events that took place at Enron. Last, it analyzes several public policy options affecting this type of behavior before making a recommendation.

The chapter does not address in detail the role of Enron's in-house counsel, since the more difficult issues relate to the outside counsel's relationship with Enron. The Enron general counsel, James V. Derrick, was not involved in off-balance-sheet transactions, the preparation of Securities and Exchange Commission (SEC) filings, or apparently any of the questionable activities that led to Enron's demise. The general counsel handled board matters and litigation. The examiner in bankruptcy, Neal Batson, found that the general counsel was guilty of malpractice for "failure to inform himself" on three specific matters. The first violation related to anonymous letters to chairman Kenneth Lay in August 2001 alleging that there were accounting irregularities at Enron. The second was his failure to become familiar with the facts of the LJM1/Rhythms Hedging Transaction. The third was failure to inform himself and then the Enron board with respect to the related party transactions. The examiner did not indicate that the facts surrounding the general counsel supported any finding of federal securities violations.[1]

The focus of the chapter is on identifying any policy changes that might provide incentives for the lawyers to further diminish the probability of corporate boards or management perpetrating another Enron.[2]

Contemporaneous with the *Central Bank* case and the Private Securities Litigation Reform Act of 1995 (PSLRA), both of which are subsequently discussed, law firms began to organize themselves in limited liability partnerships (LLPs) rather than in the traditional general partnerships. In a general partnership, each attorney is personally liable for the actions of his partners and there is a very high incentive to exert quality control and avoid litigation. In an LLP, the other partners are not liable for the actions of the miscreant, only their own. Commentators have suggested that this reduces the incentives of the law firms to oversee the actions of all of the partners. Seldom does a law firm's liability exceed it malpractice insurance. If this is true, nowhere is it more true than in the area of aiding and abetting a corporate officer's fraudulent securities transactions.

THE CURRENT REGULATORY FRAMEWORK

Law firms are "self-regulatory organizations" in that they are regulated by the state bar association, which is managed by the attorneys who are the members of the state bar association. The state bar association establishes the criteria for membership, designs and administers the test for admission, and provides administrative support. It is also the body that hears complaints against lawyers and provides sanctions for those found guilty of violating the state bar association rules. In terms of rule setting and ensuring compliance with the rules by its member lawyers, the state bar association serves as a state agency.

At the federal level, there is no agency per se that oversees or regulates lawyers. To be a practicing attorney in a federal court, an attorney must be a member in good standing of a state bar association. Hence an attorney who is disbarred for disciplinary reasons would also lose the ability to practice before any of the three levels of federal courts. Disbarment is an infrequently used practice. The state bar associations are widely perceived as little more than a trade association to buy insurance for young lawyers with children.

The American Bar Association (ABA) is a professional trade association of lawyers that lacks any authority to regulate lawyers. It has many active practice groups and is widely seen as providing quality meetings in the practice group areas. However, it can only recommend to the federal government, state governments, or state bar associations certain professional standards. It cannot cause its recommendations to be adopted nor to enforce its recommendations. It is essentially an influential, but strictly advisory, group.

At the SEC, there is no prohibition on practicing law and filling out the various documents that must be filed with the SEC. For example, S-1, 10-K, and 10-Q are often prepared by lawyers either on the staff of the filing public company or their outside law firm. There is no test or certification for the lawyers who do this work. Further, certified public accountants often do the identical work for a public company that is filing with the SEC. In fact, a lawyer is not required to prepare or file an SEC document. The SEC, on occasion, has barred individual attorneys from SEC work for securities law violations. These prohibitions are largely viewed as ineffective because the barred attorney can still draft the documents for the signature of another attorney in his firm. Attorneys can be subject to a criminal referral from the SEC to the Justice Department. These are rare, and when referred, the Justice Department is often reticent to refer the matter to a local U.S. attorney and have the attorney take it before a grand jury for fear that it will not result in an indictment or will result in the case being lost because a jury can't reach a unanimous verdict that the attorneys are guilty of criminal activity "beyond a reasonable doubt." Hence such cases are seldom brought and are often settled with only SEC civil fines prior to a possible trial.

Attorneys are often sued for damages in a civil action for "aiding and abetting" a transaction. These suits are often tied to claims of malpractice. The success of these suits is varied. These suits are often brought in expectation that the law firm will settle out of court and that most of the settlement will be paid by the attorney's insurance firm from their errors and omissions or malpractice insurance policies' coverage. Few observers conclude that relying on the trial bar to bring civil actions to discipline attorneys with monetary payments is a sound public policy.

To understand the role of the lawyers in the Enron case and to consider what an appropriate public policy might be, it is necessary to examine in depth the statutes and court cases relating to aiding and abetting. Hence there follows a rather lengthy treatment on the subject. The topics to be covered are the *Central Bank* case; the PSLRA; the current Government Accounting Office (GAO) view of the law; the ruling of Judge Melinda Harman in the Enron shareholder derivative law suit; and relevant state case laws in the states where Enron was domiciled or did significant business.

THE CENTRAL BANK CASE

Central Bank of Denver N.A. v. First Interstate Bank of Denver N.A (1994)[3] has been the most quoted case on aiding and abetting. In the case, First Interstate Bank was an indenture trustee for bonds issued to finance public improvements for the Denver building authority. First Interstate became aware that the appraisals on the land securing the bonds may have been optimistic. It decided to have the land reappraised, but postponed the reappraisal until after the bonds were issued. The building authority subsequently defaulted on the bonds.

Central Bank of Denver brought suit, claiming that the First Interstate Bank was secondarily liable under the Sec 10(b) of the Securities Exchange Act of 1934 for its conduct in aiding and abetting the building authority's fraud. There was no question that, as the indenture trustee, First Interstate Bank was a secondary actor. The court held that the Central Bank could not maintain an aiding-and-abetting suit under section 10(b). The court said the act "makes it unlawful for any person directly or indirectly . . . to use or employ, in connection with the purchase or sale of any security . . . any manipulative or deceptive device or contrivance—and does not reach those who aid and abet a violation."

In my opinion, an indentured trustee is clearly distinguishable from an attorney involved in structuring and drafting a securities offering. Notwithstanding, since 1994 attorneys have been citing the *Central Bank* case as the controlling precedent for why they should have no civil liability under section 10(b) of the Securities Exchange Act of 1934.

THE PRIVATE SECTOR SECURITIES
LITIGATION REFORM ACT OF 1995

In response to a surge of shareholder derivative suits, particularly in Silicon Valley, Congress passed the PSLRA.[4] It was strongly opposed by the trial lawyers, especially those engaged in securities derivative actions, and was passed over the veto of President Bill Clinton. Congress responded to the low level of pleadings that were required to obtain subpoena powers from a federal district court to then conduct "a fishing expedition" in a company's records. Most cases were settled on terms that had nothing to do with the merits of the accusations, e.g. "the stock dropped 10 percent." The act did several things, including establishing higher pleading standards in an effort to eliminate frivolous law suits. It also included a "safe harbor" provision that one notorious plaintiffs' securities attorney, William Lerach, said "arguably permits corporate executives to lie about future results." The legislation also specifically upheld the *Central Bank* case on aiding and abetting. Taken with the safe harbor provision, most securities attorneys took this combination to indicate that they had no potential liability since they were a "secondary actor" and not the "primary actor" who committed the 10(b) violation. The attorneys were encouraged by the fact that the act also limited the liability of "peripheral" defendants or "secondary actors" to proportional liability when they lack knowledge of fraud; that is, the attorneys are only liable for the incremental harm caused by their participation in the fraud. While the passive secondary defendants are not off scot-free, their liability is limited. This proportional liability means that the lawyers involved are not likely to face judgments that would bankrupt their firm but would only increase their malpractice insurance premiums.

By contrast, secondary defendants who actively participate in the fraud are subject to full liability. As Adam Pritchard observed, "[S]econdary defendants do not enjoy immunity from liability under current law. If they make misrepresentations upon which investors rely (such as certifying false financial statements), secondary defendants can and will be held liable. *Central Bank* only excludes liability when secondary defendants have made no false statement themselves."[5] In effect, the PSLRA reaffirmed the distinctions in *Central Bank*. The act added the protection of proportional liability for those attorneys who have not published or participated in the misrepresentation of the corporation's financial condition. This was a clear reduction of the liability for the attorneys, and they have cited the act repeatedly in their defense against aiding-and-abetting charges in subsequent shareholders' derivative class action lawsuits.

THE CURRENT INTERPRETATION BY THE GENERAL ACCOUNTING OFFICE

Testifying about Enron, the GAO rejected the *Central Bank* rationale in its March 2003 Report to the Senate Committee on Banking, Housing, and Urban Affairs and the House Committee on Financial Services when it said that the

> SEC must prove three elements in an aiding and abetting a securities law violation: (1) that a principal committed a primary violation, (2) that the aider and abettor rendered such assistance knowingly or recklessly, and (3) that the aider and abettor provided substantial assistance to the primary violator. In other words:
>
> The first legal element of aiding and abetting is the requirement that an independent, illegal act exists to which the aider and abettor can be attached. This independent illegal act or primary violation may be a misrepresentation, omission, scheme to defraud, or fraudulent course of business.
>
> The second element of aider and abettor liability is either actual knowledge of the primary violation on the part of the aider and abettor or recklessness. However, the law is ambiguous with regard to the level of knowledge needed to prove aiding and abetting liability. Some courts have required SEC to prove that the entity aiding the primary violation had actual knowledge of the violation. However, other courts have found that recklessness is sufficient. In SEC administrative proceedings, liability may be based on less than actual knowledge of the violation.
>
> The third element of aiding and abetting, 'substantial assistance by the aider and abettor in the achievement of the primary violation' has been interpreted as meaning significant assistance to the representations of others or to the fraud of others. Persons may assist primary violators in many ways—for example by repeating their misrepresentations, aiding in the *preparation of misstatements*, acting as conduits to distribute securities, executing transactions, or financing transactions.[6] (emphasis added)

It is clear that Vinson & Elkins prepared and reviewed the documents submitted by Enron to the SEC. The examiner appointed by the bankruptcy court, Batson, concluded that the appropriate legal standard was that

> Whenever corporate fiduciaries communicate publicly or directly with stockholders, they must do so honestly, candidly, and completely in all material respects. The standard of disclosure arises of more general fiduciary duties of good faith and loyalty. *The Examiner concluded in his Second Interim Report that the financial statements and disclosure of Enron did not present a fair, full, and complete picture of Enron's financial condition.*[7] (emphasis added)

THE OPINION BY JUDGE MELINDA HARMON

The 305-page opinion by Judge Melinda Harmon, the federal district judge in Houston who is overseeing the consolidated Enron class action securities suits, is likely to become the basis for a new Supreme Court opinion on the issues of aiding and abetting.[8]

An excellent summary and analysis was written by law professor Anthony Sebok and appeared in the January 2003 *FindLaw's* Legal Commentary. Rather than trying to summarize and analyze this complex opinion myself, I am pleased to reproduce Sebok's article in total with their approval.

The Recent Opinion in the Enron Shareholders' Suit: Will It Redefine Lawyers' Duties When It Comes to Securities Fraud?

. . . On December 20, 2002, Judge Melinda Harmon, the federal district judge in Houston who is overseeing the consolidated Enron securities actions, issued a 305-page opinion in the suits. (The opinion is extraordinarily long both because the applicable law is very complex and hotly contested, and because it affected a very wide range of actors, some of whom were much more intimately involved with Enron than others.)

The motion that prompted the opinion was filed by the so-called "secondary" defendants, which include the eight banks, two law firms, and one accountancy group that are alleged to have committed securities fraud. (The "primary" defendants, of course, are Enron and its officers.)

The motion asked the judge to dismiss the claims against the secondary defendants, on the ground that what they were alleged to have done did not violate the laws invoked in the complaint. Regardless of what Enron may have done, the motion argued, these defendants could not be held liable under either state or federal securities law. They themselves, it argued, were not alleged to have performed conduct that constituted fraud with regard to the purchasers of Enron securities.

In her opinion, among other holdings the judge granted the motion on behalf of one law firm, Kirkland & Ellis, and dismissed the claims against that firm. However, she also allowed the plaintiffs to maintain their federal securities fraud claims against another law firm, Vinson & Elkins.

The opinion's reasoning is interesting in part because it raises this question: Is the distinction between Kirkland & Ellis, on the one hand, and Vinson & Elkins, on the other, principled or ad hoc? The answer to that question, it turns out, is itself complex.

The High Standards for Pleading a Federal Securities Fraud Claim

To begin, it's important to realize that the law firms are being sued only under the federal—not Texas—securities law. And that means that for the claims against them to survive, they must pass a demanding test. (Over the past ten years, Congress, under the pressure of intense lobbying by corporate America, has [amended] the federal securities statute to make it harder for "frivolous" securities claims to be brought; companies had been complaining that they'd had to settle even such claims to avoid the cost of litigation.) [Author's note: this and the following discussion relate to the PSLRA.]

As of today, then, a federal securities fraud plaintiff must allege that the defendant made a misstatement or omission of a material fact, and did so intentionally (in legal parlance, with "scienter"); that the plaintiff relied on the misstatement or omission; and that the misstatement or omission direct[ly] (in legal parlance, "proximately") caused the plaintiff injury.

What counts as a "misstatement or omission"? According to Supreme Court precedent, not only a statement or silence, but also a contrivance to achieve a fraudulent end (such as market manipulation), can qualify. That may matter quite a bit in the Enron case, where the structures including offshore entities are a major issue; these seem more like "contrivances" than misstatements to me.

The Allegations of "Aiding and Abetting" By the Law Firms

So what were the law firms' alleged misstatements, omissions, or contrivances? The plaintiffs did not, in their pleadings, identify any. Instead, they alleged, in essence, that the secondary defendants, including the law firms, aided and abetted fraud by Enron and its officers.

What counts as "aiding and abetting"? The question arises in many different areas of law, civil as well as criminal. For instance, as I discussed in a recent column, the issue arises in the context of corporate violations of the Alien Tort Claims Act. (For example, when a company provides material to a government in order to facilitate security around a worksite, and knows the government will use slave labor, rape, and other such actions while trying to "maintain" security, is the corporation aiding and abetting these human rights violations?)

What about in the securities fraud context? The fact is that federal securities laws do not prohibit the aiding and abetting of securities fraud. [PSLRA]

Why not? As the Supreme Court said in *Central Bank of Denver, N.A. v. First Interstate Bank of Denver, N.A.*, Congress intended to use the laws to regulate primary fraudulent actors, who actually make the misrepresentations— not the secondary actors who, at most, have knowingly help[ed] them do so.

So why didn't Judge Harmon dismiss all the claims against the secondary defendants? After all, weren't they just that type of secondary actor? That's where it gets complicated.

When Can Professionals Be Viewed as Primary, Not Secondary, Actors?

Under the case law, professionals such as law firms and accountants need not always be secondary actors; they can sometimes be primary actors, too. As Judge Harmon noted, since 1993 a number of federal appeals courts have so held.

In the U.S. Court of Appeals for the Ninth Circuit, for example, accountants have been found liable as primary actors where there was "substantial participation" by [an] accountant in the preparation of fraudulent statements which were then presented to the public by another primary actor.

Under the "substantial participation" rule, an accountant *or a lawyer* can be a primary actor even if he or she (or, in the case of a firm, it) did not directly make a statement to the plaintiff. Indeed, the plaintiff need not even know the accountant's or lawyer's name (at the time of the fraud).

However, some federal appellate courts, most notably the U.S. Court of Appeals for the Second Circuit, have rejected the "substantial participation" rule. They have adopted, instead, [a] much more restrictive "bright line" rule. Under the "bright line" rule, the professional itself must make a misrepresentation and the plaintiff, at the moment of the fraud, must know the professional's identity as the "author" of the misrepresentation.

Judge Harmon—a district judge in a Circuit that has not yet chosen between these tests—needed to choose one herself. The Securities Exchange Commission, in a "friend of the court" brief, urged her to adopt the substantial participation rule. She did.

Her reasoning was that *Central Bank* may have properly excluded actors who may have conspired to defraud others, but that there is a difference between helping another commit fraud and "making" a fraud, even if one makes the fraud (by necessity) by working with others who are also making the fraud.

The Duty to Report Versus the Duty to Refrain From Fraud

So how did the "substantial participation" rule apply to the law firms? Again, the issue gets a bit complicated.

The law firms first argued that—regardless of whether or not the allegations of substantial participation were sufficient—they could not be held as primary actors in securities fraud because that would impose on them two conflicting duties. On the one hand, they were obliged to maintain their clients' confidences under the ABA's Model Rules of Professional Conduct (as adopted by Texas). On the other hand, "substantial participation" liability would impose on them a duty to disclose these very confidences.

Judge Harmon didn't buy the argument. The question, she ruled, is not whether the firms had an obligation to report *Enron's* wrongdoing (they may not have). It is whether they must pay damages if *their* actions meant they substantially participated in Enron's fraudulent statement.

This approach makes some sense: After all, the firms could have withdrawn from the representation without also reporting Enron; the two decisions were separate.

Looking at the Allegations Against V&E, and K&E, Respectively

Next, Judge Harmon looked carefully at the allegations against each of the two firms, respectively: Vinson & Elkins (V&E), and then Kirkland & Ellis (K&E).

V&E, she noted, had become deeply dependent on Enron's business (Enron comprised 7% of its revenues). In addition, she ruled, *the facts alleged by the plaintiff suggest that V&E was essentially "a participant making material misrepresentations . . . in order to establish and perpetuate a Ponzi scheme that was making them all very rich."* (emphasis added by McNamar)

V&E, according to the [plaintiffs'] allegations, made its own misrepresentations to the buyers of securities, the judge ruled. Specifically, it drafted "true sales" opinions for Enron that it knew were false; prepared disclosures for Enron to sign that it knew were false; and gave advice about how Enron should perform certain fraudulent acts.

[The author has researched one type of misrepresentation or, more appropriately, omission. This is the question of "materiality" in determining what is presented in the financial statements and what is not. The law and the accounting on this question are both vague. There has been a materiality test based on percentage of assets or revenues represented. Further, there has been a test of "would a reasonable investor think it was material?" V&E signed off on almost all SEC filings and so must have confronted the issues and made decisions to include or exclude SPEs, prepays, and other transactions.

For example, the Nigerian barges with electrical generators on them were sold over the period to Merrill Lynch & Co and quickly repurchased during the next period. (There was a verbal commitment from Enron's Fastow to repurchase them as soon as possible.) In terms of assets, the barges were less than 1 percent of Enron's multi-billion dollar assets, hence the sale wasn't disclosed in the 10-K. However, it represented 1 cent per share in earning, which enabled Enron to meet its earning projections. Failure to meet the projections would have had a very negative result on Enron's stock. In the author's opinion, while there is nothing in the Enron literature about determining materiality for disclosure purposes, there is an open and unresolved question about who made the materiality decisions, V&E or Enron?]

Had V&E been alleged merely to have *witnessed* the misconduct by Enron, Judge Harmon ruled, she would have had to dismiss them from the suit. But, she held, the allegations said V&E did more: When Enron spoke to the public using documents V&E had helped prepare, V&E made false statements to the public too. It didn't matter that V&E had not signed those documents; under the substantial participation rule, it was still "essentially a co-author."

What about K&E? It, too, was alleged to have known perfectly well what Enron was doing, and to have actively assisted Enron's fraudulent activities. But there was a difference in the allegations, the judge held. V&E was alleged to have helped Enron prepare documents relating to publicly traded securities. In contrast, K&E "merely" helped structure Enron's subsidiaries (the famous special partnerships with *Star Wars* and *Jurassic Park*–derived names like "Chewco" and the "Raptors").

Why the V&E/K&E Distinction Judge Harmon Made, May Not Hold Water

In the end, this may be, as lawyers often say, a distinction without a difference. As Judge Harmon notes in her opinion, these private Enron-controlled entities were necessary to Enron's "Ponzi scheme"; only because of them could Enron "hide its debt and record its sham profits." In working for these entities, K&E thus allegedly aided fraud. It also allegedly created fraudulent documents—though, like V&E, it may not have signed them.

So what's the supposed difference between V&E and K&E? V&E co-authored the documents, disclosed to the public, that contained the alleged fraudulent statements; K&E only helped make the disclosures possible by alleged[ly] creating the entities that made the whole fraudulent scheme work.

The difference, then, is this: K&E's documents, even if fraudulent, never saw the light of day. K&E allegedly worked on the secret part of the alleged fraud; V&E allegedly worked on the public part.

Of course, none—or only some—of the allegations against K&E and V&E may be true. But when deciding a motion to dismiss, judges must assume that they are. The very purpose of such a motion is to ask: If these facts are true, would they describe a law violation? It is hard to see how this question could be answered differently for K&E and V&E, as Judge Harmon answered it.

Indeed, the ruling seems somewhat ironic: V&E worked directly for Enron, a publicly traded company that committed fraud. K&E allegedly worked for Enron's non-publicly traded fraudulent subsidiaries. If creating Chewco, the Raptors, and so on wasn't fraudulent, it's hard to see how anything else could be either.[9]

Sebok's discussion of Judge Harmon's ruling not to dismiss Vinson & Elkins shows the murkiness of the laws on aiding and abetting. She was, in fact, applying federal law, which presumably abrogated aiding and abetting in the PSLRA. Reading her opinion, I conclude that she made the right decision. Other documents indicate that most often Kirkland & Ellis in fact represented the special purpose entity (SPE) in negotiations with Enron. It had no involvement in preparing Enron's SEC filings. Reading it, one has the sense that Judge Harmon wants to make new law because neither the 1995 Act nor the *Central Bank* case are good law in the aiding and abetting area. Applying federal law, not state law, she made a new distinction between "primary actors" and "secondary actors." While the distinction has logic, the current federal court decisions are simply not congruent with that distinction. Because of the length of the opinion and how well it was written, I conclude that Judge Harmon wants to make new law in this area. Assuming the Supreme Court reviews this motion, hopefully a clear and higher standard for lawyers assisting in securities fraud will emerge.

STATE LAWS

It is instructive to examine the applicable state laws on aiding and abetting. Remember that the choice of law can be a hotly contested matter. The U.S. Federal District Court in Houston can apply Texas law when appropriate. The examiner in bankruptcy for the Southern District Court in New York, sitting as a bankruptcy court, concluded that Oregon law, where Enron was incorporated, was the applicable law. Nevertheless, he concluded that Oregon, Texas, and New York all recognize a cause of action for "aiding and abetting" a breach of a fiduciary duty.

Oregon also presents a tort violation for aiding and abetting. "Legal authorities, however, virtually are unanimous in expressing the proposition that one who knowingly aids another in the breach of a fiduciary duty is liable to the one harmed."[10] Oregon, Texas, and New York law appear to be alike in requiring two elements for aiding and abetting: "knowledge" and "substantial assistance."[11] In *FDIC v. Nathan*, knowingly structuring, documenting, and closing fraudulent loans that aided a breach of fiduciary duty by their officers of a savings and loan was actionable.[12] New York appears to have more cases and be more settled. Knowing about one wrongful act does not seem to be sufficient, but raises a "failure to investigate" issue where there were indications that the company was not acting properly. Under New York law it would seem that an agent's failure to investigate is a breach of fiduciary duties.

Although redomiciled to Oregon for corporate purposes, Enron was located in Texas. Virtually all of the lawyers who worked on Enron were members of the Texas Bar Association, and almost all of the transactions in question were executed in Texas. Most of the transaction documents specified that Texas law would apply in interpreting them and that any litigation would be in Texas. Hence Texas has a strong nexus to Enron.

> Texas recognizes a claim for aiding and abetting a breach of fiduciary duty by another, and several courts in jurisdictions other than Texas have ruled that a company's outside attorneys may be liable to the company if the attorney aided and abetted an officer's breach of fiduciary duty to the corporation. Accordingly, it is appropriate to consider whether an attorney's actions constitute aiding and abetting an officer's breach of fiduciary duty to the company . . . a corporation will have an affirmative claim against its attorney for aiding and abetting the corporation's officer's breach of fiduciary duty if the attorney had actual knowledge of the wrongful conduct giving rise to such breach, if the attorney gave substantial assistance to the primary wrongdoer, and if the injury to the corporation was the direct or reasonably foreseeable result of the attorney's conduct.[13]

The above discussion should make it clear that the civil laws and court decisions on aiding and abetting are not clear. It can only be hoped that Judge Harmon's opinion in not excusing Vinson & Elkins from the civil litigation will provide the Supreme Court with an opportunity to overturn *Central Bank* so that aiders and abettors can at least be civilly liable in class action lawsuits. Such suits are a grossly imperfect method of maintaining discipline in the legal profession, but that may be about to change.

Defending his firm at a congressional hearing, Vinson & Elkins managing partner Joseph C. Dilg said that "There's nothing that I'm aware of that we would change. . . . We never saw anything at Enron that we considered illegal."[14] Granted that his firm is in substantial litigation as a defendant in the shareholders' derivative suit in the U.S. District Court in Houston and is facing major malpractice suits, you could expect no less. To lay a predicate for the policy recommendations, this chapter will examine the role of Vinson & Elkins and Enron in depth in the following sections. To begin, Batson, the examiner in bankruptcy, said: "'The Examiner concludes there is sufficient evidence from which a fact-finder could determine that Andrews & Kurth committed malpractice based on Texas Rule 1.12, aided and abetted a breach of fiduciary duty or committed malpractice based on negligence in connection with these FAS Transactions."[15] Note that, consistent with the *Central Bank* decision and Judge Harmon's rulings in the Enron class action civil case, the examiner did not find evidence of federal securities law violations because Andrews & Kurth made no "misrepresentation" regarding Enron that investors could have relied upon in buying or trading its securities.

ROLE OF THE ATTORNEYS FOR ENRON

This section summarizes some of the specific activities that the attorneys played at Enron. Vinson & Elkins is continually mentioned, but the Houston firm of Andrews & Kurth did a lot of the same work on true sales opinions on the SPE transactions. However, it was Vinson & Elkins that did all of the SEC work, and this constitutes the misrepresentation within the purview of *Central Bank* and the PSLRA. To put the magnitude of these transactions in perspective, on its third-quarter balance sheet Enron reported total debt of $13 billion. On November 19, 2001, the same day the 10-Q was filed, Enron met with its bankers at the Waldorf in New York City; Enron debt was shown as $38 billion. Thus $25 billion was "off balance sheet," but classified as something else. Approximately $13 billion of this $25 billion of additional "debt" was incurred through structured finance transactions involving the use of SPEs. Hence the role of the lawyers was key to the financial structure that Enron developed.

A true sales opinion from the company's counsel is required in all Financial Accounting Standards Board (FASB) 125 and its successor FASB 140 transactions. This is to be sure that the transaction is not simply a secured financing that must remain on the balance sheet. The objective is to ensure that in the event of bankruptcy the asset transferred by the parent to the SPE will not be included in the bankruptcy, but that it has been "*isolated*" or is "*remote*" from the parent. The accounting and legal concepts here are identical. The asset has been sold, therefore it is so remote from the company that in the event of the company's subsequent bankruptcy the asset will not be considered a part of the company's assets that its creditors can reach in bankruptcy. This is accomplished by an opinion by an outside counsel that there has, in fact, been a true sale. Such opinions are standard documentation in SPE transactions. From 1997 through 2001, Vinson & Elkins provided sixty-six true sales opinions and Andrews & Kurth twenty-eight true sales opinions.

> According to the summary of the special committee [Powers Committee] interview with Ephross [Jeol Ephross, senior attorney for Enron Global Finance], Enron lawyers believed that 'it would be easier to get an opinion from A&K than V&E.' He said V&E was concerned that its opinion letters 'were being improperly relied upon by Anderson.' A&K's Mr. Ayers says it is 'not aware of receiving any assignment from Enron that another law firm had declined.'[16]

In Enron, the facts about the attorneys and true sales opinions are not in dispute. The examiner in bankruptcy and the Senate Government Operations Subcommittee in a series of hearings all concluded basically the same thing. The shareholder derivative suit in the Southern District of Texas alleges that the attorneys were aiders and abettors in a conspiracy to commit securities fraud by Enron. The attorneys at Vinson & Elkins drafted almost all of the documents for the numerous transactions that comprised the Ponzie scheme that was the Enron securities fraud. It was not an occasional transaction that might be misunderstood out of context or possibly a standalone transaction that was close to the edge of the FASB's rules, where an attorney might not know all of the accounting. Rather, in the sixty-six transactions, Vinson & Elkins rendered the "true sales opinions" or "true issuance opinions" that were used by the bankers and Enron, even though there was no true sale of the Enron asset to the SPE that supposedly bought the asset from Enron. All of these transactions violated FASB 140 and its predecessor FASB 125 ("140/125"). Further, the examiner in bankruptcy found that the true issuance opinions failed to meet the "isolation" of the asset test in FASB 125 and 140. Hence, the SPEs should have all been consolidated on the Enron balance sheet.

The true sale opinion letters by Vinson & Elkins were written on transactions where the title of the asset did not pass in a true sale because Enron repeatedly did two things: Enron, the putative seller, guaranteed the bank debt of the SPE so that if the SPE failed to make the payments of interest and principal to the bank, then Enron would pay the interest and pay off the principal at the debt's maturity. This is a guarantee by the parent of the debt of the SPE, which is fine if the parent in turn doesn't pretend that it has sold the SPE and removed the asset from the balance sheet of the parent. Under FASB 125/140, this alone would require that the asset be shown as a part of the Enron balance sheet. Second, Enron continued to have an economic interest in the transaction through a "total return swap." A total return swap was not a derivative, but when analyzed was actually a contractual profit participation in the upside of the earnings or cash flow of the asset designed to provide Enron a continued economic interest in the asset after it had purportedly sold it to the SPE to remove it from its balance sheet. That is, Enron was contractually entitled to earn money from the asset even though it was no longer on its balance sheet. If Enron had sold the asset, how could it be entitled to earning from the asset? If Enron hadn't in fact sold the asset, how could the lawyers give a "true sale" opinion? How could the lawyers make the same mistake sixty-six times?

In fact, the examiner's interviews with a number of lawyers indicated that they did know exactly what Enron was doing:

> Wulfe (an Andrews & Kurth attorney) also recognized, at least on the FAS 140 Transaction that he was working on, that Enron, as a consolidated entity, was not shifting risk of loss and was not giving up the potential upside of the assets being transferred. Enron's obligation under the Total Return Swap to pay the loan also raised liquidity issues: ' . . . if the asset placed in the structure was sold . . . for . . . less than . . . the loan . . . [then] some Enron entity would effectively make up the shortfall.[17]

Mistakes can be made in the practice of law, as in any profession. One or two or three mistakes might be just that. The number of true sales opinions in Enron, however, doesn't seem to be a mistake, but appears to a conscious part of a conspiracy to commit securities fraud. At some point, the observer must conclude there is a suspect pattern of behavior. Batson characterized the FAS 140 transactions as follows:

> In its FAS 140 Transactions, Enron 'monetized' a variety of otherwise illiquid assets from its balance sheet while at the same time retaining control over them with a view toward better timing the final sale of those assets. In the Second Interim Report, the Examiner concluded that these transactions were improperly used by Enron to record income from gain on sale of assets and erroneously report the cash proceeds from these transactions as cash flow from operating activities (or, to lesser degree, from investment activities). Enron also failed to disclose adequately its obligations under the Total Return Swaps that were entered into as part of these FAS 140 Transactions, and to reflect the indebtedness incurred.[18]

The attorneys who wrote the Enron true sales opinions appeared to lack the ability to know the difference between renting a house and buying a house. By extension, the attorneys either didn't know the difference between renting an asset to an SPE or selling it to the SPE. Yet they continued to provide "true sales" opinions on which the bankers and accountants purportedly relied. While I lack the firsthand evidence to confirm this judgment, it is logical and totally consistent with the findings of those who have had the subpoena power to obtain the original records.

What other explanation can there be for Vinson & Elkins providing approximately sixty-six true sales opinion letters on transactions that were not true sales? Is it possible that they were mistaken that many times? Is it possible that the transactions were so complex that the lawyers just couldn't understand them? Did they keep using the same true sales opinion over and over? Or did they want to keep their client happy and make money be providing true sales opinions that they knew were false?

When Vinson & Elkins did express some reservations about some of the transactions, why was Andrews & Kurth so willing to do so? They wrote the true sales opinion on the Raptor transactions, which had neither economic substance nor represented a true sale of the Enron stock to the SPE. According to Batson,

> there is sufficient evidence from which a fact-finder could conclude that certain of Enron's attorneys involved in its SPE transactions (i) committed legal malpractice based on Texas Rule 1.12, (ii) committed legal malpractice based on negligence, or (iii) aided and abetted the Enron officers' breaches of fiduciary duty.[19]

Similarly,

> The Examiner concludes that there is sufficient evidence from which a fact-finder could determine that Andrews & Kurth committed malpractice

based on Texas Rule 1.12, aided and abetted a breach of fiduciary duty, or committed malpractice based on negligence in connection with these FAS Transactions. A fact-finder could determine that Andrews & Kurth knew that Enron had no intention to relinquish control over, or the risk and rewards of, the assets transferred in certain of the FAS 140 Transactions and therefore was engaging in the FAS 140 Transactions to produce materially misleading financial statements.[20]

An example of these transactions was Cerberus, where Andrews & Kurth rendered a true sales opinion. Again, Batson stated, "[T]he Cerberus transaction appears to be, from both an economic and risk allocation perspective, a loan rather than a sale of assets." According to his accounting experts, "Enron's disclosure of its obligations " in Cerberus was "not in accordance" with generally accepted accounting principles.[21]

Given that Vinson & Elkins also either drafted or reviewed almost all of the SEC filings that described the financial condition of Enron, including that the SPEs where they had rendered false true sales opinions were not on the Enron balance sheet, does this meet the test of aiding and abetting a securities fraud perpetrated by some of Enron's management? One is hard-pressed not to draw the conclusion that Vinson & Elkins did act as an active aider and abettor in the Enron management's securities fraud.

While the SEC has yet to act on this matter, it is instructive that Judge Harmon did not allow Vinson & Elkins' motion to be dismissed from the class action lawsuit. In my view, the *Central Bank* case is being selectively applied in the Enron case. It will certainly go to the Supreme Court, perhaps to make new state and federal law on aiding and abetting.

PREPAYS: NO SUBSTANCE TO THE TRANSACTION

Enron entered into a substantial number of transactions that had no economic substance but were bank loans disguised to look like energy swaps. Typically, these transactions were thinly disguised bank loans with no real economic effect. When netted, whether through just the bank and an Enron entity or, more typically, a third party as well, the difference in "what was owed at settlement" was the prevailing rate on a bank loan at the time expressed in cash, not an interest rate.

By disguising the bank loans as energy swaps, Enron avoided FASB No. 5, which would have required the bank loans to be booked as cash flows from financing activities rather than "cash flows from operations." Clearly these loans were cash flows from financings and not from operations. When the transactions were netted, they legally and financially operated exactly as bank loans from JP Morgan, Citicorp, CIBC, and Chase. There was a principal sum that had been borrowed and that had to be paid back, and there was an interest charge for the borrowing that was priced exactly at the current interest rate for comparable unsecured corporate credits. In fact, the banks booked them as loans even though the loan documents were titled "swaps."

By categorizing the bank loans as energy swaps, Enron avoided complying with FASB No. 5 and classifying the loans as providing cash from financing rather than operations. This helped maintain the illusion that Enron didn't have as much debt as in fact it did. The credit rating agencies didn't learn of this mischaracterization until after Enron's bankruptcy. It was clear from the internal correspondence at the banks that they knew they were bank loans. It seems incredulous to imagine that the lawyers didn't also understand these transactions were disguised bank loans.

POWERS COMMITTEE ASSESSMENT OF VINSON & ELKINS

Against this background, it is informative to review the findings of the Powers Committee. William C. Powers is the dean of the University of Texas Law School. He led a committee appointed by the post-bankruptcy Enron board to examine a number of the transactions and the related-party disclosure issues. It reviewed Enron's disclosure process, including its proxy statements and all other SEC filings, including 10-K and 10-Q reports. The committee determined that the proxy documents were drafted by Vinson & Elkins and reviewed by others and that the 10-K and 10-Q statements were drafted by others, but in all cases reviewed and signed off on by Vinson & Elkins. Members of Vinson & Elkins interviewed by the examiner in bankruptcy refute this characterization of their role. Rather, they indicated that Vinson & Elkins did draft the proxy statements, but only saw portions of the 10-K and 10-Q filings, typically the management's discussion & analysis section. The Powers Committee concluded that

> While accountants took the lead in preparing the financial statement footnote disclosures, lawyers played a more central role in preparing the proxy statement, including the disclosure of the related-party transactions . . . they [management] relied on advice from Vinson & Elkins in deciding whether the proposed disclosures were adequate, particularly with respect to related-party transactions. . . . *Overall, Enron failed to disclose facts that were important for an understanding of the substance of the transactions.*"[22](emphasis added)

SUMMARY AND CONCLUSION ON AIDING AND ABETTING

The case law and statutes on aiding and abetting are confusing. There is conflict among the federal appellate circuits. The publicly available facts in Enron are limited.

At the time of this writing, no individual lawyer or law firm has been charged with a criminal act. The SEC has not publicly announced an investigation into the role of the lawyers. The only case questioning the role of the lawyers is the shareholder derivative suit in the Southern District of the U.S. District Court of Appeals in Houston being presided over by Judge Harmon. She has granted Kirkland & Ellis's motion for dismissal, while refusing to dismiss the civil charges against Vinson & Elkins.

To obtain a criminal conviction against Vinson & Elkins or some of its attorneys, the government must obtain a grand jury indictment and proceed to trial. At the trial to obtain a conviction, the prosecution must prove "beyond a reasonable doubt" that the defendant "knowingly" committed the alleged illegal act. Further, it must convince all twelve jurors to obtain a unanimous verdict for a criminal conviction. This is a very high mountain for the prosecution to climb. In all probability, there will be no criminal convictions against Vinson & Elkins under these facts.

The Texas State Bar Association is unlikely to investigate or consider any disciplinary action. State bar associations are generally unwilling to discipline their members.

The shareholder derivative suit appears to be the only mechanism available to extract at least monetary damages from an attorney. Relying on them for attorney discipline is random at best. Yet there is the possibility of actual civil damage awards, resultant malpractice suits, and increases in the attorneys' malpractice insurance premiums as a result of the lawsuit. It is even possible that the attorneys might have to pay some of the damages from their personal assets.

The conclusion is that the attorneys in Enron are likely to escape criminal sanctions and may only face civil lawsuits, the outcome of which is in doubt at this time. Judge Harmon's ruling did not address their criminal liability, and I have no basis for an opinion on either their civil or criminal liability.

POLICY RECOMMENDATIONS AFFECTING THE LAWYERS

This section is divided into two parts. The first deals with aiding and abetting. The second deals with what professional responsibilities the lawyers should have to a corporation when they have a reasonable belief that they have found corporate wrongdoing, typically securities fraud.

The extensive prior discussion on aiding and abetting shows the confusion and conflicting statutes and court decisions about this subject. To review:

The Congress passed the PSLRA. It made it much harder to prove aiding and abetting for lawyers in securities litigation.

Subsequent to 1995, the federal appellate courts have largely ignored the PSLRA in their cases. Applying federal law, the courts are in clear conflict. The Ninth Circuit has a test for "substantial participation" in the securities fraud that makes a secondary actor (an attorney) in effect a primary actor for purposes of committing securities fraud. This flies in the face of the Supreme Court's opinion in the *Central Bank* case. It specifically held that "Congress intended to use the laws to regulate primary fraudulent actors, who actually make misrepresentations, not the secondary actors who, at most, have knowingly helped them do so."

In the Enron shareholder derivative suit, Judge Harmon, ruling on the motion to dismiss, took a different tack. She ruled that Kirkland & Ellis were secondary actors who participated in the frauds at Enron on the periphery and did not participate in the securities fraud. Hence she granted their motion for dismissal. By contrast, she found that Vinson & Elkins was guilty of "misrepresentations" in the SEC filings and had actually participated in preparing the misrepresentations. While I have no opinion as to the guilt or innocence of Vinson & Elkins in these matters, it is interesting to note that Judge Harmon's ruling is consistent with the logic of the Ninth Circuit and the *Central Bank* ruling. She simply made a finding of fact, not law, that Vinson & Elkins's preparation of the SEC materials in effect moved them from being a secondary actor to a primary actor, and preparation of the documents constituted a "misrepresentation."

State laws on aiding and abetting are fully in force, but will not apply to federal securities laws. Oregon, Texas, and New York require two elements for aiding and abetting: "knowingly" and "substantial assistance."

On the criminal side of the law, if the offense is judged aggrieved, the SEC may still make a criminal referral to the Justice Department, but the success of prosecution is problematic at best.

Against this background, it is clear that the criminal and civil laws regarding aiding and abetting need to be clarified. This raises two issues: how can they be clarified, and what is the appropriate standard?

How clarified? While congressional legislation could clarify the law in this area, the author is dubious that Congress, composed mostly of lawyers and dominated by trial lawyers, is likely to pass appropriate legislation on the matter. Bluntly put, Congress is not likely to make a lawyer's existing ethical obligations a legal obligation.

The second, and more likely, source of clarification is the Supreme Court. The *Central Bank* case was a close 5–4 decision on facts that really don't apply to lawyers in an SEC securities matter. It seems probable that Judge Harmon's ruling in the Enron civil action case will be appealed to the Supreme Court. This outcome may be the best that can be hoped for in the circumstances.

Are the lawyers exempt from the laws of the United States? This should be a rhetorical question, but isn't. The lawyers argue that they should continue to be a self-regulating organization under the state bar associations, which provide no standards of conduct that are enforceable nor discipline their members.

That said, in the case of federal securities laws, there must be accountability for the lawyers who knowingly (or a reasonable prudent lawyer who should have known) participate in a securities fraud. The SEC has only civil sanctions and no criminal authority. Prohibiting an attorney from appearing before the SEC is a laughable sanction that only attests to the influence of the securities bar.

That said, what should the standard be for lawyers? I recommend that when an attorney "knowingly" provides "substantial assistance" in preparing SEC documents that constitute a "misrepresentation," the attorney should be guilty of aiding and abetting a securities fraud and certainly civilly liable, and possibly criminally liable. In this case, "knowingly" should probably include "the failure to investigate" where there were indications that the company was not acting properly. This is essentially the current New York State law standard, which could be incorporated into the federal law.

The above policy recommendation derives from the fiduciary duties that officers of the court have to the corporation, which is managed by the board of directors and owned by the shareholders. If a corporate officer breaches their fiduciary duty to the corporation by filing false or misleading SEC documents and the lawyer knowingly provides substantial assistance in preparing the documents, it is impossible to argue that the lawyer is a secondary actor. By providing "substantial assistance" the lawyers have defined themselves as primary actors and are therefore subject to the same civil liability and prosecution standards as the corporate officer. Hopefully, the Supreme Court will adopt this policy standard, since Congress probably can't deal with it.

In the wake of Enron and other corporate scandals, there has been a lot of discussion on what lawyers should do when they have reasonable cause to believe that their client is breaking the law in some manner. In section 307 of the Sarbanes-Oxley Act of 2002 (SOA), Congress mandated that the SEC establish new standards of conduct for attorneys. It says:

> No later than 180 days after the date of enactment of this Act, the Commission [SEC] shall issue rules, in the public interest and for the protection of investors, setting forth minimum standards of professional conduct for attorneys appearing and practicing before the Commission in any way in the representation of issuers, including a rule
>
> (1) requiring an attorney to report evidence of a material violation of securities law or breadth of fiduciary duty or similar violation by the company or any agent thereof, to the chief legal counsel or the chief executive officer of the company (or the equivalent thereof); and
>
> (2) if the counsel or officer does not appropriately respond to the evidence (adopting, as necessary, appropriate remedial measures or sanctions with respect to the violation), requiring the attorney to report evidence to the audit committee of the board of directors of the issuer or to another committee of the board of directors of the issuer or to another committee of the board of directors comprised solely of directors not employed directly or indirectly by the issuer, or to the board of directors.

On November 21, 2002, the SEC published a proposed rule for a "noisy withdrawal." In its request for comments on the proposed rule, the SEC said that the noisy withdrawal would come into play when an attorney, after reporting evidence of a material violation up-the-ladder of the issuer's governance structure, reasonably believed that issuer's directors have either made no response (within a reasonable time) or have not made an appropriate response." Under these circumstances, " . . . these provisions would have permitted or required attorneys to withdraw from representation of an issuer, to notify the Commission that they have done so, and to disaffirm documents filed or submitted to the Commission on behalf of the issuer."

The SEC received many comments on the proposed rule and as of November 29, 2003, has not acted on it. There were comments that supported the noisy withdrawal as a necessary compliment to up-the-ladder reporting. However, most of the comments have been negative. This includes several law professors who are in favor of increased attorney accountability, professors Susan P. Koniak, Roger Campton, and George Cohen. They represented a group of forty-eight additional law professors, all opposed to the proposed noisy withdrawal rule.

In my opinion, the noisy withdrawal is unworkable and would be an extremely poor implementation of SOA Sec. 307, which certainly doesn't require or appear to contemplate a noisy withdrawal. The substantial opposition to the rule and the delay in SEC action suggests that it will be abandoned, although the proposed rule is still in place. The period for comment closed April 7, 2003, and no SEC action has taken place. In short, it appears dead, or at least moribund.

The two reasons why the noisy withdrawal is bad public policy are as follows. First, if it were adopted, there is a high probability that clients would exclude attorneys from meetings where information would be exchanged that could lead an attorney to believe a material securities violation had occurred or might be about to occur. Second, the noisy withdrawal directly conflicts with an attorney's obligation for attorney-client privileged information. Consider these two reasons together. The attorney-client privilege is designed so that a client is protected from publication of information as to what was discussed between the client and the attorney. Out of ignorance or to push the envelope, corporate executives often propose to conduct illegal or questionable activities. Often, even senior corporate officials are quite unsophisticated about securities matters. Under the attorney-client privilege, corporate executives can feel free to ask about all sorts of matters knowing that the attorney won't divulge them to the law enforcement authorities, IRS, etc. If an attorney had an obligation to resign and report proposed illegal activity to the SEC, it seems clear that the anticipated response by corporate executives would be to not invite the attorney to the meeting where the matter was discussed, which deprives the corporate executive of the very professional counsel that he or she may most need.

A somewhat more subtle conflict exists between the lawyer's obligation as "an officer of the court" and their fiduciary obligations to a corporate client. Some commentators say that the obligation as an officer of the court literally only applies when the attorney is in the courtroom. Others suggest that it carries over to all activities and can come into conflict with the fiduciary obligation to a corporate client or even the application of attorney-client privilege. That said, in my opinion the previous reasons for rejecting the noisy withdrawal are sufficient.

The ABA is part trade association, part educational facility, and part omni-mother to the state bar associations and its own members. It really can't be more than that, because it only has some moral suasion that some of its members might respect. Over time it has been largely ineffectual in most policy matters, but has provided excellent educational forums for its members on practice topics, e.g., securities law. Traditionally, the ABA had opposed any obligations on its state bar associations or the membership. They considered the attorney-client privilege as sacred and did not believe that the attorney had any affirmative obligation to report to the corporation possible wrongdoings that the attorney had a reasonable basis for thinking had occurred or were about to occur. They wanted no affirmative obligations placed on attorneys from the SEC or any other government entity. In the light of Enron and other corporate scandals in 2002, the ABA modified its position on the obligation of attorneys. It adopted a "permissive" disclosure policy for attorneys in situations where they had reasonable cause to believe that wrongdoing had occurred or was about to occur. This provided for an attorney to have the "option" to contact an outside board member or a partner in the law firm who is not working for the client.

While the ABA struggled with this language and it was largely opposed by the membership, it was adopted and represented a profound change on the part of the ABA. That said, if the new ABA rule were adopted by all fifty state bar associations, it would make little difference in the way that attorneys conduct themselves. And, as can be expected, there are no sanctions for not acting, because the rule is permissive. I would be hard-pressed to regard it as more than window dressing for public relations.

I believe that outside attorneys should have an *affirmative* obligation to report up in their law firm and over to the corporation's board matters that they reasonably believe represent civil or criminal wrongdoing on the part of officers of the corporation, especially potential securities fraud. The attorney's fiduciary obligations to the corporation are clear. Failure to perform the fiduciary obligations will result in the corporation having a cause of action against the attorney for malpractice. The attorney's obligations are not to management, but to the board of directors as the managing entity of the corporation and the direct representatives of the owner shareholders.

Malpractice can arise from acts committed or omission to take certain acts. Under New York law, where there are indications that the company was not acting properly, the "failure to investigate" is a breach of fiduciary duty. This failure to act can result in the corporation having a right to sue the attorney for malpractice, even though it is simply an omission rather than a commission.

Consistent with the New York case law, I recommend the following public policy for attorneys who suspect that a wrongdoing, especially an SEC securities violation, has occurred or is about to occur:

The attorney would have an affirmative obligation to report-up in his firm and over to the members of the board of the corporation.

Specifically, the attorney would first have an obligation to consult with a senior partner in the firm that is not working for the client corporation.

Second, if, after consultations with the senior partner, the attorney still believed there was a reasonable probability of a wrongdoing, he would have an affirmative obligation to report it to two outside or independent directors of the company's board, at least one of whom is a member of the audit committee.

Some have suggested that attorneys, especially junior ones, would be reluctant to pursue such a risky course of action and endanger their employment situation. The counter to this argument, the SOA provided for a five-year salary payment in the event that a whistle-blower is dismissed for acting. This is a significant financial cushion to a whistle-blower.

This affirmative reporting-up obligation would not be optional but would be mandatory. If an attorney failed to comply with the obligations, the sanctions would include: liability to the corporation for malpractice; disbarment; and civil fines by the SEC. In addition, the attorney would be subject to a new claim of malfeasance on the part of attorneys bringing shareholder derivative litigation on behalf of the corporation.

Similarly, the board members who are alerted to possible violations, especially securities violations, would have increased liability in the event of civil litigation. They have clearly been put "on notice." In terms of potential legal liability for not acting on the information, the director would have moved from a possible breach of fiduciary duty to bad faith or a failure to investigate, which should focus their attention on the issue at hand.

One should anticipate that most board members would welcome the fact that the outside attorneys are under an affirmative obligation to bring questionable activities to the attention of the board. If the two informed directors take the matter to the full board, and the full board addresses the matter in a prudent manner, the concerns about increased director liability are easily satisfied.

This policy may strike some as draconian. While it is a radical change in attorney obligations from the past, clearly the past does not represent good public policy. What happened at Enron and the fact that the attorneys with at least a reasonable suspicion, if not full knowledge, did not have any affirmative obligation to do anything about it while it was occurring warrants this change in public policy to minimize future Enron's.

In fact, one of the benefits of this affirmative obligation to report up in the law firm and to members of the board is that it is entirely consistent with the attorney-client privilege on confidentiality.

Attorneys are not only not above the law, rather they should have an affirmative obligation to see that the law is adhered to by their corporate clients. Not to do so is to commit malpractice by omission similar to "the duty to investigate" under existing New York law.

Note that the policy does not require the lawyer to contact the in-house general counsel or any executive in management. The facts in Enron clearly demonstrate why that could be a useless exercise. The general counsel ignored and threatened to fire a female attorney on his staff when she raised questions about the legality of some of the Enron transactions. Lay's ignoring Sherron Watkins and referring her letter to Vinson & Elkins, when she had specifically said they are conflicted and can't look into the matter, demonstrates that in these situations management is often the problem rather than the solution. *An attorney's fiduciary obligation is to the corporation and its shareholders, who are represented by the board of directors.* The proposed policy doesn't prohibit the outside attorney from going to management; it simply doesn't require it, since, in my view, informing management or the in-house general counsel will all too often be a useless exercise.

What happens if the two independent directors don't take the appropriate action in a reasonable time? Given the directors' liability once put on notice of the securities law violation, and the fact they know that the attorney is aware of the securities law violation, there is a very low probability that they will not act to remedy the situation. And if they do not, I would rather take that chance than impose unduly heavy compliance costs or bad policies, e.g., noisy withdrawal, on either the attorney or the director. The attorney always has the right to resign. And both the ABA rule and SOA provide for five years' salary for a whistle-blower who is fired.

This type of reporting up and over could be equally applicable to in-house counsel. When there are widespread misrepresentations of a company's financial condition to the SEC, it is unlikely that the CEO or the general counsel will be whistle-blowers, since they normally would have some complicity in the misrepresentation. In the case of Enron, the general counsel specifically did not investigate anonymous letters sent to Lay in August 2001 alleging that there were accounting irregularities at Enron. Accordingly, I believe that, as a rule, a subordinate attorney contacting management or the general counsel will be nonproductive.

By contrast, for the in-house counsel, it is feasible to have lawyers with a reasonable suspicion of wrongdoing contact two directors. The first would be an independent director not on the audit committee, and the second the chairman of the audit committee. This is a reasonable burden on the chairman of the audit committee in that the number of in-house lawyers is typically not large and most are involved in ministerial transactions, e.g., closing real estate transactions. These lawyers aren't likely to uncover securities violations on their own, but could be told of them by other in-house lawyers and acquire the obligation to report up to the two board members. If a lawyer were told of possible securities violations he would have a duty to investigate and report up to the board members.

I have above advocated an affirmative reporting responsibility by lawyers and the sanctioning of activities that "knowingly" and "substantially assist" in aiding and abetting a securities fraud. Most statutes and court cases involving aiding and abetting are state laws regarding the assistance provided a corporate officer in a breach of their fiduciary duty to the corporation. However, the SEC could use civil sanctions against attorneys who are found guilty of aiding and abetting a securities fraud.

A straightforward method of addressing these issues is by extending to the lawyers the certification requirements of the SOA section 302(a). This requires corporate officers to certify that they have read the corporate reports and that, to the best of their knowledge, they are correctly prepared and contain no misrepresentations of the company's financial condition. By extension, a similar certification could be developed for lawyers who are working on corporate transactions that have the potential to affect the accurate and fair representation of the corporate financial statements filed with the SEC.

In the Enron case, many of the individual SPE transactions would not have met the traditional accounting materiality test of representing over 3 percent of the corporate assets. However, if the exclusion of the SPE from consolidation on the balance sheet was tantamount to misrepresenting the corporate financial statements submitted to the SEC, then it clearly is material in determining whether the attorney participated in aiding and abetting a securities fraud.

While the SEC would have to publish a proposed rule, receive comments, and revise it before it becomes a final rule, it seems clear that the SEC has the statutory authority to implement this rule. And, while the rule would require refinements by the SEC, its underlying policy objectives would be the following:

For any transaction involving a public company, a lawyer would certify that, to his or her knowledge, the transaction did not cause or permit the company to not comply with FASB or to misrepresent the company's financial condition to the SEC.

The lawyer has fully complied with the reporting-up-and-over requirements as contained in the SEC rule.

Unlike SOA, there would be no requirement that the lawyer affirm that he has read the documents, but it is assumed that the lawyer drafted the documents and it would be malpractice not to have read them.

All partners and senior associates doing regular corporate work for a public company would execute the certifications on a quarterly basis. ("Regular corporate work" might be defined as more than 5 percent of the attorney's billed hours for the previous quarter.) This has the effect of reminding the lawyers on a periodic basis that they are responsible for not aiding and abetting a corporate officer's breach of their fiduciary duty to the corporation or a securities violation. While it raises the standard of conduct to include FASB violations, it provides the lawyer with the protection that a conviction requires a finding that the attorney acted "knowingly." The lawyer's quarterly certification would be disciplined by severe civil penalties imposed by the SEC. These would include the forfeiture of any salary, profits, or bonuses received during the period of the violation and a mandatory $250,000 penalty per violation.

In addition, it is reasonable to assume that any lawyer convicted of violating their certification would be subject to class action suits for malpractice and a significant increase in their malpractice insurance premium going forward. The combined effects of the above penalties should be a substantial deterrent to a lawyer aiding and abetting a securities fraud. Implementing this policy could take several possible paths. I considered the possibility of federal legislation and simply do not believe that Congress is equipped or prepared to make these difficult choices. The congressional experience with the PSLRA does not inspire confidence in Congress's ability to legislate about lawyers.

In the same vein, I do not believe that the state bar associations or the ABA are likely to play productive roles. The ABA, after great struggles with the membership, regarded its shift of position to an optional, but permissible, disclosure to the board as a major policy shift. They are unlikely to adopt an affirmative mandatory obligation to report up and over. And, if they did, their policies would have no force or sanctions. Similarly, the state bar associations are unlikely to adopt any mandatory reporting policy for attorneys and wouldn't be likely to enforce it, either.

A more innovative means of implementation must, therefore, be used. Two paths represent possible policy implementation alternatives:

The SEC could conduct rule making exercises to impose the reporting and affirmation obligations of the attorneys. They could administer the fines, etc. This appears well within the intent of SOA sections 302(a) and 307.

Second, the state of Delaware, where approximately 50 percent of the listed public companies are incorporated, could pass legislation to the effect that to retain or qualify for the Delaware incorporation privilege, the public company would only retain outside law firms that had these obligations in effect. Failure to comply with this provision could result in fines for the corporation, adverse publicity that would presumably lower the company's market capitalization, and adverse shareholder reaction. Failure to adhere to the policy could result in the company losing its Delaware charter and being forced to disclose in their SEC filings the reason that they lost it, which would be a powerful deterrent. Presumably any fines or forfeited salaries could be funneled into worthy causes in Delaware, such as education. In closing, there are ways that the lawyers could assume their rightful obligations as corporate monitors and have an affirmative mandatory reporting obligation that does not compromise the attorney-client privilege, which is good public policy and should be preserved.

I acknowledge that the issues in this chapter are difficult from an intellectual and public policy standpoint. That said, the policy recommendation for an affirmative obligation to report up and over preserves the attorney-client privilege and imposes minimal government intervention on corporate governance.

NOTES

1. Bankruptcy Examiner's Final Report, chapter 11, p. 52–53.

2. Author's note to the reader: I am not judging the criminal or civil innocence or guilt of the lawyers in the events surrounding Enron. No firsthand documents have been examined or interviews conducted with the lawyers. The conclusions describing the role of the lawyers in Enron are all based on third-party evaluations and are neither mine nor those of the Cato Institute.

3. 511 U.S. 164.

4. Chap. 10, by Adam Pritchard, is a good summary and evaluation of the PSLRA.

5. See chap. 10, page 140.

6. March 2003 Report by the General Accounting Office to the Senate Committee on Banking, Housing, and Urban Affairs and the House Committee on Financial Services.

7. Bankruptcy Examiner' Second Interim Report.

8. This opinion and other court documents related to the Enron securities litigation can be found at http://www.txs.uscourts.gov/cgi-bin/notablecases/notablecases.pl? action=chome&caseno=4:02-MD-1446.

9. This article was written by Anthony Sebok (tsebok@findlaw.com) and was published in the January 2003 issue of *Findlaw's* Legal Commentary. We are grateful to both Sebok and *Findlaw's* for approving our republication of this article. See http://writ.news.findlaw .com/sebok/20030113.html. Sebok also wrote a second part to his Enron coverage that can be found at http://writ.news.findlaw.com/sebok/20030210.html.

10. Bankruptcy Examiner's Third Interim Report, p. 43–7.

11. Bankruptcy Examiner's Third Interim Report, p. 43–7.

12. Bankruptcy Examiner Final Report: annex 1 to app. C, p. 5.

13. Ibid., p. 17.

14. Testimony of Joseph Dilg before the House Energy and Commerce Committee, March 2003.

15. Bankruptcy Examiner Final Report, chapter 11, p. 9.

16. *Business Week*, December 23, 2002, p. 61–62.

17. Bankruptcy Examiner Final Report, chapter 11, p. 40.

18. Bankruptcy Examiner Final Report, p. 27.

19. Bankruptcy Examiner Final Report, p. 1.

20. Bankruptcy Examiner Final Report, p. 9.

21. Bankruptcy Examiner First Interim Report, September 21, 2002.

22. Report of Investigation by the Special Investigative Committee of the Board of Directors of the Board of Directors of Enron Corp. February 1, 2002, p. 178.

· *13* ·

Bankers as Corporate Monitors

R. T. McNamar

$\mathcal{T}$his chapter examines the role of the bankers in Enron as actors in financing the growth of Enron's earnings, participants in what other observers have euphemistically labeled "questionable" transactions, and why they were not effective corporate monitors. The chapter will first discuss why Enron needed so much financing. It then addresses why Enron chose to finance itself off its balance sheet using special purpose entities (SPEs) and prepay contracts. Next, it discusses why the bankers were so enamored with Enron, and how modern banking structure and policies may have contributed to the actions of the bankers that eventually brought down Enron. Last, the chapter attempts to identify the lessons learned from the bankers' activities in Enron to make appropriate public policy recommendations affecting future behavior.

The focus of the chapter is on identifying any policy changes that might minimize the probability of another Enron happening or provide incentives for the bankers that would further diminish the probability of corporate boards or management perpetrating another Enron.[1]

ENRON'S FINANCING NEEDS

Enron was the merger of two pipeline transmission companies: Houston Light and Gas and Inter-North in 1985. In addition, Houston Light and Gas also had an attractive business in building power plants. Sometime after the merger, Jeffrey Skilling derisively referred to the pipelines, power plants, and water businesses as "asset-heavy businesses." Skilling eventually became the CEO of Enron on December 13, 2000.

During the 1990s, Enron pursued what can only be described as a schizophrenic corporate strategy, with neither side producing positive cash flow. Consider the bipolar nature of the company.

ASSET-HEAVY BUSINESSES

These were the pipelines that formed the original Enron. Many were fully depreciated, and it was a low-margin, low-growth business with continual cash requirements for capital expenditures and maintenance of the system. They reported profits and positive cash flow, but these varied with the increases or decreases in natural gas prices. The asset-heavy side of the business was led by the high-energy corporate jet-setter Rebecca Mark, who was an executive vice president of Enron and its chief dealmaker for major power plants and water companies. An acknowledged rival of Skilling to become CEO, she was often on an airplane, traveling around the world looking to close the next deal.

From Enron's standpoint, unfortunately, Mark was very successful in closing deals, but not profitable deals. From the Dabhol gas-fired generator plant in India to the Azuriz water company in Argentina, all of her projects lost money. Her acquisition of the Wessex water company in England became a cash drain on Enron. Even one power plant she inherited from John Wing, the legendary power plant builder, went bad on her watch. The Teesside combined-cycle gas generator in Teesside, England, appeared to have excellent profit potential and great customer acceptance. Unfortunately, to obtain the plant financing while it was being built, the lenders required a signed contract for gas supplies, a typical requirement. In 1993, Enron signed a take-or-pay contract with producers in the North Sea for gas from Block 7. Subsequently, in 1995, the price of natural gas decreased significantly and, while Enron could have purchased gas less expensively on the spot market, it was bound under its contract to take the Block 7 gas.

Mark inherited some power plants in her portfolio, but her greatest achievement was building power plants and water companies around the world. Unfortunately, not one of the deals she signed was profitable, and all were a cash drain on Enron. The cash drain came from three sources: the preconstruction development and acquisition costs; the construction costs; and the fact that the plants lost money and the operating losses had to be financed out of Enron's internal cash flow. Between 1995 and 2001, Enron's asset-heavy business is estimated to have lost $12 billion in cash. This had to be financed by Enron. As will be discussed later, Enron was reluctant to borrow in the debt markets because it wanted to retain its credit ratings and did not want to issue equity because it didn't want any dilution of earnings.

ASSET-LIGHT BUSINESSES

Skilling ran the asset-light businesses and was Mark's rival to become CEO. He had originally been a consultant from McKinsey & Company, Inc., advising Enron on strategy and new business development opportunities. He joined Enron in 1990, working initially in the nascent gas-trading business for an organization called the

Gas Bank, which provided longer-term contracts for gas delivery than were currently available without a take-or-pay clause. The Gas Bank was successful due to one major contract he signed with a New York utility. In 1997, Skilling convinced Kenneth Lay, the then CEO, to set up Enron Energy Services (EES) to begin providing long-term energy supplies to customers and trading natural gas contracts for ultimate delivery. EES was very successful and was often simultaneously on the buy and sell side.

It was not difficult to trade natural gas since the contracts are uniform, the delivery dates certain, and the place of delivery known, so that transportation differentials to the delivery point, for example, South Texas Katy, could be calculated. Skilling was building a good business long term. He reveled in announcing that Enron "wasn't a gas company, it was a logistics company." He coined the term "asset light," since, in contrast with the power business, his part of Enron did not need heavy assets at all.

There were two major problems with the asset-light strategy, and unfortunately the answer for both of them was more cash from the parent Enron. Two trends occurred simultaneously:

First, the asset-light strategy led Skilling into a number of ill-fated investments. These ranged from attempting to trade electricity futures, which the electric utilities thwarted. "They don't want us," Skilling announced when Enron withdrew from the business. Another asset-light business was video on demand in a joint venture with Blockbuster. This venture was also a cash drain, and never made money. Enamored with securitization and trading of contracts, Skilling took Enron into over a dozen asset-light businesses. With the exception of gas trading, all lost their start-up investment money and, when there was any trading volume at all, these businesses had negative cash flow, so that Enron had to infuse cash into them.

Second, Enron obtained permission to use mark-to-market accounting for its gas-trading business from the SEC's chief accountant in 1993. (As will be discussed subsequently, Enron on its own initiative extended the use of mark-to-market accounting to all of its businesses.) More importantly, from a cash-needs standpoint, the use of mark-to-market accounting led to the following anomaly:

When EES entered into a long-term contract for gas delivery, for example, five years, Enron would mark the contract's value to market and use an estimated present value of the contract as the amount of money it reported for Generally Accepted Accounting Principles (GAAP) earning purposes in the income statement. Unfortunately for Enron, this produced no current or simultaneous cash flow during the accounting period, for example, the quarter. In fact, as the trading business grew and as additional people were hired and more overhead added, the cash requirements from the parent Enron to support the trading operations became more acute.

In summary, Enron had a high and growing need for cash to build its power plants and support them with operating capital when they were not making money, and it needed cash to build and support the trading business because, while it produced reported GAAP earnings, the trading did not produce cash flow for some years. On top of this, the Enron corporate lifestyle can only be characterized as inappropriately lavish. There was a fleet of corporate airplanes, all top-of-the-line jets, extravagant cash bonuses as well as stock options, and major trips to Mexico and South America for the senior managers and star performers on the way up. The expense accounts were used to buy everything from motorcycles to strippers. All this takes cash to pay the bills.

ENRON'S FINANCING CONCERNS: THE CREDIT RATING

Enron, and particularly Skilling, was obsessed with the price of the Enron stock, which climbed steadily during the 1990s, from the mid-$20s to a high of $90 on August 23, 2000. Everyone in Enron had large stock options that were awarded annually or for special accomplishments. Stock monitors were in two and three places on each floor and not just in the finance department. There was an obsession with "making the numbers." The numbers were whatever Thompson's First Call predicted Enron would make in the quarter based on the guidance from Lay and Skilling. The analysts described Enron as a "black box," but Skilling assured the analysts and press that Enron was a new paradigm and "a totally hedged logistics company." The "Enron magic" and the "Enron legend" were born in the late 1990s and continued until mid-2001. Unfortunately, it wasn't magic. Enron needed more and ever more cash to keep the doors open and pay back the money it had previously borrowed. There was only one problem: the credit rating.

At Enron, the credit rating was of paramount concern. Enron had $13 billion of debt on its balance sheet at the time it filed its third-quarter 10-Q in 2001. Even though the stock price had been going up rapidly, the credit-rating agencies had Enron rated as a BBB, the lowest investment-grade rating. If Enron took on more debt on its balance sheet to provide operating capital, it would certainly have been downgraded to a credit watch and then to non-investment grade. Enron could not imagine the horrors of being downgraded. Several things would happen in fairly rapid order; some events would happen in a day and all within six months from a downgrade. Among the parade of horrors:

Enron would violate the covenants in its existing bonds and bank debt that it would maintain its investment-grade rating. This would be an "act of default" and some of the bondholders and banks would likely panic at the ensuing unraveling of Enron and would "declare a default" by Enron. They would then rush to bankruptcy court to try to obtain a preferential place in the bankruptcy. Pension funds and banks operating under Federal Reserve or Office of the Comptroller of the Currency cease and desist orders often are required to do this.

Enron would likely be denied any new credit outside of a bankruptcy court–supervised reorganization. As a result, Enron would not be able to sustain

its construction schedule on its power plants around the world. This would result in enormous costs and violation of covenants in the construction financing
provided by the banks that Enron would maintain an investment-grade rating.
The construction bonds on the power plants would be called and massive litigation would be sure to begin. This would be litigation around the world that Enron had no cash to support.

The most immediate consequence of Enron losing its investment-grade rating would be the loss of counterparties for trading in the gas business. In my experience, it is universally true that counterparties (banks or other energy firms) are
prohibited from trading with any company that is not investment grade. And this
stipulation almost always appears in the contract between the trading parties. Two
sets of events would happen. First, Enron would not be able to execute any new
gas trades, and all new business would stop, probably in one day for most and the
rest on the morning of day two. Second, existing counterparties would begin to
abrogate Enron's trading contracts immediately upon learning that Enron was no
longer investment grade as required in the contract. If the maturity were short
enough, some would simply demand payment in gas or a financial settlement when
the contract was due to be settled. Many more would sue for breach of contract
and most would quickly receive a summary judgment against Enron directing it to
pay what it owed under the contract. Of course, Enron would have no cash to do
so.

Some of the SPE structures that Enron entered into between 1997 and 2001
had credit triggers if Enron lost its investment-grade credit rating. On a drop in
Enron's credit rating Marlin, Osprey (or Whitewing), and Rawhide together
could have required Enron immediately to make payments of more than $4 bil-
lion. This was money Enron simply didn't have and couldn't borrow. And there
were at least a dozen other SPEs that a credit downgrade would trigger payments
of over $2 billion, for a total of $6 billion. This alone would have forced Enron
into bankruptcy.

The stock market would react extremely fast to the announcement that Enron had lost its investment-grade credit rating and that its gas-trading business was
imploding. It is highly probable that short sellers would begin to trade Enron in
volume, sensing a 75–95 percent decline from its highs. (Short sellers enter into
contracts to deliver Enron stock in the future at a price that reflects the current market. They anticipate that they will be able to cover the contract with Enron stock
purchased at a significantly lower price and pocket the difference.) This short selling accelerates the decline in a company's stock price. In instances where Enron had
used its stock as collateral or as an asset, as the stock price declined, the lenders
would call for "make whole" provisions in the contract, requiring Enron to suffer a
massive dilution at the ever lower stock prices. This would have been the case with
the Raptor transactions, which eventually brought down Enron anyway.

The management of Enron would have lost hundreds of millions of dollars
on their stock ownership and stock options. For most of the management, the En-

ron stock was almost 100 percent of their financial net worth. Many would undoubtedly be unable to retain their mansions in River Oaks, which were under construction or heavily mortgaged.

In short, the Enron management must have been frightened and afraid. Enron was executing an unsustainable business model. The asset-heavy businesses were a cash drain, the trading business produced no current cash flow, and the overhead expenses of Enron were lavish and out of control. The dilemma was clear: borrow cash to continue the business and lose the investment-grade credit rating essential to the trading activities and watch the company implode, or find a way to borrow cash without putting the debt on the balance sheet where the credit rating agencies could see it. They were in a box without an attractive alternative.

THE ENRON FINANCING SOLUTION

Enron adopted a strategy of entering into transactions with banks that would not be consolidated with the Enron balance sheet. These were principally of two types, using a special purpose entity (SPE) or entering into contracts for the future delivery of energy, usually natural gas, that were paid for by the counterparty in advance (prepays).

SPE Transactions

A brief discussion of SPEs and prepays is necessary to understand how they work. There is nothing intrinsically wrong with either SPEs or prepays. Both are legitimate financing and hedging activities. In the case of SPEs, an entity will place a particular class of asset into the SPE, which can obtain a higher credit rating than the parent entity and, therefore, reduce the financing cost for the SPE. The parent entity will book a sales profit (or loss) on the sale of the assets to the SPE. They are widely used by banks to transfer credit card receivables to an SPE and obtain a credit rating that is better than the bank's rating; subsequently the credit card receivables in the SPE are securitized and sold to investors, typically institutional investors. Properly done, the sale of assets to an SPE and securitizing them can be a very attractive financing technique.

Because banks have capital adequacy rules that require varying allocations of bank capital depending on the class of assets, it is attractive to sell the credit card debt to the SPE, because the credit card debt requires a high capital allocation. Selling the credit card receivables to the SPE allows the bank to make additional new investments with new capital. Automobile loans and mortgages are normally moved off the bank's balance sheet by the two-step process of (1) bank sale of assets to an independent SPE, and (2) securitization of the SPE's assets. In short, SPEs are a legitimate and useful tool for balance-sheet management by a company when they are legal and follow GAAP. Under GAAP, there must be a true sale by the so-called sponsoring entity (Enron) to the SPE. There must be a true sales opinion by an independent outside law firm. The assets sold to the SPE must be "isolated" or "remote" from the assets of the sponsoring entity in the event that the sponsor (Enron) subsequently went bankrupt. That is, the assets would belong to the SPE and would not and could not be construed as assets of the sponsor and subject to the sponsor's creditors suing or attaching the SPE's assets. The SPE must have a management that is independent and separate from the sponsor of the SPE. That is, the sponsor cannot be on the board of directors or involved in the management of the SPE. The management of the SPE must be truly independent from the management of the sponsor to qualify for nonconsolidation treatment under GAAP.

In addition, if the SPE had equity of at least 3 percent from an outside party unrelated to the sponsor, then the SPE should not be consolidated with the sponsor's balance sheet. While the 3 percent rule is just a guideline, it has been widely adopted. In fact, so long as the party investing the 3 percent is independent, it appears that the investment can be equity or a loan, although for liquidation purposes the loan will be subordinated and treated as equity. To qualify for nonconsolidation with the sponsoring entity, the 3 percent must be in the SPE at the end of the accounting period, although not necessarily when the SPE transaction closes. It is a GAAP rule relating to consolidation, not a legal requirement.

SPEs are widely acknowledged to be legitimate financing vehicles to achieve and report certain business results. As the chief credit officer of the Corporate Finance Group of Moody's testified during the Senate Permanent Subcommittee on Investigations hearings said, "It should be stressed that structured financing is a common risk management tool available globally to corporations, financial institutions, and state and local governments. It is a recognized method, for example, of enhancing liquidity and of transferring credit risk when appropriately implemented."[2]

Prepay Transactions

Prepay, or swap, contracts are widely used in commodity industries, for example, wheat, oil, bauxite, etc. One party wants to lock in or hedge the price of the commodity for a delivery in the future. The other party promises to deliver the commodity at a date certain, typically at the maturity or expiration date of the contract. Companies enter into these types of prepays for a variety of motives: The seller may believe the price of the commodity will decline by the time the contract matures and the seller will be able to purchase the commodity on the spot market for delivery to fulfill its obligation. The buyer may think that the price of the commodity may rise above the contract or strike price for delivery. In addition, the buyer may be concerned about shortages in the amount or grade of the commodity purchased for future delivery.

Last, the commodities are not always delivered, but rather the parties may frequently have a financial settlement of the contract. This is typically in the terms of the contract and a formula agreed to at the time the prepay is arranged so that either party knows the cost of settling the contract financially.

Prepay contracts are shown on the balance sheet of both parties if they are large enough to be considered "material" from a financial standpoint. Although there is a prepayment of cash from another company or a bank, the contracts are not shown in the "cash flow from financings" section of the balance sheet, e.g., they are not normally debt. Rather, they are shown above the financing section of the balance sheet after they are run through the income statement. Most companies disclose both sides of the contract in the income statement and show the net amount of anticipated gain or loss in their balance sheet. Again, prepay swap contracts are a legitimate hedging tool when properly used.

SCOPE OF ENRON'S OFF-BALANCE-SHEET FINANCINGS

Before considering how Enron used its off-balance-sheet financings and examining selected transactions with the bankers, it is useful to understand the size or scope of the off-balance-sheet financings that Enron did with SPEs and prepays. This is best illustrated by the post restatement-of-earnings meeting that Enron had with its bankers on November 19, 2001, at the Waldorf-Astoria in New York City. Enron met with its bankers to say that its GAAP debt at the end of the third quarter was $13 billion, but that its off-balance-sheet debt was $25.1 billion, for a total debt of $38.1 billion. Approximately $14 billion of the off-balance-sheet debt was through SPEs. The additional debt was in eight categories:

	9/30/01 Amounts (in $billions)
FAS 140 Transactions	2.087
Minority Interest Financings	1.690
Commodity Transactions with Financial Institutions	4.822
Share Trusts	3.352
Equity Forward Contracts	0.304
Structured Assets	1.532
Unconsolidated Affiliates	10.733

Hence, $10.733 billion of the off-balance-sheet debt was in unconsolidated affiliates and $13.787 billion was SPEs. The remaining $596 million was leases, for the total of $25.116 billion. By any standard, this was a staggering admission, but only the aggregate amount could have been a surprise to the individual bankers, since all of their banks had participated in many of the individual financings. Between 1997 and 2001, the banks had earned over $500 million in revenue from Enron transactions.[3] Chase (later JP Morgan Chase) and Citicorp together had loaned over $8 billion dollars to Enron in off-balance-sheet transactions between 1997 and 2001.[4]

ENRON'S SPECIAL PURPOSE ENTITY FINANCINGS[5]

Regardless of the asset putatively sold by Enron or a consolidated subsidiary to an SPE, the Enron SPEs normally had several characteristics in common. They are:

The capital of the SPE was 97 percent from a bank loan from a major bank.

Management of the SPE was not independent and separate from the management of the sponsor, and was typically the CFO Andrew Fastow or an appointee of his who worked for him but was low enough in the Enron hierarchy that his involvement did not have to be disclosed in the Enron proxy statement.

Enron directly or indirectly guaranteed that in the event the SPE could not service its debt or repay the principal, Enron would be obligated to pay the interest on the debt and would repay the debt at maturity.

Enron retained a direct interest in the financial performance of the assets sold to the SPE through a total return swap. The total return swap was nothing more than a contract between Enron and the SPE contractually guaranteeing Enron the cash flow in excess of the SPE's bank obligations and distributions to the 3 percent equity investor. Normally, these were triggered when the SPE sold or monetized the assets Enron had initially "sold" to the SPE. To be sure, the SPE's obligations to pay Enron under the total return swap placed the interests of the banks first, then the 3 percent investor, and Enron last but presumably receiving the largest proportion of the distributions.

Enron's SPE transactions all had true sales opinions from the law firms of Vinson & Elkins or Andrews & Kurth. True sales opinions are typical in SPE transactions and are relied upon by the bankers who make the loan to the SPE. In the case of Enron, Vinson & Elkins rendered sixty-six true sales opinions and Andrews & Kurth twenty-eight true sales opinions. Enron booked a profit on the "sale" of the assets to the SPE at the time of closing.

How could Enron book an accounting profit on the sale when there was no cash that came to Enron? Enron had received permission to use mark-to-market accounting for its gas-trading business in 1993, and subsequently expanded that permission and applied mark-to-market accounting for the entire business. This was rationalized in Enron by professing that all of Enron was really a "merchant bank" and, therefore, it could and should use mark-to-market accounting for all of its businesses. The SEC never approved this extension of mark-to-market accounting. Accordingly, Enron would estimate the future cash flow it would receive from the SPE and discount it back to the present and take that as profits on the sale. This went into the GAAP earnings on the income statement and subsequently into the balance sheet.

ANALYSIS OF ENRON'S SPE FINANCING PROBLEMS

In summary, when Enron "sold" an asset or assets to an SPE that it sponsored, it guaranteed the bank debt of the SPE and retained a total return swap. The total return swap was not a derivative or swap of any kind. It was actually a contract that would provide Enron a profit participation in the upside of the earnings or the cash flow of the asset(s) transferred to the SPE. This provided Enron with a continuing economic interest in the asset(s) it purportedly "sold" to the SPE. Enron did not show the SPE on its balance sheet, but did report the present value of the projected future cash flow from the SPE that Enron was entitled to under the total return swap. It then discounted the cash flow and reported this amount in its income statement as the marked-to-market value of the transaction as GAAP earnings.

A threshold question is whether Enron affected a true sale of its assets to the SPEs. By guaranteeing the debt of the SPE and retaining a participation in the cash flow of the assets of the SPE after the bank debt was paid and the 3 percent equity investors received their returns, Enron retained an equity-like upside ownership in the assets of the SPE. This was the contractual effect of the so-called total return swap between the SPE and Enron. (There were often one or two intermediate shell corporations involved, but at the end of cash flow trail, the net cash went to Enron.) It is reasonable to conclude on the facts that no true sale took place.

In each case, the SPE transferred the cash proceeds of the bank loan it received to Enron to use as operating cash for its businesses. I have not been able to determine the accounting treatment Enron used to transfer the cash from the SPE to Enron or an on-balance-sheet affiliate. However, once Enron had the bank loan at the parent, it accounted for the cash as "cash flow from operations," not "cash flow from financings." This was a clear violation of Financial Accounting Standards Board (FASB) No. 5. Somehow, Arthur Andersen signed off on this Enron accounting practice even though it isn't close to being in compliance with GAAP.

Fastow or one of his subordinates constituted the management of most of the SPEs. Certainly they managed the LJM1 and LJM2 transactions, the Raptor transactions, and many others.

As stated above, Enron received ninety-two true sales opinions from Vinson & Elkins and Andrews & Kurth. Why is this important? The bankers apparently felt that with an Enron total return swap or guarantee on their loan to the SPE, they didn't care whether there was a true sale or not, expecting that they would be repaid by the parent Enron.

True sales opinions from outside lawyers are indispensable to obtain the accounting treatment that Enron desired under FASB 125 and subsequently restated as FASB 140. FASB 140 basically said that if the sponsor (Enron) had a true sales opinion and a 3 percent equity third-party investor in the SPE, then the sponsor of the SPE did not have to consolidate the SPE on its balance sheet.

This was the accounting treatment that Enron desired. In effect, they had structured an apparent SPE transaction that complied with FASB 140, and they would not have to show what was, in essence, a disguised bank loan on their balance sheet, thereby preserving the Enron credit rating and avoiding the dire consequences previously enumerated in this chapter.

Arthur Andersen apparently acquiesced in the FASB 140 balance sheet treatment and did not require Enron to consolidate any of its ninety-four SPE financings. There were no true sales in any of the SPE transactions that I examined. In every case, Enron guaranteed the debt of the SPE, which in itself indicates no true sale. More egregious, if possible, is that Enron retained by contract (the total return swap) with the SPE the right to all of the net cash flow of the SPE. This is a contract obligation on the SPE to pay Enron its cash flow that was contractually an equity participation disguised as a derivative. There was no true sale, and there should not have been any FASB 140 accounting treatment.

ACCORDING TO A *BUSINESS WEEK* ARTICLE

Oddly enough, the players who seemed least interested in the opinion letter were those they were meant to benefit: the banks funding the SPEs. According to a report issued by Neal Batson, the examiner appointed by the federal bankruptcy court to review Enron's dealings,

> Enron employees indicated that typically these legal isolation opinions were more of a matter of importance to Enron and to Andersen but were generally not a condition to closing the financing" with the banks. Because they had the reassurance of the total return swaps, the banks felt secure. To Boston University legal expert Koniak, that should have raised a big red flag. V&E and A&K "had to have a bag over their head not to see that there was something fishy going on here," says Koniak. "The fact that the buyer did not want a true-sales opinion is not some subtlety. It is a blatant sign of possible fraud."[6]

Nor did the Senate Government Operations Permanent Subcommittee on Investigations, the General Accounting Office (GAO), or Batson find true sales that warranted Enron not consolidating the SPEs. It is true that Enron and Arthur Andersen presented Enron's financial statements and submitted them to the SEC to indicate that Enron was complying with GAAP, but they were not. It's not a close call; it's black and white. The financial statements that Enron submitted to the SEC did not accurately or remotely represent the reality of the true underlying economic and legal situation. It would be too polite to call Enron a house of cards.

PREPAYS: ENRON'S TRANSACTIONS WITHOUT ECONOMIC SUBSTANCE

According to the GAO,

> A prepay transaction involves a contractual agreement between two parties that combines the economics of a bet obligation with those of a forward contract, which is a contract for a service or product to be delivered at a later date. Forward contracts, whether prepaid or not, can be used to hedge against price moves. . . . In a prepaid forward contract, the payment for the [commodity] is made at the time of the contract, but the [commodity] is delivered [at a time in the future]; this provides immediate cash flow to the seller. If this prepay transaction is a loan in substance and intent, its accounting treatment should be that of a loan.[7]

To determine the proper accounting treatments, prepaid forward contracts must be evaluated under FASB 133, Accounting for Derivative Instruments and Hedging Activities. This states that determining whether the seller (Enron) is engaged in energy trading or securing a loan requires an "assessment of relevant facts and circumstances related to an entity's activities. However, inherent in that assessment *is an evaluation of the entity's intent* in entering into an energy contract [or obtaining a loan]" (emphasis added). In the case of Enron, it seems clear to me that the intent was to enter into a loan to finance its cash-short operations. As best as I can tell, there was never even one delivery of gas, oil, or other commodities under these prepay arrangements. All were designed to be settled financially, and the difference in settlement price for Enron was essentially the current market interest rate charged by the money-center banks to institutional-grade corporate borrowers plus an arrangement fee.

As the Enron prepays matured, Enron had to do more, because there were two cash needs: First, pay off the expiring prepays. Second, provide net additional cash to finance the Enron operations. Hence the outstanding prepays grew each year in dollar volume. And the same bank would often enter into a second prepay transaction to pay off the first. This was particularly true of Chase Bank and its offshore entity Mahonia, which entered into twelve prepay transactions with Enron totaling $3.7 billion by the third quarter of 2001. Only Citigroup had more transactions with fourteen prepays totaling $4.8 billion. Nine other banks had done prepays that totaled over $1 billion.[8]

Although the total dollar amount of the prepays is uncertain, there were a large number of misleading 10-Q and 10-K statements by Enron. Each transaction appears to violate FASB 133 and FASB 5. This means that there were a large number of potential SEC reporting violations by Enron and that banks had enough opportunities to participate in these prepay transactions to understand what they were doing. Consider a selected sample of statements in the report by the Senate Permanent Subcommittee on Investigations:[9]

- Why does Enron enter into prepays? Off-balance-sheet financing (i.e., generate cash without increasing debt load)—internal Enron presentation
- Enron loves these deals as they are able to hide funded debt from their equity analysts because they (at the very least) book it as deferred rev[enue] or (better yet) bury it in their trading liabilities.—internal Chase e-mail
- E[nron] gets money that give them c[ash]flow but does not show up on books as big D Debt.—internal Citigroup e-mail
- Enron is continuing to pursue various structures to get cash in the door without accounting for it as debt.—internal Andersen e-mail

There are literally scores of other e-mails from bankers that indicate that they understood Enron's motives and accounting treatment of the prepays. A comment in the debtor's complaint in the Enron case is an effective summary of this series of prepay transactions:

> [B]eginning in at least 1997, the Enron prepay transactions failed to qualify as typical prepay transactions, because each side did not assume commodity price risk. More specifically, when the relevant trades involved in a typical Enron prepay are pieced together, it is clear that neither party assumed commodity price risk. In fact, the commodity price was irrelevant to the transaction. . . . the Enron prepay transactions employed a structure that passed the counterparty commodity price risk back to Enron, thus eliminating all commodity risk from the transaction. As in typical prepays, Enron received cash up front. In contrast to typical prepays, however, with all elements of the structure taken together, if all parties performed as expected, Enron's future obligations were distilled to repayment of that cash with negotiated interest. The interest amount was set at the time of the contract and was independent of any changes in the prices of the underlying commodity. This was accomplished through a series of simultaneous trades whereby Enron passed the counterparty commodity price risk to a Chase-sponsored special purpose vehicle, which passed the risk to Chase, which, in turn, passed the risk back to Enron.
>
> The "trick" to the Enron prepay transactions was a circle of three. That is, each prepay transaction involved three essential parties: an Enron affili-

ate, a financial institution, and a conduit entity (usually controlled by the financial institution), each of which, at the end of the transaction, owed obligations to the others.[10]

The banks controlled the conduit entities that were typically offshore, for example, Mahonia (Chase) and Delta (Citigroup). According to Batson, when all of the obligations of the three entities were settled up, "*the prepayments to Enron simply created Enron debt*." This view that the Enron prepays were debt was strongly reinforced by the district attorney for New York, Henry Morgenthau, who reported, on completion of an eighteen-month investigation into Enron's prepay transactions with JP Morgan Chase and Citigroup, that

> In the course of our investigation, which began shortly after Enron filed its bankruptcy petition, we have interviewed hundreds of witnesses from throughout the country and abroad and analyzed more than one million documents. In addition, testimony was taken from 46 witnesses and more than 2,700 exhibits were introduced before a New York Grand Jury, which sat for six months.
>
> Prepaid commodities transactions, which involve the present sale of a commodity in exchange for future delivery, are routine and serve legitimate economic ends in commodities trading. As our investigation disclosed, however, the prepaids Chase and Citibank engage in with Enron were never designed to constitute trading in the commodities markets. Despite the banks' efforts to make these transactions look like commodities trades, they were trades only on paper. In substance, *they were loans*.[11] (emphasis added by author)

When asked why he didn't prosecute Chase and Citibank, Morgenthau said that he didn't think that he could get a unanimous jury to agree beyond a reasonable doubt that the banks were criminally guilty. He said that the civil charges of aiding and abetting were better addressed by the SEC.

In virtually all cases, the prepay transactions did not comply with GAAP under FASB 133, because it seems clear that both the "substance" and the "intent" were not to engage in a commodity trade, but to engage in a loan disguised as a commodity trade. Thus Enron should have disclosed the prepays as debt under GAAP. Further, Enron misclassified the transactions as cash flow from operations rather than cash flow from financings, violating FASB 5. Obviously, it is misleading to investors to indicate that the cash flow is from operations, making the company appear more profitable than it is, when the cash flow is from exterior financings. In the opinion of the Senate Permanent Subcommittee on Investigations, the GAO, Batson, and the other examiner, Harrison Golden, *these prepays were simply disguised bank loans*. If so, then the Enron treatment clearly violated FASB 133 and FASB 5 every time Enron published a 10-K or 10-Q.

LESSONS LEARNED

There are some lessons to be learned from observing the relationship of the commercial and investment bankers with Enron without my concluding that the bankers have either civil or criminal liability. Rather, the conclusions of third-party observers such as examiners in bankruptcy, congressional investigations and hearings, GAO reports, the filings in bankruptcy court, and the filings and judge's motions in the shareholder derivative suit in Houston offer the conclusions of observers who have seen the original documents, have taken testimony, and have the used subpoena authority to develop the facts in Enron.

Each of these groups concludes that the bankers were guilty of aiding and abetting certain Enron officers in the breach of their fiduciary duty to Enron by engaging in the SPE and prepay transactions previously described in this chapter. Both of the bankruptcy examiners recommended the judge subordinate the claims of the banks in the bankruptcy proceeding. Again, the standard for aiding and abetting is that the banks *knowingly* provided *substantial assistance* in assisting an Enron officer in breaching their fiduciary duty to the firm. It appears that all of the third-party observers felt that not only did the banks act knowingly, but that structuring the transaction, writing the documentation with Enron or its lawyers, and funding the transaction with bank debt is substantial assistance on the part of the banks.

The Enron shareholder derivative suit is ongoing, and no judgments have been rendered at this writing. If there is a criminal grand jury proceeding in Texas, its results are unknown at this time. A criminal case could take some time to develop and try. It is insightful that Morgenthau decided against attempting to indict Citigroup and Chase on criminal charges because he did not think he could get a unanimous jury conviction on the criminal standard of "beyond a reasonable doubt." The U.S. attorney in Houston must be looking at the same challenges.

Several major long-term trends have converged to change the nature of both commercial banking and investment banking. These trends have combined to virtually eliminate the role of the bankers as effective corporate monitors. Among them are:

The introduction of securitization of assets has moved the emphasis toward earning arrangement and placement fees rather than the commercial banks retaining the assets, earning interest income of the loans, overseeing their performance, and working out a distressed loan. Overall securitization of assets is a good practice and development because it has reduced the probability of a systemic risk from either a bank's failure, e.g., the failure of the Bank of the United States in New York in 1930 ushered in the Great Depression.

Securitization of assets also lessens the risk from a particular class of assets having a very high percentage of nonperforming loans, e.g., oil and gas industry loans. Securitization has spread the risk of an individual loan, a class of assets, or a bank among a large number of diversified institutional investors who purchase securitized bank loans, e.g., pension funds, life insurance companies, private equity funds, and so on. The downside of securitization is that the banks don't retain the credit risk, which appears to lessen their due diligence, credit approval, and credit oversight intensity. This is an unintended consequence of an otherwise positive development.

The development of capital adequacy rules that had the good objective of making sure that banks maintained enough capital to reflect the risks on their balance sheets has not worked particularly well. An unintended consequence of these rules is to promote the further securitization of the assets so that the capital can be redeployed either to higher yielding or lower risk-weighted assets under the capital adequacy rules. Again, it appears that when banks are not going to hold a credit to maturity, due diligence, underwriting, and credit oversight activities are not executed with the same intensity as they were when the banks were retaining the credit risk on their balance sheet.

The merger of commercial banking and investment banking has transformed both from what they used to be into new types of banks. Investment banks historically were oriented toward customer relationships, as were commercial banks. Today, the combined banks are transaction and fee driven. Transactions produce fees for advising on a transaction, arrangement fees, and placement fees. In the case of Enron, the banks received $500 million in fees between 1998 and the third quarter of 2001. Assume that the bankers got 30 percent of the fees in bonuses; that would be a pool of $150 million. If there were fifty bankers who worked on these Enron deals, that equals bonuses of $3 million apiece. These numbers are probably conservative. In short, like Rebecca Mark at Enron, the bankers were motivated to do deals regardless of their expected profits or apparent propriety.

The banks have inadequate internal credit-approval processes. The Enron congressional testimony and examiner's reports are replete with e-mails from bankers in the credit-approval process who recognized that they were participating in disguising a loan as a prepaid commodity swap. Virtually all of them recognized that there was no commodity price risk in prepays. Further, many knew that Enron was recording the cash proceeds from the bank loan as cash from operating activities, in violation of FASB No. 5. This meant that they presumably knew that the 10-Ks and 10-Qs that Enron was filing with the SEC were a material misrepresentation of Enron's financial condition. Will the grand jury in Houston find that this was a conspiracy to defraud shareholders engaged in by some Enron executives, the banks, and others? I have no basis for an opinion, but I do look forward to learning of the grand jury deliberations at some time.

SOME BANKS ARE NOT ONLY "TOO BIG TO FAIL" BUT ARE "TOO BIG TO MANAGE"

One major Chase loan that I examined is an example of this condition. No credit approval, no documentation, no signatures, nothing. Yet Chase loaned $1.1 billion dollars to Enron-related entities. The point isn't that it was repaid, the point is how can a bank like Chase assert it has any internal credit-approval process when this happens? Who has that signature authority? I am unaware of any banker, including the CEO of Chase, who could have executed this transaction within the bank's risk management or credit-approval guideline. To describe the banker who did it as a rogue gives elephants a bad name.

Bank regulators have no ability to monitor the actions of banks. The questionable activities at Enron went on for over three years. Neither the Office of the Comptroller of the Currency, the Federal Reserve, nor the New York State Banking Department had the ability to identify, analyze, and question the Enron transactions. Yet there were ninety-four SPEs and prepays, plus many other questionable transactions. Granted that the SEC was an abject failure in carrying out its enforcement mission, did the bank regulators even know that banks were disguising their lending to Enron? Did they know that Enron's GAAP numbers weren't GAAP and that mark-to-market accounting was being used to justify the GAAP numbers, but that there was no cash flow from operations? In short, the bank regulators let down the shareholders of the bank, the management and boards of the banks, and the American people. They simply were useless.

POLICY RECOMMENDATIONS RELATING TO THE BANKS

Policy recommendations relating to the SEC, the lawyers, the tax system, and other conditions that contributed to the Enron collapse are discussed in other chapters throughout this book. The failure at Enron was a systemic failure of American capitalism. All of the links in Enron's audit chain failed. Yet the bankers played a unique role in the failure of Enron. None of the deception, misrepresentations to the SEC, or the continued operation of Enron would have been possible without the complicity of the banks. The banks suggested transactions. The banks arranged transactions. The banks funded transactions. That clearly is substantial assistance within the meaning of the Texas, Oregon, and New York statutes and case law on aiding and abetting. What can be done? Banking is an honorable and important profession in the economy, and the actions of the bankers at Enron do not mean that all bankers or banks are dishonest. That said, prudent steps should be taken to minimize the probability of another Enron occurring in the future. Some possible policy changes relating to the bankers would be:

The Sarbanes-Oxley Act (SOA) includes certification provisions for corporate officers to attest to the propriety of their financial statements. The certifications are designed to create a new class of securities violation that has meaningful sanctions for its violation. The disgorgement provisions of the SOA for those who violate them are directionally correct in their intent. Without congressional action, the Office of the Comptroller, Federal Reserve, and other bank regulating agencies could pass regulations that if a bank officer engages in disguising loans or substantially assisting in knowingly misrepresenting a company's financial condition, there would be similarly severe civil consequences.

In effect, a certification system could be implemented for all loans over, say, $100 million, with a bank lending officer certifying that to the best of his knowledge based on appropriate examination, the bank's transactions for which he is responsible comply with the applicable GAAP requirements. In Enron, this would have meant FASB 140 and FASB 5 in the case of the SPE transactions and FASB 133 and FASB 5 in the case of the prepays. Note, the banker's certification does not mean that the company is following GAAP or that the bank officer is responsible for the financial statements of the company. It only means that the banker certifies that he does not know that the company is *not* complying with GAAP on his loans. In other words, the certification attests to the fact that the banker is not "knowingly" aiding and abetting.

The SEC and bank regulator sanctions for conviction of aiding and abetting should include disgorgement of any profits or bonuses received from the activities, the loss of salary from the time of the transgression until the present, and stiff civil penalties for each transgression, for example, a minimum of $250,000 per violation. This, coupled with the potential judgment in the shareholder derivative suit that would be levied, would get the bankers' attention. In effect, this policy recommendation would take the current state civil law on aiding and abetting and add real economic sanctions to the finding that the banker was guilty.

Sarbanes-Oxley has a whistle-blower provision designed for corporate executives. There should also be an affirmative obligation and whistle-blower protection for bankers who identify illegal or fraudulent transactions and report them. Without congressional action, the bank regulators could develop a bank regulatory policy so that a banker who sees a questionable transaction has an affirmative obligation to report it to the bank's chief credit officer and risk management officer (or internal auditor) and present his concerns. If they fail to act, the banker would then report this alleged wrongdoing to two outside members of the audit committee. Failure to exercise this affirmative obligation would result in the banker being terminated without severance.

By contrast, in the event the banker is dismissed by the bank for being a whistle-blower, then, if the bank regulator determines that the reporting upward was justified based on a reasonableness standard, the fired whistle-blower would receive two times their base salary and previous year's bonus for five years, paid for by the bank. If possible, these payments should be treated as a fine and made not tax deductible to the bank.

In 2004, after the banks implement the new eXtensible Business Reporting Language (XBRL) for their quarterly call reports, they should provide a direct data feed of their loan transactions over $100 million to their relevant regulators, rather than waiting for the quarterly call report. Each loan transaction would be accompanied by the banker's certification outlined above in this section. These records would be retained by the individual bank, but subject to bank examiner review. This would permit the regulators to monitor the larger loans to larger corporations and enforce the lending officers' certification about the loan. When the bank is examined, it is easy to monitor and aggregate loans to the same entity to be certain that the banks are not splitting them to avoid the reporting and certification requirement.

While it may sound trite, the federal bank regulators need advanced training in modern financing techniques. While all examiners need exposure to the advanced training necessary to understand an SPE transaction, a cadre of examiners can be trained to be experts. The Office of the Comptroller of the Currency does provide expert teams in many fields today, for example, real estate. It is not difficult to spot test to determine whether a transaction meets the criteria of FASB 140 or 133. All bankers know whether FASB No. 5 is being followed or not, and the bank examiners should also be able to test this easily.

These policy recommendations may need refinement, but they serve as a road map to minimize the probability of another Enron where the banks knowingly provide substantial assistance in the breach of fiduciary obligations and perhaps more.

The take-away from this chapter is that Enron was not complying with GAAP, and the stories that say they were are nothing more than urban legends. And that is thanks to the bankers. Alexander Pope may have said it best:

Blast paper credit! Last and best supply!
That lends corruption lighter wings to fly![12]

NOTES

1. Author's note to readers: Just as in the role of the lawyers as corporate monitors, I am not judging the criminal or civil innocence or guilt of the bankers in the events surrounding Enron. No firsthand documents have been examined except those appearing in the reports of congressional hearings. No interviews have been conducted with the bankers. The conclusions describing the role of the bankers in Enron are all based on third-party evaluations and are neither mine nor those of the Cato Institute.

2. Testimony of Pamela M. Strump to the Senate Permanent Subcommittee on Investigations, July 23, 2002, p. 28.

3. In Re Enron, September 24, 2003, p. 3.

4. Debtor's Complaint, In Re Enron, September 24, 2003, p. 23.

5. As best I can tell, Enron entered into ninety-four SPE transactions between 1997 and when it went out of business in 2001. Others, including Harrison Golden, an examiner in bankruptcy for the Southern District of New York, place the SPE transactions at approximately thirty. The difference is probably accounted for by whether some of the "parent

SPEs," such as Mahonia and LJM1 and LJM2, are accounted as three transactions or whether the multitude of transactions that were subsidiaries of the parent SPEs are counted in the total. In the case of Mahonia, many of the subsidiary transactions were, in fact, prepays. (Harrison Golden, Examiners Report, December 2, 2003.)

6. *Business Week*, December 23, 2002.

7. General Accounting Office, *The Role of Firms and Their Analysts with Enron and Global Crossing*, March 2003, p. 11.

8. Enron was financing itself largely by prepays. The net outstanding balance increased each year from $1.3 billion in June 1998 to $5.0 billion in June 2001. The Senate Permanent Subcommittee on Investigations appears to have made a mistake in calculating the total amount of prepays and the FASB125/140 sales. This is because they take the net amount of prepays outstanding at the end of the year and add it to the FASB 125/140 sales during the year. This ignores the total prepays financed during the year to refinance earlier prepays and to provide additional net new cash flow for operations. Using their methodology, the combined amount financed would rise from $1.9 billion as of December 31, 1999, to $6.6 billion at September 31, 2001. Adjusting their numbers to reflect the total prepay transactions executed during that period, the number would be approximately $21.5 billion.

9. Selected quotes are from exhibit 102 of the Senate Subcommittee on Investigations report in July 2002, p. 354.

10. Debtor's Complaint, In Re Enron, September 24, 2003, p. 33–34.

11. Debtor's Complaint, In Re Enron, p. 33–34.

12. Pope, Alexander, *Epistle to Bathurst*. Quote suggested by Paul Weaver.

• *14* •

The Credit Rating Agencies: From Cartel Busters to Cartel Builders

L. Jacobo Rodríguez

$\mathcal{T}$he collapses of Enron Corp. and WorldCom and the discovery of accounting irregularities at those and other publicly traded corporations led the U.S. Congress to pass the Sarbanes-Oxley Act (SOA) in July 2002. As President George W. Bush stated when signing the bill into law, SOA represents "the most far-reaching reforms of American business practices since the time of Franklin Delano Roosevelt."[1] In addition to the changes directly introduced by the act, Title VII of SOA directed several federal government agencies to conduct studies that could eventually lead to further transformations of U.S. business practices and of the structure of the U.S. securities markets.

One such study, as specified in section 702 (b) of SOA, instructed the Securities and Exchange Commission (SEC) to submit a report on the role and function of credit rating agencies in the operation of securities markets. The SEC submitted such a report on January 24, 2003,[2] and released a subsequent concept release (Concept Release No 33-8236) on June 4, 2003. Although the credit rating agencies were not directly implicated in any of the accounting scandals, they were heavily criticized by policy makers, regulators, and the media for their late reaction to the impending collapse of Enron. Indeed, all SEC-approved rating agencies gave Enron an investment-grade rating on its debt up until five days before the company filed for bankruptcy.[3]

The Enron scandal, the congressional investigation of the credit-rating agencies caused by it,[4] and the review mandated by SOA are just the latest events that have had the effect of shining the spotlight on this obscure but very important sector of the global financial system. Other events include the revision to the 1988 Basel Accord for minimum capital standards for banks that would put great reliance on credit ratings for the determination of bank capital requirements and the series of blunders that the rating agencies have committed over the past few years and that have called into question their privileged status.[5] Chief among those blunders are the credit defaults of Orange County, California, and the Washington Public Power Supply System, as well as the Asian financial crisis of 1997–1998. In all three instances, the credit rating agencies were late to identify the impending difficulties of the parties involved and downgrade the ratings of the parties that got into trouble.

While most market participants and commentators are familiar with the rating agencies' main product—that is, the ratings that they issue—relatively little is known about how that product is created (i.e., how ratings are determined), how the industry is structured, how credit agencies rose to prominence as the official arbiters of the creditworthiness of both private and public entities, and how regulators have come to rely more and more on the rating agencies. To the extent that the discussion concerning the role of the rating agencies is better informed and grounded in economic theory, recommendations for reform of the ratings industry will be more likely to produce, if implemented, the desired results. For that reason, this chapter will begin with a discussion of what ratings are and their role in the financial markets.

WHAT ARE CREDIT RATINGS?

Credit ratings are informed and standardized *opinions* about the creditworthiness of an obligor or of an obligation.[6] They indicate the likelihood that a debtor will make timely and full payment of principal and interest on all its obligations or on particular ones. Ratings are not audits of the entities being rated, nor are they designed to catch or prevent fraud. Rating agencies divide ratings by industry (e.g., sovereign, banking, energy), and type of instrument (e.g., corporate debt, sovereign debt, municipal securities, structured finance instruments).

In the United States the rating process is almost always initiated at the request of the issuer, although unsolicited ratings are also provided. Solicited ratings allow the raters to have access to private information that issuers deem relevant to the rating decision and to meet with senior management to discuss any factors that may affect the rating. Unsolicited ratings are usually determined by using public information only and carry a disclaimer to that effect. When the request for a rating has been received, the rating agencies will assign a lead analyst to direct the rating process. A credit committee that includes the lead analyst, other analysts, and one or more managing directors, however, is responsible for rating decisions and any subsequent revisions to them (i.e., credit upgrades or downgrades).

Worldwide there are about 130–150 credit rating firms, but most of those are local.[7] The global and, more important, the U.S. markets are dominated by a handful of firms. In the United States, Moody's and Standard and Poor's (S&P) are and have long been the dominant players, with ICBA Fitch being a distant third. (There are economic and legal/regulatory reasons, which are explained below, why those two companies have been able to achieve such a dominant position.) Table 14.1 provides some basic facts about the two industry leaders that give an indication of just how pervasive their presence is in the capital markets.

Table 14.1   Basic Facts about Moody's and S&P's

	Moody's	S&P's
Number of Analysts	1,000	1,250
Number of Securities Rated	85,000 corporate, government, and structured finance securities; 73,000 public finance obligations. Over $30 trillion in debt covered.	150,000 (over 99 percent of debt obligations and preferred stock issues publicly traded in the U.S.).
Operating Revenues	$1 billion in 2002; net income of $290 million.	$1.6 billion in 2002; net income not available.
Number of Countries Covered	Approx. 100 countries.	Approx. 70 countries.

Sources: Moody's 2002 Annual Report and S&P Senate Testimony (2002).

Rating fees, between 2 and 3 percent of the size of the issue, are agreed upon before the rating process has been initiated and the rating decision has been made. These fees make up over 85 percent of the revenues of the leading rating agencies, with the rest of the revenue coming from subscriber and ancillary services. Smaller firms and non-U.S. firms get the bulk, if not all, of their revenues from subscriber fees rather than from the rating fees paid for by issuers.

As mentioned above, ratings are standardized opinions. The scores set by rating agencies consist of letters that have well-defined meanings and that, in theory, should correlate well with other measures of risk assessment such as spreads on credit yields. Tables 14.2 and 14.3 present, respectively, S&P's and Moody's classification systems for their long-term debt ratings.[8] Other companies use variations of those two systems, so that there has been over time a general convergence in grading schemes.

WHY ARE THERE RATINGS?

Up to this point, we have only explained briefly what ratings are. This section addresses the important question of why ratings exist at all. What function do they serve in today's financial markets? Let us not forget that ratings are, after all, an opinion or, as the legal counsel of one of the leading rating agencies put it to Senate investigators, ratings are "the world's shortest editorial."[9] Why then would anyone give the credit rating agencies more than a penny for their thoughts? For that we must go back to basic economic theory.

In every lending transaction, such as those that occur when firms sell bonds to investors, there is a problem of asymmetric information. Lenders (investors) know that borrowers (firms) have private information about the uses to which loans are put and about the likelihood of repayment of those loans. They also know that some borrowers will have incentives to distort that information. Finally,

Table 14.2 S&P's Rating Categories for Long-Term Issuers and Issues

AAA	Extremely strong capacity to meet financial commitments. Highest rating.
AA	Very strong capacity to meet financial commitments.
A	Strong capacity to meet financial commitments, but somewhat susceptible to adverse economic conditions and changes in circumstances.
BBB	Adequate capacity to meet financial commitments, but more subject to adverse economic conditions.
BBB- (minus)	This is the lowest rating before non-investment grade.
BB	Less vulnerable in the near-term but faces major ongoing uncertainties to adverse business, financial, and economic conditions.
B	More vulnerable to adverse business, financial, and economic conditions but currently has the capacity to meet financial commitments.
CCC	Currently vulnerable and dependent on favorable business, financial, and economic conditions to meet financial commitments.
CC	Currently highly vulnerable.
C	A bankruptcy petition has been filed or similar action taken but payments or financial commitments are continued.
D	Payment default on financial commitments.

Source: S&P's website, http://www.standardandpoors.com.
Note: Ratings in the 'AAA,' 'AA,' 'A' and 'BBB' categories are regarded by the market as investment grade. Ratings in the 'BB,' 'B,' 'CCC,' 'CC' and 'C' categories are regarded as having significant speculative characteristics. Ratings from 'AA' to 'CCC' may be modified by the addition of a plus (+) or minus (-) sign to show relative standing within the major rating categories.

Table 14.3 Moody's Rating Categories for Long-Term Issuers and Issues

AAA	Highest quality. These issues carry the smallest degree of investment risk.
Aa	Issues judged to be of high quality by all standards. Together with Aaa bonds they comprise what are generally known as high-grade bonds.
A	Upper-medium grade obligations with many favorable investment attributes.
Baa	Medium-grade obligations. Lowest investment-grade rating.
Ba	These issues have some speculative elements.
B	Issues that generally lack characteristics of desirable investments.
Caa	Obligations of poor standing. Such issues may be in default or there may be present elements of danger with respect to principal or interest.
Ca	Obligations that are speculative in a high degree. Such issues are often in default or have other marked shortcomings.
C	Lowest class of bonds; issues so rated can be regarded as having extremely poor prospects of attaining any real investment standing.

Source: Moody's website, http://www.moodys.com.
Note: Moody's applies numerical modifiers 1, 2, and 3 in each generic rating classification from Aa through Caa. The modifier 1 indicates that the obligation ranks in the higher end of its generic rating category; the modifier 2 indicates a midrange ranking; and the modifier 3 indicates a ranking in the lower end of that generic ranking category.

lenders know that some borrowers will repay their loans on time, some will repay part of their loans, and some will just default on their obligations. In short, they know that there are several types of borrowers (say, for example, good, medium, and poor), but they may not know into which category the borrower they lend money to falls.

For most investors, figuring out *ex ante* a borrower's type (and thus the default risk or the likelihood of repayment) could be very costly. Indeed the costs often would exceed any additional benefits that may accrue to any particular investor from having that information. Consequently, no one investor may be willing to undertake the initial evaluation to determine a borrower's type and the subsequent monitoring necessary to ensure repayment.[10] Furthermore, if any one investor makes the effort of figuring out a borrower's type and acts on that information, then the information ceases to be private and other investors can become free riders. Thus, unless the private benefit is large enough, no one investor will make the effort. And if more than one investor makes the effort, then there is a duplication of efforts that leads to market inefficiencies.[11] In the end, information asymmetries can produce markets that are highly inefficient or even markets that dry up completely.[12]

Under that scenario, credit ratings can serve a useful function in the debt markets by reducing or eliminating the information asymmetries that exist between borrowers and lenders. Ratings can also help minimize the efforts undertaken by market participants to determine borrowers' types, thus making financial markets more efficient. For that to happen, at least two conditions must be met. First, the rating agency must be able to capture enough of the benefits of its credit analysis to actually conduct the analysis in the first place.[13] Second, the rating agency must have a reputation for integrity and accuracy for its ratings to be accepted. By integrity it is meant that ratings will be unbiased; by accuracy it is meant that ratings will be, on average, good predictors of default risk. Indeed, reputational capital is a rating agency's most valuable asset. It is an asset that takes a long time to develop, which is the main economic reason why there have always been just a few rating agencies.[14]

If those conditions are met, then the agencies' ratings can serve as credible signals sent to the markets that help investors identify borrowers' types.[15] By credible it is meant a signal that separates high- from medium-quality borrowers, and medium- from low-quality borrowers; in other words, a signal that creates a separating equilibrium, to use game theory terminology, by making it too costly for low-quality borrowers to obtain the signal (say, an A- or better rating). If, on the other hand, ratings do not sufficiently distinguish borrowers' types, ratings produce a pooling equilibrium and are not valuable signaling devices.[16]

In this framework, the incentive for the borrowers to obtain a rating is clear: Ratings cheaply convey information to the markets about borrowers' ability to pay their debts. Being identified as a high-quality type results in lower costs of capital, even after controlling for the costs of procuring a rating. (More accurately, borrowers will only make use of ratings if the expected savings in terms of lower costs of capital are greater than the expected costs of procuring the rating, *and* if the expected costs of obtaining the rating are lower than the expected costs of other alternative signaling devices that contain at least the same informational value as the rating.)[17]

Empirical studies show that ratings do a reasonable job of measuring relative risk. Ratings correlate well with default rates—that is, more highly rated issues have lower default rates than lower-rated issues. Initial ratings seem to correlate better with default rates than rating changes. For instance, less than 1 percent of issues rated A- or better go into default in the first year. To determine whether rating changes contain any informational value not already reflected in bond prices, one could test if announcements of rating changes are followed immediately (i.e., within a day or two) by changes in credit yield spreads. If rating changes do not lead to changes in market prices, then it could be argued that changes in ratings are just reflecting information that the markets have already processed and that ratings lag other market indicators. Based on the tests of this type that have been conducted, it appears that changes in ratings do contain some informational value.[18]

REGULATORY RELIANCE ON RATINGS:
THE BUILDING BLOCKS OF A CARTEL

A second reason why investors offer more than a penny for the rating agencies' thoughts is that ratings have been used for regulatory purposes in the United States since 1931, when the Office of the Comptroller of the Currency (OCC) and the Federal Reserve required banks to mark to market lower-rated bonds (i.e., bonds that were rated below BBB). In 1936, the first significant ratings-based regulation was approved, when the OCC, the Federal Reserve, and the Federal Deposit Insurance Corporation (FDIC) prohibited banks from purchasing "speculative securities" (defined as those securities rated below BBB), a prohibition that continues to this day.[19] Over the decades, ratings-dependent regulations in the United States increased considerably, and eventually regulators had to determine whose ratings they would approve.[20]

Of those regulations, one is particularly significant, as it is the one that led the SEC to adopt the term "nationally recognized statistical rating organization" (NRSRO). In 1975 the SEC adopted rule 15c3-1 under the Securities Exchange Act of 1934 to determine net capital requirements for broker-dealer firms. Specifically, rule 15c3-1 indicates that the percentages of the market value of securities that can be counted toward broker-dealer firms' net capital requirements will be determined by the credit ratings assigned to those securities by at least two NRSROs.

Nowhere in rule 15c3-1 is the term NRSRO defined, nor has it been since. In 1994 the SEC issued a concept release soliciting comments on the appropriate role of the rating agencies and on the formal procedures for the designation and monitoring of NRSROs. In 1997 the SEC published a rule proposal that would have adopted a formal definition of the term NRSRO and would have set specific criteria for achieving that status. Those criteria include (1) national recognition as an issuer of credible and reliable ratings by the predominant users of securities ratings; (2) adequate staffing and financial resources so it can issue credible ratings and operate independently of the firms it rates; (3) systematic use of rating procedures; (4) extent of contacts with the management of issuers; and (5) internal procedures to prevent misuse of nonpublic information and to ensure compliance with these procedures.[21]

Obviously, the criteria set forth above, which, although never implemented as a rule, guide the SEC's actions with regard to NRSRO applications, and create a catch-22 situation: To achieve NRSRO status, a credit rating firm must have adequate resources and national recognition. But national recognition and adequate resources are unlikely to be obtained unless a credit rating firm has NRSRO status. Furthermore, by concentrating on the inputs that go into the rating process (i.e., staff and resources) instead of the output (i.e., the reliability and credibility of the ratings), the SEC is likely to stifle innovation.

With no definition of NRSRO or a formal procedure for achieving such status, the SEC simply assigned the NRSRO designation to Moody's, S&P's, and Fitch Investors Service when it adopted rule 15c3-1. Since then a few other firms have received the NRSRO designation from the SEC, but these firms have subsequently merged or have been acquired by the initial three NRSROs. In February 2003, after more than a decade without granting NRSRO status to any credit rating firm, the SEC approved the application of Dominion Bond Ratings, a Canadian firm, which became the fourth NRSRO.

Thus, at the same time that the SEC and other regulatory agencies have relied more and more on credit ratings for their safety-and-soundness regulations,[22] the lack of clear procedures and criteria for achieving NRSRO status is limiting entry into the industry. Regulatory actions have likely increased the demand for the services of the credit rating agencies (as well as their profits) and limited the number of firms in the industry, thus creating a well-entrenched cartel (or duopoly).

University of San Diego law professor Frank Partnoy, one the leading critics of the status quo, claims that since the 1970s, credit ratings have contained little informational value; instead their main value comes from the granting of "regulatory licenses" associated with ratings-dependent regulations. As the number of ratings-dependent regulations has increased, so have the value of the NRSRO designation and the value of those companies that have that status. In Partnoy's view, NRSRO ratings are the key to reducing the costs associated with regulations, and that is why corporations and investors find them useful.[23]

Thus, if Partnoy is right, regulatory actions have greatly distorted the role of credit ratings in the financial markets. The next section looks at the validity of "Partnoy's Complaint," as it has come to be known, and at some other issues facing regulators today.[24]

POST-ENRON REFORM PROPOSALS

Following the Enron scandal the SEC and congressional investigators have concentrated on the following issues related to the credit rating agencies: First, whether the current NRSRO framework is limiting competition and, if so, how that framework can be modified to promote competition in the industry; second, whether the use of the NRSRO concept for regulatory purposes is desirable; third, if desirable, whether NRSROs should be regulated more closely. Finally, what conflicts of interest do the NRSROs face, and what should the SEC do about them? Relatively little attention has been given to Partnoy's Complaint and the related issue of how much the informational value of ratings is distorted by the fact that ratings are used for regulatory purposes. Or put in slightly different terms, can the informational value of ratings and their regulatory worth be separated?

Partnoy's stronger claim—that credit ratings do not contain any informational value—does not seem to be supported by the evidence. If it were indeed the case that credit ratings have value insofar as they are viewed by market participants as regulatory licenses, then the only credit ratings market participants would be interested in would be those of NRSRO firms. But there are non-NRSRO rating firms that are viable businesses, albeit much less profitable than the NRSROs. Furthermore, the majority of non-NRSROs operate as subscription-based services. So it must be the case that consumers of non-NRSRO ratings obtain some (informational) value in these ratings that they cannot obtain at a lower cost elsewhere, because these companies do not have any regulatory licenses to sell.

Partnoy's policy recommendation—that all regulatory dependence on credit ratings be eliminated—is one with which I find myself in complete agreement. That policy prescription would provide a satisfactory solution to the problems created by the current NRSRO framework, which is clearly limiting competition, and to the question of whether the NRSROs would have to be regulated more closely (there would not be any NRSROs to regulate). Eliminating the NRSRO concept and all NRSRO-related regulation would leave regulators and market participants to grapple only with issues related to conflicts of interest. Lawrence White sums up that view nicely:

> Without the rating requirements by financial regulators, the SEC would not have to certify NRSROs, and the rating firms' fates—incumbent and entrant alike—would be left to the financial markets, where they belong. The participants in the financial markets, on their own, would decide whether and which rating firms provide enough help in piercing the asymmetric information fog of these markets so as to justify the firms' costs and fees.[25]

Let us not forget that ratings are just an opinion about the creditworthiness of borrowers, but they are not the *only* opinion. Credit spreads—that is, the difference between the yield to maturity on a given security and the yield to maturity in a risk-free security of comparable maturity and structure—are another measure of the credit risk, one that is being continuously updated by all market participants;[26] financial institutions' credit risk models are another. Regulators should not be in the business of determining which measure of creditworthiness is best. Market participants should decide for themselves whether to use ratings or not and whether credit rating firms that obtain their revenues from issuers compromise the integrity of their ratings.

If the "regulatory license" view of credit ratings is the more accurate view, then elimination of ratings-dependent regulation would eliminate an implicit tax on market participants without great losses in efficiency in financial markets. If, on the other hand, the reputational view of ratings is the correct one, as the NRSROs claim, then NRSROs should have no objection to their being relieved from their quasi-regulatory role, so as to have to survive solely on the basis of the non-regulatory value they provide to market participants. Both views seem to support the adoption of policies that place *less*, not more, dependence on credit ratings for safety-and-soundness financial regulations.

CONFLICTS OF INTEREST

My view regarding conflicts of interest, a view that is subject to change if more persuasive evidence to the contrary is presented, is that the rating agencies have been able to hold the conflicts of interest that arise from charging issuers for ratings in check. Reputational concerns, an entrenched position as quasi-regulators, and fears of losing NRSRO status have provided enough discipline. Therefore, conflicts of interest are not a sufficient condition to explain the extent to which NRSRO credit ratings have declined in quality in recent years.

The rating agencies receive most of their revenue from the issuers of the securities they rate. In the view of critics, that creates a conflict of interest that tarnishes the reputation of the rating agencies. However, as stated above, rating fees are agreed upon before the determination of ratings and are based on a fixed fee schedule.[27] More important perhaps is the fact that NRSROs have a very large number of clients; the revenue the agencies obtain from any one issuer is such a small percentage of their total revenue (not more than 1.5 percent, according to the rating agencies) that any increase or decrease in revenue from a better-than-merited or worse-than-expected rating is not a strong enough incentive to compromise the integrity of the rating process. The loss of reputation that would result from rating inflation would most likely exceed any monetary gains the agencies could obtain.[28] There may be other factors that compromise that rating process, but issuer fees do not appear to be one of them. As mentioned above, reputational capital, the ratings agencies' most valuable asset, takes a long time to develop. But it takes just a short time to lose it. Thus, market pressures to maintain a good reputation have for the most part held the agencies in check.

There is another reason why the rating agencies have been very careful to preserve their reputational capital and, thus, their privileged position. NRSRO status, which is very difficult to obtain, is a source of very valuable and significant economic rents to those firms that have it. If Moody's or S&P's had seriously compromised their integrity, the SEC may have acted to withdraw their NRSRO status.[29] That would have a very significant negative effect on the rating agencies' bottom lines, an effect that would greatly outweigh any benefit that may be derived from giving out good ratings generously.

CONCLUSION

The history of the credit rating agencies closely parallels the industrialization of the United States and the development of financial markets there.[30] The rating agencies, which started as credit-reporting firms, rose to prominence in the first quarter of the twentieth century by providing information about the financial condition of firms to the public that allowed investors to determine the creditworthiness of those firms independent of the investment banks. In so doing, they broke the information monopoly that investment bankers had had with regard to the quality of the bonds these bankers underwrote just as the U.S. investor class was rapidly expanding.[31]

Over time, however, investor demand for the services of the credit agencies decreased to such an extent that the rating agencies had become of marginal importance. One of the reasons why investor demand decreased substantially was the very small number of bond defaults in the 1950s and 1960s. The turbulent conditions and financial innovations of the 1970s and, more important, the renewed use of credit ratings for regulatory purposes breathed new life into the rating agencies. But in the process the rating agencies' role was radically transformed from one as providers of information to being quasi-regulatory agencies.

There is no doubt today that the credit rating industry has been distorted by regulatory actions. On the one hand, the increased use of credit ratings for regulatory purposes has increased the demand for credit ratings above what it would be in a pure market environment. On the other, the lack of clear criteria for obtaining the NRSRO designation and, consequently, the entry barriers created by that ambiguity have limited the supply of credit rating firms. While those actions may have increased the rents of NRSRO firms, they have also created conditions that are far from optimal.

Indeed, in the absence of regulatory demand for ratings, credit ratings would be useful to market participants insofar as ratings send a credible signal about the quality of an issuer. The value of that signal would be a function of the credibility enjoyed in the markets by the sender of the signal (i.e., the rating agency) and the timeliness of the signal; credibility would, in turn, be a function of the accuracy of the ratings relative to other measures of credit risk and the integrity of the sender.

To be able to determine (a) whether rating firms provide any informational value over and above what other market signals provide such that investors or companies are willing to pay for those ratings and (b) which business model is superior—one where ratings are financed by investor fees or one where ratings are financed by the issuing companies—the SEC should eliminate the NRSRO designation and U.S. and international regulators should undertake steps to reduce and eventually eliminate their reliance on credit ratings for regulatory purposes. Those actions are the only ones that will allow us to determine with certainty whether ratings are valuable for their reputational and informational content as opposed to being valuable as regulatory licenses, and whether the reputation of credit rating agencies is tarnished because they receive the bulk of their revenues from the companies and entities whose debt they rate.

NOTES

1. White House press release, "President Bush Signs Corporate Corruption Bill." Available at http://www.whitehouse.gov/news/releases/2002/07//print/20020730.html. Accessed September 2, 2003.

2. Securities and Exchange Commission, "Report on the Role and Function of Credit Rating Agencies in the Operation of the Securities Markets as Required by Section 702(b) of the Sarbanes-Oxley Act of 2002," January 2003.

3. In their defense, the three rating agencies made Enron's maintainance of its investment-grade rating contingent on its being acquired by rival energy company Dynegy, which was a possibility until days before Enron filed for bankruptcy. Furthermore, one can argue that they were fooled, as were other market participants, by Enron's complex and opaque capital structure and, as representatives of the three agencies claimed during congressional hearings, they never gave Enron a very high rating. At any rate, there is no doubt that the rating agencies were very late in identifying problems with the failed energy company. Or, put another way, if the rating agencies did no better than other market participants, what is the point of giving them the privileged status that they enjoy?

4. See Senate Committee on Governmental Affairs, "Financial Oversight of Enron: The SEC and Private-Sector Watchdogs," Report of the Staff of the Senate Committee on Government Affairs, October 8, 2002.

5. For an analysis of the original Basel Accord as well as the proposals for revision, see L. Jacobo Rodríguez, "International Banking Regulation: Where's the Market Discipline in Basel II?" Cato Institute Policy Analysis no. 455, October 15, 2002, and references therein.

6. There are a few comprehensive studies of the ratings industry in addition to the one mandated by the SOA. See, in particular, Richard M. Levich, Giovanni Majnoni, and Carmen Reinhart, eds., *Ratings, Rating Agencies and the Global Financial System,* Norwell, Mass:

Kluwer Academic Press, 2002; Basel Committee on Banking Supervision, "Credit Ratings and Complementary Sources of Credit Quality Information," Working Paper no. 3, August 2000; Richard Cantor and Frank Packer, "The Credit Rating Industry," *Federal Reserve Bank of New York Quarterly Review* 19, no. 2, 1994, p. 1–26; and Frank Partnoy, "The Siskel and Ebert of Financial Markets? Two Thumbs Down for the Credit Rating Agencies," *Washington University Law Quarterly* 77, no. 3, 1999, p. 619–714.

7. See Basel Committee on Banking Supervision, p. 14.

8. The rating agencies also grade short-term debt (e.g., commercial paper or municipal bonds) and structured finance instruments such as asset-backed securities, special purpose entities, and mortgage-backed securities, among other instruments.

9. See Senate Committee on Governmental Affairs, p. 123.

10. The exception here may be large institutional investors, some of which have in-house credit-scoring departments. But even for these large institutional investors, whose stock of trade is to be well diversified, the marginal benefit accruing from close monitoring of the companies whose debt they hold may not exceed the marginal cost of performing that monitoring.

11. Similar arguments are made in Basel Committee for Banking Supervision, p. 12, and Lawrence J. White, "The Credit Rating Industry: An Industrial Organization Analysis," in *Ratings, Rating Agencies, and the Global Financial System*, p. 41–63.

12. The classic article here is George A. Akerlof, "The Market for Lemons: Qualitative Uncertainty and the Market Mechanism," *Quarterly Journal of Economics* 84, August 1970, p. 488–500.

13. As Lawrence J. White explains, the spread of low-cost photocopying in the 1960s led the rating agencies to change their business model in the late 1960s and early 1970s to remain viable (S&P started to charge issuers for ratings in 1968; soon, other companies followed suit). Up until that point, the majority of rating firms had derived most of their revenues from the sale of ratings reports to bondholders and other investors. As photocopying became cheaper, the demand for original reports declined (i.e., free riding increased). The leading rating firms solved the problem by starting to charge issuers for the ratings, thus spreading the costs of producing those ratings across all investors. White concludes that relying on issuer fees creates important conflicts of interest that compromise the credibility of the rating agencies. This point is discussed in greater detail below.

14. The other economic reason is the desire on the part of users of ratings to have few classifications of ratings categories that can be easily compared. In economic parlance, there are network effects that limit the number of players in the industry.

15. Although who pays for the ratings does affect the incentives faced by the rating agencies, it does not, in my opinion, invalidate framing the analysis as a signaling game.

16. There is an extensive literature on signaling that begins with Michael A. Spence, "Job Market Signaling," *Quarterly Journal of Economics* 87, 1973, p. 355–74.

17. More formally, companies will have their issues rated if the expected savings from the rating, E[S], is greater than or equal to the cost of the rating, where the expected savings from the rating is a function of the probability of achieving any particular rating and the expected savings from that rating.

18. Of course, it could also be that market movements following changes in ratings are based on the regulatory implications of the change in rating and not on any new information that the change itself actually provides.

19. This regulation was extended to thrifts in 1989.

20. See Basel Committee for Banking Supervision, p. 54; and Cantor and Packer, "The Credit Rating Industry," for a more complete list of financial regulations that depend on credit ratings.

21. See Securities and Exchange Commission, "Capital Requirements for Brokers or Dealers Under the Securities Exchange Act of 1934," Concept Release no. 34-39457, December 17, 1997.

22. For instance, rule 2a-7 under the Investment Company Act of 1940, adopted by the SEC in 1991, limits money market funds to investing only in highest quality (as determined by an NRSRO rating) short-term instruments.

23. See Frank Partnoy, "The Paradox of Credit Ratings" in *Ratings, Rating Agencies, and the Global Financial System*, p. 64–84, and Partnoy, "The Siskel and Ebert of Financial Markets?"

24. Credit rating agencies are registered with the SEC as investment advisers under the Investment Advisers Act of 1940. The SEC, thus, has sole regulatory authority over the credit rating agencies, an authority that has been used sparingly. For instance, the act does not directly address the quality or reliability of credit ratings, nor has the SEC undertaken any studies to measure the NRSROs' track records.

25. See Lawrence J. White in *Ratings, Rating Agencies and the Global Financial System*, p. 53.

26. There can be problems with credit spreads in highly illiquid markets.

27. It is not known with certainty, however, if the rating agencies negotiate volume discounts or practice some other type of price discrimination.

28. Plus, inflating ratings to obtain business makes little sense in a world where the NRSROs already have a captive market for their services.

29. Although the probability of that occurring is remote, given the SEC's poor record of enforcement, it is still greater than zero, and so it cannot be discarded entirely.

30. See Richard Sylla, "An Historical Primer on the Business of Credit Ratings," in *Ratings, Rating Agencies, and the Global Financial System*, p. 19–40.

31. As Sylla points out, it helped that the public distrusted investment bankers as the ultimate insiders, even though it appears that bankers used that privileged position to protect their reputational capital and their clients' investments. See Sylla, "Historical Primer," p. 24–25.

The SEC as a Corporate Monitor

R. T. McNamar

$\mathscr{T}$o suggest that Enron was just about a Houston company's accounting fraud is like suggesting the Cold War was just about the shooting down of Francis Gary Powers; it misses the big picture. Enron was about accounting and securities fraud and bad corporate management, but it was about much more than that. It involved a systematic failure of America's institutions of corporate monitoring.

Enron's management failed. Enron's board of directors failed. Enron's internal audit function failed. Enron's external auditors failed. Enron's attorneys failed. Enron's commercial and investment bankers failed. The credit rating agencies failed. Wall Street's securities analysts failed. The business press reporting on Enron failed. In other words, the American institutions of corporate monitoring that many had touted, indeed even preached about to the rest of the world, simply all failed.

In the Enron case, the greatest failure was the failure of the Securities and Exchange Commission (SEC). As the government's watchdog over public companies to ensure adequate and timely disclosure of relevant corporate information, the SEC simply failed in all aspects. It was not a watchdog, or a lapdog, or even involved in Enron, except in several negative ways. The watchdog did not bark. To quote Gertrude Stein, "There was no 'there' there."

If there is a major positive lesson to come out of Enron's failure, it is the opportunity for the SEC to alter dramatically how it monitors periodic corporate filings and screens them for irregularities that may deserve an investigation. If the SEC seizes this opportunity, it would take an important step to ensure that another Enron does not take place.

BACKGROUND

Enron was a true bipartisan failure on the part of the SEC. A Democrat, Arthur Levitt, chaired the commission from 1993 to 2001, when the seeds of Enron's collapse were planted and sprouted. A Republican, Harvey Pitt, chaired the commission from 2001 until 2002, when the collapse finally occurred. Congress was controlled by the Democrats until 1995, when both houses swung to the Republicans until the Democrats briefly regained the Senate in 2001.

Many supporters of the SEC contend that congressional failure to provide adequate appropriations for the SEC is the root problem of its failure. In fact, my research suggests that there was a policy management failure on the part of the SEC leadership and an oversight failure on the part of Congress. Lawmakers and their staff did not ask the right questions of the commission for a decade.

Every Four Years

Enron's 1997 10(k), which was filed in April 1998, was the last Enron periodic filing to be examined by an SEC staff member until the SEC reacted to comments in the press about the firm's problems and opened an enforcement investigation during the third quarter of 2001. Enron went bankrupt in the following quarter. In short, the SEC's failure to examine the Enron filings represents a stunning failure of public policy oversight. Worse, that failure was in compliance with the SEC's stated and congressionally approved policy of only reading a public company's periodic filings once every four years or reviewing 25 percent of all of the corporate filings each year. That was considered adequate. Enron shows that it was not.

Mark-to-Market Accounting

In a no-objection letter dated January 30, 1992, Walter P. Schuetze, chief accountant of the SEC, granted Enron permission to use mark-to-market accounting for its gas-trading operations, Enron Gas Services, beginning the first quarter of 1992. Enron responded that after "further review," it was going to begin using mark-to-market accounting for the first period of 1991 and that the "impact on earnings was not material." In fact, it was material. The year 1992 marked the beginning of the end at Enron, and the SEC never challenged the company-wide use of mark-to-market accounting over the next nine years.

Mark-to-market accounting is a valid accounting technique. Banks and insurance companies mark to market their bonds and equity portfolios quarterly for their public reports and do it daily for internal management reports. They indicate the increases and decreases in the current market value of the portfolio. The underlying accounting theory is that the current market value is a better measure of the liquid asset's value than its historical acquisition cost. It is most often used for assets for which a third-party valuation is readily available from the newspapers, Internet, Bloomberg, etc. Gas contracts are relatively uniform contracts for the future delivery of natural gas at stated volumes, prices, purity, and geographic location for delivery. Hence, the gas contracts are relatively easy to price and compare, similar to U.S. Treasury bonds. Mark-to-market accounting is not used for unique assets, project finance projects, and ongoing sales operations that do not have relatively uniform marketable assets that can be easily priced in the open market by looking at the Internet, newspaper, or trade journal publications for current market prices.

Based on the SEC no-objection letter on mark-to-market accounting for its gas-trading business only, Enron used mark-to-market accounting for all aspects of its business for SEC reporting and its public disclosures to securities analysts. Enron's SEC filings were not straightforward and obfuscated the fact that Enron was using mark-to-market accounting for all of its businesses.

There is no indication that the SEC ever responded to Enron's February 11, 1992, letter or objected to Enron adopting mark-to-market accounting a year earlier. Indeed, it does not appear that the SEC ever understood the materiality to Enron's earnings. The shift in accounting techniques permitted Enron to show earnings in 1991 that were similar to earnings it reported in 1990. In fact, the 1991 earnings would have been down if Enron had not booked two very large gas supply contracts late that year and marked them to market.

In retrospect, even though it was apparent that Enron was trying to hide what it was doing, the SEC never challenged the firm's company-wide use of mark-to-market accounting. That is a nine-year period of failure by the SEC, seven of which were while Levitt was chairman and two while Pitt was chairman.

Public Utility Holding Company Act

The Public Utility Holding Company Act of 1935 (PUHCA) was passed to protect consumers from the complex holding company structures and cross-share ownerships of many of the electric and gas utilities in the 1920s. Essentially, if a company is classified as a utility, it must file a number of additional forms for review by the SEC before issuing public securities. (The forms require the company to detail the ownership structures and percentages of ownership and inter-company debt between the parent holding company and its subsidiaries.) In October 1993, Enron petitioned the SEC to declare that power marketers were not utilities under PUHCA. In response, the SEC issued a no-action letter on January 5, 1994.

When Enron acquired Portland General Electric (PGE) in 1995, it argued that it was not operating in interstate commerce, but only in the state of Oregon. In fact, Enron reincorporated in Oregon from Delaware, where it had previously been incorporated. Consistent with its past precedents, the SEC found that Enron was not a public utility in interstate commerce. This was a classic case of the lawyers running the SEC based on what had been done before and ignoring the reality of what Enron and PGE were doing. This is another example of SEC failure in regulating Enron.

As later noted by the Senate Government Oversight Committee staff report on Enron, if the SEC had not exempted Enron from PUHCA, the firm would have been required to prepare much more detailed reports explaining the ownership connections between the parent and its many subsidiaries. The reports would have been filed and (presumably) read by the SEC utilities group. Many questions would have been raised about the nature of the ownership relations and Enron's off-balance-sheet use of the special purpose entities (SPEs).

XBRL AND THE SEC

Shortly after the accounting scandals at Enron and WorldCom, Congress passed the Sarbanes-Oxley Act (SOA). One of the purposes of the SOA was to address the deficiencies of the existing SEC corporate filing and review process. It did so in two ways:

Under section 408, the SOA mandates "enhanced review of periodic disclosures by issuers" and requires the SEC to review the filings "on a regular and systematic" basis. It then enumerates six review criteria that the SEC must consider.

Under section 409, the SOA authorizes (but does not mandate) that the SEC initiate real-time issuer disclosures from issuers of securities.

Those changes may appear to be subtle, but they are notable alterations to how the SEC had been operating.

XBRL

By chance, there is a new classification system that, if the SEC adopts it, will permit the SEC to alter its filing and analysis of periodic corporate reports in a transforming way. The eXtended Business Reporting Language (XBRL) is a new private sector scheme developed to improve the consistency, accuracy, and quality of financial reporting in the business sector. XBRL is owned by a nonprofit company, which, in turn, is owned by over two hundred member companies around the world. About fifty of the member companies are U.S.-based. Any company can join the consortium and all of them pay their own expenses to work on the project. XBRL is freely licensed to anyone who wants to use it.

In essence, XBRL is a uniform standard for the electronic distribution and comparison of business reports. It enables users to compare the financial performance of a company against a group of companies and know that the data are comparable. It has been described as an Excel spreadsheet that is preloaded on a Web server with all of the other companies in its industry. For example, in the retail sector in XBRL, "sales per square foot" will now be uniform in their comparison, whereas previously, companies could and did have different definitions of such matters as what space (restrooms? stockrooms?) should be included in the square footage. In terms of its effect on financial reporting, XBRL has been analogized to bar coding for financial statement or the introduction of containerization in world trade and shipping. Another description is that XBRL will do for financial reporting what the Dewey Decimal System did for libraries. Those analogies all seem to be apt. Mike Willis of PricewaterhouseCoopers, who also is the head of the International Steering Committee of XBRL, has claimed, "The effect that XBRL will have on the business community will be more significant than the transition from paper-and-pencil analysis of financial information to the use of electronic spreadsheets."

The standards or taxonomies underlying XBRL are expected to be available for testing and use in the fall of 2003. The standards for the banking sector are already virtually completed, and commercial and industrial standards covering 97 percent of the economy are scheduled to be completed in the fall of 2003.

Five of the six major accounting firms that audit virtually all of the U.S. public companies in the United States have led the development of XBRL, its taxonomies, and the accompanying industry standards developed by the private sector industry working groups. The accounting firms are KPMG, Ernst & Young, PricewaterhouseCoopers, Grant Thornton, and BBDO Seidman.

XBRL has been entirely developed in the private sector, and there is no government money or even government sponsorship involved. Indeed, XBRL is being adopted by the government from the private sector. The Federal Examinations Council (comprised of officials from the Federal Reserve, the Office of the Comptroller of the Currency, the Federal Deposit Insurance Corporation, and the Office of Thrift Supervision) announced in June 2003 that the government would convert the basic bank report to the government agencies, known as the call report, to XBRL. Assuming the schedule is met, a major test will occur the first quarter of 2004, and all banks will begin filing in XBRL during the third quarter of 2004. In other words, the private sector has been addressing the failures of the SEC for a decade, and improving transparency in corporate reporting so that the capital markets can function more efficiently. The government has failed to do that.

"TRUST" Reporting

I developed for the SEC a new XBRL Web-based corporate filing and screening system. This proposal was then reviewed with senior SEC staff and was refined and improved with their cooperation. The SEC was scheduled to consider it in late 2003. My recommendation is based on XBRL and is called "transparent reporting using standardized terminology," or "TRUST" for short. It is essentially an XBRL-based reporting system for the SEC to use in reviewing periodic corporate reports filed by public companies. The flow charts in figures 15.1 and 15.2 demonstrate the current SEC filing and screening system and the TRUST system.

TRUST provides the SEC with an opportunity to revise its filing and screening process for all periodic public company filings like the 10-K and the 10-Q. It enables the commission to screen electronically all of the filings and determine which ones are consistent with industry standards and which individual companies' filings require additional explanation before the SEC can sign off on them. It is like posting to the company's website, except that XBRL makes the data available for computer analysis and manipulation once it is posted. It does not have to be entered into a spreadsheet by hand.

If Enron had filed in XBRL, its reported revenues, cash flows from operations, and profits would have been compared against industry standards. Its growth rate and the growth rate of its purported cash flows from operations would have been so far above the industry norms that it would have been flagged for an SEC staff review. It looked too good to be true, and an examination by the SEC's Corporate Finance Department would have showed that it was too good to be true. In other words, using XBRL, the comparison to industry standards would have prioritized the Enron work for the SEC staff.

Second Review

Using XBRL, the SEC would be able to identify deviations from industry norms or standards. The SEC could then "comment" on the deviations and request an explanation electronically. Those deviations that the SEC determines are material and not adequately explained by the companies through an electronic e-mail would then be reviewed by the corporate finance staff, who would attempt to resolve the questions through a conference call with the firm's financial officers. That process would resolve most filing issues.

For questions that would not be resolved in the conference call, the SEC could request a second audit firm to audit the filings in dispute. This would not be a complete second audit, which would be too expensive. But, by focusing on the disputed issue, the second audit firm would recommend a resolution to the SEC and the company. Hopefully, that would lead to resolution of the matter. If resolution does not occur, the SEC would have the option of ordering a forensic audit of the company by the second auditor on the disputed matter. That should resolve the matter in virtually all cases that do not become SEC enforcement investigations.

In the case of Enron, even a cursory review of its 10-K or 10-Q disclosures by a second auditing firm would have raised serious questions as to their adequacy

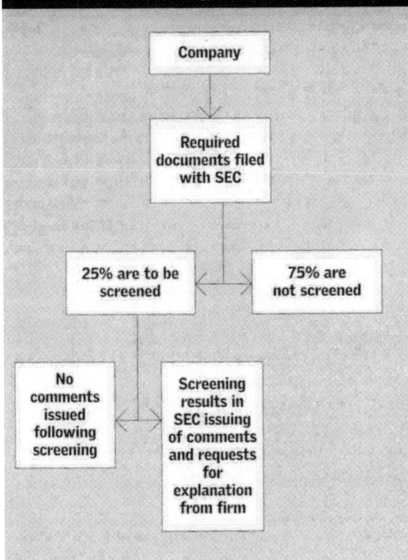

FIGURE 1

The Present

The current SEC filing and screening system

Company

↓

Required documents filed with SEC

25% are to be screened ← → 75% are not screened

No comments issued following screening ← Screening results in SEC issuing of comments and requests for explanation from firm

The Future?
TRUST Reporting

```
                    ┌──────────────┐
                    │   Company    │
                    └──────┬───────┘
                           ▼
                  ┌─────────────────┐
                  │    Required     │
                  │ documents filed │
                  │    with SEC     │
                  └────────┬────────┘
                           ▼
                  ┌─────────────────┐
                  │      100%       │
                  │   comparison    │
                  │  with industry  │
                  │    standards    │
                  └────────┬────────┘
                           ▼
    ┌──────────────┐          ┌──────────────┐
    │  Deviations  │◄─────────│ No deviations│
    │   detected   │          └──────────────┘
    └──────┬───────┘
           ▼
    ┌──────────────┐
    │ SEC requests │
    │ explanation  │
    │  from firm   │
    │ (automated)  │
    └──────┬───────┘
           ▼
    ┌──────────────┐
    │Firm responds │
    └──────┬───────┘
           ▼
    ┌──────────────┐
    │ SEC conducts │
    │  corporate   │
    │   finance    │
    │    review    │
    └──────────────┘
```

Deviations not resolved; SEC-firm conference call initiated ◄─── SEC concerns resolved

Deviations not resolved ◄─── SEC concerns resolved

Second auditor forensic audit ◄─── Second auditor review

Second auditor forensic audit ◄─── SEC concerns resolved

Informal SEC investigation ◄─── SEC concerns resolved

in describing Enron's business and the off-balance-sheet transactions Enron employed. If a second firm had been asked to review any one of Enron's 10-K filings from 1992 to 2001, the auditors would have produced a critique of the disclosures that would have caused the SEC Corporate Finance Department to initiate a serious investigation into what was going on. That would have almost undoubtedly led to enforcement actions that would have halted Enron's questionable practices several years before 2001.

The second auditor review policy has been praised by all who have examined it, including senior SEC staff and nongovernment experts on corporate reporting. In fact, Bill McDonough, the new chairman and CEO of the Public Company Auditing Oversight Board that was created under SOA, said about the second auditor review, "That puts all of the incentives in the right places for everyone."

At this time, it appears that the SEC is preparing to announce that it will convene an SEC roundtable discussion on "tagged reporting" with private sector participants. That is the normal SEC process and is similar to its recent SEC roundtable discussion on hedge funds. The discussion was expected to occur before the end of 2003. After the SEC roundtable, the commission will make a formal decision on TRUST. Discussions with SEC officials indicate that it is highly likely that TRUST will be the basis for a complete overhaul of the SEC's filing and screening process. Implementation could begin in 2004.

Benefits of TRUST

The TRUST recommendation is fully consistent with (and in some places surpasses) the requirements of the SOA. Indeed, section 408 of the SOA requires that the latest available technology be used to make filings meaningful and useful to the SEC. The TRUST proposal permits the SEC to screen 100 percent of its filings; the SOA requires only that 33 percent be reviewed annually. What is more, TRUST can work in "real time," thus satisfying the important requirement contained in section 409.

The TRUST system would provide the SEC with the screening tools that it needs to monitor corporate filings and comply with the congressionally mandated criteria for screening under SOA. The use of industry standards developed by the private sector increases the probability that they will be more accurate and effective than those that would be developed by the government. The system's greatest contribution is that the incentives for the SEC, the primary audit firm, and the chief financial officers of publicly traded firms are all aligned to avoid the use of the second auditor review, which would trigger adverse consequences, discipline, or even dismissal of the CFO and the auditor involved.

Last, at the macro level, the contribution of the TRUST system is that it would begin to close the "expectations gap" between the auditing firms and the needs of capital market participants for improved transparency. It moves away from earnings per share as the exclusive measure used by the investment community to gauge corporate performance. Enron's earnings, which supposedly followed generally accepted accounting principles, were manufactured through an elaborate Ponzi scheme and accounting fraud that the SEC did not even attempt to detect. Neither the SEC nor the Generally Accepted Accounting Principles (GAAP) reporting worked to ferret out Enron to provide private sector market discipline. I recommend that the SEC should study the addition of nonfinancial performance metrics to the SEC GAAP reporting requirements.[1]

NEED FOR TRANSPARENCY

According to a July 2002 CNN/*USA Today* poll, 77 percent of the public believes that CEO greed and corruption caused the recent U.S. financial meltdown. A survey of Main Street investors conducted that same month found that 71 percent of investors say accounting fraud is rampant. That is the real cost of the SEC's failure in Enron, and it is in no small part influenced by the constant coverage by the business news programs on cable television twenty-four hours a day, seven days a week.

Free capital markets cannot operate properly without transparency and confidence in the information they have. The current GAAP accounting and SEC reporting systems do not serve America's twenty-first century needs for transparent capital markets with trustworthy information. Fortunately, the private sector has been working to correct that problem. The SEC's adoption of TRUST would go a long way toward making GAAP reporting consistent and useful.

NOTES

1. This recommendation is also endorsed by analysts at the American Enterprise Institute and the Brookings Institution.

IV

TAXATION

· 16 ·

Our Tax System Is a
Major Part of the Problem

William A. Niskanen

Several common problems of American corporations in recent years are clearly attributable to characteristics of the U.S. tax code. The combined federal plus state corporate income tax rate is now the second highest among the industrial nations, exceeded only by that in Japan, leading to major economic distortions and undue attention to both legal and questionable means to reduce tax liabilities. A firm goes bankrupt when it does not generate enough cash flow to service its outstanding debt. But the corporate income tax invites firms to rely too much on debt finance, because interest is a deductible expense but the returns to equity are not. Prior to the effective date of the 2003 tax law, in turn, the combined effect of the corporate and individual income tax invited firms to rely too much on capital gains, rather than dividends, as the means to distribute the returns to equity, because long-term capital gains were taxed at a much lower rate than dividends by the individual income tax. The reduction of the individual tax rate on dividends has already had a substantial effect, increasing dividend payments by 30 percent in the first quarter following the effective date of the 2003 tax law.[1] A 2004 study by James Poterba estimates that the reduction in the tax rate on dividends should raise the after-tax value of dividends relative to capital gains by more than five percentage points and increase dividend payments by nearly 20 percent in the long term.[2] And an obscure provision of 1993 tax law limits the amount of an executive's salary and bonus that may be deducted to $1 million per year, substantially increasing the incentive to use stock options as a means of executive compensation. These characteristics of the U.S. tax code, in summary, increase both of the conditions that often lead to bankruptcy by encouraging an incompatible combination of too much debt and too much risk. The very complexity of the corporate income tax, in turn, is an invitation to manipulation and potential scandal.

This section develops the implications of these features of the U.S. tax system for executive compensation, the corporate debt burden, the distribution of the returns to equity, managerial preferences for risk, and the complexity of the tax code. Some of these problems were fortunately reduced by the 2003 tax law, which made the tax system more neutral between dividends and capital gains and slightly reduced the effective tax rate on the returns to corporate equity. The section concludes with a proposal to replace the very complex corporate income tax with a broad-based tax on the net cash flow of nonfinancial businesses to reduce or eliminate most of the biases of the current system.

NOTES

1. Blouin, Jennifer L., Jana Smith Raedy, and Douglas A. Shackelford, "Did Dividends Increase after the 2003 Reduction in Dividend Tax Rates?" Working Paper, October 2003.

2. Poterba, James, "Taxation and Corporate Payout Policy," National Bureau of Economic Research Working Paper no. 10321, February 2004.

· *17* ·

Compensation, Journalism, and Taxes

Alan Reynolds

$\int$hortly after the Enron bankruptcy there were several efforts to attribute the company's financial crisis to supposedly fundamental flaws in the ways in which executives in general are paid. Two distinct issues soon became confusingly intertwined. One was a broad perennial complaint about the level of compensation being excessive, using Enron as though it was a representative example of a much wider problem. The other was a narrower complaint about one particular form of such compensation—stock options—and about the way that form of compensation was accounted for and taxed. Political and media agitation about "expensing" options soon became a crusade and a symbol of virtue, as though that technical and controversial accounting procedure had some connection to accusations of actual fraud in the way Enron accounted for debts or in the way WorldCom depreciated expenses as investments.

Media and political attention to both the level and form of executive compensation in 2001–2003 began as an almost exact replay of events ten years earlier. This chapter begins with a brief history of the controversy about executive compensation in the early 1990s, showing how some intended "reforms" of that era contributed to excesses and imbalances by the end of that decade. The following section includes a critique of recent efforts to place a large share of blame for the Enron crisis on executive compensation, particularly stock options (a topic dealt with more intensively in later sections). Those first sections set the stage for a more detailed look into the complexities of measuring executive compensation, showing large differences and larger errors in the way CEO pay is reported in the press. The topic is then reexamined in the context of rents (paying more than necessary) and agency costs (trying to bring the personal interests of managers into alignment with interests of shareholders and creditors). Subsequent sections survey statistics and studies concerning both the level and particular forms of executive compensation. The chapter ends with an analysis of the ways in which stock options are or could be accounted for and taxed—a topic that has once again generated an unwarranted intensity of political and regulatory interest recently, as it did in 1991 and 1997.

Among several conclusions, two stand out most clearly. The first is that federal efforts to influence executive compensation in 1992–1993 proved counterproductive. Those efforts included Securities and Exchange Commission (SEC) disclosure rules, increased tax rates on salaries and dividends, and a million-dollar limit on the deductibility of salaries. The effect of these taxes and regulations was quite different from that promised by their advocates, including, most definitively, powerful incentives to tilt executive pay away from salaries and toward stock options.

The second conclusion is that some widely promoted efforts to have federal policy dictate future executive compensation policy, all of them inaccurately associated with Enron, are almost certain to prove as perversely counterproductive as those of a decade earlier. Efforts to further increase detailed disclosure of and shareholder voting on executive pay, for example, could put excess authority in the hands of those who represent special interests and those who have neither the information nor the incentives to negotiate on behalf of the actual owners of the firm (including nonvoting shareholders). Negotiating an executive contract could become like the U.S. government trying to negotiate an international free trade agreement while putting each proposed move online for an interactive vote.

The chapter ends by demonstrating that if the essentially unaccountable Financial Accounting Standards Board (FASB) is allowed to compel all public companies to "expense" the estimated value of stock options at the date granted, the main effects are likely (1) to reduce the transparency and pay-for-performance effectiveness of executive compensation, and (2) to make Generally Accepted Accounting Principles (GAAP) earnings even less informative for investors as a result of treating premature estimates as actual expenses.

CAUTIONARY LESSONS FROM THE 1990s

At a *Harvard Business Review* roundtable of compensation experts, New York attorney Joe Bachelder reminded everyone that

> in 1972 we were criticizing CEO pay. We were still doing it in 1982. In 1992, a raft of regulations and legislation were directed at reining in CEO compensation. Today we are still discussing it. Much of the current criticism comes from the fact that . . . nearly 80 percent of the gain in CEO pay in the 1990s is attributable to stock options. And stock markets did pretty well in the 1990s. Weren't we saying in the 1980s that we should tie CEOs to the market in order to identify them with shareholder value? We got what we asked for.[1]

BE CAREFUL WHAT YOU ASK FOR

Toward the end of prolonged economic expansions, such as 1983–1990 or 1992–2000, stock prices reach a cyclical peak and so does compensation linked to stock prices. Information about executive compensation is gathered and reported with a lag, with the result that peak compensation is reported a year or two after the economy has slipped into recession. Comparing boom pay with bust conditions then becomes irresistible fodder for media and political outrage about excessive compensation during the previous cyclical boom. In June 2001, for example, a typical issue of *Fortune* featured "The Great Pay Heist," complaining about the "highway robbery" of the year before.[2] Even in March 2002, *USA Today* erroneously reported that top executives (who are also large shareholders) "rarely felt shareholders' financial pain last year."[3] As Joe Bachelder suggested, however, the "raft of regulations and legislation" in 1992–1993 should remind us that this latest cycle of indignation could likewise inspire changes in tax and regulatory policies that end up aggravating the situation they promised to fix.

Back in 1990, the *Harvard Business Review* published a provocative and influential study by Michael Jensen and Kevin J. Murphy, who had studied compensation of CEOs at 1,400 companies from 1974 to 1988. They found that "a $1,000 change in corporate value corresponds to a [two-year] change in CEO compensation of just $2.59." They also found that "CEOs of large public companies are only slightly more likely to step down after very poor performance." With pay and job security appearing to be so insensitive to performance, Jensen and Murphy complained that "corporate America pays its most important leaders like bureaucrats." Later studies often disputed that conclusion, but that is largely because the post-1990 shift from short-term bonuses toward relatively long-term stock options has greatly improved the sensitivity of pay to stock performance. By 1998, for example, Brian Hall and Jeffery Liebman estimated that a 10 percent increase in a firm's market value added $1.25 million to the value of a median CEO's accumulated stocks and options (while it also added billions to the value of shareholders' wealth).[4]

Comparing CEO compensation in the late 1980s with the far more generous pay of partners at law firms and investment banks, Jensen and Murphy argued that CEO pay should be higher for superior stock performance. But they also thought the probability of being fired should also be higher for inferior performance. In that case, less-talented managers "would be replaced by more able and more highly motivated executives who would, on average, perform better and earn higher levels of pay." To reward "increased success fostered by greater risk taking, effort, and ability," they argued, "would eventually mean paying the average CEO more."[5] Among smaller companies, the Jensen-Murphy study found the most potent pay-for-performance incentives by far were paid to the CEO of Berkshire Hathaway, Warren Buffett, a gentleman who has been known to complain that much smaller incentives for other CEOs are excessive.

As other economists began looking into executive compensation, it seemed that Jensen and Murphy probably exaggerated the alleged inefficiency of the market for corporate leadership. Summarizing numerous studies on executive compensation produced for the National Bureau of Economic Research through 1994, Nancy Rose remarked: "We find no evidence for the popular view that boards typically fail to penalize CEOs for poor financial performance or reward them disproportionately well for good performance."[6]

The old Jensen-Murphy complaint about too few CEOs being fired looks rather quaint today. During the first five months of 2002, CEOs were being retired at the rate of two a day, eighty in May alone.[7] Another forty-four departed in the first eleven business days that June.[8] Some may have genuinely resigned or retired, even in a tough year like 2002, but an estimated 37 percent were, as they say, let go.[9] A study by Booz Allen Hamilton found that CEOs were forced out in 4.2 percent of companies surveyed in 2002, up from 2.7 percent a year earlier.[10] "The firings of CEOs when performance nose-dives has become commonplace in U.S. business," Margarethe Wiersema recently noted in the *Harvard Business Review*, but she found that it rarely improved the situation (which was often cyclical and, therefore, universal in 2002).[11] Being a CEO has become an increasingly risky job in many respects, largely due to public policy and related litigation. The more risky occupations become, the more they pay. One unexpected consequence of all the taxes, regulations, shareholder activism, and litigation aimed at reducing the compensation of corporate executives is that it almost surely has had and will have the opposite effect.

Regardless of possible exaggerations of the Jensen-Murphy study in 1990 and its certain obsolescence today (due to frequent CEO dismissal and substitution of options for salary), their powerful message that CEO pay and job security were usually unrelated to performance made CEO compensation and tenure appear *arbitrary*. And the impression that CEO compensation was arbitrary was easily abused by those who—quite unlike Jensen and Murphy—imagined CEOs to be typically overpaid. As a result, two seemingly opposed ideas—that CEO pay should be more closely tied to stock prices or that such pay should be held down by law—came together as a hot political issue in 1991 and 1992. The result was federal intervention that was intended to limit CEO pay but actually ended up having the opposite effect.

In May 1991, two months after the end of that recession, Sen. Carl Levin (D-Mich.), then chairman of an oversight subcommittee, held hearings on executive compensation in response to inflammatory articles then appearing in the press about CEO earnings a year or two before the recession. On June 4, 1991, Sen. Levin and Rep. John Bryant (D-TX) introduced the "Corporate Pay Responsibility Act" to require more disclosure of CEO pay and also to require the value of stock options to be estimated at the time they were granted and charged against earnings.[12] Congress did not act on the bill, despite subcommittee hearings on October 17. But the political pressure affected regulatory policy at the SEC and its pseudo-private subsidiary since 1973, the FASB. The FASB agreed to look into the matter of "expensing" estimated option values (as the FASB did again in 2003 for the same reasons). In May 1994, however, the Senate passed a resolution rejecting Sen. Levin's mandatory "expensing" of the estimated value of employee options by a vote of 88 to 9.[13]

On October 16, 1992, the SEC amended item 402 of regulation S-K to require much greater public disclosure of executive compensation and to facilitate shareholder voting on such compensation. This action, noted Andrew Prevost and John Wagster, "was in reaction to intense political pressure from shareholder activists, presidential candidates, the media, and the U.S. Congress." Jensen and Murphy had anticipated this development in 1990, warning that "public disclosure of 'what the boss makes' gives ammunition to outside constituencies with their own special-interest agendas. . . . How often do shareholder activists or union leaders denounce a corporate board for underpaying a CEO?"[14]

Making CEO compensation a target for litigation and political action by activist groups with quite different goals than maximizing shareholder wealth can be risky for shareholders. Prevost and Wagster surveyed several studies suggesting that managers of labor union, government, or nonprofit (e.g., TIAA-CREF) pension funds have often adopted the stance of being crusaders against big business to further their own personal interests, including running for political office. They examined several events leading up to the SEC rule change and estimated the impact on stock prices of firms targeted for institutional monitoring by the California Pubic Employees Retirement System (CalPERS). They found that firms targeted by CalPERS suffered "significant wealth losses" from the activist threat to CEO incentives caused by new SEC rules designed to make CEO pay an easier target.[15]

An earlier study by Marilyn Johnson, Susan Porter, and Margaret Shackell in 1997 noted that "pension funds like CalPERS appear to be more attuned to what is typically viewed as 'political concerns' about compensation than to what is typically viewed as 'shareholder concerns' about pay-for-performance sensitivities.'"[16] Such "institutional activists" cannot prudently be expected to represent shareholders, including shareholders in these pension funds. The evidence suggests that institutional activists constitute a new "agency problem," in which these agents (fund managers) have personal and political interests that may be the opposite of those of the principals (shareholders).

For the brief post-1993 period covered by Johnson, Porter, and Shackell, they found that some firms targeted by CalPERS responded by paying their executives like bureaucrats: "CEOs at target firms are compensated for a decrease in pay by a reduction in the riskiness of their remaining pay." That was consistent with Prevost and Wagster's finding that the market had marked down the stocks of CalPERS-targeted firms as the SEC "reforms" handed more ammunition to activists and reporters.

Although media outrage about CEO pay often quotes institutional activists as if they were disinterested observers, it appears to have had the opposite effect of

institutional activism. Johnson, Porter, and Shackell found that "firms with negative press coverage" regarding CEO pay experienced increases in "compensation
performance sensitivities." This suggests that the perennial post-recession media
indignation about executive salaries in the 1990s helped push the targets of their
indignation into increasing the share of CEO pay coming from stock options—an
unanticipated consequence that many CEOs soon learned to appreciate as stocks
soared from 1996 to early 2000.

As if such meddling in employment contracts by reporters and institutional
activists was not troublesome enough for shareholders in the 1990s, Congress decided to lend a hand.

On August 6, 1993, President Bill Clinton signed into law the Revenue Reconciliation Act of 1993. The 1993 tax law fulfilled two campaign promises in the
1992 Clinton-Gore campaign book, *Putting People First*. One was to "limit corporate deductions at $1 million for CEOs [salary and bonus]." The other was to im-
pose a "surtax on millionaires" (meaning, once in office, joint incomes above
$250,000)."[17] The million-dollar limit on the amount corporations could deduct
for executive salaries and bonuses actually passed both Houses in mid-1992 but was
vetoed by President George H. W. Bush. It was, however, reinstated in the 1993 tax
law and signed into law by its early champion, President Clinton.

The million-dollar rule, section 162(m) of the tax code, denies public companies any deduction for the cost of executive compensation in excess of $1 mil-
lion a year. This rule was never really about "fairness," since it does not apply to
other occupations, such as actors, athletes, or attorneys. And it was not really about
revenue either: The Clinton-Gore book claimed it would raise only $400 million
a year, which would have been possible only if the ceiling had been ineffective. The
main point, or at least the main effect, of this tax law was to encourage companies
to use nonsalary forms of pay to attract and keep top managers. That is because the
million-dollar rule does not apply to performance-related pay, such as grants of
stock options and restricted stock. The million-dollar rule does apply, however, to
any stock options that are "in the money" (above the market price) when granted,
thus effectively banning that type of compensation. Todd Perry and Marc Zenner
found that "many million-dollar firms have reduced salaries in response to 162(m)
and that salary growth rates have declined post-1993 for the firms most likely to
be affected."[18]

Using a more aggregated approach, Hall and Liebman found that the million-
dollar rule "led firms to adjust the composition of their pay and toward performance-
related pay" but did not decrease "the total level of compensation. . . . Any decrease in
salary brought about by section 162(m) was offset by increases in bonuses and stock
option grants."[19] Hall and Liebman examined these effects for the brief period from
1992 to 1998, which helps to explain why they found only a small substitution of options for salary resulting from the million-dollar rule alone. But the tax incentive to
shift toward options has grown stronger with every year since 1998 as the million-
dollar rule becomes more and more binding. As William McDonough points out,

"the $1 million salary cap for tax deductibility is nominal and not indexed. This means that as the average total compensation rises over time, the incentive to use stock options increases. Therefore, an increasingly large fraction of an executive's compensation in the form of stock options represents a nondiversified risk. Moreover, if the firm goes bankrupt, the options become worthless at the same time that executive's job is lost. As a result, firms may have to increase the amount of options they offer an executive to offset the increased riskiness of this form of compensation."[20]

The 1993 tax law also added a new marginal tax rate to 36 percent, up from 31 percent, on taxable income between $140,000 and $250,000. And an extra 10 percent surtax ("the millionaires' surtax") raised the top rate to 39.6 percent on incomes above $250,000.[21] That 28 percent hike in the top individual rate left the rate far above the new 35 percent corporate rate (also increased by 1 percentage point). The top marginal rate moved higher still in 1994 with the uncapping of the amount of earnings subject to the Medicare tax, increasing the top marginal tax rate on earnings to 42.5 percent. The steep new taxes on marginal salary income offered a strong incentive for high-paid professionals and managers to shift their pay packages toward deferred compensation such as stock options. And the steep tax on marginal dividend income promoted excessive (tax deductible) corporate debt and inefficient corporate acquisitions (to avoid the doubly steeper double tax on dividends).[22]

Aside from the predictably perverse impact of the million-dollar rule, the huge increase in marginal tax rates itself should have been expected to increase, rather than reduce, pretax CEO compensation—particularly the amount paid in tax-deferred forms such as stock options. "Because taxes will lead executives to provide less effort for any given level of incentive-based pay," explained Hall and Liebman, higher tax rates "should therefore increase the use of incentive-based pay."[23]

Taxes and Business Strategy by Myron Scholes and others notes that "because the corporate rate was now lower than the ordinary income tax rate [a policy ended in 2003], the corporate form offered a deferral advantage."[24] Executives facing much higher tax rates on salaries and bonuses after 1993 could exploit their employers' relative deferral advantage by switching a larger share of overtaxed CEO compensation toward the future through larger stock options, deferred income plans, and retirement perks.

Increasing the individual income tax to 39.6 percent from 31 percent also meant the double tax on dividends after 1993 was increased from roughly 55 to 60 percent at the federal level alone. That increased tax on dividends made stockholders even less interested in dividends. Benjamin Ayers, Bryan Cloyd, and John Robinson found "conditioned on dividend yield, a negative stock price reaction during the two weeks that Congress passed and President Clinton signed the increase in individual income tax rates in August 1993. . . . [And] the higher the firm's dividend yield the more negative the firm's stock price reaction to the increase in the individual income tax rate."[25] Individual investors subsequently became more inclined to favor companies that used earnings to increase assets per share through acquisitions or share repurchases, thus generating capital gains. The individual tax on capital gains was far less punitive than the tax on dividends (before 2003), particularly after 1997, when the tax on long-term gains was reduced to 20 percent from 28 percent.

The higher tax rate on corporate profits, particularly when paid out as dividends, also increased the incentive for corporate managers to use increased debt as a tax shield. John Graham at Duke University estimated that by 1994, "the present value of interest deductions averages 9.7 percent of the market value of the firm."[26] Enron and WorldCom created the appearance of rapid revenue growth largely by using retained earnings and debt to acquire companies. That may have been clever tax planning, but it proved to be fatal business planning.

John Graham, Mark Lang, and Douglas Shackelford found evidence of a trade-off "with options substituting for interest deductions" as an alternative way to reduce the bite of the unusually high 35 percent U.S. corporate tax. Corporations that "use debt conservatively also use options extensively," and vice-versa. Although the more extensive use of options among high-tech firms has been associated with more conservative use of debt (unlike Enron), the authors point out that related corporate "tax breaks" certainly did not lower total tax receipts as numerous irate press reports suggested.[27] On the contrary, "If options exercisers for our sample are in the highest individual tax bracket of 39.6 percent, we estimate a net revenue gain of $15 billion from our sample of firms . . . equivalent to increasing the corporate tax rate by 7 percent."[28]

The Clinton administration in 1993 acted on a then-popular belief that tax policy should push companies into tilting executive compensation away from the security of salaries and bonuses toward risky and illiquid stock options. A decade later, some of the same critics of CEO pay were complaining about the fact that most increases in executive pay from 1993 to 2000 came from stock-related compensation. Yet, that was precisely what the Clinton administration and many others were trying to accomplish. They simply failed to anticipate what a roaring bull market would do to the value of stock options in the late 1990s, when even the benchmark S&P 500 index was rising by nearly 30 percent per year. Companies granting CEO options in the early 1990s also did not anticipate the market's rise. Bull markets result in windfalls for stockholders, including corporate executives, and bear markets have the opposite effect.

The bull market was over by April 2000, and two years later, *Business Week* was reporting that in 2001, if a huge onetime option exercise by Oracle's CEO is left out, the drop in average CEO pay during 2001 alone "was nearly 31 percent, to $9.1 million, a level not seen since 1997."[29] CEO pay fell even further in 2002. In April 2003, *Fortune* reported that average CEO compensation among the one hundred largest companies fell by 23 percent in 2002.[30] Similarly, the *New York Times* found "total compensation of chief executives declined 20 percent."[31]

Although widely treated as indisputable facts, even by economist Paul Krug-man, press surveys of executive compensation sample different firms and use vari-ous dubious methods to count the value of stock options. In ways that varied over the years, *Fortune* bravely attempts to estimate only the value of new options granted during the previous year. While that survey was run by the overzealous Graef Crystal in the late 1980s and early 1990s, *Fortune* assumed executives held options until they expired, which greatly exaggerated the options' estimated fair value. Crystal's words continue to betray the slant of his numbers. In an April 4, 2003, *Bloomberg News* column, he boasted of having "switched sides and started to write critical articles on executive pay." More recent *Fortune* surveys just assume options are worth a third of their face value when granted. Even if such estimates had been done with more care and less bias, treating the estimated value of option grants as equivalent to cash can be as meaningless as the previously mentioned $76 million estimate for Steve Case's underwater AOL options.

Most amazing of all, *USA Today* defines a CEO's yearly pay (for the one hun-dred most valuable firms) as including both the value of old options *exercised* dur-ing a year and an estimate of the value of new options *granted* during the year. With this sort of creative accounting, a CEO's pay in 2001 might be said to consist of both options vested over the past decade (such as Larry Ellison's big sell-off while Oracle's stock was tumbling) and options that cannot be touched for another three or four years and may or may not have value after that. Armed with a definition of pay that includes both past and future stock options, *USA Today* is perpetually alarmed to find that its multiyear measure of pay is poorly matched to one year's change in the stock price. This indefensible definition of CEO pay is also the rea-son *USA Today* was the only major news source that did not notice that CEO pay fell sharply in 2001.

The *Wall Street Journal's* tables show both realized and unrealized gain on op-tions, thus calling Ellison's wealth loss a realized gain, but the accompanying reports average only the changes in "direct compensation." For 2001, the *Journal* reported "heads of the ten best-performing businesses experienced an 8.6 percent increase in direct compensation . . . [while] leaders of the ten with the poorest returns saw their remuneration sag 52.3 percent."[32] That report said CEOs were getting "stealth pay" through loans that were repaid (Enron's Kenneth Lay sold stock to repay such a loan).[33] Treating all actual loans as if they were gifts is the sort of con-fusion that led the hurried architects of the Sarbanes-Oxley (SOA) law to ban all loans to undefined "executive officers."

Lawrence Cunningham of the Boston College Law School predicts the ban on loans "will produce unintended and undesirable consequences." He notes that "loans are often tailored bonus schemes, forgiven or modified if executives achieve certain results. In that sense they resemble the incentive features of stock options, except they are better. One reason loans are better than stock options is they have a downside if targets aren't met (the borrower must pay), whereas options expiring worthless pose no penalty."[34] The idea that being paid with something that turns out to be worthless poses no penalty is certainly questionable, unless one believes (contrary to all logic and evidence) that executives who were partly paid with options would not otherwise have been paid in some other way. Still, Cunningham's point about the incentive value of loans is valid, and it means that by making this form of incentive pay illegal, the SOA law has inadvertently made stock options even more vital.

Getting back to flawed press coverage of executive compensation, it is worth emphasizing that figures about the value of past and/or future stock options have been regularly and erroneously compared to single-year stock price movements even before 1991, when Graef Crystal complained that "CEO pay rose 9.4 percent, to an average of $2.4 million. This while median share prices dropped 7.7 percent."[35] Half of that cited 9.4 percent "pay" increase resulted from Crystal's misestimate of the value of new option grants. But options granted in 1990 could not have been sensibly compared with share prices in 1990 because those new options could not be exercised until at least 1993. And the increase in CEO cash compensation barely kept pace with inflation, which averaged 4.8 percent in 1989–1991.

Long-term pay, such as stock option grants, is *forward-looking*. It is not and should not be related to previous annual moves in share prices. Yet journalists continue to make this fundamental mistake, year after year, as though (1) options granted several years ago could somehow be tied to last year's stock prices and as though (2) options that will not be vested for several more years ought to also be related to last year's stock prices. This is not what pay-for-performance is all about. If this year's shareholders only cared about last year's stock performance, they would want 100 percent of CEO compensation to be in the form of January bonuses tied to last year's stock prices. But basing pay on past performance—the journalistic definition of pay-for-performance—would offer executives zero incentive to do better in the future.[36]

Business Week recently added an estimate of the change in the value of older stock options to their own special measure of CEO pay. That could be more informative than the common practice of reporting exercised options as having been earned, rather than just cashed-in during a certain year. But the magazine stopped far short of subtracting big declines in the value of CEO holdings of stocks and options from annual income, since that would show many CEO's with negative income after 2000. Ellison, wrote *Business Week*, "earned a special place in the history of executive compensation with the $706 million he pocketed from exercising long-held options."[37] Yet Ellison certainly did not "earn" that $706 million during 2001, which makes it meaningless to suggest it was a record high for annual pay that occurred despite the company's poor stock performance. Ellison's asset position in Oracle dropped by more than $2 billion that year, so his liquidation of $706 million could hardly be described as "a special place in the history of executive compensation," unless "special" meant a record loss.

The most careless reporters (and their equally careless editors) have even described the proceeds from selling stock as though that was undisclosed CEO pay.

Why not include every sale of houses and cars, too? In a flashy *New York Times* Sunday feature, "Options Payday: Raking it in Even as Stocks Sag," David Leonhardt wrote, "At the 100 worst-performing companies in the Standard and Poor's 500 stock index, 47 executives and directors took home at least $5 million each by selling stock."[38] Leonhardt apparently did not even grasp the difference between selling stock and exercising options. Executives and directors are often required to *buy* large amounts of their company stock with their own money (which was a big reason why corporations loaned them money, before SOA prohibited doing so). Even in cases in which the stock may have been earned, it was obviously earned over many years. That makes it ridiculous to say, as Leonhardt did, that executives who sold stock in 2001, while their stocks were falling, did not suffer from that loss of wealth just as every other shareholder did. Gross proceeds from stock sales are not capital gains, much less compensation, and in 2001 such sales usually involved capital losses. In any case, including stock sales in annual compensation is total nonsense. Selling off assets is no different than selling a home—it does not make executives more wealthy and it is not "income."

Writing about "highflying executive pay" at Southwest Airlines, *Washington Post* writer Keith Alexander expected readers to be shocked that the CEO's pay "excludes the $344,000 he gained from the sale of more than 31,000 shares of Southwest stock."[39] The CEO's stock sales proved, he argued, that executives are well rewarded even when stocks fall. Yet the Southwest CEO probably purchased those thirty-one thousand shares with his own money, or they were earned over several years and not during the year they were sold. Because the stock was down, the CEO probably suffered a capital loss. In any case, calling sales of stock compensation is flatly wrong—another example of the dismal state of U.S. financial journalism and the low standards of influential editors.

In 2002, as in 1992, popular articles complaining about stock-related executive pay (even including sales of stock) began to appear long after the values of stocks and stock options had collapsed. In October 2002, Krugman wrote in the *New York Times Magazine* that CEO salaries from *Fortune*'s top one hundred had risen from $1.3 million in 1970 to $37.5 million in 1999. The latter figure, he claimed, was "more than 1,000 times the pay of ordinary workers" ($35,864).[40] Krugman's 1,000-to-1 comparison outbid even the AFL-CIO, which used similar statistical magic to claim CEO pay in 2000 was 411 times average "hourly worker" wages.[41] One problem with the CEOs' side of Krugman's 1,000-to-1 ratio is that *Fortune*'s 1999 figures on CEO pay greatly exaggerated the worth of many underwater options granted during that boom year. A far more inexcusable problem for Krugman, however, is that *Fortune*'s 1999 figures were inexcusably antique by October 2002. By then it should have been painfully obvious to Krugman's readers, if not to the author, that the wealth of CEOs must have been hugely reduced by the market's horrific decline.

For 2002, *Fortune*'s estimate of average top one thousand CEO salaries and benefits was $15.7 million—down 58 percent from the old $37.5 million figure

Krugman used—a drop of nearly 20 percent a year for three years. The other side of Krugman's ratio—ostensibly the "salaries" of "ordinary workers"—was nearly as understated as CEO pay was overstated. Average salaries certainly did not refer to average salaries within the same top one hundred firms. On the contrary, it was a national average diluted by hourly wages of many fast-food and farm workers. And unlike the figures on CEO compensation, the "pay of ordinary workers" excluded increasingly important health and pension benefits and, in many cases, stock options. Krugman's measure of average salaries (and wages) would have been $44,613 in 2000 if basic benefits were properly included, but $69,559 in finance and $75,679 in communications.[42] Industries with high CEO pay also offer higher salaries to "ordinary workers." Top one hundred firms offer even higher salaries to most workers and often provide them with stock options.

The Krugman statistical exaggerations of October 2002 were similar in spirit to equally misleading articles written in 1991–1992 by Graef Crystal and others about supposedly excessive prerecession CEO pay in 1989–1990. Such politicized and postponed misinformation was not helpful then and is not helpful now. Compensation of the leaders of America's largest enterprises is a serious subject that deserves serious statistics, not sensational misuse of creative CEO "income" statistics fabricated by the financial press.

AN IMAGINARY LINK TO ENRON

In the wake of the Enron bankruptcy, a flood of press stories about supposedly excessive executive pay echoed the media agitation of a decade earlier. Enron's failure was often attributed to corporate greed, said to be a result of what Krugman labeled "permissive capitalism." Senators Levin and John McCain (R-Ariz.) quickly seized on this media opportunity to revive their moribund 1997 proposal to arbitrarily limit employer deductions for the cost of exercised employee stock options.

On February 13, 2002, Sen. McCain attempted to tie his recycled tax plan to Enron by arguing "according to a recent analysis [a speculative one-page memo from Citizens for Tax Justice], Enron issued nearly $600 million in stock options, collecting tax deductions which allowed the corporation to severely reduce their payment in taxes." That estimated future "tax benefit" from stock options is added to cash flow rather than subtracted from taxes, and deductions occur only when options are exercised, not when issued. The senator also failed to understand that comparing corporate taxes paid with income during the same year, as his cited "analysis" had done, is meaningless, because the corporate tax is largely based on accruals rather than immediate cash flow. Depreciation is not a "loophole," and Enron's net operating losses in bad years could be carried forward or back in time.[43] In any event, Senators McCain and Levin never explained how paying larger taxes would have made it any easier for Enron to pay its bills and, thus, avoid bankruptcy.

The concocted link between Enron and the McCain–Levin assault on executive stock options was political opportunism. Yet reporters leaped for this bait-and-switch game.

The proposed Levin–McCain tax penalty on options was explained in a press release from Sen. Levin's office, also dated February 13, 2002:

> [The bill] would restrict the compensation deduction that company could claim for the exercise of a stock option by limiting the stock option deduction to the amount that company has claimed as an expense in its financial statement. This section would also make it clear that the deduction cannot be taken prior to the year in which the employee declares the stock option income.

Companies would have to expense the estimated value of options during the year they were granted, but could deduct the cost of employee stock options only years later after such options had been vested, exercised, and reported as taxable income by employees. Yet the cost deducted by the employer would *not* equal the income actually received by employees, as is the case today with this and every other form of compensation, but it would be limited to the amount that had previously been estimated to have been the "fair value" of those options to the employees when granted years before. If the actual cost to employers exceeded the early estimates of value to employees, the difference would still be taxable to employees but *not* deductible to employees. This would have been an indefensibly biased asymmetry in tax policy. Yet many press reports about this scheme in early 2002 completely ignored the tax aspects of the McCain–Levin plan and instead focused on alleged improprieties of executive stock options at Enron and, by association, at corporations in general. "What new reforms would do," claimed a *Wall Street Journal* reporter, "is shine a spotlight on companies that overuse options, in particular high-tech concerns in Silicon Valley."[44] Proposing to arbitrarily limit tax deductions for one form of compensation was never about shining a spotlight. The McCain–Levin plan, which took a free ride on the anti-Enron train, was about double taxing compensation from stock options at a 60 percent tax rate. When the plan was first floated in 1997, Sen. Levin's spokeswoman Kathleen McShea proudly told a reporter, "It's a wonderful opportunity to get some revenue."[45]

Trying to connect Enron to the McCain–Levin political complaints about stock options required considerable journalistic creativity. The first approach was to suggest that failure to "expense" employee stock options in one particular way (i.e., when granted rather than when vested or exercised) had caused Enron's earnings to be seriously overstated, with the result that investors were thought to have been deluded into paying too much for Enron stock.

On March 26, 2002, a seminal front-page *Wall Street Journal* feature by Gregg Hitt and Jacob M. Schlesinger was titled "Stock Options Come Under Fire In the Wake of Enron's Collapse." Citing Sen. Levin, the article claimed executive options "pump up the earnings figures" and, thus, deceived investors into paying too much for Enron stock. "In 2000, Enron issued stock options worth $155 million, according to a common method of valuing options [the Black-Scholes model]. Had accounting rules forced the company to deduct the cost of those options from its 2000 profit . . . Enron's operating profits for the year would have been 8 percent lower." This theme was subsequently echoed uncritically throughout the business press and broadened to lump most companies together with Enron, eventually producing a thunderous drumbeat on behalf of deducting estimates of the value of options in the year when they are granted (like that $155 million). What somehow escaped the *Wall Street Journal's* reporters and their editors, however, was the fact that stock options Enron issued in 2000 were not worth $155 million but were, in fact, completely worthless. Had accounting rules forced the company to deduct that $155 million estimate from its 2000 profit, then the resulting earnings figure would have been erroneous by $155 million.

The second effort to link Enron to stock options was to echo the claim of Senators McCain and Levin that tax deductions for the cost of stock options were the main reason Enron's U.S. taxes appeared small relative to (grossly overstated) domestic and foreign earnings. Never mind that such a claim was not even consistent with the flawed Hitt-Schlesinger calculation that options supposedly reduced income by only 8 percent. Journalists nonetheless seized on the alleged unfairness of allowing employers to deduct the cost of options as though this was another indictment of employee options in general.

On March 28, 2002—two days after the misleading *Wall Street Journal* piece—*Washington Post* staff writer Charles R. Babcock wrote, "During the boom year of 2000, some highly successful companies issued so many stock options to their executives and employees that they paid little or no corporate tax because the options were deductible." That statement was completely wrong. There is no corporate tax deduction during the year in which options are granted, so options granted during the boom year of 2000 resulted in no tax deductions. Indeed, most options granted during 2000 were so far under water by March 2002 that they were unlikely to ever produce taxable income for employees, without which there can be no deductible expense for employers.

On March 27, 2002, just one day before the Babcock blunder, *Washington Post* staff writer Alec Klein wrote that, "Despite a tough financial year, AOL Time Warner Inc's chairman and chief executive was rewarded in 2001 with stock options worth an estimated $76 million." Klein at least said "estimated," which is more than many similar reports on CEO pay have done. Half of that *estimated* $76 million depends on AOL stock rising higher than $49 a share—about four times the level of early 2003—otherwise the options will be worthless. The other $38 million of Case's supposed windfall depends on AOL stock somehow exceeding $61–73 per share. That is the trouble with estimates—they often look ridiculous within a year. Yet, proponents of "expensing" have been seriously insisting that estimates of exactly this sort "should" (in some Calvinist sense) be treated as actual expenses and subtracted from earnings. We will have more to say about this later. Meanwhile, keep in mind that subtracting Case's estimated $76 million booty from AOL's 2001 earnings would, indeed, have made that company's $4.9 billion loss look even worse. But that certainly does not mean that treating estimates as reality would have provided investors with more accurate information.

Nonqualified options become deductible only after they are vested after three or four years, in the money, and exercised. At that point, any gain on options becomes taxable to the employee and deductible to the employer. This raises income taxed by the individual tax just as much as it lowers income taxed by the corporate tax. And since the top two individual tax rates were higher than the corporate rate after 1993, the net effect was a windfall for the Treasury. Yet, the *Washington Post* mistake about tax deductions being taken in the year 2000 for options granted in that same year, and the other *Washington Post* story about Case's options being worth $76 million, and the *Wall Street Journal* blunder about the estimated value of Enron's worthless options granted during 2000, became part of a groundswell of accumulating folklore that, in turn, supported a confused and greatly exaggerated fascination with "reforming" (in one particular and rigid way) the manner and timing of stock option bookkeeping. And those three news reports are merely a two-day sampling from the flood of media misinformation about executive stock options.

In February 2003, the Joint Committee on Taxation (JCT) issued a massive report in response to political charges that Enron's problems may have been somehow connected to its executive compensation programs. They had virtually nothing to say about stock options, except that many were exercised when the stock was high and many others lost value when the stock fell. When it came to effects of taxation on CEO compensation, however, the JCT's strongest and most relevant recommendation was that

> the $1 million deduction limitation is ineffective at accomplishing its purpose, overrides normal income tax principals, and should be repealed. . . . In Enron's case, due to the existence of net operating losses [the real reason domestic taxes were low], the denial of the deduction may not have been an issue. . . . To the extent the limitation affected Enron's compensation arrangements, it may have merely placed more emphasis on the desire to increase reported earnings.[46]

It could nonetheless be argued that there really were unique peculiarities about Enron's compensation plans that might have contributed to executives' incentives to manage earnings in increasingly devious ways. But the fact that these features were unusual and not confined to stock options is the reason they cannot be plausibly converted into a generalized complaint about options. Such successful companies as Microsoft and Cisco have made much greater use of stock options than Enron ever did.

If there is a specific lesson to be learned from Enron about compensation policy, it concerns the pace and duration of *vesting*, rather than the particular *form* of incentive pay. Some critics of typical stock option plans claim that restricted stock is a superior incentive, for example, yet Enron used equal measures of both. Other critics say performance pay should be indexed—that is, made more valuable if company stock gains exceeded those of some stock index—but Enron did that, too.

Enron's compensation plan involved the usual mix of salary, annual bonuses, and long-term incentive grants, which in recent years consisted of one-half restricted stock and one-half stock options. What was unusual about Enron's restricted stock was that it had an "accelerated vesting" feature. That meant an executive would be allowed to sell restricted stock sooner than the usual four-year "cliff vesting" requirement if Enron's stock outperformed the S&P 500 average. What was unusual about Enron's stock options is that they vested in three years or less but expired in five. Other companies' stock options plans vest only gradually after three or four years, and in 85 percent of the plans, they do not expire for ten years.[47] Leaving only two years between the time options could be exercised and the time they expired, as Enron did, meant there was a narrow window of opportunity to either gain much or lose it all. To make matters worse, some stock options awards had accelerated vesting if Enron achieved 15 percent compounded growth in earnings-per-share.

"If a company wants to encourage a more farsighted perspective," suggests Harvard's Brian Hall, "it should simply extend their vesting periods."[48] Enron, unfortunately, did the opposite. The company shortened its already short vesting if executives took bigger risks and also imposed an unusually short period (two years compared with the usual six or seven) during which options could be exercised before expiring.

Although it appears plausible that accelerated vesting at Enron was an imprudent policy, even though it has been described as "optimal" by some academics, it would be equally imprudent to excuse executive activities that resulted in criminal charges and the absence of effective ethical supervision by directors as merely a sensible response to financial incentives. Leaving jewelry on the dresser when your house is being cleaned is an incentive to theft too, but housecleaners who value their integrity and reputation never steal.

Stuart Gillan and John Martin of the Center for Corporate Governance note "$100 invested in Enron stock in 1995 grew to $474.61 in 2000, compared to $227.89 for the S&P 500." Enron executives, like Enron stockholders, had comparable increases in wealth in those years, but that is the point of performance-related pay. Enron executives did not realize all those paper gains, however, so they faced substantial downside risk right up to the end. "Lay and more than 140 senior executives at Enron apparently held some $430 million of stock before the firm declared bankruptcy, of which Lay accounted for $50 million," according to Gillan and Martin; "they stood to lose a substantial amount in the event of the company's demise." They also stood to ruin lucrative careers, which is probably the best explanation why accounting tricks accelerated after the house of cards began to tumble. In the end, Gillan and Martin conclude that "many would argue that Enron's personnel and compensation programs were not only innovative, but in concert with recommended best practices."[49] Whether or not Enron's compensation plans were what experts regard as "best practices," they surely had little to do with the "worst practices" of many other professionals who are supposed to act as watchdogs and gatekeepers—directors, auditors, credit-rating agencies, and stock analysts.

The populist battle against executive pay during the early 1990s ended up saddling the United States with IRS and SEC regulations that had the unintended consequence of overpromoting stock options, thus generating huge windfalls for CEOs when the stock market boomed. The risk of surviving as a CEO was increased, with the unintended consequence of adding a risk premium (more pay or perks) to future CEO compensation. The latest, most fashionable populist crusade—namely, a backlash against stock options promoted by the last such crusade—could once again end up generating unanticipated and unwanted consequences. Executive compensation is a complex and critical topic, one in which the most mutually satisfactory arrangements are inherently subjective and differ for every firm and every executive. There is a large body of evidence suggesting that voluntary compensation agreements are remarkably efficient, on average, in terms of the interests of corporate managers and owners. Third parties, such as government regulators and self-styled activists, are unwelcome nonpartners at this bargaining table.

In a recent survey of the evidence on executive compensation for the Federal Reserve Bank of New York, John Core, Wayne Guay, and David Larcker of the Wharton School note that "in contrast to the allegations of many media pundits . . . who assert that incentive levels are random, arbitrary, or out of equilibrium, empirical evidence suggests that, on average, firms base their equity incentives on systematic and theoretically sensible factors."[50]

THEORY AND EVIDENCE OF EXECUTIVE COMPENSATION

In the language of economics, the problems of executive compensation involve agency costs and rents. Agency costs arise because corporate managers are not the firm's owners but merely agents ostensibly acting on behalf of principals who supply the firm's equity and debt capital (stockholders and creditors). Unfortunately, as Adam Smith understood very well, agents (CEOs) have interests of their own.[51] Corporate executives not only have obvious personal incentives in increasing their own income and wealth but also in wasting corporate funds on lavish perquisites and an army of executive assistants to which they delegate all arduous tasks. Executives also have personal incentives to minimize criticism and maximize job security by avoiding risks.

These agency problems are the reason for pay-for-performance elements of executive compensation, such as stock options, restricted stock, and (before SOA) loans whose repayment was tied to performance.

In this context, "rent" essentially means executives being paid more than was really required to attract, retain, and motivate them. In a sense, all highly specialized resources are likely to earn rent, such as singers, actors, and athletes being paid millions for talents consumers regard as unique. When it comes to corporate executives, however, allegations about rent involve conjectures about "managerial power" over those who hire them and renegotiate their contracts in following years. Such conjectures have been long on rhetoric and short on evidence. Hall and Murphy note, for example, that "the managerial rent-extraction hypothesis applies to incumbent executives. . . . But executives changing companies during the 1990s received large pay increases, indicating that alleged 'rents' were transferable—which suggests they are not rents at all."[52]

Lucien Bebchuk, Jesse Fried, and David Walker devoted nearly a hundred law review pages to speculating copiously that "an important factor affecting executives' ability to increase their compensation is the amount of 'outrage' their proposed pay package would create . . . [because] outsiders might become angry and upset."[53] *Wall Street Journal* columnist Holman Jenkins summarized this paper as saying, "stock options are just a ploy by CEOs and the board slaves to expand pay while evading the outrage constraint."[54] Jenkins's comment does express the tone of the tome. Yet the authors eventually say their "managerial power approach does not question the desirability of using options to compensate executives." What they question is the scarcity of what they define as "optimal contracting." They find it suspicious that the vesting of options is rarely accelerated if the stock does well (the authors do not seem to realize that Enron tried that). And they are particularly perplexed that scarcely any companies offer indexed options that pay off only if the stock beats the market. Bebchuck, Fried, and Walker conclude that the scarcity of such "optimal" arrangements proves CEOs must be using market power to rip-off rent. This is like concluding that difficulty finding extra-wide shoes proves there must be something corrupt about the shoe market because everyone knows wide feet are optimal.

The case for indexed options is usually expressed in normative terms, saying executives "should not" benefit from a general rise in the market but "should" be compensated only for doing better than some benchmark. But "should" and "should not" are concepts that have nothing to do with designing and negotiating contracts that bring the interests of managers into alignment with the interest of shareholders.

From the executive's point of view, substituting indexed options for nonindexed options greatly increases the risk of working years for nothing but salary and perks. To compensate for that risk in a rent-free competitive market either (1) the number of indexed options would have to be much greater than the number of regular options, or (2) salary, bonus, and benefits would have to be much larger.

That is, stockholders would have to sweeten the deal in ways quite likely to defeat the assumed advantage—namely, that indexing is supposed to make it more difficult for the CEO to benefit from such options. Optimality of indexing seems to assume only one party sitting at the bargaining table. It assumes that CEO pay can arbitrarily be made much more risky without cost to stockholders. It also assumes that CEOs can and should be given much greater incentives to take risk without any of that risk being borne by shareholders.

Lisa Meulbroek of the Harvard Business School uncovered a "fundamental problem: Indexed options do not function as intended. Instead, their payoff is highly sensitive to market or industry price movements."[55] For example, she shows that the estimated value of an option indexed to the S&P 500 rises by 15 percent if that stock index rises by 15 percent. So the supposedly "optimal" indexing of options does not even accomplish its stated goal—to separate movements in the value of options from general stock price movements. What it does do is offer a CEO an option that has a much greater chance of ending up worthless unless the CEO can somehow push the stock up at an above-average rate—which implies taking above-average risks. If such an offer to restrict option value to above-average stock performance was not combined with more cash, then it would have to include many more indexed options than nonindexed options.

Suppose the risk-reward hurdle could be overcome by quadrupling the number of indexed options. And assume that using the S&P 500 as the target to beat could get the indexed contract over another big hurdle—agreeing on an objective benchmark. In that case, much of the CEO's compensation would depend on getting the stock price to rise at an *unusually* rapid pace. The S&P 500 is a benchmark most professional money managers cannot beat when stocks are rising, partly because the S&P 500 is periodically reweighted by capitalization—losers are dropped from the index and winners grab a larger share.

We will later cite evidence that those who worry that conventional stock options give executives too strong an incentive to boost the stock price with risk or fraud are exaggerating that incentive. For indexed options, however, the incentive to do crazy things to hype the stock price would be much, much greater than it now is. That extra incentive toward risk arises because many more indexed options would have to be put on the table to induce executives to bear the added risk of trying to beat a difficult benchmark while the indexed options are vested.

The Bebchuk-Fried-Walker *assumption* that indexed options are optimal for shareholders is the key argument behind their *assertion* that the predominance of nonindexed options prove most CEO's have market power to collect rent. Both that assumption and that assertion could be persuasive only to those determined to be persuaded.

Many professors have compensation proposals they believe superior to the ones actually negotiated between executives and compensation committees. *Wall Street Journal* columnist Susan Lee publicized Hall's reasons for believing restricted grants of stock would be "superior" to options. One reason is that "even at the top of the bull market, one-third of options were out-of-the-money" and such options supposedly cease to motivate executives to do better.[56] Actually, Li Jin and Lisa Meulbroek at the Harvard Business School show that "the ability of options to align incentives remained remarkably intact" with "even a steep decline in stock price." That is partly because nearly all ESOs (Enron was an exception) last ten years.[57]

Burton Malkiel, like many others, wants to "require that executives who gain from the exercise of options hold onto their stock while still employed."[58] That sounds like a plan to encourage CEO's to quit while stock prices are high, which is precisely when other shareholders would suffer if they acted on that incentive.

The larger point, however, is that opinions of economists, accountants, and attorneys about how executives "should" be compensated are or should be entirely beside the point. If the academics have good advice, then it is likely to be taken.

Enron handed out plenty of restricted stock and even used performance-related vesting, which indicates that at least one firm listened to academic advice. It must have been good advice, since Enron's board of directors made *Chief Executive* magazine's list of the best five boards in the country 2000; the audit committee was even headed by a Stanford professor. And Enron was a six-time winner of the "most innovative company" award from *Fortune*, a magazine that has had much to say about CEO compensation. Who could dare to doubt that restricted stock and accelerated vesting are superior or even optimal arrangements? Whenever proponents of, say, restricted stock or indexed options propose to have their ideas cemented into accounting rules or tax laws, however, that ought to raise suspicions that few corporations or executives would voluntarily choose such theoretical visions of what someone else's "optimal" pay package ought to look like.

LIKE OTHER MARKETS, THE MARKET
FOR CEOs IS QUITE EFFICIENT

"A view that sees most firms behaving inefficiently is hard to support," wrote Core, Guay, and Larcker, whose survey on this topic effectively refutes such a view.[59] So do a number of other studies showing CEO compensation is generally quite efficient from the shareholders' point of view.

Michelle Hanlon, Shivaram Rajgopal, and Tery Shevlin, of the University of Michigan, Duke University, and the University of Washington, recently conducted a study on whether or not the value of new stock option grants to the top five executives in more than two thousand firms from 1992–2000 was associated with future operating income. What they found is, "the future operating income associated with a dollar of Black-Scholes value of an ESO grant is $3.82." Earnings rise by nearly four dollars for every dollar of option granted. They, therefore, find "little evidence [actually none] in support of rent extraction" by top managers.[60]

Studies of the relationship between boards of directors and executive pay are also consistent with market efficiency. Rachel Hayes and Scott Schaefer, of the University of Chicago and Northwestern University, found evidence that "corporate boards optimally use both observable and unobservable (to outsiders) measures of executive performance," and that compensation tends to be "more positively associated with future performance when observable measures are less useful for contracting."[61] Jennifer Milliron, at the University of Chicago, finds "the use of CEO incentive pay is positively associated with both the degree of director independence and the degree of director accountability (one component of which is the director's ownership)."[62]

Other studies have found that compensating top executives with stock options (rather than with salary or bonus) *increases* when institutional investors have a large stake in the firm. Hall and Liebman, for example, find "a strong correlation between the fraction of shares held by large institutional investors and the fraction of executive pay in the form of stock options."[63] One could easily get the opposite impression by taking seriously the comments of two or three mutual fund managers who are repeatedly interviewed in the popular press complaining about stock options.

Contradicting another common impression, Venky Nagar, Dhannanjay Nanda, and Peter Wysoki find the managers who are heavily compensated with options or stock disclose more information to shareholders: "the level of disclosure . . . is positively related to the proportion of CEO compensation based on stock price."[64] Disclosure does not simply mean conformity to FASB rules about how to report earnings and expenses (including options). Sophisticated investors find such GAAP earnings uninformative compared with free cash flow, revenue growth (for high-tech), and *pro forma* (as if) earnings. Robert Bowen, Angela Davis, and Dawn Matsumoto find that "firms with greater institutional ownership [but not those in high-tech] place greater relative emphasis on *pro forma* earnings."[65]

Augustine Duru and David Reeb find that "industrial diversification [companies that operate in more than one industry] is associated with . . . greater use of incentive-based compensation and with a greater reliance on market-based, rather than accounting measures of firm performance." They also examined companies that operate in various locations, finding only "value-enhancing geographic diversification is rewarded."[66] Once again, pay practices look remarkably efficient, even in subtle ways.

Incentive-based pay such as stock options has been shown to be closely tied to performance in other countries too. John Evans, Robert Evans, and Donna Todesco compared incentive-based executive compensation in 209 Australian firms with economic value added (a measure of value delivered to shareholders often used by professional U.S. investors): "Economic Value Added is found to be positively and significantly related to incentive-based compensation" but not to cash.[67]

What about alleged incentives to manipulate earnings in accounting statements, even though evidence is lacking that such manipulation normally works (i.e., that it fools investors into paying too much for the stock and, thus, creates CEO rents)? Bowen, Shiva Rajgopal, and Mohan Venkatachalam looked into whether managers choose "aggressive" accounting methods "for efficient shareholder maximization or in an opportunistic manner to enrich themselves." The authors "do not find evidence of systematic managerial opportunism in spite of suggestions in the popular press that the bull market and misdirected managerial incentives in the 1990s encouraged managers to choose self-serving accounting procedures."[68] Enron and WorldCom, in other words, were not at all typical.

FACTS AND CONJECTURES
ABOUT EXECUTIVE STOCK OPTIONS

Stock options give some employees the right to buy a certain number of company shares in the future, almost always at the price when the options are granted. According to a Bureau of Labor Statistics (BLS) survey, about 78 percent of executive stock options (ESOs) are "nonqualified," which means any gains will be taxed at ordinary income tax rates. "Qualified or incentive stock options (ISOs) were provided to more than 31 percent of all employees" who were granted options, notes the BLS, but with "minimal overlap."[69] Incentive stock options must be held for a year after they are exercised, so any gain between the time of exercise and sale is ostensibly taxed at the lower 20 percent rate for long-term capital gains. But ISOs can actually be taxed by the 28 percent alternative minimum tax whether there is any gain or not, which is one reason they are relatively unpopular (although they are not nearly as unpopular as several academic studies claim, assuming the BLS survey is accurate).

The current controversy is entirely focused on nonqualified options. Such options are granted at the market price at the time of the grant, called the "exercise" or "strike" price. They usually require three to five years of vesting before they can be "exercised" (which means buying the stock at the previous strike price). Vesting can be all at once (cliff vesting), but vesting more often requires a timed series of exercises, such as one-fourth per quarter. The options usually expire within ten years of the grant (Enron's five-year expiration was rare) and are most often exercised soon after they are "in the money"—that is, as soon as the stock price is significantly higher than the strike price. If the market price stays below the strike price, options are said to be under water. Employee stock options become worthless and are "forfeited" if they are not in the money between the time of vesting and expiration, or if the employee quits or is "retired" (fired). J. Carr Bettis, John Bizjak, and Michael Lemmon find that "employees exercise their options nearly five years prior to expiration," on average.[70] That usually means options are exercised five years after the grant date.

Although the controversy is focused on options granted to top executives, many companies grant options to middle managers, and a few grant options to nearly all employees. Ford Motor Company granted options to nearly 10 percent of employees, Southwest Airlines to about a third, and Amazon.com to nearly every employee. Microsoft grants options (and now restricted stock) to "everyone from administrative assistants to senior vice presidents but not the chairman and CEO."[71] Intel and Sun Microsystems also distribute most options to ordinary workers, not to senior executives. The National Center for Employee Ownership estimated that 7–10 million Americans held stock options by 2001.[72] The Execucomp database shows that in the year 2000 the top five executives accounted for only 7.6 percent of all stock options granted to employees but 12.1 percent of all such options exercised that year.[73] Any public policy mistake that risks damaging employee stock options could affect many more people than top executives who, after all, are in a better-than-average position to arrange to be paid in other ways.

Some argue that it would be fairer to distribute options—that is, risk—even more broadly among lower-level employees. Thomas Donlan, the editor of *Barron's*, finds it an "egregious mismatch" that at Coca-Cola "only about 8,200 employees out of 38,000 received options in 2001."[74] Sen. Joseph Lieberman (D-Conn.) proposed to "prohibit companies from deducting the cost of options when exercised if they do not offer the majority of them to rank and file workers."[75] But paying rank and file workers more in the form of options necessarily means paying them less in salaries and benefits. Since options are extremely risky, the Donlan-Lieberman definition of fairness means making people with modest incomes bear more personal risk if their bosses perform poorly.

This is not meant to suggest that companies should be prevented from offering risky pay packages to people with modest compensation, as many high-tech companies did during the "new economy" boom to keep golden handcuffs on mobile young techies.[76] Guay and Core study stock options plans among nonexecutive employees at 756 firms, finding that these firms were successfully "using options to attract certain types of employees, provide retention incentives, and create incentives to increase firm value."[77] If it works for some businesses, that's their business. The efficient government policy in this market, as in others, is to maximize individual freedom and choice and to minimize collective meddling. That is, let decisions about the mix of salary and options be made between those directly involved—potential employees and prospective employers. This is an issue that demands less FASB and more MYOB.

Hamid Mehran and Joseph Tracy of the Federal Reserve Bank of New York found that because a larger number of companies were granting stock options to a wider mix of employees, stock options were accounting for a larger share of compensation and salaries for a smaller share. Citing a supporting study by Sandra Black and Lisa Lynch, they suggested, "This restructuring of the wage contract between a firm and its workers may be contributing to the upturn in labor productivity."

Mehran and Tracy also argued that "an increased reliance on stock options may also increase overall pay flexibility in the U.S. labor market."[78]

The dramatic bankruptcies of Enron and WorldCom were temporarily covered up with accounting deceptions. Since stock options also involve accounting, and since Senators McCain and Levin spent years trying to change that accounting, that seemed to be all the connection needed to inspire a flurry of press reports speculating about all sorts of sins that might be attributed to executives being paid in this way, rather than another.

On June 27, 2002, the *Washington Post* reported, "Many corporate watchdogs believe options create an incentive for company executives to inflate profits to keep their stock prices up so they can cash in their options." These "corporate watchdogs" were twice cited as the source of such beliefs, but not one name was mentioned, except that of Sen. Levin. Whoever these corporate watchdogs may be, they are surely not shareholders, so their unexplained beliefs about options and incentives represent unwelcome interference in contracts to which they have committed nothing but words.

Hall of the Harvard Business School is a serious corporate watchdog, so he and other compensation experts are rarely mentioned in the popular press unless they have something critical to say about stock options. After studying the use of option grants for many years, Hall concludes: "Option grants do not promote a selfish, near-term perspective on the part of businesspeople. On the contrary, options are the best compensation mechanism we have for getting managers to act in ways that ensure the long-term success of their companies and the well-being of their workers and stockholders."[79] Hall demonstrates that options "provide far greater leverage" than grants of restricted stock (companies can typically offer three for the price of one), and "even greater downside risk" for executives (option values often drop to zero, which only happens to stock if companies go bankrupt).

In March 2003, for example, Apple Computer awarded CEO Steve Jobs 5 million shares of restricted stock "to replace 27.5 million options made worthless by a three-year slide in Apple's share price."[80] Since restricted stock can only become worthless if the company goes bankrupt, it offers much less risk to Apple's CEO than the previous stock options did and, therefore, greater certainty of expense (dilution) for other shareholders, regardless of how the stock performs. In comparison with stock options, restricted stock shifts more of the downside risk from executives to ordinary shareholders.

Several other companies switched from stock options to restricted stock, including Microsoft and Amazon.com (which provides investors with *pro forma* figures excluding the expense of these stock grants). Microsoft also began paying dividends which, since they are now taxed at the same rate as long-term capital gains, made restricted stock more attractive for employees (Microsoft is unique, since top executives never received options or restricted stock). A newly fashionable assertion is that restricted stock, which often vests within two years, encourages executives to be more focused on the long term than do stock options, which typically vest in three or four years.

Many articles in the popular press assert that all executive stock option plans (regardless of vesting or expiration) encourage executives to take reckless chances, as though stockholders prefer zero risk (in which case they would just own Treasury bills).[81] As William Sahlman points out, "Any compensation system that is based on performance has the potential to encourage cheating."[82] But that does not mean stockholders would be better off paying executives like bureaucrats, because risk and reward are often inseparable. Besides, Hanlon, Rajgopal, and Shevlin found that "ESO risk incentives are associated with [only] modest increases in firm risk."[83] That modest trade-off also works in reverse. That is, executives recruited to manage firms with unstable stocks generally ask for and get more cash in their pay package and fewer options. Rajesh Aggarwal and Andrew Samwick "find that executives in companies with the lowest [stock price] variance have pay-performance sensitivities that are an order of magnitude greater than executives in companies with the highest variance." That is, "executives in firms with more volatile stock prices will have less performance-based compensation" [more cash relative to options].[84]

ESTIMATING OPTIONS MEANS ESTIMATING EARNINGS

In 2003, the seven-member FASB voted unanimously to again reconsider requiring U.S. corporations to treat employee stock options as an estimated expense when the options are granted. A draft proposal was expected in 2004. London's International Accounting Standards Board was contemplating similar regulations.

Many business reporters have described this topic as merely a moral battle with greedy executives and lobbyists on one side and heroic defenders of honesty and virtue on the other. Expensing of options has become, as Michael Kinsley put it, "an obsession of high-minded scolds and bores."[85] *Fortune* columnist Geoffrey Colvin, for example, wrote, "Today's [option accounting] rules hurt investors by concealing the truth. . . . The forces of logic got clobbered by brute force and that's probably what will happen again. Big companies have a lot of power in Washington." But Colvin was proud of "being on the right side of a lost cause."[86] The issues are more complicated than that, and there are always interest groups involved on both sides of any issue. Institutional investors such as CalPERS—and lobbying groups to which CalPERS and similar funds belong, such as the International Corporate Governance Network and Council of Institutional Investors—do not necessarily represent the interests of individual investors. Although reporters automatically count managers of huge public and union pension funds among the "good guys" favoring expensing, it would be dangerously naïve to allow such organized interests to dictate legally-imposed executive compensation policy for the nation (through FASB) or for the industrial world (through the IASB). Even private mutual fund managers, who face neither the disclosure requirements that corporate executives do nor the million-dollar limit on their ample pay, are also not the most disinterested observers of CEO compensation.[87] Fund managers are agents, not owners.

The actual problems with the obsessive "lost cause" of mandated expensing of options can be boiled down to two simple points: First of all, a possible future expense is not the same as an actual current expense. Second, the estimated fair value of options to employees when they are granted is not the same as the actual expense to employers if and when those options are later exercised.

On the surface, the issue of how and when to account for employee stock options may look like a trivial bookkeeping detail. Yet the idea has generated a heated debate, even among academics. Distinguished economists Burton Malkiel of Princeton and William Baumol of New York University warned that this politicized accounting crusade risks "destruction of equity compensation instruments that have been engines of innovation and entrepreneurship." Another prominent economist, Hal Varian, wonders if "subtracting an imprecise estimated value of options" might "just confuse things more." He adds, wisely, that "much of the problem would go away if people paid attention to diluted earnings per share rather than basic earnings per share." But, perhaps, they already do.

Professors of economics may view this issue differently from the way professors of finance and accounting do. Economists tend to focus on such issues as economic incentives and information costs, while accountants focus on reaching "generally accepted" principles about how best to keep the books. The latter perspective was aptly illustrated by a March 2003 *Harvard Business Review* article, "For the Last Time: Stock Options Are an Expense," by Professors Zvi Bodie, Robert S. Kaplan, and Robert C. Merton.[88] That title and much of the text seemed to challenge an argument no serious critic of expensing ever made—namely, to suggest that options are either worthless to employees or a free lunch for employers. The real debate has to do with just what that expense is, when it occurs, and how and when it should be reported on company books.

Companies with a highly mobile labor force and a highly uncertain future like to offer stock options precisely because there is an excellent chance those options will cost the firm nothing. Executives put up with that downside risk for the same reason people buy lottery tickets—options offer a slim chance of becoming very rich.

Before the Bodie, Kaplan, and Merton article appeared, the December 2002 *Harvard Business Review* published "Expensing Options Solves Nothing" by Sahlman of the Harvard Business School. Sahlman emphasized that the issue of expensing options has been a huge distraction from serious issues of deceptive accounting. He noted that "options have the earmarks of an investment in the future, rather than an operating expense." On balance, Sahlman concluded, options should not be expensed, "particularly if it entails disclosing less information in their footnotes."[89] Under current FASB rules, companies that expense options are not required to provide the information that others do about how many options were granted, outstanding, forfeited, or exercised and at what prices. Expensing estimated costs thus "increases reporting complexity and decreases transparency," according to Robert Blicker, professor of accounting at Case Western Reserve University.

Before investors allow FASB, an unelected and largely unaccountable agency, to compel all U.S. companies to replace transparency with estimates, we need to think seriously about the nature of the cost of employee options to shareholders, including when that cost occurs. Until we agree on what the cost is, we cannot agree on how and when to report it.

Advocates of expensing options at the time they are granted (as opposed to when they are exercised) often gloss over the fact that they are advocating treating an *estimate* as an actual expense. To require companies to estimate costs is to require them to estimate earnings. That just adds a new element of whimsy to measured earnings. It does not make reported earnings more honest; it just makes them more indecipherable.

Bodie, Kaplan, and Merton echo investor Warren Buffet's familiar argument that companies have to estimate depreciation too. But that is a weak analogy. When depreciating the cost of a machine, the exact cost of the machine is known, and only the pace at which it must be written off is uncertain. When granting employee stock options, nobody knows if those options will eventually be worth millions or nothing. The finance professors reply that "financial statements should strive to be approximately right," but these particular estimates cannot be even approximately right unless cost is defined in a uniquely academic way.

The debate has focused on technical problems of valuation, meaning the relevance and accuracy of the 1973 Black-Scholes model for estimating the value of short-term tradable options. But even if Black-Scholes could flawlessly estimate the subjective value of options to employees on the day the options were granted, that has literally nothing to do with the actual cost to employers several years later, when some unknown fraction of those options may or may not become vested and exercised. What advocates of expensing are saying, in a somewhat ambivalent way, is that the cost of exercised options does not really matter. What matters, they say, is the "opportunity cost" on the day options are granted: "The value of the stock option to the company is its cost—the cash forgone by granting the options to an employee rather than selling them to external investors."[90]

The key question about accounting for options, in short, is whether this novel concept of cost has any practical value. If the "cost" of ESOs to shareholders is really the money a company could have raised by selling call options at a fixed price—options that cannot be traded for several years and which have no value if employees quit or get fired—then who are those "external investors" who might buy such options and how much would they pay?

Any Black-Scholes estimate depends on the stock price, volatility, and interest rates when the estimate is made, and all of those things change constantly. The model also assumes options are held to maturity, although employee options are almost never held that long and the duration before exercise is subjective and unpredictable. Some scholars, therefore, recommend revising the estimates quarterly, which is called "mark-to-market." But that means the estimated value of granted options would rise and fall with the stock market. Using a mark-to-market method would have made reported earnings look smaller as stocks and profits rose in 1998–1999, and larger in 2001–2002 as stocks and profits fell, but it is difficult to see how introducing such random feedback between stock prices and reported earnings would have made the earnings reports more informative for shareholders. At the end of this undulating process, the sum of all those continuous corrections would merely wind up with the actual cost at the time of exercise, which is already automatically reported as reduced earnings per share (or, if options are financed by share repurchases, as a reduction in cash on hand). The fact that all estimates prior to exercise had to be revised to conform with the actual cost at the time of exercise clearly demonstrates that all previous estimates were incorrect and that basing reported earnings on such estimates therefore made the earnings figures incorrect.

Proponents of expensing estimates at the time options are granted, such as Bodie, Kaplan, and Merton, say granting options to an executive is no different from granting stock. But options, unlike company shares, have two big strings attached: they cannot be sold until after a few years of vesting and they become worthless if the stock falls or the executive quits or is fired. Indeed, this is why options are considered so important by *employers* (that is, shareholders and their directors), particularly in firms with a highly uncertain future. How executives feel about options depends on their taste for risk, which is as variable as personality. Employers in new or volatile lines of business have obvious reasons to value the prospect that they will never have to make good on options if an executive gets sacked before vesting, or quits, or does such a bad job that the stock price falls.

Granting an employee the right to buy shares at the current price after a few years of vesting creates a contingent liability to provide those shares to employees if (1) the stock price goes up and (2) the employee remains with the firm long enough to be vested. If and only if those two contingencies are met, the company must either issue more shares or it must dip into cash to repurchase shares in the stock market. Dilution obviously reduces earnings per share—the only measure of earnings that matters when it comes to stock prices *per share*. And share repurchases obviously reduce company cash and (because that cash would otherwise have been invested) future earnings.[91] The common claim that the cost of employee options to shareholders is never reported in financial statements is clearly untrue.

Those who agree that the cost of options consists of dilution (or share repurchases) at the time of exercise should not expect that cost to be even approximated by a Black-Scholes estimate of value at the time options are granted. Estimating the value of options when they are granted is not at all the same as *forecasting* the cost if and when they are exercised. The Black-Scholes model is based on information available at a particular moment in time. It was never intended to forecast the future value of stocks or options. The value of options today is not the same as the future cost of deferred and contingent compensation, and estimates of the former are not forecasts of the latter.

Potential dilution from all outstanding options that are in the money is prominently displayed in every earnings report as *diluted* earnings per share. Aside from the possibility that underwater options might float back to the surface, diluted earnings per share provides a useful but exaggerated summary of the worst investors might expect as a result of all the options being eventually exercised (all outstanding options are *never* exercised, partly because people resign or die before the options are vested).

Bodie, Kaplan, and Merton, however, resist defining the cost of stock options as potential dilution of earnings per share as a result of having to issue more shares if the options pay off. They prefer a far more academic definition of cost, one which is not remotely comparable to the way companies measure other costs. They say the "opportunity cost" of granting stock options consists of the cash the company could otherwise have received by selling those options to investors. This, they claim, is "exactly" like giving stock to employees rather than selling it. But is it? No option market is remotely comparable to employee option grants. Giving options to employees is not at all comparable to giving them stock, because the options (unlike stock) will have value only if the employee remains employed at least long enough to be vested and (if the stock has not risen before then) possibly for ten years. No investor purchasing stock or options has to worry about being fired before the option can be exercised, but employees holding stock options certainly do. Besides, selling options to buy a company's stock several years from now at today's price would be like announcing that management expects the stock to fall. And it is obviously impossible to sell an option to a third party when the payoff on that option depends on the executives' decision not to quit and the employers' decision not to fire them. The whole idea of an opportunity cost in this context is fanciful—it relies on an opportunity that does not and could not exist.

Before 2002, only two companies (Boeing and Winn Dixie) thought it made sense to count the estimated value of option when granted as if that was either a current expense (obviously not) or an estimate of a predictable future expense (also untrue). In 2002, several companies in which Warren Buffet happens to be a major shareholder (recall that Jensen and Murphy had awarded him top honors for the best-rewarded small business CEO) decided to adopt this curiously trendy accounting convention. To judge by the way the press lionized this bookkeeping adjustment, it could easily be confused with a public relations stunt. *USA Today* headlined the first such move as "Coke toughens its accounting rule" with a subtitle (from Buffet) describing this as a "classy move." The story said Coke's accounting change "follows an outcry by many investors, economists, and politicians who believe that options should be expensed." What does "an outcry by many . . . who believe" really mean? Coke first said it would do the arithmetic by estimating the value of options on the day they were granted (rather than the following day) and then write off that cost over the period in which the options vest (conveniently more quickly than the options are likely to be exercised). Would they do the same with millions of outstanding options and, therefore, restate past earnings downward? Nobody asked and nobody told. FASB allowed companies that took this "classy" step to stop providing the same information about older options that every other corporation does. Let bygones be bygones. Coca-Cola first tried to get investment banks to value the options but, after having just received a few overpriced Black-Scholes estimates, soon reverted to its own estimating game. The company announced a 15 percent quarterly increase in profits that same week, but the stock dropped to about $45 from $52.[92] Fed Chairman Alan Greenspan was widely reported as having seen this as proof the market prefers this sort of opinionated and obfuscated bookkeeping.

On August 13, 2002, Standard and Poor's put out a press release intended to praise sixty-eight companies for announcing an intention to expense the estimated value of any options granted in the future. Few reporters noticed that only four of those sixty-eight companies were in the S&P Small Cap 600 index. Nearly all companies embracing the new expensing fad were established "old economy" giants such as General Electric, General Motors, Procter & Gamble, and several Wall Street financial conglomerates. That was instructive because smaller, cash-starved new enterprises argue that they must rely on the risky upside potential of options to lure talented executives and skilled technicians away from the high salaries, bonuses, and perks offered by the largest industrial and financial firms.

Hall and Murphy found that "smaller companies are more likely to offer options to a broader base." They also found that the estimated average value of options granted by "new economy" firms was $18,882 in 2001, compared with $2,856 among "old economy" firms.[93] Little wonder that old economy firms remain/are relatively indifferent to how such a small expense is reported.

Another reason many large companies may have suddenly become more willing than before to expense new option grants in late 2002 is that they planned to use this opportunity to grant fewer options, particularly to midlevel employees. A 2003 survey of thirty-three large companies by Mercer Human Resource Consulting found that half were reducing the number of options granted and the number of employees who would receive them. "Employees who fall below middle management are likely to see option awards sliced by anywhere from 30 percent to 100 percent, according to the Mercer survey. Top executives are likely to see their awards sliced by just 20 percent to 30 percent."[94]

The fact that option cutbacks for lower-level employees were announced shortly after announcing an intent to expense such dwindling options may not have been unanticipated by the large companies involved, though it may have surprised proponents of mandatory expensing. They may have been even more surprised by the cutbacks in employee-stock purchase plans. Companies that expense the estimated cost of option grants must also expense the cost of selling shares to employees at a discount. As a result, Mellon Financial reduced the employee discount to 5 percent from 15 percent, and Bank One limited discounted stock sales to $5,000 a year (down from $21,500). Other companies that expensed options were expected to eliminate stock purchase plans.[95]

Critics of expensing typically focus on the technical difficulties of putting a value on options the day they are granted. Gurupdesdh Pandher found that when you take severance risk into account, "Black-Scholes valuation . . . dramatically overstates the cost of the options to the firm (e.g., 28–29 percent)."[96] Steven Huddart found "the employer's cost is much less than the options' Black-Scholes value."[97] Jude Rich used several FASB-acceptable models to study stock options for nearly two hundred top firms, finding that options granted at $100 share could be estimated to be worth somewhere between $10 and $97, depending on the company and subjective assumptions.[98]

The main problem with estimating earnings by estimating the cost of employee stock options is not simply that estimates derived from Black-Scholes or binomial models are extremely subjective and wildly inaccurate (which they are), but that such estimates are essentially irrelevant to the actual cost of exercised options. Veteran accounting professor Alfred Rappaport of Northwestern University says, "The cost [of options] is the dilution of ownership interest when employees exercise their options and purchase shares at a discount to the market price."[99] That is how most people surely define the cost. But cost in this sense (dilution at exercise) has literally no connection at all to a Black-Scholes or other estimate at the time options are granted. Whatever the value that options may have to employees on the day they are granted (which is an inherently subjective issue), that estimate is not a *forecast* of the actual cost to corporations if and when those options are eventually vested, in the money, and exercised. Unless you can somehow believe the true cost of vested, job-contingent options consists of all the loot that might have been raised if that sort of option could be sold to some outsider, the endless fuss about "expensing" stock options has been about nothing more than making GAAP earnings even more useless to investors by adding one more capricious bit of guesswork to the FASB official definition of corporate income.

CONCLUSION

What began in 1990 as an academic complaint that CEO pay was insufficiently linked to company stock performance soon turned into changes in regulations and taxes designed to entice companies to pay less in salaries and more in stock options. When all these "reforms" happened in 1992–1993, nobody—including corporate directors and executives—could possibly have imagined that grants of executive options during the next few years would end up being unbelievably valuable after only three or four years of vesting. If offered a less government-biased choice in 1993, most CEOs and corporate directors in 1992–1995 would surely have agreed on deals that involved fewer risky options and more cash.

Thanks to the bull market of 1996–1999, populist tax and regulatory reforms of 1992–1993 had the decidedly unintended consequence of making CEOs far more wealthy than they would have been if salaries and bonuses had been negotiated as before—when there was not so much pressure against paying competitive salaries from the IRS, the SEC, the FASB, public and nonprofit pension fund managers, and two media-wise senators.

It is one thing to recommend to corporate boards that they should make executive compensation more dependent on stock prices, as scholars such as Jensen and Murphy were doing in the early 1990s and many other scholars still do. But it is quite another for the government to use tax penalties or heavy-handed accounting mandates to tilt the playing field either in favor of stock options (as in 1993) or against them (the latest fad). The shift from paying executives like bureaucrats to making their pay much more dependent on improving shareholder wealth was surely a good thing, on balance. But, perhaps, there can be too much of a good thing. Executives became a great deal less eager to trade salary for stock options after Wall Street's bull fell off a cliff in April 2000, showing once again that markets have their own ways of correcting excesses.

The massive bankruptcies during the past recession, particularly the relatively unexpected downfall of Enron, generated a media blitz on behalf of greatly increased regulatory empowerment and activism (i.e., unpredictability) at both the federal and state level. Most of these efforts had no relationship whatsoever to Enron's collapse, particularly the intemperate verbal assault on executive and employee stock options. In this respect and others, we have shown through numerous examples that leading U.S. newspapers and financial journals have long been inexcusably careless when claiming to report facts about executive compensation, even to the extent of counting stock sales as pay.

Efforts to impose any one-size-fits-all regulations on employment contracts—including proposed FASB rules to require uniformly dubious accounting for stock options—risk adding many unexpected costs for no clear benefit. Like many studies finding the compensation plans vary quite efficiently among different types of firms, Stuart Gillan, Jay Hartzel, and Laura Starks conclude that "regulatory actions applying a one-size-fits-all criterion may be suboptimal, and increase contracting costs for some firms."[100] Milliron, citing other studies that came to the same conclusion, finds that even "the same set of board governance characteristics may not be appropriate for all types of firms."[101]

Executive compensation is certainly a legitimate concern of significant shareholders, directors, and creditors. But introducing third parties into compensation negotiations (such as the FASB, the IRS, activists, or trial lawyers) is apt to introduce rigidities that lead to suboptimal arrangements from the point of view of both executives and shareholders. One-size-fits-all federal rules affecting compensation negotiations may have impeded the flexibility needed to deal with the inherently individualized, subjective process of negotiating customized contracts to attract and retain highly specialized managerial skills and talents.

NOTES

1. "What's Wrong with Executive Compensation? A Roundtable Moderated by Charles Elson," *Harvard Business Review,* January 2003, p. 69.

2. Colvin, Geoffrey, "The Great CEO Pay Heist," *Fortune,* June 25, 2001, p. 64.

3. Strauss, Gary, "Why are These CEOs Smiling? Must Be Payday," *USA Today,* March 25, 2002, p. B1.

4. Hall, Brian J. and Jeffery B. Liebman, "The Taxation of Executive Compensation," National Bureau of Economic Research Working Paper no. 7596, March 2000, p. 3.

5. Jensen, Michael C. and Kevin J. Murphy, "CEO Incentives: It's Not How Much You Pay, but How," *Harvard Business Review,* May–June 1990, p. 138–153.

6. Rose, Nancy L., "Executive Compensation," National Bureau of Economic Research, *NBER Reporter,* winter 1994–95, p. 11.

7. Jones, Del and Gary Strauss, "CEOs Are Going, Going, Gone," *USA Today,* June 10, 2002. The figures are from the prominent placement firm Challenger Gray and Christmas.

8. Challenger, Joseph A., "Where Have All the CEOs Gone?" *Wall Street Journal,* June 25, 2002.

9. "The Curse of Charisma" *Economist,* September 7, 2002, p. 58.

10. Plitch, Phyllis, "CEO Turnover Declines in U.S. Amid Global Rise," *Wall Street Journal,* May 21, 2003. The overall decline in turnover was because fewer CEOs were removed because of mergers and takeovers, even though more CEOs lost their jobs for poor performance.

11. Wiersema, Margarethe, "Holes at the Top: Why CEO Firings Backfire," *Harvard Business Review,* December 2002, p. 70.

12. Bachelder, Joseph E., "Proposed Tax Changes: Stock Options," *New York Law Journal,* March 29, 1993.

13. "FASB Rule Rejected," *San Francisco Chronicle,* May 5, 1994, p. D2.

14. Jensen and Murphy, "CEO Incentives."

15. Prevost, Andrew K. and John D. Wagster, "Impact of the 1992 Changes in the SEC Proxy Rules and Executive Compensation Reporting Requirements," mimeo, Wayne State University School of Business Administration, September 1999.

16. Johnson, Marilyn F., Susan Porter, and Margaret B. Shackell, "Stakeholder Pressure and the Structure of Executive Compensation," May 1997. http://papers.ssrn.com/id=41780. Accessed May 23, 2003.

17. Clinton, Bill and Al Gore, *Putting People First,* New York: Times Books, 1992, p. 31.

18. Perry, Todd and Marc Zenner, "Pay for Performance? Government Regulation and the Structure of Compensation Contracts," *Journal of Financial Economics* 62, 2001, p. 453.

19. Hall and Liebman, "Taxation of Executive Compensation." Also in James Poterba, ed., *Tax Policy and the Economy,* National Bureau of Economic Research 14, 2000.

20. McDonough, William J., "Issues in Corporate Governance," Federal Reserve Bank of New York, *Current Issues in Economics and Finance,* September/October 2002, p. 4–5.

21. "Clinton is expected to . . . impose a surtax on those making more than $1 million a year," John A. Byrne, "Clinton Starts a Stampede," *Business Week,* December 14, 1992, p. 38.

22. Stein, Steve, "Taxes, Dividends, and Distortions," *Policy Review,* June 2002. In the spirit of full disclosure, Steve Stein is Alan Reynolds's brother-in-law, but Reynolds had zero input into this chapter.

23. Hall and Liebman, "Taxation of Executive Compensation."

24. Scholes, Myron S., Mark A. Wolfson, Merle Erickson, Edward L. Maydew, and Terry Shevlin, *Taxes and Business Strategy*, 2nd ed., Englewood Cliffs, N.J.:Prentice Hall, 2002, p. 77.

25. Ayers, Benjamin C., C. Bryan Cloyd, and John R. Robinson, "Capitalization of Shareholder Taxes in Stock Prices: Evidence for the Revenue Reconciliation Act of 1993," mimeo, Tull School of Accounting, University of Georgia, October 20, 2000. http://papers.ssrn.com/sol2/papers.cfm?abstract_id=324501. Accessed May 15, 2003.

26. Graham, John R., "How Big Are the Tax Benefits of Debt?" *Journal of Finance,* October 2000, p. 1919.

27. For example, "Cisco, Microsoft Get Income Tax Breaks on Gains from Employee Stock Options," *Wall Street Journal,* October 10, 2000. The many irate news reports about corporate "tax breaks" always failed to mention that this was simply income shifting from the corporate to the individual tax base.

28. Graham, John D., Mark H. Lang, and Douglas A. Shackelford, "Employee Stock Options, Corporate Taxes and Debt Policy," National Bureau of Economic Research Working Paper no. 9289, October 2002, p. 32.

29. Lavelle, Louis, "Executive Pay," *Business Week,* April 16, 2002, p. 80.

30. Useem, Jerry, "Have They No Shame?" *Fortune,* April 28, 2003. The article describes an increase in median compensation "more telling" than the mean average, but that is dubious spin. The only way the median could have risen while the mean fell was for the largest pay packages to have been deeply cut.

31. McGeehan, Patrick, "Executive Pay: A Special Report," *New York Times,* April 6, 2003.

32. Lublin, Joann S., "Under the Radar: As CEO's Reported Salaries and Bonuses Get Pinched, Many Chiefs are Finding Hidden Ways to Increase Their Compensation," *Wall Street Journal,* April 11, 2002.

33. Stealth compensation has been used to refer to perks such as use of corporate jets and such, but that accounts for less than 1 percent of CEO compensation. Journalists have suggested that deferred compensation plans are both deceptive and a tax dodge, although they are not secret and no different in principle from an IRA, 401k, or Keogh plan, except that they can be larger.

34. Cunningham, Lawrence A., "The Sarbanes-Oxley Yawn: Heavy Rhetoric, Light Reform (and It Might Just Work)," Boston College Law School Research Paper no. 01, 2002, p. 31. See also Stephen M. Bainbridge, "The Creeping Federalization of Corporate Law," *Regulation,* Spring 2003.

35. Crystal, Graef S., "How Much Do CEO's Really Make?" *Fortune,* June 17, 1991.

36. "Future income implications of good performance are as important, if not more important, than the contemporaneous effect. . . . Attempting to strengthen the pay-performance sensitivity by monitoring the contemporaneous relation may be dysfunctional." John F. Boschen and Kimberly J. Smith, "You Can Pay Me Now and You Can Pay Me Later: The Persistent Effects of Firm Performance on Executive Performance," 2002, http://papers.srn.com/sol3/papers.cfm?abstract_id=5401. Accessed May 1, 2003.

37. Lavelle, "Executive Pay."

38. Leonhardt, David, "Options Payday: Raking It In, Even as Stocks Sag," *New York Times,* December 29, 2002, p. BU1, 10.

39. Alexander, Keith L., "As Carriers Sought Help, Top Tier's Pay Soared," *Washington Post,* April 12, 2003.

40. Krugman, Paul, "For Richer: How the Permissive Capitalism of the Boom Destroyed American Equality," *New York Times Magazine,* October 20, 2002, p. 64. On the widespread misuse of income distribution statistics, by Krugman and others, see Alan Reynolds, "Economic Foundations of the American Dream" in Lamar Alexander and Chester E. Finn, Jr., eds., *The New Promise of American Life,* Indianapolis: Hudson Institute, 1995, p. 194–220.

41. AFL-CIO, "Trends in Executive Pay," http://www.alfcio.org/corporateamerica/paywatch/pay/index.cfm? Accessed May 15, 2003.

42. U.S. Census Bureau, *Statistical Abstract of the United States* (2002), table 607, p. 400.

43. "For . . . Citizen for Tax Justice purposes, the effective tax is defined as taxes paid currently divided by net income before tax. The numerator includes not only implicit taxes but also tax deferrals," Scholes et al., *Taxes and Business Strategy,* p. 495n.

44. Whitman, Janet, "Stock Option Awards Undergo Scrutiny in Wake of Outcry for More Accountability," *Wall Street Journal,* April 3, 2002.

45. Hitt, Gregg, "Stock Options May Be Curbed by House Panel," *Wall Street Journal,* June 6, 1997.

46. Joint Committee on Taxation, "Report of Investigation of Enron Corporation and Related Entities Regarding Federal Tax and Compensation Issues, and Policy Recommendations," February 2003, vol. 1, p. 723.

47. Hall and Liebman, "Taxation of Executive Compensation."

48. Hall, Brian, "What You Need to Know about Stock Options," *Harvard Business Review,* March–April 2000.

49. Gillan, Stuart L. and John D. Martin, "Financial Engineering, Corporate Governance, and the Collapse of Enron," University of Delaware Center for Corporate Governance, Working Paper WP 2002-001, November 6, 2002, p. 29–32.

50. Core, John E., Wayne R. Guay, and David F. Larcker, "Executive Equity Compensation and Incentives: A Survey," Federal Reserve Bank of New York, *FRBNY Policy Review,* April 2003, p. 32.

51. "The directors of such companies, however, being the managers rather of other people's money than of their own, it cannot well be expected that they should watch over it with the same anxious vigilance with which the partners in a private co-partnery frequently watch over their own. . . . Negligence and profusion, therefore, must always prevail, more or less, in the management of the affairs of such a company." Adam Smith, *The Wealth of Nations,* New York: Modern Library, 1937, p. 700.

52. Hall, Brian J. and Kevin J. Murphy, "The Trouble with Stock Options," National Bureau of Economic Research Working Paper 9784, June 2003, p. 28.

53. Bebchuk, Lucian Arye, Jesse M. Fried, and David I. Walker, "Managerial Power and Rent Extraction in the Design of Executive Compensation," *University of Chicago Law Review,* 2002. Available online at http://www.law.harvard.edu/faculty/bebchuk/pdfs/2002.Bebchuk-Fried-Walker.Olin.No366.Managerial.Power.pdf.

54. Jenkins, Holman W., Jr. "Outrageous CEO Pay Revisited," *Wall Street Journal,* October 2, 2002.

55. Meulbroek, Lisa K., "Executive Compensation Using Relative-Performance-Based Options: Evaluating the Structure and Costs of Indexed Options," Harvard Business School Working Paper no. 01-021, July 10, 2001. http://papers.ssrn.com/sol3/papers.cfm?abstract_id=281028. Accessed May 22, 2003.

56. Lee, Susan, "Toil and Trouble, Options Lead to a Scary Bubble," *Wall Street Journal,* July 29, 2002.

57. Jin, Li and Lisa Meulbroek, "Do Underwater Executive Stock Options Still Align Incentives?" Harvard Business School, 2001. http://papers.ssrn.com/sol3/papers.cfm?abstract_id=29157. Accessed May 22, 2003.

58. Malkiel, Burton, "The Market Can Police Itself," *Wall Street Journal,* June 28, 2002.

59. Malkiel, "The Market Can Police Itself," p. 28.

60. Hanlon, Michelle, Shivaram Rajgopal, and Terry Shevlin, "Are Executive Stock Options Associated with Future Earnings?" December 20, 2002, http://papers.ssrn.com/sol3/papers.cfm?abstract_id=318101. Accessed May 22, 2003.

61. Hayes, Rachel M. and Scott Schaefer, "Implicit Contracts and the Explanatory Power of Top Executive Compensation for Future Performance," *Rand Journal of Economics,* summer 2000.

62. Milliron, Jennifer, "Board of Director Incentive Alignment and the Design of Executive Compensation Contracts," mimeo, University of Chicago Graduate School of Business, May 2000, p. 28.

63. Hall and Liebman, "Taxation of Executive Compensation."

64. Nagar, Venky, Dhannanjay Nanda, and Peter Wysocki, "Compensation Policy and Discretionary Disclosure," June 2001, http://papers.ssrn.com/sol3/papers.cfm?abstract_id=224143. Accessed May 23, 2003.

65. Bowen, Robert M., Angela K. Davis, and Dawn A. Matsumoto, "Spin in Earnings Press Releases? Determinants of Emphasis on Pro Forma versus GAAP Performance," mimeo, University of Washington Business School, draft, February 12, 2003.

66. Duru, Augustine and David M. Reeb, "Geographic and Industrial Diversification: The Level and Structure of Executive Compensation," *Journal of Accounting, Auditing and Finance,* winter 2002.

67. Evans, John, Robert Evans, and Donna Todesco, "An Examination of Economic Value Added and Executive Compensation," mimeo, Curtin University of Technology, Perth, Australia, 2002.

68. Bowen, Robert M., Shiva Rajgopal, and Mohan Venkatachalam, "Accounting Choice, Corporate Governance, and Firm Performance," mimeo, University of Washington, January 5, 2002, p. 33.

69. Crimmel, Beth Levin and Jeffrey L. Schildkraut, "Stock Option Plans Surveyed by NCS [National Compensation Survey]," U.S. Bureau of Labor Statistics, *Compensation and Working Conditions,* spring 2001, p. 5.

70. Bettis, J. Carr, John M. Bizjak, Michael L. Lemmon, "The Cost of Employee Stock Options," mimeo, Arizona State University, March 2003.

71. Opdyke, Jeff D. and Michelle Higgins, "What the New Option Rules Mean for Your Pay: Employees Will Bear the Brunt of Drive to Expense Them," *Wall Street Journal,* August 7, 2002, p. D1–D2.

72. Lieberman, Joseph I., "The Best Way to Spread the Wealth," *Washington Post,* July 21, 2002.

73. Desai, Mihir A., "The Divergence between Book and Tax Income," October 2002, table 2.

74. Donlan, Thomas G., "Optional Equity," *Barron's,* July 22, 2002, p. 31.

75. Lieberman, "The Best Way to Spread the Wealth."

76. Since broad ownership of options was most common in places like Silicon Valley and Redmond where stocks exploded in the 1990s, it should not be surprising that companies with broad ownership of options did well in the 1990s. Joseph Blasi and Douglas Kruse of

Rutgers, longtime apostles of employee stock option plans (ESOPs), used this boomtime connection to claim broad ownership of options raises stock returns (*In the Company of Owners*, Basic Books, 1992). But that theory raises questions about causality: Tech companies whose stocks were soaring could have been more willing to share the capital gains without much fear of diluting earnings per share (some had no earnings anyway), and employees in such companies would surely have been more willing than other workers to accept options in place of cash.

77. Guay, Wayne R and John E. Core, "Stock Option Plans for Non-Executive Employees," October 2000, http://papers2.ssrn.com/paper.taf?ABSTRACT_ID=249511. Accessed June 5, 2002.

78. Mehran, Hamid and Joseph Tracy, "The Impact of Employee Stock Options on the Evolution of Compensation in the 1990s," Federal Reserve Bank of New York, *Economic Policy Review*, December, 2001, p. 17–34.

79. Hall, Brian, "What You Need to Know about Stock Options," *Harvard Business Review*, March–April 2000, p. 122.

80. "Business in Brief," *Washington Post*, March 26, 2003.

81. Murphy, Matt, "Options Frenzy: What Went Wrong? Executives' Ownership Stake Put Extreme Focus on Stock, Creating a House of Cards," *Wall Street Journal*, December 17, 2002.

82. Sahlman, William A., "Expensing Options Solves Nothing," *Harvard Business Review*, December 2002, p. 96.

83. Hanlon, Michelle, Shrivaram Rajgopal, and Terry Shevlin, "Large Sample Evidence of the Relation between Stock Option Compensation and Risk Taking," October 30, 2002, p. 23.

84. Aggarwal, Rajesh K. and Andrew A. Samwick, "The Other Side of the Tradeoff: The Impact of Risk on Executive Compensation," National Bureau of Economic Research Working Paper no. W6634, June 1998.

85. Kinsley, Michael, "Stock-Option Cure-All," *Washington Post,* July 19, 2002.

86. Colvin, Geoffrey, "Losing the Good Fight," *Fortune,* April 15, 2002, p. 75.

87. "Portfolio managers and chief investment officers may make significantly more than a corporation's top executives." John Shipman, "Fund Executives See Paycheck Cut," *Wall Street Journal,* April 24, 2003.

88. Bodie, Zvi, Robert S. Kaplan, and Robert C. Merton, "For the Last Time: Stock Options Are an Expense," *Harvard Business Review*, March 2003, p. 63–71.

89. Sahlman, "Expensing Options Solves Nothing," p. 91–96.

90. Bodie, Zvi, Robert S. Kaplan, and Robert C. Merton, "Options Should Be Reflected in the Bottom Line," *Wall Street Journal,* August 1, 2002.

91. Bens, David A., Venky Nagar, Douglas J. Skinner, and M. H. Franco Wong, "Employee Stock Options, EPS Dilution, and Stock Repurchases," July 2002, http://papers.ssrn.com/sol3/paprs.cfm?abstract_id=301405. Accessed May 23, 2003.

92. "Another Week, Another Plunge in Stocks," Data Bank, *New York Times,* July 21, 2002.

93. Hall, Brian J. and Kevin J. Murphy, "The Trouble with Stock Options," p. 6–7. Hall and Murphy argue that expensing is desirable because of its anticipated results. They believe that as a consequence of expensing, "stock options are likely to be reduced and concentrated among those executives and key technical employees who can plausibly affect company stock prices" (p. 34). Whether or not that would be a desirable result, changing accounting

rules in order to influence compensation packages would be a questionable precedent. And anything that reduces stock options is apt to tilt the market for executives and technical employees in favor of "old economy" firms.

94. Simon, Ruth, "Companies Get Stingy with Stock Options," *Wall Street Journal,* July 30, 2003.

95. Simon, Ruth, "Popular Stock Perk Faces Cutbacks," *Wall Street Journal,* September 4, 2003.

96. Pandher, Gurupdesdh S., "Executive Stock Option Valuation under Multiple Severance Risks," DePaul University Department of Finance, May 2002, http://papers.ssrn.com/sol3/papers.cfm?abstract_id=314761. Accessed May 1, 2003.

97. Huddart, Steven J., "Employee Stock Options," Pennsylvania State University, June 1994.http://paper2.ssrn.com/paper.taf?ABSTRACT_ID=5440. Accessed May 19, 2003.

98. Rich, Jude, "FASB's Stock Options Blunder," *Forbes,* January 1, 2003.

99. Rappaport, Alfred, "Choosing a Useful Option," *Wall Street Journal,* September 24, 2002. The author favors a mark-to-market approach, which, he argues, would show that the FASB method of expensing would have overstated Yahoo's expenses (and understated earnings) by $1.3 billion in 2001.

100. Gillan, Stuart L., Jay C. Hartzell, and Laura T. Starks, "Industries, Investment Opportunities, and Corporate Governance Structures," Center for Corporate Governance, Working Paper WP 2003-003, November 2002, p. 28.

101. Milliron, "Board of Director," p. 28.

18

Replace the Scandal-Plagued Corporate Income Tax with a Cash-Flow Tax

Chris Edwards

$\mathscr{T}$he corporate income tax will raise about $150 billion in fiscal 2003, which accounts for about 8 percent of total federal tax revenues.[1] Despite some popular perceptions that large corporations are able to evade much of their tax liability, most large corporations pay a huge amount of tax to the federal government. Consider Wal-Mart. It paid $3.02 billion in current federal income taxes in 2002 on pretax U.S. profits of $9.52 billion.[2] That works out to an effective tax rate of 31.7 percent.

Of course, Wal-Mart and other corporations do not actually bear the burden of the corporate tax; they simply act as tax collectors for the government. The actual burden of corporate taxes falls on individuals as workers, consumers, and shareholders. The extent to which the burden falls on each group is subject to much debate with no clear answers.[3] Suppose that Wal-Mart's $3 billion tax in 2002 was fully borne by its 1.1 million U.S. workers. The effect would be to reduce each worker's annual wage by $2,727. But no matter which group actually bears the burden, corporate income taxes create the fiction that $150 billion of federal spending is "free" because the cost is invisible to the general public.

The corporate income tax is generally considered the most complex and distortionary of all federal taxes. Jane Gravelle of the Congressional Research Service concludes that the "one fundamental aspect of the tax law that appears to cause the greatest tax distortions is the double tax on corporate income," which occurs because corporate profits are taxed at both the corporate and individual levels.[4] That distortion has caused concern since the beginning of the income tax, but the costs are rising in today's competitive and globalized economy. The observations that Stanford economists Myron Scholes and Mark Wolfson made in 1991 are still true today:

> The United States is out of sync with most of the rest of the world in taxing corporate income so heavily relative to non-corporate income. In most other countries, corporate income is taxed more favorably by allowing

shareholders to take a tax credit for corporate taxes they pay indirectly as shareholders, by imposing low shareholder-level tax rates, or by imposing relatively low corporate-level tax rates.[5]

Scholes and Wolfson concluded that "unless the tax system is changed to make U.S. corporations less tax disfavored relative to partnerships, investment bankers and other organizational designers will continue to search for ways to gut the corporate tax."[6] That comment was prescient given the subsequent aggressive tax avoidance efforts by Enron and other companies. The U.S. corporate tax is not gutted yet, but policy makers largely have themselves to blame for recent corporate tax avoidance scandals. After all, policy makers have not responded to the reality that nearly every major industrial nation has cut its statutory corporate tax rate to below the U.S. rate.[7]

The recent tax bill passed by Congress included shareholder tax cuts that are a first step toward solving the corporate tax problem. The Jobs and Growth Tax Relief Reconciliation Act of 2003 (JGTRRA) reduced the top tax rates on dividends and long-term capital gains to 15 percent.[8] However, those tax cuts are set to expire after 2008, and the tax bill did not address many serious distortions in the corporate income tax. For those reasons, Congress needs to pursue a major corporate tax overhaul or a full corporate tax repeal. Former treasury secretary Paul O'Neill's musings about abolishing the corporate income tax were not far-fetched, given the growing strain the tax is under in the competitive global economy.

That growing strain was highlighted in the recent 2,700-page report on Enron Corp.'s tax-sheltering activities by the congressional Joint Committee on Taxation (JCT).[9] Enron is just one company, but it took a team of JCT investigators a year to figure how all its tax shelters worked. And the JCT was still unable to determine how much tax Enron should have paid between 1995 and 2001, because the Internal Revenue Service (IRS) needs to spend many more hours auditing those returns.[10] The efforts of the JCT team were a mirror image of the huge efforts of the experts at Enron, the accounting firms, and investment banks that put Enron's tax shelters into place to begin with.

The brainpower spent on Enron's taxes is a just a fraction of the vast brainpower spent on the 2.2 million corporate income tax returns filed each year.[11] Most of the 54,846 pages of federal tax rules relate to business income taxes.[12] The JCT concluded that Enron "excelled at making complexity an ally."[13] Although it was an ally to Enron, tax complexity is an enemy to productive business management and sound investment decisions. A typical large corporation spends tens of millions of dollars per year on tax planning and paperwork. This chapter draws on the numerous Enron tax shelter deals to highlight the serious efficiency and complexity problems of the corporate income tax.

Enron-style tax sheltering has not been the only type of corporate tax scandal in the news. Attention has also focused on the growing number of U.S. companies moving their place of incorporation to low-tax jurisdictions, such as Bermuda. U.S.

firms can save taxes on their foreign operations by creating a foreign parent company for their worldwide operations. At the same time, there are growing incentives for foreign companies to acquire U.S. companies because the United States has a bad tax climate for multinational headquarters.[14]

Those developments have prompted knee-jerk denunciations of corporate wrongdoing and a batch of ill-conceived Band-Aids from Congress. But something more fundamental than a sudden decline in ethical standards or patriotism in corporate boardrooms is going on. The more fundamental issues include the high U.S. corporate tax rate, the uncompetitive and complex corporate tax rules, globalization, and tax reforms by foreign governments. In addition, Wall Street "financial innovation is growing rapidly and the tax law has not kept pace," as the Treasury Department noted in a major study of tax shelters in 1999.[15] For example, the total value of financial derivatives issued is estimated to have jumped from $3 trillion in 1990 to $127 trillion today.[16] A recently decided case in the U.S. Tax Court involving Bank One's use of derivatives concluded an eight-year battle and a trial that produced a 3,500-page transcript and 10,000 exhibits.[17] Clearly, the complex modern economy is creating unprecedented pressure on the antiquated income tax system.

In the next section I examine how the corporate tax shelter issue has developed in recent years and contrast legalistic and fundamental economic solutions to the problem. Then I discuss the three fundamental structural problems with the U.S. corporate tax: the high statutory tax rate; the inherent complexity of an income tax that relies on capital gains taxation and capitalization; and the gratuitous inconsistency that Congress has injected into the income tax, such as the different rules for corporations and other types of businesses.

In the final part of this chapter I consider two reform options. First, I consider full corporate tax repeal. Second, I examine replacement of the corporate income tax with a low-rate business cash-flow tax. A cash-flow tax would eliminate many current complexities (e.g., depreciation) and distortions (e.g., debt favored over equity) that haunt the current tax code. Cash-flow taxation has been part of numerous reform plans over the years, including a Brookings Institution tax plan from the 1980s and then House majority leader Dick Armey's (R-Texas) flat tax of the 1990s.[18] I conclude that recent scandals and rising tax competition make this an excellent time to repeal the corporate tax or replace it with a business cash-flow tax.

TAX SHELTERS: LEGALISTIC VS. FUNDAMENTAL ECONOMIC SOLUTIONS

Every few years, the income tax generates another cycle of tax avoidance scandals. In the 1970s and 1980s, the main focus was on individual tax shelters. Wealthy taxpayers sheltered income in real estate deals, movie projects, and exotic ventures such as jojoba bean farming.[19] The shelters involved strategies such as accelerating deductions, converting ordinary income to capital gains, and use of limited partnerships. A series of tax laws in the 1970s and 1980s mitigated those problems by closing loopholes and substantially cutting tax rates. The top individual income tax rate was cut from 70 percent to 50 percent in 1981, and then to 28 percent in 1986.[20] With that low rate, it made more sense for dentists, doctors, and other high earners to make sound investments rather than dodge the IRS with elaborate schemes.

In recent years, concern has shifted from individual to corporate tax avoidance. By most accounts, corporate tax avoidance has been on the upswing, though there are no firm estimates of the magnitude of those activities. The upswing has been spurred by sophisticated tax planning made possible by advanced computers and software, Wall Street financial innovation, global competitive pressures, and the high U.S. corporate tax rate. The first three factors are realities that will only intensify in the years ahead. But Congress can do something about the high corporate tax rate, as discussed in the next section.

Competitive pressures and financial innovations have also given rise to the manipulations of financial statement earnings that have been much in the news. Many corporate financial manipulations have created the dual benefit of tax reduction and a reported earnings boost at the same time. The rising gap between financial statement income and income reported for tax purposes seems to be caused by both tax avoidance efforts and efforts to inflate book earnings to please financial markets.

The increase in corporate tax avoidance has been costly in time and money for both companies and the government. Accounting and Wall Street firms have developed high levels of expertise at combining disparate parts of the tax code to engineer tax savings. But that expertise costs money: tax shelter promoters have been paid as much as $25 million for a deal sold to a single company.[21] Enron paid $88 million for advice on twelve tax shelter deals between 1995 and 2001.[22] These business costs are mirrored by the added costs on government administrators and enforcers. For example, it can cost the government $2 million just to litigate a single tax shelter case.[23] The IRS, the Treasury, and the courts are kept busy as each new tax shelter is discovered and then squelched through statutes, regulations, enforcement, and litigation. In 1999, the Treasury Department noted that at least thirty new narrow provisions had been added to the tax code in the previous few years in response to particular abuses.[24] Those new rules, in turn, force taxpayers and their advisers to abide by growing lists of anti-abuse statutes, reporting requirements, and disclosure rules.

TAX CODE AMBIGUITY MAKES
LEGAL CRACKDOWN INEFFECTIVE

One might think that these wasteful efforts could be reduced if corporations simply stopped acting improperly. But there is usually no clear-cut right or wrong in the income tax avoidance cat-and-mouse game. Most corporate tax disputes involve different interpretations of the rules, not straightforward cheating.[25] Indeed, taxpayers often win court cases when the IRS challenges them on their tax law interpretations. Some recent IRS wins against corporate tax shelters in the U.S. Tax Court were reversed by the Federal Court of Appeals.[26] Tax lawyers often come to widely different conclusions when they examine the same facts in particular cases. Many issues are so gray that tax disputes between companies and the IRS can remain unsettled for ten years or more.[27] The IRS's estimate of the correct tax liability across all corporations can be tens of billions of dollars different from what U.S. corporations believe to be the correct amount owed.[28]

Given this level of legal uncertainty, companies have strong incentives to push the tax code's limits. After all, no taxpayer has an obligation to pay more than what is owed, and the government cannot tell taxpayers for sure what an illegal tax shelter is. One tax law professor noted that "virtually all tax shelters comply with the literal language of a relevant (and perhaps the most relevant) statute, administrative ruling, or case."[29] With regard to Enron's tax shelter activities, the then JCT chief of staff Lindy Paull testified, "I don't know if you could call it illegal."[30] Though they are not clearly illegal, Paull did think that the IRS should challenge many Enron-style tax shelters.

The courts have followed various general principles or doctrines to challenge tax shelters, such as "substance over form," "business purpose," and "economic substance." For example, "substance over form" basically means a taxpayer cannot simply label equity as debt and deduct dividends as if they were interest. That makes sense, but the Treasury Department notes that the "substance over form doctrine is highly subjective and fact dependent, and thus is uncertain."[31] The economic substance and business purpose doctrines attempt to deny tax benefits for transactions that do not have a nontax business purpose. But ambiguity comes into play because it is not clear how broadly a "transaction" should be defined or how much nontax business purpose is needed for a transaction to pass muster.[32]

In speaking of anti-tax-shelter legal approaches, the 1999 Treasury Department report noted that the "application of these doctrines to a particular set of facts is often uncertain."[33] Indeed, courts often come to different conclusions in seemingly similar cases. Nonetheless, the Treasury Department created its own list of the general characteristics that may identify an unjustified tax shelter. Those include transactions that lack economic substance, create inconsistencies between tax and financial statement income, make use of nontaxable counterparties, are sold confidentially, have high or contingent fees, or involve widespread marketing efforts by the shelter creator.[34]

There is much debate regarding the best way to crack down on tax shelters from a legal point of view. Some experts support imposing more detailed rules; others support stronger general standards. Some lawyers actually call for vague tax rules and large amounts of IRS discretion to intimidate companies, but that seems to be hostile to the rule of law and may inhibit legitimate business activities.[35] Numerous superficial antishelter ideas are currently being implemented. For example, the Treasury Department recently issued regulations that require that taxpayers and promoters of dubious tax avoidance transactions register them with the IRS. In addition, there is a movement to ban accounting firms from doing tax work for their audit clients, especially the marketing of tax reduction ideas. Obviously, such rules would not eliminate the underlying economic incentives to avoid high taxes. Thus, large companies will probably just do more tax planning in-house or purchase shelters from nonaccounting firms. Ultimately, a large and sustained reduction in tax sheltering can be achieved by changing fundamental economic incentives, not by adding endless layers of new rules.

FUNDAMENTAL ECONOMIC SOLUTIONS NEEDED

The development of detailed legal rules is certainly necessary for any tax system. But the tax shelter discussion in the past few years has been far too much a conversation between lawyers, without any focus on economic solutions. The tax shelter discussion has been about which legal doctrines should be used to enforce bad laws, rather than about reforming the bad laws. The 1999 Treasury Department study on tax shelters identified the many "discontinuities" in the income tax as a key cause of shelters: "[Tax] shelters typically rely on some type of discontinuity in the tax law that treats certain types or amounts of economic activity more favorably than comparable types or amounts of activity."[36] These discontinuities can arise in the basic structure of the federal income tax system or in specific provisions of the code and regulations. The development of sophisticated financial instruments, such as derivatives, has facilitated the exploitation of these tax law discontinuities.

Yet the Treasury study spent only a few paragraphs discussing fundamental reforms that would remove those discontinuities and focused instead on ways to better police them. For example, the tax code favors debt over equity financing by allowing corporations a deduction for interest payments but not for dividend payments. That discontinuity has spurred companies to design complex financial structures that have many features of equity but are treated as debt for tax purposes. If Congress eliminated such inequities, tax authorities could save much time and effort now spent on policing the tax avoidance activities that have arisen in response. The American Bar Association (ABA) noted that "parties to a tax-driven transaction should have an incentive to make certain that the transaction is within the law."[37] However, it would be much better to reduce "tax-driven" transactions altogether by creating a more neutral tax code.

Unless basic economic incentives are changed, narrow limitations on tax-driven activities may simply spawn new tax avoidance techniques. The Treasury Department report notes that a vicious cycle is created as "legislative remedies themselves create the complexity that the next generation of tax shelters exploits, which leads to more complex responses, and so on."[38] For example, the private sector created new tax shelters in response to the repeal in 1986 of General Utilities Doctrine (which had allowed firms to avoid capital gains tax on some transactions), the restrictions on foreign tax credits in 1986, and the more recent implementation of mark-to-market securities rules.

Legalistic approaches to tax shelters usually frame the issue as if Congress should imperiously be able to impose any bad tax policy it wants on Americans without any consideration of the damage it may do. That attitude is seen in the 1999 Treasury Department report, which states that tax shelters "breed disrespect" for our "voluntary tax system." But surely it is the compulsory, complex, and ungainly tax system that breeds disrespect and gives rise to tax shelters. If we do not have a transparent and straightforward way of complying with the system, Congress is responsible, not the taxpayers.

One trap that Congress repeatedly falls into is carving out narrow benefits targeted at special interests. Nontargeted taxpayers will often find the new loopholes and exploit them. A classic example was recently reported by the *New York Times*.[39] Decades ago, Congress carved out a tax exemption for small insurance companies—those with less than $350,000 in premiums—in order to help farmers and others get coverage. The *Times* reports that a host of millionaires and non-insurance companies have seized the opportunity to set up insurance company shells that do little actual insurance business. Those tax avoiders transfer billions of dollars of assets to those shells in order to generate tax-free earnings—all legally.

As long as Congress perpetuates such distortions in the tax code, legalistic solutions to shelters will fail. Another dead end is the belief that more money and more aggressive enforcement by the one-hundred-thousand-worker IRS will solve the problem. The reality is that the IRS will always be outgunned by highly paid tax experts in the private sector.[40] As Congress makes the rules ever more complex, private-sector tax experts will have an even bigger advantage. The government is already using every kind of legal tool in its arsenal—legislative, regulatory, and judicial—to combat tax shelters.[41] But the distortion-laden income tax is too complex for any bureaucracy to administer accurately.

Instead, it is time that Congress pursued a fundamental economic solution to the problem. That means reducing the corporate tax rate and building the tax code on a neutral and transparent base to make administration and compliance easier for taxpayers and the government. Another advantage to a neutral tax code is that it would reduce tax inequalities between companies. An important cause of aggressive corporate tax sheltering has been the pressure on executives to ensure that their firms' effective tax rate reported on financial statements is no higher than competitors' tax rates.[42] As the Treasury Department notes, effective tax rates are "viewed as a performance measure, separate from after-tax profits. That has put pressure on corporate financial officers to generate tax savings through shelters."[43] Thus, more neutrality in the tax code would equalize tax rates between firms and reduce pressures to pursue tax sheltering.

A HIGH RATE EXACERBATES ALL CORPORATE TAX PROBLEMS

After the United States cut its corporate tax rate from 46 percent to 34 percent in 1986, other countries followed suit and tax rates tumbled across the industrial nations of the Organization for Economic Cooperation and Development (OECD). Corporate tax rate cutting has continued in recent years, with the average top rate in the OECD countries falling from 37.6 percent in 1996 to just 30.8 percent by 2003.[44] That compares to a 40 percent rate in the United States, including the 35 percent federal rate and an average 5 percent state rate. The United States now has the second-highest statutory corporate tax rate in the OECD, next to Japan.[45]

More countries are realizing that high corporate tax rates discourage inflows of foreign investment and encourage domestic companies to invest abroad. As world direct investment flows soared from about $200 billion to $1.3 trillion during the 1990s, countries sought to attract their share of investments in automobile factories, computer chip plants, and research facilities.[46] Extensive empirical research has concluded that tax rates are important in channeling cross-border investments.[47] As just one current example, the world's third-largest memory chipmaker, Infineon Technologies, recently announced that it may move its headquarters out of Germany, partly because of that country's high tax burden.[48]

Indeed, an important conclusion of public finance research is that in an open world economy countries should reduce tax rates on capital income to zero.[49] Higher tax rates raise the required pretax return on investments, which reduces a country's capital stock and wages. In that situation, it would be more efficient for a country, and better for workers, to tax wages directly. It is true that the zero tax rate conclusion depends on certain assumptions and is subject to various academic debates. But in general, it is efficient to tax highly elastic items more lightly than other items. Corporate profits are highly elastic or mobile in today's economy and thus should be taxed very lightly in order to maximize U.S. gross domestic product.

The mobility of the corporate tax base is illustrated by the number of U.S. companies that are "inverting," or reincorporating in low-tax foreign jurisdictions such as Bermuda. By doing so, U.S. firms have found that they can reduce taxes paid to the U.S. government on their foreign operations. In a typical corporate inversion transaction, the U.S. firm places itself under a new foreign parent company formed in a lower-tax jurisdiction. Such transactions generally have no real effect on the company's U.S. business operations; the company just pays less tax to the U.S. government.

Many politicians and pundits have found corporate inversions to be scandalous, and a number of bills have been introduced in Congress to stop them. Unfortunately, those efforts offer only a superficial response to the issues raised by inversions and do not tackle the underlying uncompetitiveness of the U.S. corporate tax.[50] It is certainly sad that venerable American businesses such as Stanley Works and Ingersoll-Rand feel that the U.S. tax code is so bad that they must consider incorporating abroad.[51] The decisions to undertake such transactions are not taken lightly by U.S. companies, because inversions need complex planning and can involve large upfront tax costs.[52] Thus, U.S. firms would not be pursuing inversions unless there was something seriously wrong with the U.S. tax system.

This issue highlights the two-sided game that some politicians play with regard to the tax code. First, they attack the tax code's inefficiency and complexity, and then they turn around and attack the taxpayers who logically try to take advantage of the tax mess that the government created. For example, in the mid-1930s President Franklin Roosevelt and Treasury Secretary Henry Morgenthau launched a campaign to energize their constituents by attacking tax loopholes used by the rich.[53] The Treasury Department vilified famous wealthy people as tax cheaters and introduced a string of proposals to increase taxes on the rich and big corporations.[54] Yet in the previous few years, the government had jacked up the top individual tax rate from 25 percent to 79 percent, thus encouraging the rich to aggressively hunt for new tax shelters. Meanwhile, Roosevelt railed against income tax rules "so complex that even certified public accountants cannot interpret them."[55]

Today it is the same with the corporate income tax. The high rate and the distortions work hand in hand to give companies a strong incentive to pursue tax reduction schemes. The high corporate rate exacerbates every distortion in the income tax code, such as the bias in favor of debt. Indeed, high tax rates increase the "deadweight losses" caused by such distortions more than proportionally as tax rates rise.[56] Thus, even modest rate reductions can substantially increase the efficiency of the tax system. As marginal tax rates fall, tax distortions become less important and executives become less interested in taking the risks and paying the high fees involved in tax shelter transactions.

In today's global economy, it is not just the absolute level of the corporate rate that is important. A firm's tax rate compared to those of its competitors based in other countries is also very important. For example, today there is much concern about "earnings stripping," which occurs when parent firms and their affiliates use intercompany borrowing to shift profits from high-tax to low-tax countries. The benefits of such transactions depend on the tax rates in the two countries. Thus, as our trading partners have cut tax rates in recent years, it is not surprising that the U.S. corporate tax is feeling pressure from such tax avoidance techniques.

The United States needs to update its tax policies to keep pace with changes in the rest of the world. Cutting the U.S. corporate rate from 35 percent to, say, 20 percent would increase capital investment, reduce corporate activities aimed at avoiding U.S. taxes, and encourage companies to restructure themselves to move more of their global tax base into the United States.

FLAWS INTRINSIC TO THE CORPORATE INCOME TAX

The corporate income tax began in 1909, masquerading as an "excise" tax.[57] Ever since the Supreme Court had struck down the income tax in 1895, attempts had been made to work around the Court's decision and somehow apply taxes to an income base.[58] The Corporation Tax Act of 1909 applied a 1 percent tax on corporate net income, on the theory that it was an excise on the "privilege" of organizing in the corporate form.[59] Supporters of the tax took advantage of the populist anti-wealth and anti-big business attitudes that had been gaining steam since the 1890s.[60] Support for the corporate tax also came from opponents of tariffs who wanted to find a substitute revenue source.[61] The corporate income tax was seen as a first step toward broader income taxation that would be adopted a few years later. After the adoption of the Sixteenth Amendment to the U.S. Constitution in 1913, the corporate tax was rolled into the new income tax system.

Even before 1909, there was a history at the state level of taxing corporations more heavily than other types of businesses. State corporate taxes had been supported because corporations were seen as too powerful or as beneficiaries of privileges conferred on them by the government. Politically, special taxes on corporations made sense because they allowed governments to hide funding for additional spending out of sight of the voters. But taxing corporations differently from noncorporate businesses never had a sound economic justification.

Congress compounded the mistake of imposing a special tax on corporations by applying the tax to the very troublesome base of net income or profits. The tax base of net income created substantial complexity from the beginning. Civil War administrators had trouble measuring income and capital gains under the income tax that lasted from 1861 until 1872.[62] Soon after the corporate income tax was enacted in 1909, the tax base began creating confusion and inefficiency. The congressional JCT was created in 1926 to study income tax simplification and the complex tax administration problems that had already arisen. By the 1930s, experts were lamenting all the fundamental income tax problems that cause distortions and complexities today. A major report by the Treasury Department in 1934 noted with regard to the corporate income tax:

> The irregularity of income, the taxation of capital gains, the definition of the time of "realization," the handling of depreciation and appreciation, the cash versus accrual method of accounting, the holding and distributing of corporation earnings in the form of dividends, all raise serious difficulties in the definition of income and administration of a net income tax.[63]

Despite hundreds of statutory and regulatory changes to these provisions during the subsequent decades, all these problems persist today. A key problem is that the income tax superstructure has been built ever higher on a very problematic base. The problems begin with the Haig-Simons income concept, which underpins the tax, named after economists Robert Haig and Henry Simons writing in the 1920s and 1930s.[64] In abstract, Haig-Simons income equals consumption plus the rise in market value of net wealth during a year. In practice, it includes all forms of labor compensation, including fringe benefits, and all sources of capital income, such as interest, dividends, and capital gains.

A Haig-Simons tax would tax income very broadly and would tax it on an accrual basis. Taxing on an accrual basis means taxing income when earned, not when cash is actually received. For example, individuals would be taxed each year on all stock market gains whether or not any stocks were sold. Also, individuals would be taxed on items such as the buildup of wealth in their life insurance policies and the implicit rent received from owning their homes.

It would be completely impractical to tax such a broad accrual income base.[65] For example, many individuals would not have any cash available to pay capital gains tax if they did not sell any stock. As a consequence of the impracticality of full Haig-Simons taxation, the income tax system is a jumble of ad hoc rules based on different theories and various practical realities. David Bradford, a former Treasury official and current Princeton professor, has examined the complexity of income taxation and concluded:

> It is simply very difficult to design rules that can be administered by ordinary human beings that will provide an acceptable degree of approximation to the accrual-income ideal. That is why the tax system requires continual patching—one year, tax straddles; another year, self-constructed assets; another year, installment sales; another year, discount bonds; and so on.[66]

Under the current income tax, corporations generally capitalize long-lived assets used for production. That means that such assets may not be deducted when purchased, but their cost is deducted over time under rules for depreciation, amortization, and inventory. In addition, the income tax generally uses accrual accounting, meaning that income is included in the tax base when earned, not when cash is received, and expenses are deducted when incurred, not when cash is paid. Capitalization and accrual accounting involve the creation of many artificial accounting constructs that open the doors to manipulation and distortion of the income tax.[67] (By contrast, under cash-flow accounting businesses deduct all expenses when paid and include income when received). Capitalization and accrual accounting are also the building blocks of financial statement income, based on Generally Accepted Accounting Principles (GAAP). Recent corporate accounting scandals illustrate that GAAP-based income suffers from large manipulation problems, similar to the problems faced by the current income tax. It is occasionally suggested that income for tax purposes be conformed to GAAP income as a simplification measure. However, recent accounting scandals suggest that that would not produce a less problematic tax base. Also, a tax base of GAAP income would retain the anti-investment bias of the current income tax. For example, it would still require depreciation of capital purchases rather than immediate deduction ("expensing").[68] Also, conforming tax to GAAP income may cause corporate executives' tax considerations to distort their financial statements and upset the efficiency of financial markets.[69]

NET CASH FLOW IS AN ALTERNATIVE TAX BASE

An alternative to income taxation based on accrual accounting is consumption taxation based on cash-flow accounting.[70] A cash-flow tax would be imposed on net cash flow of businesses, not net income or profits. The most commonly proposed type of cash-flow tax (an "R-based" tax) would have a tax base of receipts from the sale of goods and services less current and capital expenses. Under an R (real) base, financial items such as interest, dividends, and capital gains would be disregarded—they would not be included in income or allowed as deductions.[71] (Alternately, an R+F base, real plus financial, would include financial flows.) Under cash-flow accounting, businesses would include receipts when cash is received and deduct the full costs of materials, inventories, equipment, and structures when they are purchased.

Business cash-flow taxes have been discussed in academic and policy circles for years and have formed the basis of numerous legislative proposals since at least the 1970s. (Going back further, Treasury Secretary Andrew Mellon's chief tax adviser in the 1920s, Thomas Adams, suggested replacing the income tax and its "incurable inconsistencies" with a consumption-based tax.)[72] In 1985, the Brookings Institution's Henry Aaron and Harvey Galper proposed an R+F-based cash-flow tax on businesses within a comprehensive tax plan.[73] In 1981, the Hoover Institution's Robert Hall and Alvin Rabushka introduced their "flat tax," based on an R-based business cash-flow tax.[74] Interestingly, it was former Sen. Dennis DeConcini of Arizona and former Rep. Leon Panetta of California, both Democrats, who first introduced the Hall-Rabushka Plan in Congress in 1982, illustrating that tax reform was more of a bipartisan concern in the 1980s than now.[75] In the 1990s, Armey and Steve Forbes proposed Hall-Rabushka-style tax reform plans.

Economists from Aaron to Armey agree that many basic income tax distortions would be eliminated under a business cash-flow tax. Those distortions include the different treatment of debt and equity, the different treatment of corporate and noncorporate businesses, the bias against saving, and distortions caused by inflation.[76] As time goes by, the business cash-flow tax becomes more appealing compared with the deepening swamp of complexity and inefficiency under the corporate income tax.[77]

INCOME TAXATION IS SENSITIVE TO TIMING

Timing is everything under the income tax, which relies on capitalization and accrual accounting. The basic idea is to match expenses against corresponding income when earned. If cash is spent this year that creates benefits in future years, the expense should not be currently deducted. Instead, the cost must be capitalized and deducted later. Alternatively, rules are needed to deal with cash received this year that relates to economic activity in other years. Thus, in any given year under the income tax there are numerous income and deduction items on corporate tax returns that do not coincide with flows of cash but are based on tax law definitions determining the proper timing of recognition.

Examples of noncash tax return entries are depreciation and amortization. For example, goodwill is created as an artificial asset under some corporate acquisition transactions. The acquiring company in an acquisition amortizes the goodwill asset (takes a noncash deduction) over the subsequent fifteen years. Such noncash items may only be rough measures of underlying economic reality. In addition, inflation throws a wrench into the accurate matching of income and expenses, since deductions slated for future years lose their value with inflation. As a result, the income tax code is rife with distortions that are roadblocks to efficient investment and offer opportunities for tax avoidance transactions.

The Treasury Department notes that "it is extremely difficult, and perhaps impossible, to design a tax system that measures income perfectly . . . even if rules for the accurate measurement of income could be devised, such rules could result in significant administrative and compliance burdens."[78] Capital gains is a good example. In theory, broad-based income taxation would tax capital gains on an accrual basis. But since that is not feasible, the income tax falls back on taxing most, but not all, gains when realized. Recent tax shelters have exploited the fact that some gains are taxed on a realization basis and other gains, such as foreign currency contracts, are taxed on a mark-to-market, or accrual, basis. That discontinuity has been exploited by Wall Street experts who have devised a variety of tax shelters.[79] Apparently, firms subject to mark-to-market tax treatment are able to enter into mutually beneficial transactions with other taxpayers subject to realization treatment to absorb their capital gains.

Many tax avoidance techniques exploit the income tax's sensitivity to timing. One technique is to take advantage of tax code provisions that accelerate income recognition. Installment sale shelters and lease strips (both of which are now banned) used that approach. Those shelters worked by having a corporation set up a partnership with a nontaxpayer (such as a foreigner). A transaction would be performed through the partnership that generates up-front income; that income would be mainly allocated to the nontaxpayer; then the partnership would be dissolved. Under the lease strip shelter, the partnership would buy an item such as an airplane, lease it out under a prepaid lease, and then allocate the up-front money to the nontaxpayer.[80] The partnership would then be dissolved, leaving the corporation with no income to report but with annual depreciation deductions to take on the airplane or other assets.

A number of Enron deals exploited various timing-sensitive income tax rules. For example, "commodity prepay" transactions were used to reduce taxes. In one deal, Enron sought to generate income in order to use section 29 tax credits before they expired. Those credits are special-interest benefits designed to encourage fuel production from unconventional sources.[81] Enron designed transactions to enable it to receive up-front payments, so that it could use the tax credits, in exchange for later delivery of oil and gas. But no oil and gas were actually delivered, and the transaction was later reversed with a complex flow of money after the tax benefits had been realized.

Most such manipulations with regard to the timing of income and expenses would be eliminated under a cash-flow tax. Income would be included in the tax base when received. Deductions would be taken when cash went out the door. That treatment would not only be more economically efficient, it would remove a great many tax avoidance opportunities that exist under the current tax regime.

CAPITALIZATION

Under the income tax, business costs for assets that generate revenues in future years are typically not deducted at the time of purchase. Instead, such items as buildings, machines, and intangible assets are capitalized and deducted over future years. Under income tax theory, the purchase price of buildings and machines should be deducted, or depreciated, over time to match the loss in economic value of the asset. When intangible assets are purchased, they are amortized over a specified period of time. Materials purchased for inventory and related inventory expenses face special rules to determine when deductions should be taken.

There are two key problems with capitalization: figuring out which assets need to be capitalized and figuring out the period over and method by which to take future deductions. With regard to the first problem, any asset that produces benefits in future years should be capitalized in income tax theory. But that principle becomes extremely ambiguous in practice. For example, the IRS has battled companies over whether management consultant expenses should be immediately deducted if they relate to long-term improvements in a company's productivity. Taxpayers say yes, but the IRS has held that such expenses must be written off over future years. The tax code contains no consistency on such rules. Advertising and research and development expenses are immediately deducted under current rules, yet they produce benefits in future years. On the other hand, the tax law requires capitalization of numerous expenses that taxpayers think of as current expenses, such as interest costs related to inventory.

Capitalization is probably the greatest weakness of the corporate income tax. University of Chicago law professor David Weisbach notes that capitalization is "unbelievably complex" and "extremely uncertain" for companies.[82] In recent years, the IRS has been aggressive in forcing companies to capitalize all kinds of expenses that it unilaterally determines yield long-term benefits. One rough estimate was that up to one-quarter of IRS examination resources in some industries are used for capitalization issues alone.[83] Capitalization is a heavily litigated part of the tax code, with taxpayers winning about half the cases against the IRS.[84] Weisbach notes that the outcome of court cases is essentially random because of the ambiguity.[85] The Supreme Court has weighed in on the ambiguity of capitalization: "If one really takes seriously the concept of a capital expenditure as anything that yields income, actual or imputed, beyond the period . . . in which the expenditure is made, the result will be to force the capitalization of virtually every business expense."[86]

The problems of capitalization are evident in the tax rules for inventory. Businesses may not simply deduct the costs of materials when purchased; rather, costs must be capitalized and deducted later when products are sold. A range of indirect costs related to inventories, such as interest, must also be capitalized. These rules are so complex that a top Treasury Department official thinks that many companies are simply guessing to get the correct inventory deduction on their tax returns.[87] The 1986 tax act was supposed to "reform" the corporate tax by measuring income better, but with inventory accounting and other items the rules became more complex.

The second key problem with capitalization is determining the time period for and method by which each asset should be deducted over future years. In income tax theory, depreciation deductions should match an asset's obsolescence over time. But every asset is different, and new types of assets are being invented all the time. Rough approximations are used to place assets in categories that determine the length of the period for deductions and which formula to use in calculating deductions.[88] For example, cars, farm buildings, racehorses, shrubbery, and tugboats may all have different depreciation time periods and other rules. For newer technologies, the asset classification system is long out of date, resulting in incorrect treatment of such items as computers.[89] But even up-to-date depreciation schedules would be wrong because of inflation distortions.

Depreciation plays an important role in many tax shelters, including a number of Enron deals. A basic shelter strategy is to artificially raise the basis of an asset to increase future depreciation deductions. ("Basis" is generally the original cost less accumulated depreciation. For example, a machine that was purchased for $100 and had $40 depreciation taken against it would have a basis of $60.) That strategy was used in 1997 in Enron's Teresa tax shelter, which involved a synthetic lease, which is a lease treated differently for tax purposes and financial statements.[90] Enron and an investment bank set up a partnership to which Enron contributed its Houston North office building and other assets, as well as preferred shares of an affiliate. In the early years of the deal, Enron paid additional tax from receipt of dividends, but that cost would be outweighed by added depreciation deductions in later years. Tax benefits were gained by shifting $1 billion in basis from a nondepreciable asset (the preferred shares) to depreciable assets including the office building.

The partnership tax rules, combined with the shifting of basis from nondepreciable to depreciable assets, was also the key to other Enron tax shelters.[91] Enron shelters Tammy 1 and Tammy 2 involved shifting about $2 billion in basis to the Enron South office building and other assets. Again, tax benefits were gained by increasing future depreciation deductions.[92] (Ultimately, those deals were not completed as planned because of the subsequent Enron meltdown.)

A business cash-flow tax would eliminate capitalization and all related concepts such as depreciation. Basis could not be shifted from some assets to others as in the Enron deals because asset basis is always zero under a cash-flow tax. Businesses would include the full price of asset sales in taxable receipts and would deduct the full cost when purchased. All business purchases would be treated the same way and immediately deducted. Partnerships would be taxed the same as other business entities so there would be no advantages in shifting assets to them. Expensing would create tax neutrality across all types of assets. Inflation would not distort marginal tax rates under a cash-flow tax as it does under the income tax. The rules under a cash-flow tax would be simple and durable over the long term.

CAPITAL GAINS

Capital gains taxation has caused complexity and distortion throughout the history of the income tax. As early as 1944, a Treasury Department report noted that "the treatment of capital gains has long been a source of controversy in federal taxation."[93] Under consumption-based taxes, such as a cash-flow tax, capital gains taxation would disappear. But under the income tax, Congress cannot seem to find a stable and efficient treatment for capital gains: it repeatedly changes the rates, exclusion amounts, holding periods, and treatment of losses. Capital gains taxation gets more complex as Congress adds more rules whenever new financial products are developed. For example, complex "constructive sale" rules were added in 1997 to prevent investors from using short selling to lock in gains without paying tax. But the new rules prompted private-sector development of other techniques to allow investors to accomplish the same thing, such as strategies using puts and calls.

While Congress has made capital gains taxation more complex than it needs to be—for example, by imposing multiple tax rates—most of the complexity is intrinsic. For example, practicality dictates than most gains be taxed on a realization basis, yet that treatment "stimulates an almost infinite variety of tax planning."[94] Since gains are taxed when assets are sold, taxpayers need to optimally plan, matching their gains with losses. That planning has prompted the government to create a large apparatus of rules to police realization strategies.

One example of intrinsic capital gains complexity for businesses is the difficulty in drawing distinct lines between assets sold as a part of regular sales, which are taxed as ordinary income, and assets sold by investors for speculation, which are taxed as capital gains.[95] For industries such as real estate, this classification of receipts as ordinary or capital gains is a continuing area of complexity and conflict.

For corporations, net capital gains are taxed at the regular corporate rate, generally 35 percent.[96] Capital losses may be deducted only against capital gains, not ordinary income. Net capital losses may be carried back three years or forward five years. These basic rules necessitate large amounts of tax planning. Companies have an incentive to avoid realizing gains unless they have losses available. Also, they generally prefer income to be characterized as capital gains, not ordinary income, and losses to be characterized as ordinary losses, not capital losses, because of the limitations on capital losses.[97] In addition, the international tax rules provide incentives to characterize income or gains as foreign-source, but deductions or losses as U.S.-source.

Corporations pay capital gains on sales of capital assets, such as shares of other corporations. But gains on the sale of depreciable assets involve other rules. Sales of personal property, such as machinery, are taxed partly as capital gains and partly as ordinary income. The overall taxable amount is the difference between the sales price and basis, which is generally the original cost less accumulated depreciation. That amount is taxed as ordinary income to the extent of previous depreciation allowances (depreciation is "recaptured"). Sales of real property, such as buildings, are also taxed partly as ordinary income and partly as capital gains, but different rules apply.

In a nutshell, the corporate capital gains rules are complex and compel substantial tax minimization planning. In addition, they create distortions, such as "locking in" corporate investments in other companies. That occurs because built-in gains face corporate taxation when shares are sold. Thus, companies may avoid selling shares and be stuck holding old investments with low returns or be unable to reallocate their capital when business conditions change.

A key goal of German corporate tax reforms put in place in 2002 was elimination of this lock-in effect. In an effort to improve the economy's competitiveness, Germany cut the federal corporate tax rate to 25 percent and eliminated the corporate capital gains tax on sales of other firms' stock.[98] Incestuous cross-holdings between German companies are thought to have sapped the dynamism from the economy. Capital gains taxes stood in the way of needed divestitures and corporate restructuring. The tax reform was designed to allow corporations to unwind their unproductive investments without a tax penalty. The Netherlands has also gained a competitive edge by having no corporate capital gains tax on sales of shareholdings. As a result, the Netherlands is a favored location for holding companies and multinational headquarters.[99]

By contrast, the United States dissuades efficient business reorganizations by taxing corporate capital gains at a high rate. To give one example of the size of the lock-in effect, consider SunTrust and Coca-Cola. SunTrust owns roughly $2 billion in Coca-Cola company shares, which it has held since 1919. If SunTrust wanted to unload those shares, it would face corporate capital gains taxes of roughly $700 million at the 35 percent corporate tax rate.[100]

Not surprisingly, the high corporate capital gains tax has caused U.S. corporations to devise elaborate strategies to avoid it. Corporations have developed techniques to effectively divest holdings in other firms while retaining legal ownership and deferring capital gains tax until later years.[101] For example, *Times Mirror* wanted to unload its holding of Netscape Communications without paying the corporate capital gains tax in 1996.[102] With help from Wall Street, *Times Mirror* designed and issued "PEPS," which allowed it to put off until later years capital gains taxes on the sale, to get cash up front, to push Netscape risk onto PEPS holders, and to receive an interest deduction for its PEPS payments.[103]

Deals to avoid corporate capital gains taxes come in many flavors. *Tax Notes* columnist Lee Shepard wrote sarcastically a few years ago: "It has finally happened. Wall Street has run out of macho acronyms for securities that purport to be debt. We already have LYONS and TIGRS and CATS and PRIDES and ELKS. We have securities with meaningless names, like MIPS and DECS and PEPS. And now we have PHONES."[104] PHONES are financial derivatives that give companies the benefit of selling their holdings without actually selling stock and incurring capital gains tax. PHONES were used a few years ago by Comcast when it unloaded its AT&T holdings and by Tribune Company to unload its AOL holdings. Such large stock sales could generate a huge tax at the 35-percent rate; thus companies have big incentives to devise complex strategies, such as PHONES, to avoid the tax.

A number of tax avoidance strategies involve companies buying assets with built-in losses that can be used to offset other income. One strategy popular in the late 1990s involved companies putting profitable activities into their foreign subsidiaries and then acquiring losses from foreigners to offset their profits.[105] For example, a foreign entity might have a built-in loss stemming from owning a financial security worth $10 million that had been bought for $50 million. A subsidiary of a U.S. company could devise a strategy to buy the security for, say, $11 million, and acquire the asset's high basis and, thus, built-in loss. Using various provisions of the tax code, the subsidiary could sell the security and take a $40 million ordinary loss and use it to offset other income.

Enron built a number of tax shelters around the capital gain and loss rules. Enron's tax shelter deal Tanya aimed to generate capital losses that it could use to offset gains it had created in other activities.[106] In 1995 Enron had a large gain from the sale of Enron Oil and Gas. Arthur Andersen came up with a transaction that moved assets and liabilities to an Enron subsidiary, Enron Management Inc. Then Enron sold its holding in the subsidiary to create a capital loss of $188 million for Enron to use to offset gains from other activities. The deal also managed to create duplicate tax deductions in later years. Project Valor was similar, creating a $235 million capital loss for Enron that it used to offset gains from further sales of holdings in Enron Oil and Gas in 1996.[107]

Steele and Cochise were deals in which Enron acquired built-in losses from another company in order to offset some of its income. The Steele tax scheme involved setting up a new entity, ECT Partners, and then transferring assets with built-in losses from Bankers Trust to the entity. The assets involved were REMIC residual interests, which are particularly suited to such deals.[108] The assets had a basis of $234 million and a market value of only $8 million. Since ECT Partners was part of Enron in its consolidated tax return, Enron was able to use the losses to reduce taxable income by $112 million between 1997 and 2001.[109]

This deal and others generate tax benefits by moving "tax attributes," such as built-in losses, net operating losses, and credits, from the firms that generate them to other firms that can better use them. Income tax rules try to limit the transfer of tax attributes, and IRS policing is required to challenge deals where there seems to be no nontax purpose to such transfers.[110] But how much nontax purpose is needed to pass IRS inspection is ambiguous. In these Enron deals, the nontax purpose was to increase financial statement income that came about from the reduction in taxes—a clearly circular logic. Nonetheless, in these shelters and others, prestigious law and accounting firms signed off on the deals, usually charging a fat fee for writing opinion letters.[111]

Another tax shelter incentive created by capital gains taxation is to increase asset basis before a sale in order to reduce taxable gain. Enron used this strategy with the Tomas deal, which involved increasing the basis of a portfolio of assets it wanted to dispose of, including leased airplanes and rail cars. The deal eliminated $270 million of taxable gain on the disposition of those assets.[112] Enron set up a partnership with Bankers Trust in 1998, to which it transferred assets that had high market value but low basis (i.e., the assets had been nearly fully depreciated). Once the partnership held the assets, it used various transactions and tax provisions to shift basis from stock it held to these depreciable assets. The deal was able to increase the assets' basis enough to reduce Enron's taxable income by $270 million. Later, Enron liquidated its interest in the partnership. The partnership and Bankers Trust were able to sell the high-basis assets without gain. As in other deals, use of the partnership structure was crucial. Enron paid Bankers Trust $13 million for the deal.

These tax shelters illustrate the extensive incentives and opportunities that capital gains taxation creates for corporate tax planning and avoidance. Under a business cash-flow tax, capital gains taxation would be eliminated. Businesses would generally not collect "tax attributes," such as built-in losses, that could be traded to other companies in tax avoidance schemes. Asset basis would not be a variable to manipulate up or down to create gain or loss. Businesses would simply include the market price of asset sales in taxable revenue and symmetrically expense assets when purchased. That would create an enormous simplification of business tax planning, close many tax shelters, and reduce the need for government rules and enforcement efforts.

MERGERS AND ACQUISITIONS

The tax law controlling the world of corporate reorganizations—mergers, acquisitions, and other transactions—is a messy interaction of the income tax rules for capital gains, depreciation, interest deductions, net operating losses, goodwill, and other items. Many tax experts echo Cleveland State University professor Deborah Geier's views on this area of tax law:

> The current state of the law regarding corporate reorganizations is incomprehensible. The law in this area is not the result of a grand, coherent scheme but rather is the end result of a long accumulation of cases, statutory amendments, and IRS ruling positions, the sum total of which is a system that is staggering in its complexity and unpredictability. Moreover, the system exacts extremely high and inefficient transactions costs, as deals must be structured in ways that make sense only to the tax lawyers.[113]

Tax law stifles economic growth if it stands in the way of flexible business restructuring. Indeed, as noted in a study of the recent German corporate tax reforms, "The freedom to buy, sell, and refocus and reallocate assets in response to changing economic forces is potentially one of the most critical features of competitive market economies."[114] Conglomerates may find that they need to refocus on their core mission and spin off some divisions. Growing firms may want to acquire weaker firms to build greater economies of scale. Industries facing foreign competition may need to restructure to survive. Tax rules should not be a hurdle to those transactions.

Tax rules should also not encourage transactions that make no economic sense. For example, the more favorable treatment of debt than equity may encourage firms to pursue ill-advised debt-heavy acquisitions. There was much concern in the 1980s that the preferential tax treatment of debt was helping fuel the leveraged buyout spree, which was financed by high-yield, or junk, bonds. For example, part of the game plan of the famous 1989 RJR–Nabisco buyout was to wipe out the company's taxable income for years to come with interest deductions from a huge high-yield bond issue.[115]

Although buyouts are often a big plus for improving corporate management, the tax code should not be setting the parameters in the market for corporate control. But as tax laws change, so do the incentives for mergers and acquisitions (M&As). The 1981 tax act encouraged M&As, but then the 1986 tax act reversed course and discouraged them. One change in 1986 was the repeal of the General Utilities Doctrine, which had allowed firms to avoid capital gains tax on certain distributions of assets to shareholders. That change caused firms to innovate and find new ways to avoid capital gains on appreciated property they held.[116]

The complexity of the tax rules on corporate reorganizations spurs companies to create elaborate strategies for tax avoidance. Those strategies provide great fodder for antibusiness cynics in the media. The *Washington Post*'s Allan Sloan makes it seem as if every business reorganization he reviews is robbing Uncle Sam blind. Some of his column headlines have been "GM Finds a Hole in the Tax Code Big Enough to Drive Billions Through" and "Northrop Grumman Deal Scores a

Direct Hit on Taxes."[117] But the critics rarely consider whether there is something fundamentally wrong with a tax system that turns nearly every M&A into a supposed scandal.

The problems that create M&A scandals and complexity are rooted in the basic structure of the income tax. A brief overview of M&A tax rules illustrates the importance of two key income tax problems—capital gains taxation and capitalization.[118] Shareholders of companies being bought (target firms) may be paid either in cash or in shares of the acquiring firm. A tax-free transaction generally occurs when the target's shareholders receive shares. In these deals, target shareholders do not pay capital gains taxes in the transaction. (They will pay capital gains taxes later when they sell their shares.) By contrast, under taxable transactions the target firm shareholders receive cash and may face current capital gains taxes. Deals are sometimes partially stock and partially cash, in which case target shareholders may pay some taxes.

Different transaction structures (called A, B, C, etc.) provide rules for different amounts of stock and cash, different classes of shares, and other specifics. For example, Allan Sloan criticized General Motors in 2001 for a deal that used multiple classes of shares to get around capital gains taxes on the sale of GM's Hughes Electronics to Echostar.[119] On this deal, GM was apparently able to get around restrictive new rules put in place in 1997. In turn, the 1997 rules had been put in place to prevent transactions of a type for which GM had been able to avoid taxes on in a prior deal. What is Sloan's solution to these endless tax avoidance games? He does not have one.

Another key tax issue for M&As is how much depreciation companies will be able to deduct on target assets after reorganization. Under some types of transactions, particularly taxable ones, the basis of the target's assets is stepped up to market value. If a target firm's assets have a market value higher than their current tax basis, the assets will be worth more to another company, which will be able to take larger depreciation deductions than the current owner. That fact creates incentives for acquisitions.

All in all, the tax rules for corporate reorganizations are "immensely complicated," notes tax guide publisher CCH.[120] While Sloan criticizes firms for navigating the tax rules to the best of their ability, consider what one judge said in an M&A tax case. A 1999 Tax Court case involved an energy company acquisition that seemed to be tax driven because the acquiring firm would gain $84 million of the target firm's losses. The court ended up siding with the taxpayer and concluded, "In the complexity of today's business and tax jungle, a corporate president who does not obtain tax advice before an acquisition or merger or substantial dollar transaction ought to be fired."[121]

Most of the tax rules for business reorganization would be swept away under a business cash-flow tax. Indeed, a study on tax reform by the American Institute for Certified Public Accountants (AICPA) concluded that "the notoriously complex rules surrounding corporate distributions, liquidations, and reorganizations would become almost entirely obsolete" under a business cash-flow tax such as the Hall-Rabushka flat tax.[122] Generally, business reorganizations that involve an exchange of shares—the purchase of stock of one firm by another—would not be taxable events.[123] However, sales of assets for cash between businesses would be taxable events. The market value of assets would be included in the seller's tax base, which provides symmetrical treatment to the expensing of asset purchases. The concept of "basis" that is behind capital gains and depreciation under the income tax would disappear under a cash-flow tax.[124] There would be no step up in asset basis during restructuring, no future streams of depreciation or goodwill deductions to consider, and no distinctions between debt and equity for financing. American businesses could merge, split up, spin off, and reorganize any way that was efficient without the tax distortions that plague business restructuring today.

GRATUITOUS FLAWS IN THE CORPORATE INCOME TAX

On top of the intrinsic problems of income taxation, such as capitalization and capital gains taxation, are the gratuitous flaws added by Congress. Corporate and noncorporate businesses are taxed differently. Earnings paid out as dividends face taxation at both the corporate and individual levels, but interest does not. Retained earnings face double taxation insofar as they generate capital gains, but they are favorably treated compared to dividends. The corporate income tax imposes different marginal tax rates on different types of capital investment. All those factors result in investment being misallocated—investment is reduced, too little investment flows through corporate businesses, too much debt is used in financial structures, and corporate profits are retained rather than paid out.

How much do such corporate tax distortions cost? Gravelle summarized the extensive research on the issue and concluded that corporate income tax distortions probably cost more than is collected in corporate tax revenue.[125] Thus, the corporate tax will impose a direct cost of about $150 billion this year in tax liability, and distortions (or deadweight losses) will cost Americans an additional $150 billion or so.[126] Note that the cost at the margin is greater than implied in this 1-to-1 ratio. In other words, a cut in the corporate rate that reduced revenues by $20 billion would save the private sector much more than $20 billion in deadweight losses.[127] In addition, corporate tax distortions are rising over time as a result of the increasing openness in the world economy and greater capital mobility.

These figures summarize the costs that can be measured in formal economic models. In addition, the corporate tax creates other costs that are harder to measure. For example, the bias toward debt probably causes increased bankruptcy, but the destabilizing effects of bankruptcies are difficult to put a dollar value on. Also, complexity and frequent changes in the tax law waste a great deal of executives' time and energy on tax avoidance and business restructuring. It is hard to estimate how much higher GDP might be if executives focused instead on creating better products.

The following sections summarize some of the major distortions of the corporate income tax that are gratuitous or unwarranted under any tax system.

MULTIPLE BUSINESS STRUCTURES

The largest business enterprises in the United States are organized as "subchapter C" corporations and are subject to the corporate income tax. The corporate income tax forms a second layer of tax on investment returns in addition to individual income taxes. Noncorporate businesses face just a single layer of income taxation. As a result, the overall marginal effective tax rate on corporate income is about twice that on the noncorporate sector.[128] Thus, "despite the critical role played by corporations as a vehicle for economic growth, the [U.S.] tax law often perversely penalizes the corporate form of organization," concluded the Treasury Department's major 1992 study on tax reform.[129] As a result, fewer businesses take advantage of the benefits of the corporate structure, such as limited liability, ease of ownership transfer, access to public capital markets, and rapid growth potential.

The list of competitors to C corporations includes sole proprietorships, partnerships, subchapter S corporations, limited liability corporations (LLCs), limited liability partnerships (LLPs), real estate investment trusts (REITs), regulated investment companies (RICs), real estate mortgage investment conduits (REMICs), and financial asset securitization investment trusts (FASITs). Each of these structures avoids the double taxation of earnings, but each is subject to an array of special tax code rules. As a result, entrepreneurs and investors must consider the unique limitations of each structure when starting, expanding, or investing in a business.[130] One simple example is that S corporations can only issue a single class of stock and can have no more than seventy-five shareholders.

The pros and cons of the various business tax rules have resulted in different business structures being popular in different industries. Also, the complex rules have resulted in a multiplicity of business lobbyists in Washington, each looking for narrow changes in the rules for particular businesses. Often, American businesses do not speak with one voice because the tax code has carved them up into multiple constituencies.

As the tax rules affecting each business structure have changed, industry has evolved to fit the incentives created by Washington. For example, changes in the top tax rate for individuals relative to corporations affect the attractiveness of the corporate form. After the Tax Reform Act of 1986 (TRA86) cut the top individual rate to below the corporate rate, there was strong growth in the number of S corporations, whose owners are taxed at individual rates.[131] Further liberalization in S corporation rules has caused the number of such companies to grow from 0.7 million in 1985 to 1.6 million in 1990 and to more than 2.7 million today.[132] Also, federal and state law changes have created rapid growth in LLCs in the 1990s.[133] In general, alternatives to C corporations have grown in popularity during the past decade or two. Indeed, some observers think that C corporations may whither away from "self-help integration" as the rules for other business types are liberalized. That does seem to be the case for small and mid-sized firms, and it is a positive trend. But it would be much more efficient if Congress took the lead and directly eliminated the double layer of taxation on C corporations.

The existence of different business structures creates tax planning opportunities for businesses since the same activity can be undertaken in different ways with different tax results. Tax shelters used by Enron and others have made extensive use of alternative business structures to conceal debt, change the form of financial flows, and confuse tax authorities and investors. In particular, the interaction of the partnership and corporation rules seems to be a key focus of many tax avoidance efforts. The idea behind partnerships is that income, gains, and losses are not taxed at the partnership level but passed through to individual partners on the basis of the parameters in the partnership agreement. One basic tax sheltering idea is for a corporation to set up a partnership with a tax-exempt entity and to then allocate the tax-exempt partner most of the income, while the corporation is allocated the losses to offset other income it may have.

The "partnership rules often act as chemical plants creating artificial tax losses and distilling them out to U.S. corporations . . . the variations on the idea are infinite."[134] We saw this with Enron. Partnership rules were used in a number of its tax shelters, including Tomas and Condor, often with the goal of moving assets between entities to engineer increases in asset basis. If deals can be structured to increase asset basis, taxes can be cut either by reducing capital gains on sales or generating higher depreciation deductions.[135]

The problem is not that the tax code has partnership rules. Rules for partnerships and other structures are in the tax code to relieve the double taxation that faces C corporations. Partnerships allow corporations to enter into deals with other companies without an additional layer of tax acting as a hurdle. The underlying problem is that the government has imposed a double tax on C corporations to begin with, creating an incentive for the nation's biggest businesses to continually hunt for tax relief.

Partnerships were not the only business structure used in Enron tax shelters. The Apache deal used a FASIT, a business structure created by Congress in 1996.[136] FASITs are similar to REMICs, which were created by Congress in 1986. They are both flow-through, or nontaxable, vehicles used in the securitization of debt. REMICs are mainly used to securitize mortgage debt, whereas FASITs hold a broader array of debt, such as automobile loans. One indication of how complex the tax code has become is that one tax guide on the Federal Income Taxation of Securitization Transactions covers REMICs, FASITs, and similar investments and spans 1,309 pages![137] Despite the length, the authors claim it is written in "plain English" and is not just for specialists, which makes one wonder how long the specialist version would be.

In Enron's Apache deal, a FASIT structure was used to get around some punitive parts of the tax code, including the subpart F rules on inclusion of foreign income.[138] Using a foreign subsidiary, Enron created a financial structure that allowed it to deduct both interest and principal payments to a foreign lender. Enron was able to avoid the subpart F rules that would usually require some of the deal's income to be included in taxable income. The deal provided Enron with interest deductions of $242 million in 1999 and 2000, yet a big circular flow eventually sent the money back to Enron. A FASIT was a crucial middleman in the Apache deal, designed to stand between the Enron foreign subsidiary and U.S. Enron.[139]

Enron used other types of business structures as middlemen in tax shelters. A REMIC was used in Steele and a REMIC and a REIT were used in the Cochise deal.[140] A particular form of REIT, a "liquidating REIT," was exploited by a number of companies as one popular tax shelter in the 1990s.[141] But Congress did not create special interest business structures such as FASITs, REMICs, and REITs for companies such as Enron to exploit. Nonetheless, since Congress created them, financial engineers have swooped in to help every company extract what tax benefits it can from Congress's narrow tax provisions.

The alternative is to establish a single form of business organization across all industries and every type of business big or small. Indeed, that is one of the principles of a business cash-flow tax, such as the Hall–Rabushka flat tax. It would treat all business activity equally and eliminate special forms of business organization. However, the flat tax would not tax income twice because it would tax only labor income to individuals and only capital income to businesses. Thus, it would integrate individual and business taxation so that income from all types of business activity would be taxed only once. Princeton's David Bradford notes that such "uniform treatment of all businesses, whether corporate or in other form, automatically deals with a vast array of complex issues that are intractable under present law."[142] There would be no need for special pass-through entities such as REITs because all income would be taxed only once. Marginal investments would produce the same after-tax return no matter which type of business undertook them.

In addition, a single type of business structure would eliminate the ability of large companies to structure fancy deals that are tough for tax authorities and investors to figure out. Investors would not have to hunt for suspicious special purpose entities (SPE) on financial statements, which use the rules for partnerships, LLCs, and other entities. Companies would not be able to arbitrage the tax rules on different structures. Tax planning for new investments would be a breeze, and all businesses would compete on a level playing field.

DOUBLE TAXATION OF CORPORATE EQUITY

A Treasury Department report said: "Double taxation of corporate profits is the principal problem raised in connection with the corporation income tax. At the present time corporate profits are taxed first to the corporations, then again to the stockholders when they are distributed as dividends."[143] That assessment was not from the Bush Treasury but from Roy Blough, director of tax research at the Treasury Department in 1944. The double taxation of dividends was a long-festering problem that Congress has just taken the first step to fix in this year's tax bill with the reduction of dividend and capital gains tax rates.

Corporate earnings distributed as dividends face both the 35 percent corporate income tax and the individual income tax, which had a top rate of 38.6 percent before reductions in this year's tax law. The JGTRRA reduced the maximum individual rate on dividends to 15 percent through 2008.[144] Earnings retained in the corporation also face double taxation. Retentions generally increase a corporation's share price, thus imposing a capital gains tax on individuals when the stock is sold. In contrast to dividends and retained earnings, interest is deductible to the corporation and thus only taxable at the individual level. JGTRRA reduced the maximum individual tax rate on capital gains to 15 percent until 2008.

The 1944 Treasury Department report suggested some of the same dividend tax reforms that were considered this year, including a corporate deduction, an individual exclusion, and an individual credit.[145] In the 1980s, the Reagan Treasury proposed a 50 percent corporate dividend deduction as part of a major tax reform plan.[146] More recently, the Treasury Department's 1992 report on tax reform discussed various methods of corporate integration to eliminate the double taxation problem.[147] That report's recommendations were the basis of President George W. Bush's proposal for an individual dividend exclusion. The Bush plan would have allowed individuals to exclude from tax dividends on which corporate taxes had already been paid and provide shareholders capital gains relief on corporate earnings retained.[148]

This year's dividend tax reduction is not an untried or risky scheme. Indeed, nearly all major industrial countries have partly or fully alleviated the double taxation of dividends. Currently, twenty-eight of thirty countries in the OECD, including the United States with this year's tax cut, have adopted one or more methods of dividend tax relief.[149] Only Ireland and Switzerland do not relieve double taxation, but Ireland and Switzerland have substantially lower corporate tax rates than does the United States.

The economic distortions created by the current tax bias against corporate equity are briefly reviewed here. These distortions were reduced, but not eliminated, by JGTRRA. As discussed below, a cash-flow business tax would fully eliminate all these distortions. A cash-flow tax would equalize the treatment of debt and equity and remove the bias against dividend payouts. A cash-flow tax would create neutrality in corporate financial and investment decisions.[150]

Increased Cost of Capital

High dividend taxes add to the income tax code's general bias against savings and investment. Dividend taxes raise the cost of capital, which is the minimum pretax rate of return that firms must earn to proceed with a new project. Income taxes on individuals and corporations place a wedge between the after-tax return enjoyed by individual savers and the gross return on corporate investment that their money finances. The tax wedge pushes up the cost of capital and reduces the number of profitable business investments. Reduced business investment means reduced output and reduced family incomes in the long run.

Nonetheless, there are differences of opinion among economists as to exactly how dividend taxes affect the cost of capital and marginal investment decisions.[151] The traditional view contends that the dividend tax burden falls heavily on marginal investment and thus creates large economic distortions. The new view, which was developed a couple of decades ago, contends that most firms finance marginal investments through retained earnings or debt, and thus dividend taxation does not have a large marginal investment effect (retained earnings face double taxation as well, but less so than dividends). Differences in these two positions affect policy views regarding the effects of dividend taxes on stock market valuation, dividend payout, and other items. Empirical studies lean toward favoring the traditional view.[152] In a recent analysis of the administration's dividend proposal, the Congressional Budget Office assumed an effect midway between those two views.[153] However, there is general agreement that the cost of capital for investment financed by new share issues is increased by dividend taxation. As a result, heavy dividend taxation certainly hurts new, growing companies that may not have substantial retained earnings to harness for growth and need to tap equity markets.

Excessive Debt

When corporations borrow money to finance investment they are able to deduct interest payments and reduce their tax liability. By contrast, when new investment is financed by equity, dividend payments cannot be deducted. That means that a corporation needs to earn $1.54 pretax in order to pay $1 in dividends but needs to earn just $1 to pay $1 in interest. As a result, the tax system favors debt, and U.S. corporate structures have become over-leveraged.[154] There are varying empirical estimates of the extent of this distortion. A 1999 study by Roger Gordon and Young Lee found that a 10-percentage point reduction in the corporate tax rate would reduce the share of assets financed with debt by about 4 percentage points.[155] The authors conclude that this is a large distortion, given that the share of assets financed by debt has been about 19 percent historically.

Numerous studies have examined why corporate debt levels are not even higher, given the big tax advantage of debt. The reason appears to be that there are substantial nontax costs to over-leveraging. The marginal cost of debt rises with increases in debt load, which curtails debt issuance. This occurs because added debt increases the risk of financial difficulty and bankruptcy and thus affects credit ratings. Excessive debt can also restrict management flexibility, which may be suboptimal. Finally, there are nontax advantages to equity financing that offset equity's tax disadvantage.

Taxation is just one factor that affects corporate financial structure, but it is an important factor. To the extent that taxes distort corporate decisions, the costs can be large, given that corporations are the dominant business organization in the country. If tax rules favor excessive debt, the entire economy may be destabilized as more corporations are pushed into bankruptcy during recessions. As profits turn to losses during recessions, dividends can be suspended, but interest payments must be paid. Since equity provides a cushion against the ups and downs of the business cycle, penalizing it is a poor policy choice.

Excessive Retained Earnings

When a corporation earns a profit, it has the choice of retaining earnings or paying them out as dividends. Prior to the 2003 tax cut, dividends faced ordinary tax rates of up to 38.6 percent when paid out to individuals. The 2003 tax law dropped the top dividend rate to 15 percent through 2008. When earnings are retained, they also generate a layer of individual taxation when they push up the share price and create a capital gain. The 2003 law imposed a maximum capital gains tax rate of 15 percent, but gains are taxed only when realized. The effect of this deferral of tax is to further reduce the effective tax rate. Thus, retained earnings face a lower tax rate than earnings paid out as dividends, thus creating a bias toward earnings retention. However, this bias was reduced by the 2003 tax law.

The precise effects of dividend taxation on earnings payout has been subject to dozens of studies over the years but with few concrete results.[156] The traditional and new views of dividend taxation provide different perspectives on dividend incentives. But it is clear that there has been a downward trend in dividend payments by U.S. corporations. Between 1925 and 2002, the average dividend payout as a share of corporate earnings was 55 percent.[157] Today, the payout ratio hovers around 30 percent. One study found that the share of corporations paying dividends has fallen from about 90 percent in the 1950s to about 20 percent today.[158] Newer firms, in particular, avoid paying dividends. One reason is that corporations are paying out earnings in the form of share repurchases, which avoid the individual dividend tax (but do generate capital gains tax). Repurchases have accelerated since the mid-1980s.[159] Another factor to consider is that a substantial share of dividends are paid to nontaxable entities, such as pension funds.

While dividends are down, they are not out. In 2000, $142 billion of taxable dividends were reported on tax returns.[160] Economists have asked why corporations pay dividends at all, given the heavy tax penalty. The answer is that there are important nontax benefits to dividends. Dividends help reduce the "principal-agent" problem caused by the separation of ownership and control in large corporations. Retained earnings allow corporate executives to more easily make imprudent investment decisions and fund wasteful projects. If high dividend taxes cause excessive earnings retention, executives become the default investment managers for shareholders by making decisions that should be made by individual investors. Higher dividends reduce the discretionary cash that executives can pour into pet projects. Forcing executives to go to the market to raise money provides an added check on their investment strategies. The bias in favor of retentions has also put undue emphasis on stock option compensation, which may lead executives to overemphasize short-term financial results.

Dividends signal to shareholders that a corporation is earning solid profits and making good decisions. Dividends help investors accurately judge the financial health of companies because they are paid in hard cash and cannot be fudged or manipulated, as financial statement earnings can be. Financial markets are thought to reward firms that generate rising dividend payouts.[161] As Jeremy Siegel notes, before today's regulatory agencies were created, dividends were the old-fashioned—but probably superior—way to ensure that earnings were solid.[162] Indeed, nearly all corporate earnings were regularly paid out as dividends during the nineteenth century.[163]

The upshot is that dividends make good sense from a corporate governance perspective, and high dividend taxes stand in the way of this important investor protection. The problems caused by the tax bias against dividends have been recognized for decades. For example, the issue was discussed in the 1930s when the Revenue Act of 1936 imposed an "undistributed profits tax" on retained earnings to encourage a higher payout. A Treasury Department staff report from 1937 foreshadowed today's debates about corporate management:

> The earnings of a corporation belong to its stockholders; and stockholders are entitled to exercise a choice . . . with respect to the disposition of those earnings. [Tax changes] that encourage corporate managements to obtain the consent of their stockholders for capital expansion, and to give stockholders—the real owners of the corporation—a greater control over the dispositions of their earnings, this effect is altogether desirable. It has often been remarked that corporate managements are far more prudent in the use of capital funds obtained through formal financing with the aid of investment bankers than in the use of capital funds arising out of reinvested earnings.[164]

The 1930s undistributed profits tax was a bad solution to the problem and was short-lived, but it is interesting that the corporate governance problems of the income tax were noticed right from the beginning. As discussed below, replacement of the corporate income tax with a cash-flow tax would eliminate those problems by creating neutrality in corporate financial and investment decisions.

WASTEFUL FINANCIAL ENGINEERING

The tax advantage of debt has spurred corporations to design complex transactions that are treated as debt for tax purposes but as equity for financial statements.[165] In turn, financial innovations have forced Congress and the Treasury Department to add more and more tax rules to police the debt-equity distinction. Disputes between taxpayers and the government on securities that have both debt and equity characteristics have gone on for years.[166]

Corporations have long sought securities that combined the tax advantage of debt and the financial statement advantage of equity.[167] In the 1980s, the debt preference apparently helped fuel the binge in leveraged buyouts financed by high-yield bonds. In a 1990 study, Lawrence Summers and his co-authors complained about debt securities that were "equity in drag." These securities helped fuel leveraged buyouts such as the RJR-Nabisco deal and allowed companies to cut or wipe out their taxable income with interest deductions.[168]

In the 1990s, Enron and other companies discovered hybrid securities called monthly income preferred securities (MIPS), which fit within a broader category of "tiered preferred securities."[169] Under one deal, Enron set up a subsidiary, Enron Capital LLC, in the Turks and Caicos in 1993.[170] This SPE issued $214 million of preferred shares, then lent the money to Enron to be paid back over fifty years. Enron began deducting interest payments to the SPE on its tax return. But on its financial statements, Enron counted the transaction as equity called "preferred stock in subsidiary companies." Therefore, Enron reduced its taxes but was able to avoid increasing its financial statement debt, which might have hurt its credit rating.

MIPS highlight the use of noncorporate business structures in tax shelters. Enron used an LLC in this deal as an SPE to transform the character of the deal's financial flows. Partnerships and trusts can also play the role as a middleman in a tax shelter. For Enron, the SPE was not part of its consolidated tax return; thus it could deduct interest paid to it. But the SPE was part of its consolidated financial statement.[171] During the 1990s, the use of hybrid securities such as MIPS exploded. By 2002, a total of $180 billion of tiered preferred securities was outstanding, with Enron accounting for about $800 million of the total.[172]

While many commentators find MIPS and tiered preferred securities very dubious, other tax experts have argued that they are reasonable from a tax and a financial accounting perspective.[173] They argue that Enron's financial statement disclosures on these hybrids were sufficient and that credit rating agencies should have been able to figure them out.[174] Either way, a legal battle over these hybrids raged between taxpayers and the Treasury Department throughout the 1990s.[175] All in all, such hybrids have surely cost hundreds of millions of dollars in lawyer and accountant fees—pure waste from the perspective of the broader economy. The JCT notes that with MIPS Enron was pursuing self-help corporate integration, or finding a way to get around the double taxation of corporate equity.[176] That cut the cost of capital for Enron, but it would be better to cut out all the game playing and treat all companies the same by real integration under major tax reform.

MIPS are not the only type of tax shelter that preys on the debt-equity distinction. There were also "step-down preferreds," which, like MIPS, used a noncorporate middleman structure.[177] In this shelter, a U.S. corporation would set up and fund a real REIT in an agreement with a nontaxpayer, such as a foreigner, an American Indian tribe, or a company with losses. The REIT lends the corporation money, which the corporation pays back over time and deducts interest. The REIT is a flow-through entity and uses interest received to generate an income stream to the nontaxpayer. The effect is to allow the corporation to reduce taxes from an interest deduction with no offsetting taxable income reported elsewhere.

The government has typically used narrow Band-Aids to close these sorts of tax shelters. Yet Glenn Hubbard and William Gentry note, "As financial markets become even more sophisticated, the line between debt and equity for tax purposes is likely to be tested more often."[178] As long as tax distinctions, such as debt versus equity and corporate versus noncorporate, remain, companies will have incentives to keep pushing against the legal definitions. It makes more sense to end the game playing and create a lasting economic solution with fundamental tax reform.

MARGINAL TAX RATE DISTORTIONS

The federal income tax imposes different marginal effective tax rates on different economic activities. (Effective tax rates take into account statutory tax rates plus such items as depreciation deductions and tax credits.) These tax rate differences cause investment to be misallocated across industries and across types of capital equipment. Industries produce too much or too little, and they use the wrong combination of inputs to produce it. Research has found that intersectoral and interasset distortions create large deadweight losses, or inefficiency costs, under the current income tax.

The TRA86 narrowed the range of marginal effective tax rates across the economy, but it did so by broadly pushing up tax rates. To provide one example, Gravelle found that before TRA86 the tax rate on a corporate investment in electric transmission equipment was 21 percent, but the rate on communications equipment was just 4 percent.[179] After TRA86, those tax rates jumped to 36 percent and 22 percent, respectively. Thus after TRA86, corporate investment was subject to higher tax rates, and there are still substantial tax rate differences between assets and industries. Similarly, in a 2002 study, Treasury economist James Mackie estimated effective tax rates across industries and types of assets and found fairly substantial differences.[180]

A key factor causing marginal tax rates to diverge across different economic activities is depreciation. Even if broad-based income taxation—which mandates use of depreciation instead of expensing—made economic sense, it is very difficult to design depreciation schedules that accurately track the true depreciation rates of thousands of different assets in the economy. A much better idea is to expense all capital investment, as under a business cash-flow tax. That would eliminate investment distortions as it equalized marginal tax rates across industries and different types of assets.

TAX RULES ON INTERNATIONAL INVESTMENT

The tax rules on international investment are perhaps the most complex part of the corporate income tax. Most large U.S corporations have dozens, sometimes hundreds, of foreign branches and subsidiaries, and they must do a great deal of planning to minimize their global tax burden. A key source of complexity is the application of the corporate tax to the worldwide income of U.S. companies. For example, a U.S. company that owns a winery in France or an oil rig in Iraq must report that foreign income on its U.S. tax return.

An alternative method, used by about half of the major industrial nations, is the "territorial" approach, under which active foreign business income is generally not taxed.[181] Business cash-flow tax proposals, such as the Hall-Rabushka flat tax, generally adopt the territorial approach. Territorial business taxation would allow for a much simplified set of international tax rules.

Simplification is badly needed.[182] For example, profits earned abroad by majority-owned subsidiaries are generally not taxed until repatriated—taxation is deferred. But there are overlapping sets of anti-deferral rules that do tax certain types of foreign income as soon as it is earned. On top of those rules, a complex system of foreign tax credits provides relief from taxation when income is taxed in both the U.S. and a foreign country. But foreign tax credits are subject to complicated limitations. For example, firms may average out income earned in high-tax and low-tax countries in order to maximize their tax credits. But the tax code limits such cross-crediting by dividing up foreign income in nine different categories, or "baskets," that cannot be blended.

The U.S. international tax rules have been widely criticized for complexity, uncompetitiveness, and "stimulating a host of tax-motivated financial transactions," as Glenn Hubbard and James Hines put it.[183] Business groups, the ABA, and the AICPA have repeatedly called for reform.[184] For companies, the international tax rules create a very complex tax-planning climate. For example, a California computer company must perform extensive tax calculations and projections of its U.S. tax situation before deciding where in Europe, if anywhere, to build a new European facility.

Enron provides interesting illustrations of the problems with the international tax rules. Enron was particularly concerned with its situation vis-à-vis the foreign tax credit, the rules that allocate interest deductions between domestic and foreign income, and the tax disincentive to repatriating earnings from abroad. JCT's Enron report found that "the company faced the possibility of significant double taxation of its foreign source income. This potential for unmitigated double taxation was of paramount concern in Enron's international tax planning and significantly influenced the structures of Enron's international operations and transactions."[185]

Enron's aggressive global expansion strategy was one source of its tax problems. As the firm expanded abroad by buying power plants and other assets, the U.S. rules threatened it with double taxation. One strategy it used to deal with the problem was to avoid repatriating its foreign earnings. "In Enron's case, the U.S. international tax rules (particularly the interest expense allocation rules) combined with the relevant financial accounting standards, created a significant incentive for the company not to repatriate foreign earnings to the [U.S.]," the JCT concluded.[186] The tax disincentive to repatriate foreign earnings is a negative for the U.S. economy since it may reduce domestic investment or cause a smaller dividend payout to U.S. shareholders.

Some pundits zeroed in on Enron's use of hundreds of foreign affiliates as proof of tax evasion activity. But the JCT found instead that "prudent tax planning typically requires a U.S.-based multinational enterprise to use a combination of many different entities in many different jurisdictions, even if the enterprise's tax planning goals are limited to . . . generally unobjectionable ones."[187] Enron had 1,300 foreign entities in its structure, although only about 250 were used for ongoing business. An important reason for the existence of so many affiliates was Enron's inability to use foreign tax credits, which gave the company strong incentives to defer tax on foreign earnings through use of complicated affiliate structures.[188] Tax planning for a foreign project often requires creating a complex tier of foreign entities to minimize the risk of excess U.S. taxation.

The JCT also found that media reports far overcounted the number of Enron affiliates in low-tax Caribbean nations. It noted that companies that have affiliates in places that do not have corporate income taxes, such as the Cayman Islands, are not necessarily illegally or unethically avoiding taxes.[189] Overall, Enron's international tax planning did not particularly push the legal limits. Instead, it simply took part in the usual, grossly complex tax planning that most large U.S. corporations deal with under the U.S. worldwide tax system. For investors, the fact that tax rules encourage such complex business structures is an impediment to transparency and accurate assessments of firms' financial health.

The complexity of the international tax rules makes fertile ground for tax shelters, and it makes government enforcement more difficult. Congress makes it worse by greedily squeezing as much tax as it can out of foreign income under the pretense of closing tax shelters. But that greediness can backfire. For example, the 1999 Treasury Department tax shelter report noted:

> The 1986 Act included a complex set of restrictions on the use of foreign tax credits. Attempts to avoid these restrictions seem to be at the heart of certain types of tax shelters. . . . Efforts by Congress to rein in specific tax shelters often make the Code more complex, creating a vicious cycle. The

legislative remedies themselves create the complexity that the next generation of tax shelters exploits.[190]

The vicious cycle of international tax complexity can be ended by fundamental tax
reform. A territorial cash-flow tax would greatly simplify business planning by eliminating most international tax rules.[191] There would be no need for foreign tax credits and numerous other parts of the international tax apparatus. A territorial tax
would allow U.S. businesses to compete in foreign markets without the burdens imposed by the U.S. tax code. The United States would become an excellent location
for multinational corporate headquarters because foreign affiliates could repatriate
their profits free of U.S. tax.[192] The current disincentive for repatriation—a key tax-
planning factor for Enron—would be eliminated. Finally, capital expensing under a
consumption-based cash-flow tax would create strong incentives for domestic and
foreign companies to locate investment in the United States.

REPEAL THE CORPORATE INCOME TAX

The corporate income tax has survived for more than ninety years, despite having
little support in economic theory.[193] Indeed, most economists agree that the cost
of the corporate income tax in terms of distortions created is very high.[194] Conservative economists have tended to favor a consumption-based tax system, which
has no place for a corporate tax on net income. Liberal economists have tended to
favor the Haig-Simons ideal of broad-based income taxation, but that ideal does
not require a corporate income tax either. The Haig-Simons approach could be
implemented by imposing a broad tax on capital income at the individual level. In
his 1977 classic, *Blueprints for Basic Tax Reform*, Bradford sketched out both a consumption tax and a broad-based income tax model for fundamental reform, and
neither included a tax on corporations.[195]

With no compelling economic rationale, then Treasury Secretary O'Neill and
others have suggested repealing of the corporate income tax. But there are some administrative and political hurdles to corporate tax repeal. The politics are easy to
understand. Corporations provide a concentrated pool of cash that government can
tap to fill its coffers—governments tax corporations "because that is where the
money is." Trillions of dollars of revenue flow through U.S. corporations each year,
providing an irresistible target for politicians. Indeed, the country adopted the corporate income tax in 1909, not because of any economic principle, but mainly because of the anti-big-business political atmosphere at the time.

Corporations are an easy target because they do not vote, and corporate taxes
are invisible to individuals. Corporate taxes get passed along to consumers, workers, and investors, but those individuals do not observe the burden that falls on
them.[196] Tax invisibility is beneficial to politicians, but it creates a basic dishonesty

in democratic government. It denies individuals the ability to make informed and efficient choices since government spending appears to be partly "free." If $150 billion of corporate taxes is invisible, citizens will likely support a large government.

Of course, the ability to fuel a bigger government by invisible corporate taxation is appealing for some on the political left. Nonetheless, some liberal economists have supported corporate tax repeal as part of an overall tax reform package. One problem they see is that the corporate tax does not allow the fine-tuning of income redistribution that they favor. Recipients of corporate income include both low-income retirees and high-income investors, but they will both be hit by the same 35 percent corporate tax rate.[197] Thus, some advocates of progressive taxation might support corporate tax repeal with the substitution of more individual taxation of capital income (but that is still an inferior option to moving to a consumption-based system).[198]

Aside from politics, there are some administrative hurdles to consider in repealing the corporate tax. The corporate income tax is supported as a backstop to individual taxation of capital income. Corporations are essentially withholding agents for capital income that flows through to individuals. Under the Haig-Simons ideal, businesses would not need to be taxed if all capital income were taxed on an accrual basis at the individual level. But that is extremely impractical (in addition to being bad economic policy). Instead, the current income tax system settled on using corporations as pre-collectors of income taxes. That structure prevents individuals from accumulating income within corporations tax-free, which would violate accrual income tax theory. Also, corporations are used to prevent evasion since they generate information about dividends and interest paid out.

However, there would be no need for a corporate-level tax under some proposals for consumption-based tax reform. "Savings-exempt" or "consumed-income" tax proposals would apply a comprehensive tax at the individual level without need for a business-level tax. One model is the saving-deferred cash-flow tax proposal developed by Norman Ture at the Institute for Research on the Economics of Taxation.[199] This proposal would replace the individual and corporate income taxes with a flat rate individual tax on a base of income less net savings. Individuals would defer tax on saving by deducting saving (and debt repayments) from taxable income but would include withdrawals from savings (and borrowing) in their tax base. The result would be that business earnings would be taxed at the individual level when not reinvested by individuals. A similar proposal is the model cash-flow consumption tax included in *Blueprints for Basic Tax Reform*. The *Blueprints* model would eliminate the corporate-level tax and allow individuals a choice of two treatments for saving.[200] Saving in qualified accounts would be deducted upfront with withdrawals taxed later, like regular IRAs. Alternately, saving could be made from after-tax earnings with the returns received tax-free, like Roth IRAs.

Corporate tax repeal would involve some tricky issues with regard to international investment. As one public finance scholar notes, "One reason most countries tax corporate profits is because most countries tax corporate profits."[201] Cross-border investments by multinational corporations have caused tax systems to become entangled with one another. For example, corporate tax repeal could result in the federal government ceding tax revenue to foreign governments because, if the United States did not tax the U.S. profits of foreign companies, other countries would have an incentive to do so. Suppose a Japanese car company earns $100 million in its U.S. subsidiary and pays $35 million in U.S. corporate tax. When the company filed its Japanese corporate tax return, it would receive a foreign tax credit, which is designed to prevent taxation of the same income in both countries. But if the United States repealed its corporate tax, Japan's worldwide system would still tax the U.S. profits, but no tax credit would be provided. The end result might be that the car company paid tax on $100 million of U.S. profits to the Japanese government but paid no tax to the U.S. government.

However, a number of factors would mitigate that possible problem. The Japanese government might face pressure to reduce taxes on Japanese firms' U.S. profits so as not to put those firms at a competitive disadvantage in the U.S. market. The firms would be at a disadvantage to firms headquartered in countries that have "territorial" tax systems, which would not tax U.S.-source profits.[202] One step the United States could take with corporate tax repeal would be to place a withholding tax on profits when paid to parent companies of foreign firms. That would generate revenues to the U.S. government and would not necessarily impose higher overall taxes on companies operating here, since they would get a credit for the withholding tax on their home-country tax return.

Federal corporate tax repeal may have a precursor at the state level. The share of state tax revenues coming from corporate income taxes has fallen from more than 9 percent to about 6 percent in the past two decades.[203] State-level tax competition has been intense as mobile corporations organize their activities to minimize their state tax payments. States have responded with cuts and various tax base changes.[204] State corporate tax competition has also led to tax complexity and litigation as companies spanning numerous states have had to fight each state tax authority over the proper amount owed. As a result, a growing number of economists are supporting state corporate tax repeal because the tax is highly inefficient and collects little revenue. The liberal contributing editor of *State Tax Notes*, David Brunori, came out for state corporate tax repeal last year because the state tax "consumes an inordinate amount of intellectual firepower and economic resources in terms of planning, compliance, and administration."[205]

Similar pressures and inefficiencies are growing under the federal corporate income tax as international tax competition increases. Revenues from the corporate income tax have fallen from more than 30 percent of federal revenues in the early 1950s to just 8 percent today.[206] As a highly inefficient tax that collects only a small fraction of federal revenue, the corporate income tax is a high-priority tax for Congress to repeal.

OR REPLACE THE CORPORATE INCOME TAX
WITH A BUSINESS CASH-FLOW TAX

If a corporate-level tax is retained, reforms should focus on reducing the rate and creating a transparent and uniform base to maximize efficiency and minimize tax sheltering. One idea is to retain an income tax but eliminate some of the inconsistencies. For example, the corporate tax could be "integrated" with the individual tax to reduce the disparities between debt and equity and between corporate and noncorporate businesses. In 1992, the Treasury Department issued a major study on corporate tax reform options that included various integration proposals to eliminate the double taxation of corporate equity.[207] One proposal was to exempt dividends from individual taxation, which also formed the basis of President Bush's dividend proposal in 2004.

A more ambitious proposal in the 1992 report was for a comprehensive business income tax (CBIT). The idea behind the CBIT was to tax capital income only once—at the business level. Neither dividends nor interest would be deductible by businesses. But individual taxes on interest, dividends, and capital gains would be repealed. All businesses (corporate and noncorporate) would be taxed under the same rules. The CBIT would equalize taxes on corporate and noncorporate businesses, equalize taxes on interest and dividends, eliminate the lock-in distortion of capital gains, and remove the bias against dividend payouts.

Although such a tax reform would be far-reaching, key distortions would remain. The CBIT would retain core problems of income-based taxation, particularly capitalization, inflation-caused distortions, and a bias against savings and investment. Those remaining distortions could be eliminated by replacing the corporate tax with a cash-flow tax. That would be like taking the CBIT reforms and adding capital expensing (rather than depreciation) and cash accounting (rather than accrual accounting).

Substituting a cash-flow tax for the corporate income tax has been discussed by economists for years. Fundamental reform along these lines would "dramatically reduce the incentives for tax planning," concluded Glenn Hubbard and William Gentry.[208] A cash-flow tax would "make it easy to write rules that hold to a minimum tax distortions in financial and business affairs," concluded Bradford.[209] Recent scandals and the growing uncompetitiveness of the current corporate tax make now an excellent time for Congress to take a fresh look at the idea.

A cash-flow tax would be imposed on net cash flows of businesses, not net income. Net cash flow is calculated as the receipts from the sale of goods and services less current and capital expenses. Financial flows such as interest income and interest expense would be disregarded.[210] Accrual accounting under the income tax would be replaced with simpler cash accounting. Businesses would include receipts when cash is received and deduct materials, inventories, equipment, and structures when purchased. The cost of both a $1 pencil and $10 million machine would be deducted immediately.

Various proposals for cash-flow taxes have differed with regard to whether employee compensation would be deductible. If compensation deductions were disallowed, the tax would be a value-added tax (VAT). Such a tax would capture the value added by both labor and capital at the business level. The broad base of a VAT would need only a low tax rate to raise the same amount of revenue as the current corporate tax. For example, an 11-percent VAT formed part of the "USA" tax proposal of former Sen. Sam Nunn (D-GA) and Sen. Pete Domenici (R-N.M.).[211] A recent estimate suggests that a VAT would need a rate of between 5 and 7 percent to replace the revenue generated by the corporate income tax.[212]

However, that raises a key problem with a VAT—it would be a money machine for the government because the tax base is so broad. While the rate might start out low, each rate increase would sound modest yet would raise a huge amount of fresh government revenue. That problem would be exacerbated because VATs, like all business-level taxes, could be hidden from the view of individuals, thus tempting politicians to continue raising the rate over time. Since individuals ultimately bear all tax burdens, taxes should be visible to them so they can best judge how big the government ought to be. As a general rule, tax reforms should keep the bulk of tax collections at the individual level to promote visibility and frugality in government.

The flat tax proposed by Robert Hall and Alvin Rabushka of the Hoover Institution is structured to reap the efficiency benefits of a cash-flow business tax while keeping the bulk of taxes visible and payable by individuals.[213] Versions of the Hall-Rabushka plan were proposed by former House majority leader Armey and by former presidential candidate Steve Forbes. Under the Hall-Rabushka plan, individuals would be taxed on wages and pension benefits at a flat 19 percent, with large basic exemptions provided. Individuals would not be taxed on interest, dividends, or capital gains. Businesses would pay a 19 percent tax on receipts from sales of goods and services less wages and purchases of materials, equipment, buildings, and other expenses.[214] Businesses would disregard interest, dividends, and capital gains. For example, interest would not be deductible, nor would it be taxable. This exclusion of financial flows means that the flat tax has a real, or "R base," as did the Treasury's CBIT.[215] (Alternately, a cash-flow tax could have an R+F base—real plus financial—where firms take into account all flows of cash, other than to their own shareholders, when calculating their tax base.)[216]

The flat-tax business structure would be similar to the CBIT except businesses would expense capital purchases rather than depreciate them. It is that difference that makes the CBIT an "income tax," and the Hall-Rabushka tax a "consumption-based tax." Consider the basic economic formulation: income = consumption + investment. Given that, a tax on income with a full deduction for investment is said to be a consumption-based tax. Some observers conclude from this that a cash-flow tax would not tax business profits or capital income at all. That is not correct; the issue is more tricky.

It turns out that business expensing exempts only the "normal" risk-free rate of return (also called the return to waiting) but fully taxes "above-normal" returns (also called "economic rents" or "inframarginal returns").[217] The normal risk-free rate of return is usually measured by the Treasury bill interest rate. "Above-normal" returns are profits made through monopoly profits, unexpected windfalls, and other unique factors. Because it is thought that above-normal returns account for most of total business profits, a cash-flow tax with expensing would continue to tax most business profits.[218]

However, while a cash-flow tax would continue to tax most business profits, it would do so much more efficiently. That is because marginal investments yielding the normal return would not be taxed. In present value terms, the upfront tax benefit of expensing fully offsets future tax payments on normal returns. As a result, the tax would not distort marginal investment choices, thus spurring greater capital formation.[219] Investment decisions would not be distorted by inflation, depreciation, or other factors that affect marginal effective tax rates under the income tax.

Economists generally agree that a business cash-flow tax would be simpler and more efficient than the corporate income tax. However, there are various implementation concerns that would need to be ironed out with the adoption of a cash-flow business tax:

A cash-flow tax would close a huge array of tax shelters, but it may open some new ones. One point of trouble for a cash-flow tax with an R base is the separation of financial from nonfinancial flows, which would create a source of tax avoidance opportunities. For example, businesses would try to characterize normal sales receipts as interest in order to exclude them from taxation. Some tax lawyers have explored more complex financial strategies that might develop to exploit the sharp divide between financial and nonfinancial.[220] One solution would be to adopt an R+F-base cash-flow tax, rather than the R-base tax of the Hall-Rabushka model.[221]

A number of tax avoidance problems under the current tax system would continue to be problems under some cash-flow taxes. An example is transfer pricing by multinational corporations. That refers to the shifting of profits from high-tax to low-tax countries using the prices of goods, services, and intangibles traded between corporations and their subsidiaries. Transfer pricing would continue to be a problem under a Hall-Rabushka cash-flow tax, although it would be eliminated under cash-flow taxes that are "border adjustable."[222]

Note that tax reform is designed to cut marginal tax rates, which in itself would reduce tax avoidance. For example, the Hall-Rabushka flat tax would have a broad tax base and no tax credits, thus allowing for lower rates than currently. For example, an analysis of all nonfinancial corporations for the period 1998 to 1992 found that the Hall-Rabushka tax at 19 percent would have raised about the same revenue as the current corporate income tax.[223] With a rate only about half of the current 35 percent corporate rate, the incentive to engage in all forms of tax avoidance, such as transfer pricing, would be greatly reduced.

Businesses with net operating losses create a challenge for any tax system.[224] In theory, losses should be refundable to create fair and symmetrical treatment between profit and loss firms and between firms with fluctuating and stable profit patterns. The current income tax allows losses to be carried backward two years and forward twenty years to offset profits, but without interest. Limitations on losses invite tax avoidance efforts because businesses will try to move losses to profit-making firms. A related issue is whether affiliated entities should file as consolidated units. Consolidation is advantageous since it allows business units to offset profits and losses. To deal with these issues, the Hall-Rabushka plan would allow unlimited carryforward of losses with interest.[225] That favorable treatment would reduce tax avoidance efforts and retain strong incentives for capital investment by companies with losses.

Financial businesses, such as banks and insurance companies, would require special rules under any tax reform plan, just as they do under the current income tax. Special rules would be needed under an R-based cash-flow tax because it does not include financial flows, such as interest, in the tax base. One solution would be to simply exclude financial businesses under a new consumption-based tax system, as is the case under most state retail sales taxes and foreign VATs.[226] Another option would be to tax financial businesses on an R+F cash-flow tax basis.[227]

A tax reform challenge will be to create transition rules to move from the old tax system to the new one.[228] A key issue is treatment of the existing tax basis in assets (that portion of the asset's cost not yet recovered by depreciation deductions). Trillions of dollars of machines and buildings would be only partially written off at the time of switching to a new tax system. Not allowing the remaining deductions on this old capital would impose large losses on owners. On the other hand, allowing full and immediate deduction for basis in old assets would involve a large short-term government revenue loss. Ultimately, creating some middle-ground rules for basis and other transition items is essential to generating support for reform.[229] Transition relief is a hurdle, but given that a new tax system might last even longer than the current one has lasted, it is worth the trouble.

CONCLUSION

The flawed structure of the corporate income tax is a key driver of inefficient and wasteful business activities. The income tax distorts corporate investment and financial choices, and its complexity and inconsistency stimulate an aggressive pursuit of elaborate tax shelters.

Three fundamental flaws of the corporate income tax would be addressed by the adoption of a low-rate cash-flow tax. First, a lower corporate tax rate would reduce wasteful tax-sheltering activities, mitigate the economic distortions caused by business taxation, and respond to the rising global competition faced by U.S. businesses.

Second, a business cash-flow tax would eliminate key flaws intrinsic to the income tax, particularly capitalization and capital gains taxation. These features of the income tax create complexities and distortions that seem to get worse over time. Enron and other companies zeroed in on these weaknesses and exploited them with elaborate tax shelters. A business cash-flow tax would eliminate capital gains taxation and would substitute expensing for capitalization to create simple and efficient treatment of business capital investment.

Third, the great number of gratuitous inconsistencies in the corporate income tax would be reduced or eliminated under a cash-flow tax. All businesses would be treated equally, the tax treatment of corporate financing would be neutral between debt and equity, and there would be little incentive or ability of companies to create complex transactions to avoid tax.

Today's combination of corporate management problems and rising global competitive pressures make this an excellent time to fundamentally rethink U.S. business taxation. A cash-flow tax holds out hope of dramatically reducing the complexity, distortions, and scandals that mark the current corporate tax system.

NOTES

1. Congressional Budget Office, "An Analysis of the President's Budgetary Proposals for FY2004," March 2003, p. 36.

2. Wal-Mart Stores Inc., Form 10-K as filed with the SEC. The "current" income tax expense reported on financial statements often differs, sometimes substantially, from actual liability reported on the 1120 tax return filed with the Internal Revenue Service. Wal-Mart's federal tax rate on U.S. income was 28.7 percent in 2001 and 34.7 percent in 2000.

3. Estimates of incidence differ depending on such factors as the length of the time period considered and the international openness of the economy. A good survey is John Whalley, "The Incidence of the Corporate Tax Revisited," Canadian Department of Finance, Technical Committee Working Paper no. 97-7, October 1997.

4. Gravelle, Jane, *The Economic Effects of Taxing Capital Income,*

5. Scholes, Myron and Mark Wolfson, "The Role of Tax Rules in the Recent Restructuring of U.S. Corporations," *Tax Policy and the Economy* 5, Cambridge: National Bureau of Economic Research and MIT Press, 1991, p. 2.

6. Scholes and Wolfson, "Role of Tax Rules," p. 24.

7. KPMG, "Corporate Tax Rate Survey," January 2003, www.in.kpmg.com/pdf/2003CorporateTaxSurveyFINAL.pdf.

8. For a description, see Joint Committee on Taxation (JCT), "Summary of Conference Agreement on H.R. 2., the Jobs and Growth Tax Relief Reconciliation Act of 2003," JCS-54-03, May 22, 2003.

9. JCT, "Report of Investigation of Enron Corporation and Related Entities Regarding Federal Tax and Compensation Issues, and Policy Recommendations," Vol. 1, JCS-3-03, February 2003.

10. JCT, "Report of Investigation of Enron," p. 6.

11. Internal Revenue Service, *Statistics of Income Bulletin,* Washington, D.C.: IRS, summer 2002, table 13. This is the total number of corporate returns, excluding S corporation returns.

12. This is the 2003 page count for the CCH "Standard Federal Tax Reporter," which includes the tax code, tax regulations, and various IRS rulings. See www.cch.com/wbot2003. For the business share of the burden, see Scott Moody, "The Cost of Complying with the U.S. Federal Income Tax," Tax Foundation, November 2000.

13. JCT, "Report of Investigation of Enron Corporation," p. 16.

14. For example, the decision to headquarter Daimler-Chrysler in Germany as opposed to the United States was apparently partly motivated by tax considerations. See discussion in Chris Edwards and Veronique de Rugy, "International Tax Competition: A 21st-Century Restraint on Government," Cato Policy Analysis no. 431, April 12, 2002.

15. U.S. Department of the Treasury (U.S. Treasury), "The Problem of Corporate Tax Shelters: Discussion, Analysis, and Legislative Proposals," July 1999, p. 17, 27, 30.

16. Berry, John, "Divided on Derivatives," *Washington Post,* March 6, 2003, p. E1.

17. Simpson, Glenn R., "Derivatives Traders, IRS May Be near a Truce," *Wall Street Journal,* June 10, 2003, p. C1.

18. See Aaron, Henry and Harvey Galper, *Assessing Tax Reform,* Washington, D.C.: Brookings Institution, 1985. Aaron and Galper propose an "R+F-based" cash-flow tax.

19. U.S. Treasury, "The Problem of Corporate Tax Shelters," p. 19, 55, 58.

20. The 50 percent rate enacted in 1981 was effective for 1982. The 28 percent rate enacted in 1986 was effective for 1988.

21. U.S. Treasury, "The Problem of Corporate Tax Shelters," p. vi, 23.

22. JCT, "Report of Investigation of Enron Corporation," p. 107.

23. U.S. Treasury, "The Problem of Corporate Tax Shelters," p. v.

24. U.S. Treasury, "The Problem of Corporate Tax Shelters," p. iv.

25. For example, in comparing differences in amounts perceived as wed by the IRS and large corporations, the GAO found that "the difference is substantial and, in large part, attributable to ambiguity and complexity in tax law." GAO, "Reducing the Tax Gap," GAO/GGD-95-157, June 1995, p. 4.

26. See a summary in Steven Toscher and Charles Rettig, "A Once in a Lifetime Opportunity: The Tax Shelter Controversy Continues," 2002, www.taxlitigator.com.

27. GAO, "Reducing the Tax Gap," p. 4.

28. For example, in 1992, the IRS estimated that after audit, large corporations owed $142 billion in taxes, but corporations themselves figured they owed just $118 billion. See GAO, "Reducing the Tax Gap," p. 4.

29. Bankman, Joseph, "Bankman Examines the New Market in Corporate Tax Shelters," *Tax Notes,* June 21, 1999, p. 1775.

30. Quoted in Peter Behr, "Enron Skirted Taxes Via Executive Pay Plan," *Washington Post,* February 14, 2003, p. E1.

31. U.S. Treasury, "The Problem of Corporate Tax Shelters," p. 48.

32. Bankman, "New Market in Corporate Tax Shelters," p. 1778, 1787.

33. U.S. Treasury, "The Problem of Corporate Tax Shelters," p. 46.

34. U.S. Treasury, "The Problem of Corporate Tax Shelters," p. v.

35. See related comments of Lester Ezrati of the Tax Executives Institute, "Statement before the U.S. Senate Committee on Finance Hearing on The Clinton Administration's Proposals relating to Corporate Tax Shelters," April 27, 1999.

36. U.S. Treasury, "The Problem of Corporate Tax Shelters," p.6, 9.

37. The recently passed tax law, which reduced individual tax rates on dividend income, will partly solve this problem.

38. Cited in U.S. Treasury, "The Problem of Corporate Tax Shelters," p. xiv.

39. Johnston, David Cay, "Help for Bad Times Now Helps Rich," *New York Times*, April 1, 2003, p. C1.

40. Bankman notes that many attorneys believe the IRS is currently far outgunned on corporate shelters. Bankman, "New Market in Corporate Tax Shelters," p. 1786.

41. For a good summary of corporate tax sheltering, see Bankman, "New Market in Corporate Tax Shelters."

42. U.S. Treasury, "The Problem of Corporate Tax Shelters," p. 7, 14.

43. U.S. Treasury, "The Problem of Corporate Tax Shelters," p. 28.

44. KPMG, "Corporate Tax Rate Survey."

45. KPMG, "Corporate Tax Rate Survey."

46. For a discussion of cross-border investment, see Edwards and de Rugy, "International Tax Competition."

47. See Hines, James, ed., *International Taxation and Multinational Activity*, Chicago: University of Chicago Press, 2001. See also James Hines, "Lessons from Behavioral Responses to International Taxation," *National Tax Journal*, June 1999, p. 305.

48. Nagl, Hans, "Infineon CEO Mulls Moving HQ, Plans Job Cuts," Reuters, April 29, 2003.

49. For a brief survey of the issue, see Eric Engen and Kevin Hassett, "Does the U.S. Corporate Tax Have a Future?" *Tax Notes*, 30th anniv. ed., 2002.

50. For a discussion, see Veronique de Rugy, "Runaway Corporations: Political Band-Aids vs. Long-Term Solutions," Cato Tax & Budget Bulletin no. 9, July 2002.

51. Ingersoll-Rand reincorporated in Bermuda in 2001. Stanley Works ultimately backed down on its plan to reincorporate abroad.

52. U.S. Treasury, "Corporate Inversion Transactions: Tax Policy Implications," May 2002, p. 21.

53. Thorndike, Joseph, "Civilization at a Discount: The Morality of Tax Avoidance," *Tax Notes*, April 29, 2002. See also W. Elliot Brownlee, *Federal Taxation in America: A Short History*, Cambridge: Cambridge University Press, 1996, p. 72–82.

54. Ibid.

55. Thorndike, Joseph, "Historical Perspective: Wartime Tax Legislation and the Politics of Policymaking," Tax History Project at Tax Analysts, 2002, p. 5. www.taxhistory.org/Articles/wartaxes.htm.

56. Boskin, Michael, "A Framework for the Tax Reform Debate," in Michael Boskin, ed., *Frontiers of Tax Reform*, Stanford, Calif.: Hoover Institution Press, 1996, p. 14. See also Gravelle, *The Economic Effects of Taxing Capital Income*, p. 30.

57. For a summary of the early law, see Roy G. Blakey, "The Federal Income Tax," U.S. Treasury, September 20, 1934, sec. I, www.taxhistory.org.

58. The income tax law of 1894 was struck down in *Pollock v. Farmers' Loan and Trust Company*, 157 U.S. 429 (1895).

59. It is often stated that the corporate business form exists only because of government "privileges." But that view has been challenged. For example, see Norman Barry, "The Theory of the Corporation," *Ideas on Liberty* 53, no. 3, March 2003.

60. Brownlee, *Federal Taxation in America*, p. 36–46.

61. Webber, Carolyn and Aaron Wildavsky, *A History of Taxation and Expenditure in the Western World,* New York: Simon and Schuster, 1986, p. 420.

62. Blakey, "The Federal Income Tax," sec. I.

63. Blakey, "The Federal Income Tax,"sec. VIII.

64. For further discussion, see Art Hall, "The Concept of Income Revisited: An Investigation into the Double Taxation of Saving," Tax Foundation, February 1997.

65. For a further discussion, see Chris Edwards, "Simplifying Federal Taxes: The Advantages of Consumption-Based Taxation," Cato Institute Policy Analysis no. 416, October 17, 2001.

66. Bradford, David, *Untangling the Income Tax,* Cambridge, Mass.: Harvard University Press, 1999, p. 313.

67. For a discussion of the basic problems with income taxation, see Bradford, *Untangling the Income Tax*. See also David Bradford, *Blueprints for Basic Tax Reform*, 2nd ed., Arlington, Va.: Tax Analysts, 1984, p. 22.

68. Note that the measure of net income for tax and GAAP can be quite different. For example, depreciation for tax purposes is generally accelerated compared to GAAP depreciation.

69. Johnson, Calvin, "Using GAAP Instead of Tax Accounting Is a Bad Idea," *Tax Notes*, April 19, 1999. Johnson calls GAAP accounting "a pretty sick puppy."

70. For a discussion of cash-flow vs. income taxes, see Jack Mintz and Jesus Seade, "Cash Flow or Income? The Choice of Base for Company Taxation," *World Bank Observer*, July 1991, p. 180.

71. Most cash-flow tax proposals have an "R base" as they consider just real, not financial, transactions. An R+F cash-flow tax base has been considered for the taxation of financial institutions under a consumption-based tax.

72. Brownlee, *Federal Taxation in America,* p. 64.

73. Aaron and Galper, *Assessing Tax Reform*. The authors call their plan a "cash-flow income tax." The plan would combine a personal consumed-income tax, a business cash-flow tax, and taxation of estates and gifts.

74. Hall, Robert and Alvin Rabushka, *The Flat Tax*, 2nd ed., Stanford, Calif.: Hoover Institution Press, 1995.

75. Hall and Rabushka, *The Flat Tax,* p. 47. For another good discussion of cash-flow business taxation from the 1980s, see Mervyn King, "The Cash Flow Corporate Income Tax," National Bureau of Economic Research (NBER) Working Paper no. 1993, August 1986.

76. These distortions are discussed in Aaron and Galper, *Assessing Tax Reform*.

77. There has also been substantial interest abroad in cash-flow business taxation. For example, the New Zealand Treasury has produced a number of studies on the issue. A good recent study is Peter Wilson, "An Analysis of a Cash Flow Tax for Small Business," New Zealand Treasury, Working Paper no. 02/27, December 2002.

78. U.S. Treasury, "The Problem of Corporate Tax Shelters," p. 113.

79. U.S. Treasury, "The Problem of Corporate Tax Shelters," p. 16.

80. Bankman, "New Market in Corporate Tax Shelters," p. 1780.

81. JCT, "Report of Investigation of Enron Corporation," p. 346.

82. Weisbach, David, comments at the Invitational Conference on Tax Law Simplification, sponsored by the ABA, AICPAs, and the Tax Executives Institute, Washington, D.C., December 4, 2001.

83. Weisbach, Comments.

84. IRS National Taxpayer Advocate, "FY2002 Annual Report to Congress," December 2002, p. 288, 290. The IRS's aggressive position grew out of the 1992 INDOPCO case. See also Lawrence Lokken, "Capitalization: Complexity in Simplicity," *Tax Notes*, May 28, 2001.

85. Weisbach, Comments.

86. Quoted in JCT, *Study of the Overall State of the Federal Tax System and Recommendations for Simplification,* Washington: Government Printing Office, April 2001, JCS-3-01, vol. 2, p. 324.

87. Olson, Pamela, comments concerning tax code section 263A at the "Invitational Conference on Tax Law Simplification."

88. Under the Tax Reform Act of 1986, businesses depreciate tangible property under the Modified Accelerated Cost Recovery System (MACRS), sec. 168 of the tax code, which determines recovery periods, placed-in-service rules, and depreciation methods.

89. Neubig, Tom and Stephen Rhody, "21st Century Distortions from 1950s Depreciation Class Lives," *Tax Notes*, May 29, 2000. They note that the current classification system is partly based on guideline lives from a 1959 Treasury study.

90. JCT, "Report of Investigation of Enron Corporation," p. 165, 173, 174.

91. JCT, "Report of Investigation of Enron Corporation," p. 181.

92. JCT, "Report of Investigation of Enron Corporation," p. 221, 234.

93. Blough, Roy, "Postwar Tax Structure: Capital Gains Tax," staff memo, U.S. Treasury, Division of Tax Research, December 5, 1944. www.taxhistory.org.

94. The New York State Bar Association, cited in U.S. Treasury, "The Problem of Corporate Tax Shelters," p. 10.

95. JCT, *Study of the Overall State of the Federal Tax System,* vol. 2, p. 37.

96. For a discussion, see JCT, "Tax Treatment of Capital Gains and Losses," JCS-4-97, March 12, 1997, p. 7. Prior to 1986, the corporate capital gains rate was generally less than the ordinary rate.

97. U.S. Treasury, "The Problem of Corporate Tax Shelters," p. 36.

98. Lang, Mark, Edwards Maydew, and Douglas Shackelford, "Bringing Down the Other Berlin Wall: Germany's Repeal of the Corporate Capital Gains Tax," January 2001, p. 11. In the reform, Germany also eliminated its dividend imputation system and went to a 50-percent dividend exclusion for individuals.

99. Lodin, Sven-Olof, "The Competitiveness of EU Tax Systems," International Bureau of Fiscal Documentation, *European Taxation*, May 2001, p. 169.

100. Lang, Maydew, and Shackelford, "Bringing Down the Other Berlin Wall," p. 10. Example recalculated at today's share price.

101. Lang, Maydew, and Shackelford, "Bringing Down the Other Berlin Wall," p. 6.

102. Browning, E. S., "Hybrid Stock Issue Skirts Tax, Securities Laws," *Tax Notes*, April 8, 1996, p. 223.

103. "PEPS" stands for premium equity participating securities.

104. Sheppard, Lee, "Rethinking DECS, and New Ways to Carve Out Debt," *Tax Notes*, April 19, 1999, p. 347.

105. Bankman, "New Market in Corporate Tax Shelters," p. 1777. This is a very brief sketch of Bankman's "High-Basis Low-Value" example.

106. JCT, "Report of Investigation of Enron Corporation," p. 118, 128.

107. JCT, "Report of Investigation of Enron Corporation," p. 124.

108. JCT, "Report of Investigation of Enron Corporation," p. 146.

109. JCT, "Report of Investigation of Enron Corporation," p. 136.

110. JCT, "Report of Investigation of Enron Corporation," p. 159.

111. For example, see JCT, "Report of Investigation of Enron Corporation," p. 142.

112. JCT, "Report of Investigation of Enron Corporation," p. 189, 201.

113. Geier, Deborah, "A Proposal for Taxing Corporate Reorganizations," *Tax Notes,* February 10, 1997, p. 801.

114. Lang, Maydew, and Shackelford, "Bringing Down the Other Berlin Wall,"p. 1.

115. Bulow, Jeremy, Lawrence Summers, and Victoria Summers, "Distinguishing Debt from Equity in the Junk Bond Era," in John Shoven and Joel Waldfogel, eds., *Debt, Taxes, and Corporate Restructuring,* Washington, D.C.: Brookings Institution, 1990, p. 135.

116. U.S. Treasury, "The Problem of Corporate Tax Shelters," p. 26, 31.

117. Sloan, Allan, "GM Finds a Hole in the Tax Code Big Enough to Drive Billions Through," *Washington Post,* January 28, 1997, p. C3; and Allan Sloan, "Northrop Grumman Deal Scores a Direct Hit on Taxes," *Washington Post,* February 27, 1996, p C3.

118. For an overview, see Patrick Gaughan, *Mergers, Acquisitions, and Corporate Restructurings,* 3rd ed., New York: John Wiley & Sons, 2002. See also Merle Erickson, "The Effect of Taxes on the Structure of Corporate Acquisitions," *Journal of Accounting Research* 36, autumn 1998, p. 279–298.

119. Sloan, Allan, "GM Follows Zero-Percent Financing With a Zero-Tax Sale of DirecTV," *Washington Post,* November 6, 2001, p. E3. Sloan describes a "reverse Morris Trust" deal.

120. Maydew, Gary, *Small Business Taxation,* 2nd ed., Chicago: CCH, 1997.

121. The case was *Plains Petroleum Co. and Subsidiaries v. Commissioner,* T.C. Memo 1999-241, 1999, cited in Vivian Hoard, "Corporate Tax Shelters: Is Every Generation Doomed to Repeat History?" *Tax Practice & Procedure,* June–July 2000, p. 24.

122. Sullivan, Martin, "Flat Taxes and Consumption Taxes: A Guide to the Debate," American Institute of Certified Public Accountants, December 1995, p. 7, 99. For a discussion of M&A issues under a flat tax, see David Weisbach, "Ironing Out the Flat Tax," John M. Olin Law & Economics Working Paper no. 79, University of Chicago, August 1999, p. 36–44.

123. For a further description of rules that might apply under a cash-flow business tax, see Alliance USA, "USA Tax System," January 24, 1995, p. 275–284. This tax reform group was chaired by Paul O'Neill and Robert Lutz.

124. However, determining the best treatment of current law asset basis during transition to a new tax system is a difficult problem. For a discussion of transition issues, see Alliance USA, "USA Tax System," p. 55.

125. Gravelle, *The Economic Effects of Taxing Capital Income,* p. 90.

126. For a summary of the many estimates of the efficiency costs of the corporate income tax, see John Whalley, "Efficiency Considerations in Business Tax Reform," Canadian Department of Finance, Technical Committee, October 1997.

127. Whalley, "Efficiency Considerations in Business Tax Reform," p. 13.

128. Gravelle, *The Economic Effects of Taxing Capital Income,* p. 52. "Effective" tax rates take into account statutory rates and other tax items such as depreciation deductions.

129. U.S. Treasury, *Integration of the Individual and Corporate Tax Systems: Taxing Business Income Once,* Washington, D.C.: Government Printing Office, January 1992, p. v.

130. For a discussion, see John Lee, "Choice of Small Business Tax Entity: Facts and Fictions," *Tax Notes,* April 17, 2000, p. 417.

131. Scholes and Wolfson, "Role of Tax Rules," p. 5.

132. IRS, "SOI Bulletin," spring 2002, p. 297.

133. The Treasury's "check-the-box" regulations in 1996 simplified the tax classification of LLCs and generally allowed most non-publicly traded entities to avoid the corporate income tax. See JCT, "Report of Investigation of Enron Corporation," p. 368.

134. Johnson, Calvin, "Corporate Tax Shelters, 1997 and 1998," *Tax Notes*, September 28, 1998, p. 1603.

135. JCT, "Report of Investigation of Enron Corporation," p. 181.

136. JCT, "Report of Investigation of Enron Corporation," p. 244.

137. Peaslee, James M. and David Z. Nirenberg, *Federal Income Taxation of Securitization Transactions*, 3rd ed., New Hope, Pa.: Frank J. Fabozzi Associates, 2001, www.securitization-tax.com.

138. JCT, "Report of Investigation of Enron Corporation," p. 255.

139. JCT, "Report of Investigation of Enron Corporation," p. 244.

140. JCT, "Report of Investigation of Enron Corporation," p. 115.

141. U.S. Treasury, "The Problem of Corporate Tax Shelters," p. 4, 135.

142. Bradford, David, "An Uncluttered Income Tax: The Next Reform Agenda," John M. Olin Program Discussion Paper no. 20, Princeton University, July 1988.

143. Blough, "Postwar Tax Structure: Capital Gains Tax."

144. Note that about half of corporate dividends do not face double taxation because they go to tax-exempt entities such as pension funds.

145. Blough, "Postwar Tax Structure: Capital Gains Tax."

146. This was the "Treasury I" proposal. See Bradford, *Untangling the Income Tax*, p. 291. The original proposal was contained in U.S. Treasury, *Tax Reform for Fairness, Growth, and Simplicity*, Washington, D.C.: Government Printing Office, 1984.

147. U.S. Treasury, *Integration of the Individual and Corporate Tax Systems*.

148. U.S. Treasury, "General Explanations of the Administration's Fiscal Year 2004 Revenue Proposals," February 2003.

149. Edwards, Chris, "Dividend Taxes: U.S. Has the Second-Highest Rate," Cato Tax & Budget Bulletin no. 12, January 2003. Based on data from the Organization for Economic Cooperation and Development.

150. For a discussion, see Mervyn King, "The Cash Flow Corporate Income Tax," NBER Working Paper no. 1993, August 1986, p. 14–21.

151. See Sinn, Hans-Werner, *Taxation and the Cost of Capital: The Old View, the New View, and Another View*, Tax Policy and the Economy 5, Cambridge, Mass.: NBER and MIT Press, 1991, p. 25. See also U.S. Treasury, *Integration of the Individual and Corporate Tax Systems*, p. 116.

152. For a summary of studies, see George Zodrow, "On the Traditional and New Views of Dividend Taxation," *National Tax Journal* 44, December 1991, 497.

153. Congressional Budget Office, "President's Budgetary Proposals for FY2004," p. 23.

154. For a discussion, see U.S. Treasury, *Integration of the Individual and Corporate Tax Systems*, p. 3–14, 115.

155. Gordon, Roger and Young Lee, "Do Taxes Affect Debt Policy? Evidence from U.S. Corporate Tax Return Data," NBER Working Paper no. 7433, December 1999.

156. For a survey, see Franklin Allen and Roni Michaely, "Payout Policy," Wharton Financial Institutions Center, April 2002, http://fic.wharton.upenn.edu/fic/papers/01/0121.pdf.

157. Brown, Ken, "Will Stock Dividends Get Back Their Respect?" *Wall Street Journal*, December 10, 2002. Based on Ibbotson Associate's data.

158. Allen and Michaely, "Payout Policy," fig, 2, p. 8, 134.

159. Allen and Michaely, "Payout Policy," p. 116.

160. Gale, William, "About Half of Dividend Payments Do Not Face Double Taxation," *Tax Notes*, November 11, 2002, p. 839. Gale notes that $62 billion of payments were interest payments from mutual funds that the IRS records as dividends.

161. Allen and Michaely,"Payout Policy," p. 10, 117.

162. Siegel, Jeremy, "The Dividend Deficit," *Wall Street Journal*, February 2, 2002, p. A20.

163. Brown, "Will Stock Dividends Get Back Their Respect?"

164. Haas, George, "Rationale of the Undistributed Profits Tax," staff memo, U.S. Treasury, Division of Tax Research, March 17–18, 1937. www.taxhistory.org.

165. Gentry, William and R. Glenn Hubbard, "Fundamental Tax Reform and Corporate Financial Policy," NBER Working Paper no. 6433, February 1998.

166. JCT, "Report of Investigation of Enron Corporation," p. 327.

167. Reid, John, "MIPS Besieged—Solutions in Search of a Problem," *Tax Notes*, December 1, 1997, p. 1057.

168. Bulow, Summers, and Summers, "Distinguishing Debt from Equity in the Junk Bond Era," p. 135.

169. MIPS were the Goldman Sachs version of this financial structure, while TOPRS were Merrill Lynch's version. See John Reid, "MIPS Besieged: Solutions in Search of a Problem," *Tax Notes*, December 1, 1997, p. 1057.

170. McKinnon, John and Greg Hitt, "Double Play: How Treasury Lost in Battle to Quash a Dubious Security," *Wall Street Journal*, February 24, 2002, p. A1.

171. JCT, "Report of Investigation of Enron Corporation," p. 314.

172. McKinnon and Hitt, p. A1. See also JCT, "Report of Investigation of Enron Corporation," p. 313.

173. For a defense of MIPS, see Edward Kleinbard, "Lee Sheppard's Misguided Attacks on MIPS," *Tax Notes*, June 8, 1998, p. 1365.

174. Kleinbard, "Lee Sheppard's Misguided Attacks on MIPS."

175. McKinnon and Hitt, "Double Play," p. A1.

176. JCT, "Report of Investigation of Enron Corporation," p. 332.

177. See Bankman, "New Market in Corporate Tax Shelters." See also Lee Sheppard, "Treasury Steps on Step-Down Preferred," *Tax Notes*, March 3, 1997, p. 1102.

178. Gentry and Hubbard, "Fundamental Tax Reform and Corporate Financial Policy," p. 18.

179. Gravelle, *The Economic Effects of Taxing Capital Income*, p. 55.

180. Mackie. James B., III, "Unfinished Business of the 1986 Tax Reform Act: An Effective Tax Rate Analysis of Current Issues in the Taxation of Capital Income," *National Tax Journal* 60, no. 2, June 2002, p. 293.

181. Dubert, Carl and Peter Merrill, *Taxation of U.S. Corporations Doing Business Abroad: U.S. Rules and Competitiveness Issues,* Morristown, N.J.: Financial Executives Research Foundation and PricewaterhouseCoopers, 2001, table 10-2.

182. For a summary of U.S. rules, see Dubert and Merrill, "Taxation of U.S. Corporations Doing Business Abroad." See also National Foreign Trade Council, *The NFTC Foreign Income Project: International Tax Policy for the 21st Century,* Washington, D.C.: NFTC, 1999, part 1.

183. Hubbard, Glenn and James Hines, "Coming Home to America: Dividend Repatriations by U.S. Multinationals," NBER Working Paper no. 2931, April 1989.

184. For example, see American Bar Association, "Tax Simplification Recommendations," February 2001. See also National Foreign Trade Council, *The NFTC Foreign Income Project*.

185. JCT, "Report of Investigation of Enron Corporation," p. 370.

186. JCT, "Report of Investigation of Enron Corporation," p. 371.

187. JCT, "Report of Investigation of Enron Corporation," p. 373.

188. JCT, "Report of Investigation of Enron Corporation," p. 377.

189. JCT, "Report of Investigation of Enron Corporation," p. 375.

190. U.S. Treasury, "The Problem of Corporate Tax Shelters," p. 30.

191. For a further discussion, see Edwards and de Rugy, "International Tax Competition.

192. For a discussion, see National Foreign Trade Council, *The NFTC Foreign Income Project*.

193. A number of economic justifications have been given for a corporate tax, but they do not seem to be crucially important. For example, it may be efficient in theory to correct certain externalities through corporate taxes. For a discussion, see Richard Bird, "Why Tax Corporations?" Canadian Department of Finance, Technical Committee Working Paper no. 96-2, December 1996, p. 4.

194. For example, Bird notes that the high distortions are "sufficiently persuasive to convince most economists that there is little, if anything, to be said for corporation taxes." Bird, "Why Tax Corporations?" p. 1. However, Bird concludes that there are reasons for retention of the corporate tax, at least within an income tax system in a smaller economy such as Canada's.

195. Bradford, *Blueprints for Basic Tax Reform*, p. 4.

196. Despite endless debate, economists do not agree on which group bears the burden of the corporate income tax. Probably, it changes over time and falls variously on consumers, workers, or investors depending on the openness of the economy and market conditions in various industries.

197. The federal corporate rate is not precisely flat. Indeed, it has rates of 15, 25, 34, and 35 percent, but the large bulk of business activity occurs in the top two brackets that apply to companies with taxable income of more than $75,000 and $10 million, respectively.

198. My view is that proportional taxation is both fairer and more efficient than progressive taxation, thus one of the few virtues of the current corporate tax is its essentially flat rate. Also, note again that the actual burdens of capital income taxation may fall on individuals other than the stockholders who mail tax payments to the IRS.

199. See Stephen Entin, "The Inflow-Outflow Tax: A Savings-Deferred Neutral Tax System," Institute for Research on the Economics of Taxation, undated, www.iret.org. Another version of a savings-exempt tax is the individual portion of the "USA" tax introduced in 1995 by Senators Nunn and Domenici.

200. Bradford, *Blueprints for Basic Tax Reform*, p. 13.

201. Bird, "Why Tax Corporations?" p. 7.

202. Note that even under worldwide systems, foreign active business profits are usually not taxed until repatriated.

203. Hoffman, David, "State Tax Collections and Rates," Tax Foundation, February 2002.

204. Stark, Kirk, "The Quiet Revolution in U.S. Subnational Corporate Income Taxation," *State Tax Notes*, March 4, 2002. The author discusses the apportionment formulas that determine the corporate tax base, and he advocates corporate income tax repeal.

205. Brunori, David, "Stop Taxing Corporate Income," *Tax Notes*, June 25, 2002.

206. *Budget of the United States Government, Fiscal Year 2004, Historical Tables,* Washington, D.C.: Government Printing Office, February 2003.

207. U.S. Treasury, *Integration of the Individual and Corporate Tax Systems*. See also discussion in Gentry and Hubbard, "Fundamental Tax Reform and Corporate Financial Policy."

208. U.S. Treasury, *Integration of the Individual and Corporate Tax Systems*, p. 30.

209. Bradford, *Untangling the Income Tax*, p. 314.

210. Most cash-flow tax proposals have an "R" tax base. Alternatively, a cash-flow tax could have an "R+F" base, which would be calculated using both real and financial income and expense amounts.

211. The proposal included a subtraction-method VAT, which differs from the credit invoice VATs that are common in Europe. For a discussion of these two types of VATs, see Sullivan.

212. Engen and Hassett, "Does the U.S. Corporate Tax Have a Future?" p. 29.

213. Hall and Rabushka, *The Flat Tax*.

214. Business expenses that would not be deductible under the Armey plan include interest, dividends, nonpension fringe benefits, employer's share of payroll taxes, and bad debts.

215. The terminology of cash-flow taxes, R-base (real) or R+F (real + financial), follows from the British government's Meade Commission report on tax reform in 1978.

216. For a discussion, see Bradford, *Untangling the Income Tax*, p. 119.

217. Gentry, William and R. Glenn Hubbard, "Distributional Implications of Introducing a Broad-Based Consumption Tax," NBER Working Paper no. 5832, November 1996. Gentry and Hubbard define this issue precisely by breaking down capital income into four parts: (1) the opportunity cost of capital or the return to waiting, (2) the return to risk taking, (3) inframarginal returns or economic profit, and (4) realizations differing from expectation or unexpected windfalls. The income tax taxes all four components. A consumption-based tax taxes only the last three components. See also Gentry and Hubbard, "Fundamental Tax Reform and Corporate Financial Policy," p. 8.

218. See discussion in David Bradford, *Taxation, Wealth, and Saving,* Cambridge, Mass.: MIT Press, 2000, p. 91–3.

219. Mintz, Jack and Jesus Seade, "Cash Flow or Income? The Choice of Base for Company Taxation," *World Bank Observer*, July 1991, p. 180. See also King, Mervyn, "The Cash Flow Corporate Income Tax," NBER Working Paper no. 1993, August 1986, p. 14–21.

220. For a discussion of some possible administrative problems with the flat tax, see Weisbach, "Ironing Out the Flat Tax." See also Parthasarathi Shome and Christian Schutte, "Cash-Flow Tax," in Parthasarathi Shome, ed., *Tax Policy Handbook*, Washington, D.C.: International Monetary Fund, 1995, p. 172. See also Gentry and Hubbard, "Fundamental Tax Reform and Corporate Financial Policy," p. 29.

221. McLure, Charles and George Zodrow, "A Hybrid Approach to the Direct Taxation of Consumption," in Michael Boskin, ed., *Frontiers of Tax Reform*, Stanford, Calif.: Hoover Institution Press, 1996, p. 76. The authors propose a hybrid tax that would tax individuals under the Hall-Rabushka-style individual tax but businesses under an R+F cash-flow basis.

222. A border-adjustable tax would exempt exports from U.S. taxation and symmetrically deny a deduction for imported inputs. The USA tax is a border-adjustable cash-flow

tax. By contrast, the Hall-Rabushka tax is "origin-based" and would tax income on exported goods but allow a deduction for imported inputs.

223. Price Waterhouse LLP, Economic Policy Consulting Services, "Tax Liability of Nonfinancial Corporations under the USA and Flat Taxes: An Industry Analysis," June 29, 1995. I adjusted the study's 17 percent results up to the 19 percent rate specified under the Hall-Rabushka plan.

224. These issues have been around since the beginning of the income tax. For a discussion from the 1930s, see Blakey, "The Federal Income Tax," sec. VIII.

225. For a discussion, see Weisbach, "Ironing Out the Flat Tax," p. 36.

226. See Grubert, Harry and James Mackie, "An Unnecessary Complication: Must Financial Services Be Taxed under a Consumption Tax?" U.S. Treasury, January 30, 1996. Note that countries with VATs often impose a separate type of tax on financial institutions.

227. See Peter Merrill and Chris Edwards, "Cash-Flow Taxation of Financial Services," *National Tax Journal*, September 1996. See also Peter Merrill and Harold Adrion, "Treatment of Financial Services under Consumption-Based Tax Systems," *Tax Notes*, September 18, 1995. Note that Armey's flat tax legislation recognized the need for special rules for "financial intermediation services" but did not specify any details.

228. Schwarz, Melbert, Peter Merrill, and Chris Edwards, *Transitional Issues in Fundamental Tax Reform: A Financial Accounting Perspective,* Tax Policy and the Economy 12, Cambridge, Mass.: NBER and MIT Press, 1998. Also see Bradford, David, "Fundamental Issues in Consumption Taxation," American Enterprise Institute, 1996.

229. The Nunn-Domenici USA cash-flow tax plan did include detailed transition rules. Generally, the plan allowed for the amortization of remaining asset basis over a period of years.

V

CORPORATE GOVERNANCE

19

Corporate Governance

William A. Niskanen

THE RULES OF CORPORATE GOVERNANCE

$\mathcal{T}$he rules of corporate governance—in effect, the constitution of a corporation—are a complex combination of federal and state laws, court decisions, and regulations; the rules of the stock exchanges and the major creditors to a corporation; and the rules approved by each corporate board. These rules describe the structure of the corporation, the authority of the major officers in that structure, and the decision rules for selecting these officers and approving major decisions.

The single most important lesson from the collapse of Enron and other large corporations is that the rules of corporate governance do not now adequately protect the general shareholder against the discretionary behavior of corporate managers. In other words, the "agency problems" from the separation of ownership and control first recognized by Adam Smith (1776)[1] and developed by Adolf Berle and Gardiner Means (1932)[2] have not yet been adequately solved and may have recently increased.

At this point, one should recognize the revival of a view that corporate managers should also be accountable to other "stakeholders" affected by their decisions—such as employees, creditors, the local community, the environment, etc. From this perspective, the failure of Enron is supposed to demonstrate a lack of "corporate social responsibility." May I acknowledge that I am wholly unsympathetic with this view. Enron collapsed because its managers were not sufficiently responsive to the interests of its general shareholders, and the losses to the several groups of stakeholders were unfortunate side effects of this agency problem. Although I recognize that a corporation's contracts with these other constituencies are not complete, they are *far* more complete than the open-ended contract with shareholders. Good managers will pay attention to the interests of the several types of stakeholders to the extent that this attention is consistent with the interests of the general shareholders. But making corporate managers accountable to multiple constituencies would substantially increase managerial discretion, increasing the prospect that they would not serve any constituency very well. For these reasons, I conclude that the rules of corporate governance should be evaluated solely in terms of how well they serve the general shareholders.

This chapter summarizes and evaluates the major changes in the effective rules of corporate governance over the past several decades. These include the development of the monitoring model of the corporate board, the increased role of institutional investors, the reduced monitoring role of banks, the major changes in the formal rules of corporate governance, and the consequent erosion of the market for corporate control.

THE DEVELOPMENT OF THE MONITORING MODEL OF THE CORPORATE BOARD

As late as 1970, most corporate boards served primarily in an advisory capacity. Most board members were current or former executives in the firm, specialists in the industry or the financial markets, and friends of the CEO. The implicit assumption of the advisory board is that it should trust and support the management, offering information and counsel only as it bears on the general conduct of the firm. An audit committee for each corporate board had been recommended as early as 1939 by the New York Stock Exchange (NYSE) and 1940 by the Securities and Exchange Commission (SEC), but the creation of audit committees spread slowly and without much public attention.

The major proposals that led to a new monitoring model of the corporate board date from the 1970s. In 1976, SEC Chairman Roderick Hills suggested that the NYSE change its listing standards to require that all listed corporations have an independent audit committee, a suggestion approved by the NYSE in 1978. Later that year, the Committee on Corporate Law of the American Bar Association (ABA) endorsed the developing model of the corporate board "in its role as reviewer of management initiatives and monitor of corporate performance."[3] Even the major CEOs in the Business Roundtable (BRT) endorsed this general model, although they maintained that the appropriate relation between the board and management was one "of mutual trust . . . challenging yet supportive and positive . . . arm's length but not adversarial."[4] In 1980, a report on corporate accountability by the staff of the Senate Banking Committee reflected this broader consensus as follows:

> The consensus is moving strongly toward greater participation by directors independent of management, currently calling for a board composed of at least a majority of independent directors, with properly functioning independent audit, compensation, and nominating committees, as essential to enhanced and effective corporate accountability.[5]

Over the next twenty years, the developing consensus for the monitoring board evolved slowly with recommendations for a majority of independent directors, a stricter definition of the conditions that would qualify a director to be independent, audit committees composed only of independent directors, and a stronger role for the audit committee in selecting and monitoring the firm's external auditor. This process culminated in the summer of 2002, after the collapse of Enron and WorldCom, with new recommendations by the BRT and new listing standards by the NYSE and NASDAQ, most of which were incorporated in the Sarbanes-Oxley Act (SOA). The BRT, reflecting the evolving consensus, described the appropriate relation of the board and management as "constructive skepticism . . . [leading them to] ask incisive, probing questions and require accurate, honest answers"[6]—very different from their "mutual trust" perspective of 1978. The new listing standards of the NYSE, for example, include the following:

- All listed companies must have a majority of independent directors with a tighter definition of director independence,
- Audit, nominating, and compensation committees must consist solely of independent directors,
- Director compensation must be the sole compensation of members of the audit committee,
- Audit committees would have the sole authority to select the independent public auditor and to approve any significant non-audit work by the auditor,
- The CEO would be required to attest to the accuracy, completeness, and understandability of information provided to the investors,
- All equity-based compensation plans must be approved by the shareholders, and
- The NYSE would be authorized to issue public reprimand letters in addition to suspension and delisting.

My guess is that the measures approved in the summer of 2002, with the exception of a few more SEC regulations authorized by the SOA, will be about the end of the evolution toward a monitoring model of the corporate board. The new listing standards and the provisions of the SOA represent a significant nationalization of the rules of corporate government, measures that until recently were authorized primarily by the state corporate chartering laws.[7]

EVIDENCE BEARING ON THE MONITORING MODEL

What is one to make of the monitoring model of the corporate board after several decades of a developing consensus toward this model?

The first, chastening response to this question is that the Enron board was a model board, even by the tighter standards approved in 2002; when Enron declared bankruptcy, for example, it was in full compliance with the corporate governance provisions of the SOA, with the exception of loans to some officers. Prior to Enron's collapse in late 2001, the Enron board was composed of Kenneth Lay, Jeffery Skilling, and twelve independent directors. Many had advanced degrees, some were heads of major corporate or nonprofit organizations, and others had significant governmental and regulatory experience. All of the audit committee members were independent, the chairman was a respected former dean and accounting professor at the Stanford University Graduate School of Business, and another was a doctor of economics who had chaired the Commodity Futures Trading Commission. In 2000, one year before the Enron bankruptcy, Enron's board was judged one of the five best boards in the country by *Chief Executive* magazine. A question had been raised about financial ties between Enron and some of the independent directors but, upon examination, any financial relations in addition to board compensation, with one exception, were *de minimis*. Moreover, all of the other major firms charged with accounting scandals through 2002 were also in full compliance, at least formally, with the standards for board and audit committee independence. Monitoring by independent board directors has at least not proved to be sufficient to deter or detect the conditions leading to numerous accounting scandals, the explosion of executive compensation, and the bankruptcy of some major firms.

For those who view most corporate problems as a consequence of conflicts of interest, the ideas that led to the board as a monitor of corporate performance are plausible and have become more generally shared. As it turns out, however, there is *no* evidence that firm performance is related to the proportion of independent directors. Over the past twenty years, many studies have tested this relation and reach a common conclusion. As summarized by Benjamin E. Hermalin and Michael S. Weisbach (2001), "[o]verall, there is little to suggest that board composition has any cross-sectional relation with firm performance."[8]

The increase in the proportion of independent directors over this period appears to reflect the appeal and momentum of an idea without any evidence of a beneficial effect. The increased role of independent directors over this period was strongly supported by the institutional investors, but this support does not appear to have served its intended purpose. Institutional investors also supported the separation of the positions of the chairman and the CEO, but again without any evidence of a beneficial effect. Another tenet of the monitoring model of corporate boards is also inconsistent with the evidence: A study by Stephen P. Ferris, Murali Jagannathan, and A. C. Pritchard (2003) finds that there is no significant evidence that the number of director appointments by a board member affects firm performance, service on board committees, or the probability of securities fraud litigation.[9] On the other hand, these studies broadly support a conclusion that firm performance is negatively related to board size, a conclusion more consistent with the reduction of the average size of corporate boards over this period.

These two types of evidence should lead to broader questioning of the monitoring model of corporate boards. As Alton Harris and Andrea Kramer conclude,

> by turning the corporate board into the "monitor" of corporate management, we do not appear to have been able to stop the scandals and flagrant abuses, and we may well be closing the vision, advice, and competitive perceptiveness that a good board should be providing the CEO. Surely there must be better ways to deal with the consequences of the separation of ownership and control in the modern corporation. The time has come, we believe, to think outside the "consensus" box.[10]

THE LIMITED MONITORING ROLE OF INSTITUTIONAL INVESTORS

In parallel with the evolution of the monitoring model of the corporate board, there has been a large increase in the proportion of shares managed by institutional investors—from about 20 percent in 1970 to over 50 percent in 2000. As late as October 2001, for example, more than 60 percent of Enron stock was owned by large institutional investors. Large independent shareholder blocs have been rare in U.S. corporations for many years, and for many corporations the largest outside shareholder is now some fund. These funds have the potential for an effective voice in the corporations in which they are invested, acting alone or in concert, but, for various reasons, shareholder activism by these funds is both low and without significant effect. One reason why one should not expect the managers of funds to be effective monitors of the firms in which the fund is invested is that the funds are also subject to an agency problem; the interests of fund managers are quite different from the interests of those who have invested in the fund. Another reason is that the managers of most mutual funds are not allowed to sell short. The other obvious reason is that it is usually more efficient for a fund to be diversified than to invest in the knowledge and activism necessary to be to be an effective monitor of an individual firm. Bernard S. Black (1998), in a survey of the studies of this issue, concludes;

> A small number of American institutional investors, mostly public pension funds, spend a trivial amount of money on overt activism efforts. They don't conduct proxy fights, and don't try to elect their own candidates to the board of directors. Legal rules, agency costs within the institutions, information costs, collective action problems, and limited institutional competence are all plausible partial explanations for this relative lack of activity. The currently available evidence, taken as a whole, is consistent with the proposition that the institutions achieve the effects on firm performance that one might expect from this level of effort—namely, not much.[11]

Roberta Romano (2000) agrees with Black in concluding that

> shareholder proposals, although an increasingly prominent feature of insti-
> tutional investor corporate governance activism since the mid-1980s, have
> not had a significant impact on firm performance, [but she contends that]
> [t]he most plausible explanation for the absence of a discernible positive ef-
> fect has been large-scale misdirection in the form that such activism has
> taken; many proposals have focused on reforming board composition and
> structure and limiting executive compensation, yet empirical studies of such
> reforms consistently indicate that they do not improve performance.[12]

As a consequence, most fund managers, who have the greatest potential for
effective shareholder activism but little of their personal wealth at stake, are inclined
to behave much like individual investors—to be so diversified that they do not care
much what happens to any single corporation and to sell, rather than fight, in response to information about mismanagement of a firm. No apparent change in
government policy is likely to change this condition. Maybe that is just as well;
much of the shareholder activism by public pension funds in recent years has been
as representatives of various stakeholder groups, not of the general shareholders.

The primary value of the increased role of institutional investors, however,
appears to be better investment decisions rather than shareholder activism. A 2001
study by Paul Gompers and Andrew Metrick, for example, found that the stock returns from 1980 through 1996 were higher for companies with greater institutional ownership.[13]

THE REDUCED MONITORING ROLE OF BANKS

Commercial banks now have a much smaller potential role in monitoring large
corporations for two reasons: Most large corporations are now much less bank dependent than in the past, with the ability to borrow at all maturities and risk
categories from commercial paper to junk bonds. And banks have much less incentive to monitor large corporations because they no longer bear most of the
credit risk of large loans. Bankers are now more likely to make more of their income from fees for making loans than from the long-term performance of these
loans. For these reasons, few American corporations—even those, like Enron, that
are unusually bank dependent—have a banker on their board. As documented in
chapter 13, some of the nation's largest banks were part of the problem at Enron,
not part of the solution. A change in law that would authorize prosecutors to
charge individual bankers with aiding and abetting securities fraud would reduce
the approval of bad loans, but there is no obvious change in policy that would induce bankers to be more effective monitors on an ongoing basis.

THE EROSION OF THE MARKET FOR CORPORATE CONTROL

The major changes in the legal rules of corporate governance began with congressional approval of the Williams Act in 1968, roughly coincident with the beginning of the evolution toward the monitoring model of the corporate board and the increasing role of institutional investors. The Williams Act, the only major federal measure to protect incumbent corporate managers from a takeover bid, requires that any person or group that acquires more than 5 percent of the outstanding shares of a firm inform both the firm and the SEC within ten days of the following information: the background of the purchaser, the source and amount of the funds used in the purchase, the purpose of the acquisition, the number of shares owned, and the number that the purchaser has a right to acquire. The act also requires that target shareholders be accorded substantially equal treatment in such matters as the right to tender their shares and in the price that they receive. This act, reenforced by subsequent SEC rules, substantially increased the cost of successful tender offers and completely eliminated the potential for surprise. The Williams Act, followed by a proliferation of state anti-takeover statutes, substantially reduced hostile takeover activity in the 1970s.

A combination of conditions, however, led to a resurgence of hostile acquisitions in the 1980s—specifically the change in antitrust enforcement by the Reagan administration, the development of new financing techniques such as junk bonds, and economic changes that made it profitable to restructure several industries. A 1982 U.S. Supreme Court decision in the case of *Edgar v. MITE*[14] also restricted the authority of the states to implement anti-takeover statutes. In response, the value of mergers and acquisitions increased from $44 billion in 1980 to $226 billion in 1988.

In 1987, however, the Supreme Court reversed their prior position in the case of *CTS Corp. v Dynamics Corp. of America*,[15] permitting states to implement control share acquisition statutes affecting corporations incorporated in that state. As of mid-1999, forty-two states had implemented one or more takeover defenses. The primary types of takeover defenses are the following:

- Control share acquisition statutes require any shareholder who acquires more than some threshold percent of the outstanding shares to have the approval of a majority of the other nonmanagement stockholders to exercise the voting rights of his shares.
- Fair price provisions typically require a bidder to pay to all shareholders the highest price paid to any shareholder during a specified period before a tender offer, but do not apply if the deal is approved by the board of directors or a supermajority of the target's shareholders.
- Merger moratorium statutes prohibit any shareholder who has acquired more than some threshold percent of the outstanding shares from causing

the target company to enter into any merger with the bidder for several years without the prior approval of the board or the subsequent approval of the board and two-thirds of the other shareholders.

- Share purchase rights plans ("poison pills") allow target shareholders to acquire the stock of the bidder at a fraction of its value or to dilute the bidders's stake in the target by issuing additional stock that the bidder is not allowed to buy. These plans may be lifted only by the approval of the target board.
- Director's duties plans authorize boards to resist a potential change in control of the corporation if it does not serve the interests of other stakeholders such as employees, suppliers, customers, and the local community.

Finally, staggered board plans require a bidder to win two or more successive elections to replace the incumbent board. A study using data on hostile bids in the years 1996–2000 finds that a staggered board increases the probability of remaining independent following a hostile bid from 34 percent to 61 percent and reduces the returns to the target shareholders by 8–10 percent in the nine months after the hostile bid was launched.[16]

The general effect of these and other takeover defenses, by interposing a third party between the bidder and an individual target shareholder, is to require shareholders to act collectively by using their vote to remove the impediment to their rights to sell their stock. The one exception to this pattern of increasing management protections was a 1992 rule by the SEC that reduced the cost of challenging incumbent management. Under the old rule, a shareholder had to file a proxy statement with the SEC before *even talking* with more than ten other shareholders; the new rule allows any form and extent of shareholder communication as long as they send a copy of the substance of the communication to the SEC after the fact. The net effect of these increased management protections and the SEC rule, however, was that the number of effective hostile tender offers dropped sharply in the 1990s. Marco Becht, Patrick Bolton, and Alisa Roell (2002) conclude their massive survey of the studies of corporate governance by stating that

> starting in the early 1990s the market for corporate control in the U.S. has essentially collapsed. Indeed, following the wave of anti-takeover laws and charter amendments introduced at the end of the 1980s, most U.S. corporations are now extremely well protected against hostile takeovers. Their control is generally no longer contestable.[17]

Joseph Grundfest (1993), a former SEC commissioner and now a professor at the Stanford University Law School, similarly concludes that "[t]he takeover wars are over. Management won. . . . As a result, corporate America is now governed by directors who are largely impervious to capital market electoral challenges."[18]

Very few corporate boards now include a member with a sufficient portion of the total shares to be a credible threat to replace the incumbent management.

In testimony to Congress in March 2002, Sara Teslik of the Council of Institutional Investors observed:

> Our system allows executives to pick the boards who are supposed to police them. . . . Frauds are bigger and more frequent because the laws that were passed 65 years ago to protect shareholders have been steadily worn down by special interests. Indeed, our laws now protect executives, accountants, and financial wheeler dealers at shareholders' expense, instead of the other way around.[19]

Henry Manne (2002), the founding scholar of the market for corporate control, concludes:

> It should come as no surprise that, as hostile takeovers declined from 14 percent to 4 percent of all mergers, executive compensation started a steep climb, eventually ending for some companies with bankruptcy and management scandal. . . . Enron is a predictable consequence of rules that inhibit the efficient functioning of the market for corporate control.[20]

A CAUTIONARY PUZZLE

For all the accumulation of takeover defenses over the past several decades, there is reason to believe that *the number of corporate acquisitions may still be too high*! The evidence for this surprising conclusion, from a large number of careful studies, is that the average gains to the shareholders of the bidding firms are close to zero and are probably negative for large public firms, with a very high variance of the gains from individual acquisitions. A 2003 study by Dennis Mueller and Mark Sirower, for example, concludes that "for the average merger the acquiring firms' shareholders lose, because the premium offered for the target is more than the potential gains from acquiring it."[21]

Another 2003 study by Sara Moeller, Frederik Schlingemann, and Rene Stulz, based on a much larger sample, concludes that

> takeovers by large firms have destroyed $226 billion of shareholder wealth over 20 years. In contrast, small firms, defined as companies whose market capitalization is equivalent to the smallest 25 percent of companies listed on the NYSE each year, created $8 billion of shareholder wealth through their transactions.[22]

There appears to be no consistent evidence of postmerger synergy between the bidding and target firms. In that case, what explains the continued level of acquisitions?

One explanation of why most acquisitions do not increase the stock of the bidding firm is that the acquisition may be interpreted by investors as a signal that the firm has exhausted any profitable internal growth opportunities. This may be true, but it fails to explain why the firm uses spare capital to finance an acquisition rather than a stock buyback or a special dividend.

An alternative, more disturbing, explanation is that most acquisitions serve the interests of the managers and board members of large bidding firms even when not that of their shareholders. This may be primarily a consequence of rules that make the compensation of managers and board members a function of firm size, a rule usually based on an accounting measure of total revenues that, in turn, invites a manipulation of this measure. This explanation suggests that there may be a bias in favor of acquisitions, even those that do not serve the interests of the shareholders of the bidding firms. More careful study, of course, is needed, but the appropriate change in corporate governance may be to require approval of all acquisitions by the owners of a majority of the shares not owned by managers and members of the board. The revival of a productive market for corporate control may require both a tighter rule in the acquiring firms for approving a proposed acquisition and less restrictive takeover defenses by the target firms.

FIRM PERFORMANCE AND THE RULES OF CORPORATE GOVERNANCE

What is the relation between the performance of a firm and the rules of corporate governance by which it operates? Fortunately, an important 2003 study by Paul Gompers, Joy Ishii, and Andrew Metrick addresses just that question. The authors first develop a governance index, based on the number of corporate governance rules that protect management, for about 1,500 large U.S. firms with only one class of common stock in 1990. The study then estimated the relation between the stock market performance of these firms over the 1990s and the level of this index in 1990. The results are dramatic! An investment strategy that bought shares in the top decile of the shareholder-friendly firms and sold shares in the top decile of the management-friendly firms would have earned an additional nominal return of 8.5 percent a year during this period. The authors also find

> that firms with stronger shareholder rights had higher firm value, higher profits, higher sales growth, lower capital expenditures, and made fewer corporate acquisitions. . . . The results for both stock returns and firm value are economically large and are robust to many controls and other firm characteristics.[23]

The results of this study are consistent with a hypothesis that each additional rule protecting management significantly reduces the market value of the firm, but the study is not able to sort out whether some other unobserved condition related to the governance index might explain this result. One other condition deserves special examination: The 1990s were an extended period of a stock market boom; even the top decile of the management-friendly firms earned an annual nominal return of 14 percent. Maybe no one minds the store in good times, when even indifferent management can earn a satisfactory return. It would be especially valuable to test the relation between stock market returns and the governance index during the extended bear market after March 2000. At a minimum, this important study should stimulate more such studies and lead both state legislators and corporate boards to question whether the proliferation of management protections since the late 1980s serves the interests of the general shareholders.

WHAT TO DO?

This chapter describes a serious problem about the current rules of corporate governance but without a very clear sense about what, if anything, should be done about it. Some pension or mutual fund is now often the largest outside shareholder of American corporations; the managers of these funds have the potential, but little incentive, to be more effective monitors. Most large corporations are no longer very dependent on bank credit, and bankers have a reduced incentive to be effective monitors because banks no longer bear much of the credit risk from large loans. American corporations are now increasingly dependent on monitoring by their boards, but this has proved insufficient to discipline corporate managements that are increasingly protected by management-friendly rules of corporate governance. The only alternative appears to be the restoration of an effective market for corporate control.

One obvious change in policy would be to repeal the federal Williams Act. That would help restore the market for corporate control but would have limited benefit without unwinding the snarl of state anti-takeover statutes and board-approved management protections, and it is much less obvious how to unwind this snarl.

The occasional proposals to replace this snarl with federal corporate chartering legislation, however, should be strenuously opposed. Many specialists in corporate law believe, maybe correctly, that they could write better federal corporate chartering legislation than now exists in any state, but that begs the point. Federal politicians, not these specialists, would write any federal corporate legislation; such legislation would probably include some takeover defenses to reflect the political demands of the time, and federal legislation would lose the benefits of the choice and diversity of state legislation in a choice-of-law regime. Most of the advocates of federal corporate law describe the choice-of-law regime of state corporate charters as "a race to the bottom" in terms of investor protection, but that is a mistaken perception.

Starting with the influential 1993 book by Roberta Romano,[24] most special-ists in corporate law now seem to agree that competition among the states in the production of corporate law leads to better law. Competition among the states has led more than half of public corporations to incorporate in Delaware, not because it is especially protective of management but because of the dispute-settlement services of its Chancery Court and the clarity of its laws. Delaware has only one anti-takeover statute, a merger moratorium that has proved to be relatively easy to overcome. (In April 2003, however, the Delaware Supreme Court validated "lockup" agreements between a bidder and a corporate board that foreclose an of-fer by a second bidder; even this ruling, however, can probably be countered by paying the first bidder a termination fee.) And the evidence is now overwhelming that firms incorporated in Delaware are both more valuable than similar firms in-corporated elsewhere and more likely to receive takeover bids and be acquired.[25] For whatever its relevance, Enron and WorldCom were not incorporated in Delaware but in Oregon and Georgia, respectively.

The benefits of a choice-of-law regime seem larger than those of a uniform federal charter that is also likely to include some anti-takeover measures. So an agenda for reform of the rules of corporate governance should try to unwind the snarl of anti-takeover measures rather than to replace this snarl with a federal cor-porate charter. Maybe there is some legal basis for reversing the Supreme Court decision in the *CTS* case. Maybe state legislatures and corporate boards would be impressed with the dramatic evidence of the Gompers, Ishii, and Metrick study that management protections appear to reduce the market value of firms. Sugges-tions are welcome.

More likely, however, some major new technique will be necessary to restore the market for corporate control. That technique, I suggest, would be to allow bid-ders who are seeking control of a firm to buy (or, more accurately, to rent) the *voting* rights of other shareholders for a limited time and for a specific purpose, a proposal first made in 1964 by Henry Manne.[26] The reason why such a howitzer is necessary to break up the snarl of takeover defenses is that the several major types of takeover defenses, as explained above, require a collective decision by the target board and/or by other shareholders to lift the takeover defense before a bidder is allowed to buy enough shares to control the firm. The bidder's incentive is to rent the votes of just enough other shareholders to lift the takeover defense or, if nec-essary, to win a proxy contest to control the board. The incentives of a shareholder are to limit his offer to lease his voting rights to the votes on these specific issues, retaining his voting rights on all subsequent issues.

This process of vote renting would benefit bidders by making it possible to gain control of firms where that opportunity would otherwise be precluded by some takeover defense. The general shareholders of the target firm would benefit in one or two ways: the temporary lease of his voting rights even if the takeover bid is not successful and the increased value of his shares if the bid is successful. The average price of the voting shares of U.S. firms with two classes of shares, for example, has been about 5 percent above the price of nonvoting shares.[27] And several event studies indicate that the average premium to the target shareholders has been about 24 percent for all U.S. acquisitions with an even higher premium for hostile takeovers.[28] General shareholders of the target firms clearly have a lot to gain by restoring the market for corporate control.

What does it take to create a legal market for renting votes? There is apparently no federal legislation that bears on this issue. The SEC "one share, one vote" rule has been interpreted "merely as a prohibition against the disenfranchisement of existing shareholder's voting rights."[29] In effect, however, the many state antitakeover statutes greatly restrict the voting rights of large shareholders. State laws in New York and a few other states explicitly prohibit vote buying for the shares of corporations incorporated in those states.

As is often the case in corporate law, rulings by the Delaware court may be the best guide to this issue because more than half of all public corporations are incorporated in Delaware. A careful examination of the Delaware court decisions by Thomas J. Andre Jr. (1990) leads him to conclude:

> The broad lesson to be drawn from these cases is that, at least in Delaware, public policy no longer voids transactions in which individual stockholders voluntarily surrender the power to vote their shares in exchange for benefits (pecuniary or otherwise) that other stockholders do not share. In essence, the Delaware courts have recognized that the separation of the voting rights from the residual interests might well serve perfectly reasonable and legitimate corporate ends and that there is no reason to assume ex ante that every vote buying scheme is unlawful. Rather, whether vote buying is lawful in a given case must be determined by reference to well-established corporate principles, including full disclosure in the transaction, the lack of any fraudulent purpose, and compliance with fiduciary duties when applicable . . . at the very least it can be said that in the current state of the law not all vote buying is prohibited.[30]

Andre's article also provides a valuable analysis of the effects of vote buying as a means to lift the several major types of takeover defenses, and he concludes that such a market for votes would benefit general shareholders even if the target management also bids for the votes of the target shareholders as part of a takeover defense.

The policy actions that would be helpful to restore an effective market for corporate control in the United States, therefore, appear to be the following:

A repeal of the federal Williams Act would help restore the market for corporate control, primarily by allowing a bidder to buy a larger proportion of shares without disclosure. A repeal of this act, however, would not be sufficient, because it would leave the accumulation of state and board-approved anti-takeover measures in place, measures that are specifically designed to limit the voting power of large shareholders. A repeal of the Williams Act is probably also not necessary; the many mergers and acquisitions in the early 1980s, for example, were consistent with this act. The primary value of repealing the Williams Act would be to put Congress on record as endorsing a restoration of the market for corporate control.

The SEC should clarify the "one share, one vote" rule to assure potential bidders that the voluntary and temporary lease of shareholder votes to lift a takeover defense is not inconsistent with this rule. This might seem like not much of a change, but it may be necessary to offset the limits in state anti-takeover statues on the rights of large shareholders.

A repeal of the New York State legislative prohibition on vote buying would be helpful, but is not necessary. Only about 5 percent of public corporations are incorporated in New York, and a change in policy in other states that clearly benefits general shareholders would probably lead to a repeal of such prohibitions in New York and a few other states.

Finally, the Delaware courts should clarify the conditions for which they are likely to approve a market for the votes of a target company, a clarification that some corporate bidder would probably have to force by investing in a carefully structured lease of target shareholder votes as part of a takeover bid.

Most important, the case for restoring a market for corporate control must be made to the general public, the media, and politicians. There is reason for some optimism that this is possible. More than half of U.S. households now own some equity. And the accounting scandals, the explosion of executive compensation, the gross mismanagement of too many large U.S. corporations, and the large decline in U.S. stock markets after March 2000 should make them receptive to the argument and evidence that the current rules of corporate governance do not serve us very well.

NOTES

1. Smith, Adam, *An Inquiry into the Nature and Causes of the Wealth of Nations*, New York: Modern Library, originally published 1776.

2. Berle, Adolf and Gardiner Means, *The Modern Corporation and Private Property*, New York: Macmillan, 1932.

3. ABA, Section of Business Law, "Corporate Directors' Guidebook," *Business Lawyer* 33 (April 1978).

4. BRT, "The Role and Composition of the Board of Directors of the Large Publicly Owned Corporation," January 1978.

5. Senate Committee on Banking, Housing, and Urban Affairs, Staff Report on Corporate Accountability, September 4, 1980.

6. BRT, *Principles of Corporate Governance*, May 14, 2002.

7. Bainbridge, Stephen M., "The Creeping Federalization of Corporate Law," *Regulation* 26, no. 1, Spring 2003.

8. Hermalin, Benjamin E. and Michael Weisbach, "Boards of Directors as an Endogenously Determined Institution: A Survey of the Economic Literature," National Bureau of Economic Research Working Paper no. 8161, March 2001.

9. Ferris, Stephen P., Murali Jagannathan, and A. C. Pritchard, "Too Busy to Mind the Business? Monitoring by Directors with Multiple Board Appointments," *Journal of Finance* 58, no. 3, June 2003.

10. Harris, Alton B. and Andrea S. Kramer, "Corporate Governance: Pre-Enron, Post-Enron," in Christopher L. Culp and William A. Niskanen, eds., *Corporate Aftershock*, Hoboken, N.J.: John Wiley and Sons, 2003.

11. Black, Bernard S., "Shareholder Activism and Corporate Governance in the United States," in Peter Newman, ed., *The New Palgrave Dictionary of Economics and the Law*, 1998.

12. Romano, Roberta, "Less is More: Making Institutional Activism a Valuable Mechanism of Corporate Governance," *Yale Journal of Regulation* 18, 2001.

13. Gompers, Paul A. and Andrew Metrick, "Institutional Investors and Equity Prices," *Quarterly Journal of Economics*, 2000.

14. 457 U.S. 624, 1982.

15. 481 U.S. 69, 1987.

16. Bebchuk, Lucian, John Coates, and Guhan Subramanian, "The Powerful Anti-takeover Force of Staggered Boards: Theory, Evidence, and Policy," National Bureau of Economic Research Working Paper no. 8974, 2002.

17. Becht, Marco, Patrick Bolton, and Alisa Roell, "Corporate Governance and Control," National Bureau of Economic Research Working Paper no. 9371, December 2002.

18. Grundfest, Joseph A., "Just Say No: A Minimalist Strategy for Dealing with Barbarians inside the Gates," *Stanford Law Review* 45, 1993.

19. Teslik, Sarah, Testimony to the U.S. Senate Committee on Banking, Housing, and Urban Affairs, March 20, 2002.

20. Manne, Henry G., "Bring Back the Hostile Takeover," *Wall Street Journal*, June 26, 2002.

21. Mueller, Dennis C. and Mark L. Sirower, "The Causes of Mergers: Tests Based on Gains to Acquiring Firms' Shareholders and the Size of the Premia," *Managerial and Decision Economics* 24, 2003.

22. Moeller, Sara, Frederik Schlingemann, and Rene Stulz, "Do Shareholders of Acquiring Firms Gain from Acquisitions?" National Bureau of Economic Research Working Paper no. 9523, August 2003.

23. Gompers, Paul, Joy Ishii, and Andrew Metrick, "Corporate Governance and Equity Prices," *Quarterly Journal of Economics,* February 2003.

24. Romano, Roberta, *The Genius of American Corporate Law*, Washington, D.C.: AEI Press, 1993.

25. Daines, Robert, "Does Delaware Law Improve Firm Value?" *Journal of Financial Economics* 62, 2001.

26. Manne, H.G., "Some Theoretical Aspects of Share Voting," *Columbia Law Review* 64, 1964.

27. Lease, Ronald C., John J. McConnell, and Wayne H. Mikkelson, "The Market Value of Differential Voting Rights in Closely Held Corporations," *Journal of Business* 57, 1984.

28. Andrade, Gregor, Mark Mitchell, and Erik Stafford, "New Evidence and Perspectives on Mergers," *Journal of Economic Perspectives* 15, 2001.

29. SEC, One Share–One Vote Release, at 89, 225.

30. Andre, Thomas J., Jr., "A Preliminary Inquiry into the Utility of Vote Buying in the Market for Corporate Control," *Southern California Law Review*, March 1990.

VI

MAJOR POLICY LESSONS FROM THE COLLAPSE OF ENRON

20

Major Policy Lessons from the Collapse of Enron

William A. Niskanen

$\mathcal{W}$hat to do? Any response to this question should be based on an understanding of the *general* problems illustrated by the collapse of Enron and other large corporations and of the comparative advantage of the several monitoring institutions in addressing these problems. At this point, may I acknowledge that I have a general bias against increasing the role of government to resolve these problems. All too often, as with the hurried passage of the Sarbanes-Oxley Act of 2002 (SOA), it seems more important for government officials to be seen to address some problem of popular concern than to be held responsible over time for resolving this problem. Most large general declines in equity prices have been followed by increased government regulation of the securities markets without any significant evidence that the perceived problems have been reduced. The most important role for the government is to reduce or end those policies that have contributed to these problems. There remain important residual monitoring and sanctioning roles for the government, but most of the general problems illustrated by the collapse of Enron, I suggest, are best resolved by private institutions.

THE SARBANES-OXLEY ACT

The SOA was the most important political response to the collapse of Enron and several other large corporations. My own evaluation of this act is much like that in chapter 3 by Alan Reynolds, who described the SOA as "unnecessary, harmful, and inadequate."

Unnecessary—because the stock exchanges had already implemented most of the SOA changes in the rules of corporate governance in their new listing standards; the Securities and Exchange Commission (SEC) had full authority to approve and enforce accounting standards, the requirement that CEOs certify the financial statements of their firms, and the rules for corporate disclosure; and the Department of Justice had ample authority to prosecute executives for securities fraud. The expensive new Public Company Accounting Oversight Board (PCAOB) is especially unnecessary. Its role is to regulate the few remaining independent public auditors, but it has no regulatory authority beyond that already granted to the SEC. Moreover, the audit firms still have a potential conflict of interest, because they are selected by and paid by the public corporations that they audit; a much more effective change would have been to have each stock exchange select, monitor, and compensate the auditors for all firms listed on that exchange. The PCAOB may also be unconstitutional, because it is a private monopoly that has been granted both regulatory and taxing authority.

Harmful—because the SOA substantially increases the risks of serving as a corporate officer or director, the premiums for directors and officers liability insurance, and the incentives, primarily for foreign and small firms, not to list their stock on an American exchange. The ban on loans to corporate officers eliminates one of the more efficient instruments of executive compensation. And the SOA may also reduce the incentive of corporate executives and directors to seek legal advice.

Inadequate—because the SOA failed to identify and correct the major problems of accounting, auditing, taxation, and corporate governance that have invited corporate malfeasance and increased the probability of bankruptcy. What to do?

At a minimum, Congress should clarify that the criminal penalties in the SOA require proof of malign intent and personal responsibility for some illegal act. The major potential problem of the act is the awesome threat that senior corporate managers may be held liable for an illegal action the senior manager did not direct, condone, or even know about. No large organization can operate under such a threat. Congress has wisely refrained from applying this standard to government managers even though the General Accounting Office (GAO) reported in 1998 that "significant financial systems weaknesses . . . prevent the government from accurately reporting a large portion of its assets, liabilities, and costs."[1]

Any SOA cleanup legislation should address the potential problem of delisting by foreign and small firms from the American stock exchanges, maybe by exempting such firms from the regulatory requirements. Such delisting would reduce both the information about and the liquidity of the firms delisted. The current application of SOA to foreign firms represents a significant extraterritorial extension of U.S. regulations that is also likely to cause other problems.

A wise Congress would also eliminate the expensive new and wholly unnecessary PCAOB, preferably before it establishes new precedents and creates some new special interest. This should probably be accompanied by amending the SOA to shift the authority to select, monitor, and compensate the independent public auditors from the audit committee of the corporate board to the stock exchange on which the corporation is listed.

A Congress that is both wise and brave would repeal the SOA—lock, stock, and barrel. The SOA adds no necessary authority to those previously granted, creates the potential for substantial harm, and does not address the major policies that lead to problems in the U.S. corporate economy.

ACCOUNTING

For the several reasons described in chapter 4, current financial accounting is often not a very good guide to either corporate managers or investors. The primary policy issue is whether accounting standards should continue to be set by the Financial Accounting Standards Board (FASB) and approved by the Securities and Exchange Commission (SEC). I suggest not, for the following reasons:

There is no obvious reason why any one set of accounting standards is best for all firms in all industries or stock exchanges.

There is no evidence that the FASB, the SEC, and Congress have any comparative advantage in setting accounting standards.

As a private monopoly, the FASB has been slow to develop standards for new types of financial transactions and conditions, has allowed the U.S. standards to become unusually complex and vulnerable to subjective interpretation, and has been vulnerable to several controversial accounting doctrines. The SEC has no comparative advantage to review and approve the changes recommended by the FASB, except to interpret the balance of current political demands. In response to a congressional order to study the comparative value of rules-based and principles-based accounting, for example, the SEC straddled the issue. As reported in the *Wall Street Journal*, the SEC staff observed that

> U.S. accounting rules can reward those willing to engineer their way around the intent of the standards . . . leading to financial reports that stress compliance over meaningful communication. At the other extreme . . . a principle-based approach could give companies and accountants too much leeway and too little structure, resulting in inconsistent treatment that would make it hard to compare financial results at different companies. [And, quoting from the staff report] We believe that neither the U.S. nor the international accounting standards as presently comprised are representative of the optimum principle-based standards.[2]

As an alternative, the staff endorsed an objectives-oriented approach that would set broad goals backed by enough detail to produce meaningful, informative financial statements. In conclusion, the SEC staff recommended an entirely new and yet undefined concept of objectives-oriented accounting standards. Gee thanks, fellows, for all your help. And Congress, with neither the professional expertise nor the incentive to establish generally accepted accounting principles, is more inclined to defend or create some special interest.

Again, what to do? At a minimum, as suggested by George Benston's chapter 5, the SEC should approve the proposal by the American Institute of Certified

Public Accountants (AICPA) to limit fair valuation of nontraded securities to separate registered investment companies, no owner of which owns more than 20 percent of its financial interests. More important, Benston recommends that Congress or the SEC permit corporations with publicly traded stock to base their financial accounting statements on either the U.S. or international accounting standards. My one continuing minor disagreement with Benston is his unqualified support for the expensing of stock options.

The primary policy lesson bearing on accounting, however, should be to eliminate the existing roles of the FASB, the SEC, and Congress in setting accounting standards, allowing, as described in the next section, each stock exchange to set the accounting standards for corporations listed on that exchange.

Another accounting lesson that was highlighted by the failure of several large corporations is that the best possible financial accounting should be complemented by reporting the primary *nonfinancial* indicators of the earnings potential of a firm. Such indicators are typically industry specific and may best be developed by the relevant trade association. The market value of most contemporary firms is a multiple of the book value, and many types of changes can affect the market value of a firm, for better or for worse, that are not reported on the balance sheet. The major current challenge to accountants may be to develop the types of nonfinancial indicators of earnings potential that are most useful to both managers and investors. And the most valuable new role of the SEC, as suggested by R. T. McNamar in chapter 15, may be to convene a series of industry meetings to start the process of identifying the most useful industry-specific nonfinancial indicators.

AUDITING

As documented in part III, *every* link in the Enron audit chain failed. And this condition is common among many other firms that declare bankruptcy. The problem, apparently, is that no private or public institution has a sufficient incentive to detect vulnerable financial conditions and to act on this information in time to limit a further loss of wealth.

The more general problem is that any one major financial scandal reduces the market value of all corporations, by increasing the uncertainty about the behavior of other corporate managers and the accuracy of other corporate accounts. One bad apple may spoil the barrel. The corresponding condition is that no one institution now captures the third-party benefits of accurate, transparent, and timely audits.

One might hope that one or more of the links in the audit chain could capture enough of these benefits to assure a good audit, but the experience of the major recent corporate failures is not encouraging. Each of the now "final four" independent public auditors, as well as Arthur Andersen, had previously been subject to major frauds by one or more of their corporate clients. The market analysts, the business press, major creditors, and the credit rating agencies have a record of discovering a financial problem too late to take effective action. The SEC should bear a considerable responsibility for failing to deter or detect the major recent corporate failures, but the administration rewarded this failure by doubling the SEC budget over the next three years.

THE STOCK EXCHANGES

The one institution that has the greatest potential to capture the third-party benefits of a good audit, I suggest, is the stock exchange on which the corporation is listed. Investors would prefer trading on an exchange that develops a reputation for good audits, and corporations would prefer to be listed on that exchange if the benefits of a good audit are higher than the cost. Competition among the exchanges may lead some exchanges to require less complex accounting rules, less demanding disclosure rules, a less expensive audit, etc., but only if the reduction in benefits is smaller than the reduction in cost. Some exchanges may choose to specialize in the rules and procedures that best serve the investors in a specific industry, others may specialize by region, firm size, etc.

This leads me to recommend a radical increase in the authority of stock exchanges in the United States to include the following four roles:

1. *Each exchange would choose the accounting rules for the corporations listed on that exchange.*

In the United States, of course, each exchange would start with the Generally Accepted Accounting Principles (GAAP) but would have the authority to add, delete, or amend any of these rules. There would continue to be a role for the Financial Accounting Standards Board (FASB) and other accounting advisory groups, but their proposed changes would be subject to approval by each exchange, not by the SEC.

Over time, the set of accounting rules chosen by each exchange would probably diverge somewhat, better reflecting the preferences of a subset of investors and the corporations listed, but a professional specialty and software would almost surely develop to report the financial accounts on alternative accounting standards. This first proposal would be a role for the exchanges for which they have no history and which they had not previously considered in their internal deliberations. Our initial interviews with officials of the exchanges, however, suggest that there is some interest in this proposal. The New York Stock Exchange (NYSE) is concerned that the extraterritorial reach of the SOA may lead some foreign firms to delist rather than bear the increased costs and potential liability of listing on an American exchange; the European Union, in response, has sought exemption from the SOA.[3] For similar reasons or to avoid a potential FASB requirement to expense stock options, the NASDAQ is concerned that smaller firms may delist by going private; six firms with a value of $100 million or more had already gone private by May 2003.[4]

2. *Each exchange would choose the disclosure rules for the corporations listed on that exchange.*

In effect, each exchange would establish and monitor the disclosure rules and any exchange-specific rules of corporate governance for the corporations listed on that exchange. In fact, the exchanges had a long history in this role prior to the federal securities legislation of the 1930s; when the SEC was established, most of the first regulations were those then in place at the NYSE. The case for restoring the authority of the exchanges to establish the disclosure rules is that they have a private incentive to choose those rules for which the value to the investors is highest relative to the cost to the listed corporations.

Monitoring the disclosure rules would be shared by the exchanges and the SEC. The exchanges apparently have all of the data that are routinely available to the SEC. Both the exchanges and the SEC are well advised to establish a computer scan of these data to identify those corporations that are most likely to have misrepresented their financial condition, as described by R. T. McNamar in chapter 15. As I write, NASDAQ is working with Microsoft and PricewaterhouseCoopers to test this type of routine. If an exchange identifies a likely violation of the disclosure rules, they either request more information from the corporation or refer the case to the SEC for further investigation and possible sanction. The SEC has a larger potential to monitor violations of the disclosure rules because of its authority to order a forensic audit and to subpoena corporate records, although it has not been very effective in this role. Some competition between the exchanges and the SEC in the monitoring role would probably be productive.

The exchanges, however, have a limited capability to enforce the disclosure rules. Their primary potential sanction is delisting, a penalty that is too high for small violations of the disclosure rules and too low for major violations; a corporation in serious financial trouble is more likely to risk delisting than to disclose its financial weakness. This problem is best addressed by the proposal made by Paul Mahoney in chapter 9 to maintain the authority of the SEC to monitor disclosure and to impose civil sanctions for violations of these rules.

This proposal, in summary, would restore the authority of the exchanges to choose and monitor the disclosure rules and would maintain the authority of the SEC to monitor and enforce these rules. Our initial interviews with officials of the exchanges suggests that they were uneasy about this division of authority between the exchanges and the SEC, some believing that an exchange's own sanctions may be sufficient.

3. *Each exchange would select the public auditors for the corporations listed on that exchange and would set the rules for any other business with the corporations they audit. The auditors, in turn, would be paid by the exchange and would report to the exchange. The exchanges would recover the costs of audits in their listing fees.*

The primary case for this proposal is that the public auditors will always have a potential conflict of interest as long as they are paid by the corporations that they audit. An exchange has a much larger incentive to assure a good audit than an individual corporation because of the benefits of each good audit to other corporations listed on that exchange. In addition, each exchange would probably have a better judgment about whether other business by the public auditors is likely to compromise their audits, so there is no obvious reason for the government to set a common rule limiting the other business of the public auditors. This proposal was apparently considered by the exchanges in the deliberations that led to their positions on the bills that were consolidated in the SOA.

4. *Each exchange would have the authority to allow investors in the corporations listed on that exchange to sell their voting rights separately from their ownership rights and to establish a market in these voting rights.*

This is clearly the most radical of the four proposals, may not now be legal, and would trigger strong opposition by many corporate managers. But that should not be a sufficient reason to dismiss this proposal. The effect of this proposal would be to allow those who want to have a voice in the major decisions of a corporation to increase their vote without increasing their share of the ownership rights. The objective of this proposal is to offset the rules that protect corporate managers that have accumulated over the past several decades, as documented in part III. Corporate democracy has become somewhat of a sham over this period, increasing the incentives of both individual and institutional investors to sell their shares rather than to contest the major decisions and, potentially, the tenure of the incumbent board and senior managers. The only effective discipline on corporate managers has become a large decline in the share price, but this is usually after the major bad business decisions were revealed.

This proposal would almost surely benefit the general shareholders, few of whom value the voting rights in their corporate shares as much as others may pay for these rights. In addition, an increase in the concentration of voting rights is likely to increase the value of their ownership shares, increasing the role of voice relative to exit as a means to protect their interests. Yes, this proposal would increase the number of contentious board meetings and potentially hostile takeovers. That is the reason that the proposal would probably be opposed by many corporate managers. That is also the primary reason why this proposal should be given serious consideration by the broader investor community.

One side benefit of these proposals is that they would substantially reduce the monopoly powers of the FASB and the SEC and would *eliminate* any need for the expensive new PCAOB. The FASB would become only one of potentially several accounting advisory groups, and their proposed accounting rules would be subject to the approval by each stock exchange rather than by the SEC. The SEC would lose the authority to determine the disclosure rules but would retain the authority to monitor and sanction violations of the rules established by the exchanges. The role of the new PCAOB would be completely replaced by authorizing each stock exchange to select, monitor, and compensate the public auditors of firms listed on that exchange. More generally, there is no reason for the government to approve and enforce accounting rules, the rules for executive compensation, and such rules of corporate governance as whether the same person can serve as both the chairman and the CEO; the size, composition, and tenure of corporate boards and committees; the process for nominating new board members; the responsibilities of corporate lawyers and those for whom the corporation is a client; the rotation of audit partners or firms; and the allowable range of activities by the major accounting firms—all of which are current or likely regulatory outcomes of the SOA. An individual investor may have preferences concerning one or more of these issues, but there is no obvious reason that any one set of such preferences should be imposed on all firms. There is no one right answer to these questions for all firms and no significant third-party effects of decisions on these issues that would not be captured by the exchanges. This set of proposals promises to both reduce the role of the government and increase the performance of private economic institutions, a win–win combination that merits serious consideration and support.

For this set of proposals to be effective, of course, the stock exchanges must be willing to accept these roles, rather than to continue to operate as a quasi-bureaucracy under the detailed authority of the SEC. That may take new, more creative leadership of the exchanges. That may also take exchange boards that have better judgment than was reflected by the 2003 decision of the NYSE board to approve the extraordinary compensation of their chairman, especially in a year when a former NYSE chairman was chairman of the SEC. The implicit premise of our proposal to replace some of the authority of the government with an increased role of the stock exchanges, of course, is that the leadership of the exchanges would prefer to operate an innovative private business rather than a quasi-bureaucracy. I hope, but without great confidence, that is the case.

Maybe this is not such a radical agenda. Canada has a thriving securities industry and has had few financial scandals. In Canada, however, accounting standards are set by the Accounting Standards Board, the decisions of which are reviewed only by the new Accounting Standards Oversight Council, both of which are fully under the control of the private Canadian Institute of Chartered Accountants. Only the provinces and territories have any authority for securities regulation, much of which they delegate to self-regulatory organizations such as the exchanges, which have a long history of regulating and supervising financial market intermediation in Canada. The accounting and regulatory institutions in Canada may not be best for the United States, but they demonstrate that a strong federal government role in setting accounting standards and securities regulations is not necessary to protect investors from financial misrepresentation and manipulation. And the U.S. experience to date suggests that such a strong federal role has not been sufficient for this purpose.

THE ROLE OF SHAREHOLDER SUITS

For many years, there has been a heated controversy about whether securities laws are better enforced by public sanctions or by shareholder suits. A recent study, fortunately, finally sheds some light on this issue. The authors compare the securities laws in forty-nine countries to estimate the effects of differences in these laws on various measures of stock market development. The study finds that

> public enforcement appears to play a small role in the development of stock markets. For example, the supervisor's investigative powers and the strength of criminal and civil sanctions matter for only a narrow set of outcomes. But stock market development is strongly associated with such private enforcement measures as extensive disclosure requirements and a relatively low burden of proof on investors claiming improper or inadequate disclosure from issuers. [And the authors conclude that] . . . the most effective arrangement is private enforcement of public rules, which encourages private recovery of damages by investors harmed by promoters.[5]

In 1995, however, Congress passed the Private Securities Litigation Reform Act (PSLRA) to curtail class action lawsuits by the plaintiff's bar. In particular, the high-technology industry, accountants, and investment bankers thought that they had been unjustly victimized by class action lawsuits based on little more than a decline in a company's stock price. Prior to 1995, the plaintiff's bar had free rein to use the discovery process to troll for evidence to support its claims. Moreover, the high costs of litigation were a powerful weapon with which to coerce companies to settle claims.

Given the evidence of the general superiority of private actions relative to public enforcement of the securities laws, should the PSLRA be repealed? Chapter 10 by Adam Pritchard concludes that the PLSRA should *not* be repealed, based on his study of the post-1995 effects of this law. Pritchard finds that securities class action suits are being filed at a record pace. And although a higher percentage of these lawsuits are being dismissed now than before the act, those that survive lead to larger settlements. The combination of higher settlements and a smaller percentage of such cases getting to trial suggests that the class action lawsuits under the PSLRA are doing a more efficient job of deterring corporate fraud. This conclusion is bolstered by the fact that post-PSLRA complaints have more particularized allegations that are more highly correlated with factors related to fraud. And Pritchard concludes that the PSLRA is working well, although not as well as intended, and there do not appear to be grounds to repeal or significantly amend it. A better course for reform would be to change the damages remedy in securities fraud cases to focus on deterrence.

I recognize that class action lawsuits are a major burden to corporations, but so are government regulations. And I agree with Pritchard that the PSLRA has led to a better focus of class action lawsuits in securities law cases. My own suggestion to reduce frivolous civil suits is a general rule that the losers pay the winners for their litigation costs. More effective private enforcement of the securities laws, in turn, should lead one to question whether the appropriate next step was to increase the public enforcement of the securities laws, such as in the SOA. For reasons that I have already spelled out earlier in this chapter, I suggest not.

THE MARKET SPECIALISTS

Market specialists in the stock of a corporation have no formal role in the audit chain. But they have a substantial potential role in disciplining corporate malfeasance if they are able to detect misleading accounting or other breaches of fiduciary duty by the management and board, issue an unbiased report on this information to individual or institutional investors, or act on this information as a short seller. Unfortunately, there is little evidence that the many bright people engaged in such analysis make much of a difference. Despite the implicit assumption of the charges brought by New York State Attorney General Eliot Spitzer, there is no broad evidence that stock price forecasts by independent sell-side analysts are significantly more accurate than those by analysts working for investment banking firms. The superior market performance of stock funds may indicate that the analysts for these funds have a better record, but this analysis is not accessible by the individual investor. In the Enron case, the record of the independent analysts was only slightly less misleading than that of analysts for the investment banking firms. In the early fall of 2001, most market specialists in Enron stock maintained a buy recommendation and institutions owned 60 percent of Enron stock; the only market specialists with a superior record were those that started to sell short beginning in the fall of 2000.

For all of the fuss that was made about misleading market analysis during the bear market, no improvements in public policy with respect to the market analysts are apparent to me. The SEC's general disclosure rule of 2000 may reduce the bias of the corporate information available to different parties at the expense of reducing the information available to everyone. The Spitzer charges were settled out of court and are not likely to be a precedent for further charges. The major development affecting the market analysts, I suggest, will be a general decline in the demand for sell-side analysis, and a lot of bright people will find something more productive to do. So be it.

THE BUSINESS PRESS

The business press also has no formal role in the audit chain. But succinct, accurate, and timely reports of corporate behavior can also be an important part of the process of monitoring corporations. As described in chapter 11 by Paul Weaver, however, the business press is subject to a number of biases:

- An article about people, as either heroes or villains, is generally more newsworthy than an article about accounting, auditing, or corporate governance.
- Some publications may be biased by their dependence on business advertising.
- And, like market specialists, most journalists will not write a critical article about a corporation more than once unless they are no longer dependent on inside information.

For all that, the business press, with the cooperation of some short sellers, proved to be the most effective link in the audit chain in the Enron case. The first serious public question about Enron accounting was in an insert to the Texas edition of the *Wall Street Journal* in September 2000. The first general question about the value of Enron stock was in a February 2001 edition of *Fortune*. The first article to explain the misleading accounting in any detail, including the first to identify Andrew Fastow as a villain of the story, was in a May 2001 edition of the online TheStreet.com. All of this was months before any of the shocking accounting information was released and before any investigations were initiated by the formal parts of the audit chain.

Some public recognition of the important role of the business press in opening up the Enron story would be valuable, but no change in public policy affecting the business press is apparent to me.

BANKERS AS CORPORATE MONITORS

Enron was unusually bank dependent and was heavily indebted to some of the nation's largest banks. As documented in chapter 13 by R. T. McNamar, however, most of this debt was not on the Enron balance sheet, largely in the form of prepay transactions and loans to special purpose entities. Moreover, most outside observers have concluded that the bankers who structured these transactions were party to aiding and abetting Enron officers in a breach of their fiduciary duty. The accounting scandals and bankruptcies of Enron and several other large corporations raise two types of questions about bankers:

Why are bankers no longer very effective monitors of the corporations to which they have made huge loans? McNamar, with experience as a senior bank officer, attributes this development primarily to the securitization of bank loans to reduce the credit risk of their portfolio and the consequent reduction in their due diligence, credit approval, and credit oversight intensity. Bank earnings are now more dependent on loan arrangement and placement fees than on the interest income on the bank portfolio. This condition has been magnified by the recent merger of commercial and investment banks. Other conditions, including the failure of the bank regulators, have also contributed to this development but have a longer history.

And, what, if any, policy changes should be considered to reduce the role of bankers in aiding and abetting corporate officers in a breach of their fiduciary duty? One approach is to sanction the bank in cases for which its officers have been judged as having substantially and knowingly assisted in misrepresenting a corporation's financial condition by making its loans to the corporation subordinate to all other creditors in a bankruptcy proceeding. But that may not be enough to discipline the behavior of individual bankers. In that case, McNamar's primary recommendation is to broaden the certification provisions of the SOA to include the bankers who structure the loans to a corporation as well as the senior corporate officers. I am less comfortable with this recommendation, but the role of some of the nation's largest banks in the Enron debacle suggests that it merits serious consideration.

LAWYERS AS CORPORATE MONITORS

As documented in chapter 12 by R. T. McNamar, lawyers for whom Enron was a client also had a substantial role in structuring many Enron securities offerings that were later alleged to be fraudulent. We have no basis for judging whether any one security offering was fraudulent or whether any one lawyer was guilty in helping structure that offering; that is a problem for the courts to resolve. The Enron experience, however, has led many to question (1) the conditions for which a lawyer should be judged as guilty in aiding and abetting a securities fraud, and (2) the obligation of a lawyer to report some activity by a client that he or she believes may be illegal.

For many, a 1994 decision by the Supreme Court seems to have answered the first question. In *Central Bank of Denver N.A. v. First Interstate Bank of Denver N.A.*, the Court ruled that section 10(b) of the Securities Exchange Act of 1934 does not reach those who aid and abet a violation. This decision seems to have immunized the accountants, bankers, and lawyers from civil prosecution for aiding and abetting a securities fraud if they had not made a false statement themselves, and this decision became their primary defense in shareholders derivative class action lawsuits.

This interpretation of the *Central Bank* decision, however, began to unravel when several federal appellate courts ruled differently on whether substantial participation in the preparation of misrepresentations was a sufficient basis for considering these professionals as primary actors for purposes of committing securities fraud. The most recent of these decisions was issued in December 2002 by Judge Melinda Harmon, the federal district judge in Houston who is overseeing the consolidated Enron securities actions. Judge Harmon's careful and extensive decision, which endorses the substantial assistance standard, is very likely to be appealed to the Supreme Court. We endorse this process as the best way to resolve this issue.

The collapse of Enron and other large firms also provoked a range of responses about the professional obligation of lawyers to report an activity by a client that he or she believes may be illegal. In 2003, the American Bar Association (ABA) endorsed a *permissive* disclosure policy that would give a lawyer the option of reporting a client's act that may be illegal to a senior partner in the law firm who is not working for the client or to an independent member of the client's board of directors; with no sanction for not acting, this proposed rule is not likely to have any significant effect. In contrast, the SEC proposed a noisy withdrawal rule in November 2002, such that lawyers would be expected to end their representation of the client, notify the SEC to that effect, and disaffirm any documents submitted to the SEC on behalf of the client; this rule, which would breach the privacy of attorney-client information, provoked strong opposition and has not been implemented as of the end of 2003.

Our judgment is that the proposed ABA rule would be ineffective and that the proposed SEC rule would be much more stringent than necessary. In contrast, we endorse a rule such that a lawyer *must* report a possible illegal act by his client, first to a senior partner in the firm who does not work for the same client and second to two independent members of the client's board, at least one of which is a member of the audit committee, but with no obligation to terminate the relation with the client or to report to the SEC. This proposed rule does not breach the privacy of lawyer-client information, maintains the incentive for corporate managers to seek legal advice, and shifts the direct liability for potential malfeasance to the corporate board.

One other potential problem has been revealed by our investigation. Beginning in 1992, interestingly in Texas, all of the state governments have authorized limited liability professional partnerships. As a consequence, most accounting firms and law firms changed their legal status from general partnerships to limited liability partnerships (LLPs). In 1994, for example, all of the then Big Six accounting firms adopted the LLP legal status as soon as it was approved by the New York State government. In a general partnership, each partner is liable for the malfeasance of his partners, and there is a strong incentive to maintain quality control within the firm to avoid litigation. In a limited liability partnership, in contrast, each partner is liable only for one's own malfeasance, not for that of the other partners, reducing the incentive to monitor the potential malfeasance by other partners. The increase in LLPs, accounting scandals, and legal malfeasance during the same period may be just a coincidence, but maybe not. Some other scholar should explore this potential relation to determine whether the reorganization of accounting and law firms as LLPs contributed to these adverse effects.[6]

THE CREDIT RATING AGENCIES

The Enron collapse also focused attention on the credit rating agencies, because the three SEC-approved rating agencies maintained an investment-grade rating for Enron debt until five days before Enron filed for bankruptcy. As documented in chapter 14 by Jacobo Rodriguez, there are three problems with the market for credit rating services:

As of 2001, the SEC had approved only three nationally recognized statistical rating organizations (NSROs) without any formal definition of the characteristics of a firm that would be so recognized, so there is very little competition in this market. (A Canadian firm was approved as the fourth NSRO in 2003.)

For many years, federal financial regulators have prohibited banks and money market funds from purchasing debt instruments that are not rated as investment grade, so there is a lot at stake to the issuing firm for its debt to be favorably rated by one of the NSROs.

The NSROs are compensated for their credit rating services by the firms whose debt that they rate, so there is a potential conflict of interest.

Rodriguez concludes, I believe correctly, that

> the SEC should eliminate the NSRO designation and U.S. and international regulators should undertake steps to reduce and eventually eliminate their reliance on credit ratings for regulatory purposes. The actions are the only ones that will allow us to determine with certainty whether ratings are valuable for their reputational and informational content as opposed to being valuable as regulatory licenses, and whether the reputation of credit rating agencies is tarnished because they receive the bulk of their revenues from the companies and entities whose debt they rate.[7]

THE SECURITIES AND EXCHANGE COMMISSION

The final link in the audit chain that failed to deter or detect the collapse of Enron was the SEC, the government agency that has the primary responsibility to ensure adequate and timely disclosure of relevant corporate information. More accurately, the SEC did not fail; it was not even a part of the audit chain during the critical period.

The last financial report by Enron examined by the SEC was Enron's 10-K for 1997, filed in April 1998. The SEC did not open an enforcement investigation of Enron until the third quarter of 2001, only *after* substantial information about Enron's financial weakness was in the press and the market price of Enron's stock had dropped by more than 50 percent. Moreover, this was consistent with the SEC's congressionally approved schedule of reviewing a public company's financial filings only once every four years. SOA authorized a once-every-three-years target schedule and a substantial budget increase for the SEC but, without much more frequent review by a more effective process, that will also not be enough.

This book recommends a combination of reducing the role of the SEC and increasing its effectiveness. As described earlier in this chapter, each stock exchange would establish the disclosure rules for all corporations listed on that exchange and would have the authority, in parallel with the SEC, to monitor the performance against these rules. The competition between the exchanges and the SEC should improve the monitoring effectiveness of each institution. The SEC would maintain the authority to sanction firms when it detects a violation of the securities laws not detected by the exchanges or on the request of an exchange. As described in chapter 15 by R. T. McNamar, however, the SEC needs to modernize its reporting and review process. A new eXtensible Business Reporting Language (XBRL) would permit more frequent and more effective monitoring by either or both the exchanges and the SEC. This system is now being tested by a number of federal regulatory agencies, and the early reception, including by the SEC, is quite favorable. I am not qualified to determine whether this is the best new reporting and review process, but there is broad support for at least an experiment with an XBRL-based process. There is also broad support for the SEC to encourage the development of industry-specific nonfinancial measures of firm performance to augment the required financial reports, a recommendation that I strongly endorse.

EXECUTIVE COMPENSATION

Almost every recession or substantial decline in equity prices has been followed by increased popular and political concerns about the compensation of corporate executives. Some of this surely reflects a common envy about anyone whose income is many times one's own income, some reflects a search for someone to blame for one's own losses. Given a one- or two-year lag in reporting compensation, moreover, this concern is often amplified by careless journalism, which too often compares prior peak compensation with current recession conditions. And this problem is compounded by inconsistent measures of compensation; various articles reporting total compensation as salary and bonus plus some combination of the value of old options exercised, an estimate of the value of new options granted, loans, and even the sale of stock. There is no reason to deny what was clearly an explosion of executive compensation through 2000. Some of this was the consequence of public policies that increased the use of stock options, most of which was due to the unexpected and unsustainable bubble in equity prices from 1998 through early 2000, and some of which was surely due to the combination of demanding executives and compliant boards. The primary focus of public attention should be on policies that bias the magnitude and structure of executive compensation, not on the outcomes of approved compensation rules. The second condition was surely unanticipated by both corporate executives and board members and is often offset by an unexpectedly large decline in equity prices, whose effects on executive compensation do not generate much general concern. The third condition merits attention primarily because the rules of corporate governance are often insufficient to induce board members to be effective monitors of executive compensation.

Some form of equity compensation is necessary to align the interests of shareholders and senior corporate managers. But there are several reasons to be concerned about the rapid increase in the use of stock options. Stock options, in effect, are a one-sided bet, because an option has no value at any market price below the strike price; for any expected value of a stock, thus, the value of an option *increases* with the variance of the stock price, and this may lead to unduly risky behavior by option owners. And all too often in bear markets, the strike prices of options have been reduced to increase their value even if the market price of the stock has declined. The problems with options are best resolved by substituting restricted stock for options; this would make incentives more symmetric with respect to gains and losses in the market value of the stock and would eliminate the perverse effect of repricing options. No apparent change in accounting or tax provisions is necessary to encourage the increased use of restricted stock, and an increasing number of firms, now including Microsoft, have shifted equity-based compensation from options to restricted stock.

As documented in chapter 17 by Alan Reynolds, the conditions affecting executive compensation often lead to changes in public policy that are later recognized as counterproductive even by their initial advocates. In 1992, for example, the SEC amended their regulations to require more disclosure of executive compensation and to encourage greater shareholder voting on such compensation, the net effect of which was to increase shareholder activism by institutional investors and a decline in the stock value of firms targeted by this activism. The 1993 tax law included two provisions that strongly increased the use of stock options and other forms of equity-based compensation: a $1 million limit on the salary and bonus that could be deducted as a current expense and a large increase in the top marginal tax rate on individual income. This effect was compounded by the 1994 extension of the Medicare tax rate to all earnings and the 1997 reduction in the capital gains tax rate. Many of those who supported these measures are now promoting the required expensing of stock options, in the hope to reduce the relative use of stock options. But the ban on all loans to corporate officers in the SOA will only increase the relative importance of stock options as a form of executive compensation.

The most careful studies of these issues conclude that the structure of executive compensation is quite efficient in aligning the interests of corporate executives and shareholders, subject, of course, to the biases introduced by public policies and the rules of corporate governance. The important implication of this conclusion is that public policy should not bias this structure one way or another. Fortunately, the

2003 tax law reduced two of these biases by reducing the individual tax rates on both capital gains and dividends to 15 percent and by reducing the individual rates on other income.

This perspective leads to the following guidelines to public policies that directly affect executive compensation:

Repeal the $1 million limit on the amount of salary and bonus that may be deducted as a current expense, a proposal endorsed by the Financial Economists Roundtable in November 2003.

Repeal the ban on loans to corporate officers.

Do not require shareholder approval of executive compensation.

And do not require the expensing of stock options. In general, do not use regulations or tax measures to limit or favor any specific form or level of executive compensation.

THE MANY PROBLEMS OF THE CORPORATE INCOME TAX

The U.S. corporate income tax grossly distorts many types of economic decisions and should be replaced by a cash-flow tax. The major problems of the corporate income tax, as documented in chapter 18 by Chris Edwards, are the following:

The combined federal and state statutory rate is now among the highest in the industrial world, exceeded only by that in Japan. This high rate reduces investment, encourages firms to choose another form of organization or to move profits abroad, and provides incentives to push the legal margins with complex tax-driven deals.

The corporate income tax base has become as complex and subjective as the GAAP and for many of the same reasons. The tax rules for capitalized assets and capital gains cannot be made simple and neutral and are repeatedly exploited in corporate tax shelters. These rules also cause economic distortions by interfering with economic decisions on capital investment and business organization.

The third fundamental flaw is the gratuitous inconsistency that Congress has injected in the tax code. One example is the different tax treatment of equity and debt, leading to the double taxation of corporate equity. Another example is the different tax rules imposed on corporations and other forms of business organization. And a third is the taxation of U.S. corporations on their worldwide income, rather than only on their U.S. income. Such inconsistencies have played a major role in the tax shelters exploited by Enron and other firms. More generally, they have created large costs to the economy by channeling investments into less productive uses and by encouraging U.S. firms to incorporate in foreign tax havens.

All of these biases would be reduced or eliminated by replacing the corporate income tax with a broad-base tax on the net cash flow of all nonfinancial businesses. And this should be the focus of the next major tax reform, a position now endorsed by many public finance economists. According to one estimate, a tax rate on the net cash flow of nonfinancial firms of 19 percent would have raised about the same revenue as the current corporate income tax. The primary benefit of a cash-flow tax would be to improve the allocation of capital. Another benefit would be to eliminate most of the complex tax shelters exploited by Enron and other large corporations. Since all income from capital would be taxed at the source, a third benefit would be to set the stage for *eliminating* the taxes on all income from capital on receipt.

CORPORATE GOVERNANCE

My own chapter 19 on corporate governance is a collection of puzzles. Over the past several decades, the monitoring model of the corporate board has gained broad acceptance, as reflected in the new corporate governance rules of the stock exchanges and the Sarbanes-Oxley Act; there is no significant evidence, however, that firm performance is a function of the major rules, other than the value of small boards, suggested by this perspective. Institutional investors now have a much greater potential to monitor the corporations in which their fund is invested, but the small amount of shareholder activism by the managers of these funds is more often addressed to the interests of various stakeholders rather than the general stockholders. Banks still have a great deal at stake in the financial soundness of the firms to which they have made major loans, but most banks are no longer effective monitors of large firms. The management of most firms is now protected by one or more various takeover defenses, even though firm performance is *negatively* related to the number of such defenses. There are still a substantial number of mergers and acquisitions, despite the proliferation of takeover defenses and the evidence of significant negative payoffs to the shareholders of the bidding firms. And, for all of these problems, the average growth of productivity and equity value of American corporations has been better than those of any other industrial economy, both recently and since 1982.

There are plausible, even if not wholly convincing, explanations of some of these puzzles. Some of these conditions, moreover, seem inconsistent with the economist's standard model of the corporation as a wealth-maximizing firm. For that reason, the major policy lesson that I draw from this experience is that the federal government should withdraw from *any* role in establishing the rules of corporate governance and disclosure, returning this role to the state governments and stock exchanges. State governments and the exchanges, of course, will also make mistakes, but they are not likely to make the same mistakes, and competition among the states and exchanges is likely to lead to a more rapid correction of mistakes.

As is often the case, the appropriate next steps by the government are to repeal some of its authorities and to clarify others. As spelled out in part V, the policy actions that would be most helpful to restore an effective market for corporate control are the following:.

Congress should repeal the Williams Act.

The SEC should repeal or clarify its one share, one vote rule to assure potential bidders that the voluntary and temporary lease of shareholder votes to lift a takeover defense is not inconsistent with this rule.

The New York State legislature should repeal is prohibition on vote buying.

The Delaware courts should clarify the conditions for which they are likely to approve a market for the votes of a target firm.

The rules of corporate governance should be selected to maximize the value of corporate equity to general shareholders—not to serve the interests of managers, employees, the government, or other stakeholders. Private self-regulatory organizations such as the stock exchanges, plus a choice-of-law regime among the state governments, should be sufficient to this task.

CONCLUSION

The collapse of Enron imposed large losses on its shareholders and stakeholders. And the various civil and criminal investigations of the parties responsible for this collapse will take years to sort out. On the other hand, the Enron case should teach us many lessons about the types of policies, the decisions that we make together as a political community, that would reduce the frequency and magnitude of such future cases. For these lessons to be valuable, however, we must learn the right lessons, not only those that are consistent with our prior prejudices.

The American corporation is one of our most important institutions. Like all human institutions, both corporations and governments are subject to some bias, some errors, some exploitation by their leaders. An eyes-open perspective on both the corporation and the government is necessary to draw the right lessons from the Enron collapse. That has been the objective of this book.

NOTES

1. *Washington Post*, April 21, 1998.

2. *Wall Street Journal*, July 28, 2003.

3. Guerrera, Francesco and Gary Silverman, "Europe May Hit Back at U.S. Audit Rules," *Financial Times*, May 16, 2003.

4. Kahn, Jeremy, "The Burden of Being Public: Bound by New Regulations and Changes in Wall Street, More Firms are Breaking Free—by Going Private," *Fortune*, May 12, 2003.

5. Rafael La Porta, Florencio Lopez-de-Silanes, and Andrei Shleifer, "What Works in Securities Laws?" NBER Working Paper no. 9882, *NBER Digest*, November 2003.

6. For a view that is skeptical of this perspective, see Larry E. Ribstein, "Limited Liability of Professional Firms after Enron," draft, April 2003.

7. See p. 228.

Index

ABA (American Bar Association), 16, 172, 179, 192, 194, 196, 288, 338, 367; Accounting and Auditing Enforcement Releases (AAERs), SEC, 75; accounting firms' change to LLP status, 94, 367; Accounting Oversight Board (*See* Public Company Accounting Oversight Board); accounting practices, 55–56, 357–58; authority to set standards, 48, 49–53, 80, 81, 357–60; Canada, 362; conservatism, 66; corporations other than Enron, problems associated with, 74–76; critical accounting policies as defined by SEE, 27; economically meaningful numbers, obtaining, 60–61; effective discipline of violators, 73–74, 80–81; Enron, problems specific to, 47–48, 68–73; general problems with current system, 50–52; historical background, 56–58; intangible assets, 51–52; managerial manipulation, 66–68, 82n7, 265–66; mark-to-market accounting, 150, 154, 163, 200, 232–33, 272, 323; net income, measuring, 63–66; nonfinancial indicators of corporate worth, 358; reasons for corporate collapses laid at

feet of, viii–ix, 6, 18–19; responsibility for problems in, 76–77; rule-based versus principle-based nature, 79–80, 89–90; S&P's new measure of corporate earnings, 13; standards, role of, 68; stock options, expensing of, 48–49; summary of policy lessons, 357–58; trustworthiness of statements and IPA attestations, 59–61; value and usefulness of audited financial statements to investors, 58–59, 61–63. *See also* fair value accounting; Generally Accepted Accounting Principles

acquisitions, 301–4. *See also* market for corporate control

activists and special interests: class action reform, 125; executive compensation policy, 249–50, 261, 269–70; multiple alternative business structures, 305

Adams, Thomas, 294

Adelphia Communications, 19, 31, 158

agency costs and problems, 261–64, 337

Aggarwal, Rajesh, 269

Ahold, 2

AICPA. *See* American Institute for Certified Public Accountants

aiding-and-abetting liability, 173; banks, 212, 214–16; class action reform and

375

monopoly issues, 107, 108, 109–11; summary of policy lessons, 359–62, 373

stock market analysts: effect of SOA and Wall Street settlement on quality of analysis, 22; role of market specialists in audit chain, 101–4, 364; Wall Street firms, settlement with, 18, 21, 22, 34–40, 103, 360

stock market prices: class action reform and PSLRA, response to, 136–37; credit ratings, sensitivity to, 201–3; Enron collapse, effect of, vii, 2, 7, 22–24; SOA's effect on, 32–33

stock options as executive compensation, 245–88, 370; accounting practices, 49, 83n28; approval/disapproval, cycle of, 246, 250–56, 261; Black–Scholes stock option pricing model, 48, 77, 90, 258, 264, 271–75; business press commentary on, 268–69; class actions targeting, 142–43; dilution from, 272–73, 275; Enron's dependence on, 201; imperfect nature of, 99n4; indexed options, 262–64; market efficiency, 264–66; nonqualified options, 259, 266; qualified or incentive stock options (ISOs), 266; responsibility for corporate scandals, 138–39; restricted options, 263–64, 267, 268; summary of policy lessons, 370; vesting rules, 260, 262, 264, 266

stock options, expensing, 245–46; accounting practices, 48–49; auditing practices, 90; estimation problems arising from, 269–75; FASB, 48, 49, 249; moral issue, viewed as, 269; summary of policy lessons, 358, 370, 371

stock options for nonexecutive employees, 267, 274, 280–81n76

Stulz, Rene, 345

Stymiest, Barbara, 33

substance over form doctrine, 287

"substantial assistance" standard, 190, 214

"substantial participation" rule, 178, 188–89

Sullivan, Scott, 19

Summers, Lawrence, 312

Sun Microsystems, 267

Sun Trust, 299

Sunbeam Corporation, 96, 142

swap contracts (prepay transactions), 186–87, 204–5, 209–11, 217n8

Switzerland, 308

Tax Notes, 300

Tax Reform Act of 1986 (TRA86), 305, 313

tax shelters, 285–89; alternative business structures, 306–7, 312–13; ambiguity of tax code, problems created by, 286–87; capital gains, 300–301; cash-flow tax, effects of, 321; depreciation, role of, 297; fundamental economic solutions required for, 288–89; international investment tax rules, 315–16; partnerships, 297–98; timing sensitivities, 295–96. *See also specific boards, commissions, etc.*

taxation, 243–44; ambiguity of tax code, problems created by, 286–87; executive compensation, attempts to manipulate, 250–52, 276; "flat tax," 294; historical background, 291–92; JGTRRA, 243, 283–84, 308; marginal tax rates, 251, 313–14, 321; millionaires' surtax, 250, 251; Revenue Reconciliation Act of 1993, 250–52. *See also* corporate income tax

Teesside combined cycle gas generator, U.K., 199

Telecommunications Act of 1996, 8

telecommunications industry, special problems of, 8–9

territorial approach to international investment, 314, 316

Teslik, Sara, 345

Texas aiding-and-abetting laws, 181–82, 214

About the Editor and Contributors

William A. Niskanen organized and edited this book and is the author of nine of the chapters. He is also a co-editor of the prior Cato Institute book on this general topic, *Corporate Aftershock*, which was published in June 2003. An economist, he has been chairman of the Cato Institute since 1985. His prior positions include service as a member and acting chairman of the Council of Economic Advisers under President Ronald Reagan and as director of economics of the Ford Motor Company. He holds degrees in economics from Harvard and the University of Chicago. His e-mail address is wniskan@cato.org.

Contributors

George J. Benston is a professor of finance at the Goizueta Business School at Emory University. He is both an economist and a certified public accountant; his areas of specialization include bank regulation and financial disclosure. He is the co-editor of the *Journal of Financial Services,* an associate editor of several other professional journals, and a member and founder of the Shadow Financial Regulatory Committee. He previously served on the faculties of the University of Rochester and the University of Chicago. His e-mail address is gjb@bus.emory.edu.

Chris Edwards is the director of fiscal policy studies at the Cato Institute, with over a decade of experience in tax and budget policy analysis. His most recent Cato study is "War between Generations: Federal Spending on the Elderly Is Set to Explode." Prior to joining Cato, he worked at the Joint Economic Committee, PricewaterhouseCoopers, and the Tax Foundation. He has a master's degree in economics from George Mason University. His e-mail address is cedwards@cato.org.

Paul Mahoney is a professor of corporate law at the University of Virginia Law School. He teaches securities regulation, corporate finance, contracts, and quantitative methods at the law school and introduction to business law at the Darden School of Business Administration. He previously practiced law with a New York law firm and served as a law clerk for Judge Ralph K. Winter of the U.S. Court of Appeals for the Second Circuit and for Justice Thurgood Marshall of the U.S. Supreme Court. He is a graduate of the Massachusetts Institute of Technology and the Yale Law School. His e-mail address is pgm9h@virginia.edu.

R. T. "Tim" McNamar is now a consultant to PricewaterhouseCoopers LLP on XBRL and enhanced accounting topics, following a year as a visiting fellow at Cato. He had an extensive prior career in financial services as a consultant, chief financial officer, regulator, international investment banker, and vice chairman of the turnaround team for the Bank of New England. He also served as the deputy secretary of the Treasury during the first Reagan administration. His e-mail address is tim.mcnamar@us.pwc.com.

Adam C. Pritchard teaches corporate and securities law at the University of Michigan Law School. After completing his own law training at the University of Virginia, he served as a clerk for Judge J. Harvie Wilkinson III of the U.S. Court of Appeals for the Fourth Circuit, on the staff of the solicitor general of the Department of Justice, and as senior counsel in the Office of the General Counsel of the Securities and Exchange Commission. He has also been a visiting fellow in capital market studies at the Cato Institute. He can be contacted at acplaw@umich.edu.

Alan Reynolds is a senior fellow at the Cato Institute and a syndicated columnist. He previously served as the director of economic research at the Hudson Institute and as chief economist at Polyconomics and the First National Bank of Chicago. One of the original "supply side" tax economists, he worked on one of the Reagan transition teams in 1981 and as research director of the National Commission on Tax Reform and Economic Growth in 1986. He is a graduate of the University of California at Los Angeles and of California State University in Sacramento. His e-mail address is areynolds@cato.org.

L. Jacobo Rodriguez, formerly a financial services analyst at the Cato Institute, is now at Dimensional Fund Advisers in Santa Monica. His research interests include banking regulation, deposit insurance reform, financial regulation, monetary policy, and public pension privatization. His articles have appeared in newspapers in the United States, Latin America, Europe, and Japan, in publications such as the *Wall Street Journal, Investors Business Daily,* and *Foreign Policy.* He was the book review editor of the *Cato Journal.* He holds degrees in economics from the University of California at Berkeley and Johns Hopkins University. He can be contacted at jacobo.rodriguez@gmail.com.

Paul H. Weaver, the author of *News and the Culture of Lying* and *The Suicidal Corporation*, is a freelance journalist who has written extensively about business, media, and politics. After earning a Ph.D. in political science at Harvard, he served as a staff writer and assistant managing editor at *Fortune* magazine, a member of the public affairs staff at Ford Motor Co., and a media fellow at the American Enterprise Institute and the Hoover Institution. His articles have appeared in the *New York Times Magazine, Reason, Public Interest*, and other publications. His e-mail address is paulhweaver@comcast.com.